Advances in Human-Machine Interaction, Artificial Intelligence, and Robotics

Advances in Human-Machine Interaction, Artificial Intelligence, and Robotics

Editors

Juan Ernesto Solanes Galbis
Luis Gracia
Jaime Valls Miro

MDPI

Basel • Beijing • Wuhan • Barcelona • Belgrade • Novi Sad • Cluj • Manchester

Editors

Juan Ernesto Solanes Galbis
Universitat Politècnica de València
València
Spain

Luis Gracia
Universitat Politècnica de València
València
Spain

Jaime Valls Miro
University of Technology Sydney
Sydney
Australia

Editorial Office
MDPI AG
Grosspeteranlage 5
4052 Basel, Switzerland

This is a reprint of articles from the Special Issue published online in the open access journal *Electronics* (ISSN 2079-9292) (available at: https://www.mdpi.com/journal/electronics/special_issues/New_Industrial_Revolution_HMI).

For citation purposes, cite each article independently as indicated on the article page online and as indicated below:

Lastname, A.A.; Lastname, B.B. Article Title. *Journal Name* **Year**, *Volume Number*, Page Range.

ISBN 978-3-7258-2389-5 (Hbk)
ISBN 978-3-7258-2390-1 (PDF)
doi.org/10.3390/books978-3-7258-2390-1

Contents

About the Editors

Juan Ernesto Solanes Galbis

Juan Ernesto Solanes Galbis received his B.S. degree in Industrial Electronics Engineering, his B.S. degree in Industrial Automatics, his M.S. degree in Automatics and industrial informatics, and his Ph.D. in Robotics, Automatics and Industrial informatics from the Universitat Politècnica de València (UPV), Spain, in 2007, 2009, 2011, and 2015, respectively. He is currently an Associate Professor with the Department of Systems Engineering and Control (DISA), UPV. His research interests include nonlinear and robust control, extended reality, human–machine interaction, and robotics.

Luis Gracia

Luis Gracia received his B.Sc. degree in Electronic Engineering, his M.Sc. degree in Control Systems Engineering, and his Ph.D. in Automation and Industrial Computer Science from the Universitat Politècnica de València (UPV), Spain, in 1998, 2000, and 2006, respectively. He is currently a Professor at the Department of Systems Engineering and Control (DISA) of UPV, where he has worked since 2001. His research interests include mobile robots, robotic manipulators, sliding-mode control, collaborative robots, and system modeling and control.

Jaime Valls Miro

Jaime Valls Miro received his B.Eng. and M.Eng. degrees in Computer Science (Systems Engineering) from the Universitat Politècnica de València (UPV), Valencia (Spain), in 1990 and 1993, respectively. He received his Ph.D. from Middlesex University, London (UK) in 1998. His thesis examined the use of full dynamics for trajectory planning and optimal control of industrial manipulators. He worked for 5 years as a software and control systems analyst for a London-based company designing ROVs (remotely operated underwater vehicles). He has been an Associate Professor at the Centre for Autonomous Systems of the University of Technology Sydney (Australia) since 2011.

Preface

This reprint brings together a collection of groundbreaking research articles that explore the latest advancements in human–machine interaction (HMI), artificial intelligence (AI), and robotics. The contributions featured in this reprint highlight innovative solutions developed by leading experts from around the world, pushing the technological boundaries of what is possible in these fields. From enhancing collaborative robots' cognitive abilities to integrating augmented and virtual reality into everyday robotics applications, these studies offer a comprehensive look at how emerging technologies are shaping a future where robots and AI systems work alongside humans in a more intuitive, efficient, and inclusive manner.

Juan Ernesto Solanes Galbis, Luis Gracia, and Jaime Valls Miro
Editors

electronics

Editorial

Advances in Human–Machine Interaction, Artificial Intelligence, and Robotics

Juan Ernesto Solanes [1,]*, Luis Gracia [1] and Jaime Valls Miro [2]

1 Instituto de Diseño y Fabricación, Universitat Politècnica de València, 46022 València, Spain
2 Centre for Autonomous Systems (CAS), Faculty of Engineering, University of Technology Sydney (UTS), Sydney, NSW 2007, Australia
* Correspondence: esolanes@idf.upv.es

1. Introduction

The convergence of artificial intelligence (AI), robotics, and immersive technologies such as augmented reality (AR), virtual reality (VR), and extended reality (XR) is transforming the way humans interact with machines. Human–machine interaction (HMI) has evolved from simple command-based systems to complex, intelligent interactions that leverage AI to understand and respond to human behavior in real time. As robots become integral to everyday life and industry, there is a growing need to make these interactions more intuitive, efficient, and human-centered.

Recent advances in AI have played a pivotal role in enhancing robotic capabilities, allowing robots to perceive their environment, make decisions, and learn from interactions. Deep learning models, such as convolutional neural networks (CNNs) and large language models (LLMs), have significantly improved robots' abilities in perception, language processing, and decision-making [1]. These models enable robots to recognize objects, understand human speech, and even detect emotions, making HMI more seamless and natural. However, these advancements also bring challenges, such as ensuring the ethical use of AI, managing data privacy, and mitigating biases inherent in AI algorithms [2].

The integration of AR, VR, and XR into robotics further enhances HMI by creating immersive environments where humans and robots can interact in more intuitive and engaging ways. AR technology overlays digital information onto the physical world, enhancing user awareness and control over robotic systems. For instance, AR can be used in industrial settings to provide real-time data visualization, helping operators monitor robot performance or guide robots through complex tasks [3,4]. VR creates fully simulated environments that are invaluable for training and prototyping, allowing users to experiment with robotic behaviors without the constraints of the physical world [5,6]. XR, which encompasses both AR and VR, provides flexible and scalable solutions that blend real and virtual environments, enabling new forms of collaborative robotics [7,8].

This Special Issue brings together cutting-edge research that addresses these multifaceted challenges in HMI, AI, and robotics.

Citation: Solanes, J.E.; Gracia, L.; Valls Miro, J. Advances in Human–Machine Interaction, Artificial Intelligence, and Robotics. *Electronics* **2024**, *13*, 3856. https://doi.org/10.3390/electronics13193856

Received: 26 September 2024
Accepted: 26 September 2024
Published: 29 September 2024

2. The Present Issue

For this Special Issue, 15 submissions were received, and each was carefully evaluated by at least one of the Guest Editors to determine its alignment with the theme of human–machine interaction, artificial intelligence, and robotics. Submissions deemed relevant underwent a thorough review process involving at least two external reviewers, while those that did not meet the criteria were rejected. After a rigorous peer-review process, 11 articles were selected for publication. The accepted contributions explore a diverse array of applications within the fields of human–robot interaction, AI, and robotics, including predictive modeling, immersive technologies, and collaborative decision-making systems. A summary of the findings and conclusions of each article is presented below.

In the first contribution, Al-Yacoub et al. present a data-driven approach for modeling human–human co-manipulation using force and muscle surface electromyogram (EMG) activities. The study investigates the use of EMG sensors to enhance the mapping between force/torque data and displacements during collaborative manipulation tasks. The authors compare data-driven models, mathematical models, and hybrid approaches, demonstrating that the inclusion of EMG data significantly improves the prediction accuracy of human–robot interaction. Their results highlight the potential of using EMG-enhanced data-driven models to teach robots more intuitive and human-like behaviors in co-manipulation scenarios.

In the second contribution, Martí-Testón et al. propose a novel methodology for producing augmented-reality guided tours in museums using mixed-reality headsets. The study focuses on developing an interactive and immersive visitor experience, specifically designed for the Almoina archeological museum. The authors combine augmented reality with scenographic and theatrical techniques to create a natural and emotive storytelling approach. Their results from usability tests and observational studies demonstrate that this methodology significantly enhances user engagement, making historical content more accessible and personalized. The findings suggest that integrating augmented reality in museum contexts can revolutionize how heritage is experienced, offering a more intuitive and emotional connection to the past.

In the third contribution, Kim et al. explore the dynamics of human and AI speaker interaction, focusing on communication failures categorized into system, semantic, and effectiveness errors. Using data from major AI speaker users in South Korea, the study investigates how different types of communication failures impact user satisfaction and continued use of the AI speakers. The findings reveal that system and semantic errors negatively affect sustained usage, while effectiveness failures, surprisingly, do not deter users, especially among single-person households, such as elderly users. The study concludes that AI speakers can significantly alleviate loneliness in these demographics and highlights the importance of designing AI systems that effectively manage communication failures to maintain user engagement.

In the fourth contribution, Castillo-Vergara et al. explore the acceptance of Industry 4.0 technologies among technical students from rural areas, using an extended Technology Acceptance Model (TAM). The study aims to understand how factors like technological optimism, subjective norms, and facilitating conditions influence students' perceived usefulness, ease of use, and intention to adopt these technologies. The results indicate that technological optimism positively impacts perceived usefulness and ease of use, though it does not directly affect the attitude towards using the technology. Facilitating conditions and subjective norms also play crucial roles in shaping students' intentions to use Industry 4.0 technologies, suggesting that a supportive environment and positive social influences are critical for successful adoption. The findings provide valuable insights for policymakers and educators aiming to enhance technology integration in educational settings.

In the fifth contribution, Xie and Shen develop a lightweight KD-EG-RepVGG network for detecting surface defects in strip steel using structural reparameterization, efficient channel attention (ECA), and Gaussian error linear units (GELU). The study aims to enhance the speed, accuracy, and stability of defect identification in industrial applications. The proposed model demonstrates a high defect recognition accuracy of 99.44% and a rapid detection speed of 2.4 ms per image. Compared to traditional and other deep learning models, the KD-EG-RepVGG network achieves superior performance while maintaining a low computational cost, making it highly suitable for deployment in real engineering environments.

In the sixth contribution, Castiblanco Jimenez et al. compare user engagement (UE) between advergames and traditional advertising using electroencephalography (EEG) to assess its influence on purchase intention. The study explores how interactive advertising formats like advergames can enhance user engagement compared to passive formats such as TV commercials. The findings reveal that advergames significantly increase engagement levels, as measured by EEG, compared to traditional advertisements. Furthermore, the study concludes that higher engagement levels positively influence the user's purchase intention, suggesting that more interactive and engaging advertising strategies can be more effective in driving consumer behavior.

In the seventh contribution, Mandischer et al. propose an adaptive human–robot collaboration system aimed at including people with disabilities (PwD) in manual labor tasks. The study introduces a novel approach that uses a two-stage reasoning system combined with a matchmaking ontology to align the capabilities of PwD with specific task requirements. The methodology involves real-time assessment of individual capabilities using sensor data, which then guides task allocation between the human and the robot. The results highlight that this system allows robots to autonomously adapt to the user's in situ capabilities, significantly enhancing the inclusion of PwD in the workforce by making collaborative workplaces more flexible, accessible, and economically viable.

In the eighth contribution, Mourtzis et al. propose a novel approach for optimizing the reliability of robotic cells using digital twin (DT) technology and predictive maintenance (PdM). The study focuses on improving the reliability of critical components within robotic cells by leveraging real-time data monitoring and machine learning algorithms to predict failures before they occur. The authors developed a DT model that integrates with a predictive maintenance framework, allowing for continuous monitoring and assessment of component health. Results demonstrated that implementing this approach significantly reduces unexpected downtimes and maintenance costs, thereby enhancing overall system reliability and performance in manufacturing environments.

In the ninth contribution, Burčiar et al. present a methodical approach to enhancing proactivity in production processes using a digital twin (DT) integrated with a simulation-based decision-making framework. The study focuses on integrating a DT with a Manufacturing Execution System (MES) to enable real-time analysis and proactive order management. The proposed Manual Order Rearrangement (MOR) method demonstrates the ability to simulate and optimize production scenarios before execution, significantly reducing downtime and resource waste. Experimental results show that the implementation of DT technology improves process efficiency by optimizing production schedules and minimizing potential errors, highlighting the potential of DTs in advancing smart manufacturing practices.

In the tenth contribution, Lee et al. introduce a mission-conditioned path planning approach using a Transformer Variational Autoencoder (CVAE) to integrate mission specifications through Linear Temporal Logic (LTL) into robotic path planning. The proposed framework combines the CVAE with a Transformer network to generate control sequences that meet LTL specifications while optimizing trajectory costs. The study demonstrates that the approach outperforms traditional sampling-based and deep-learning methods in terms of computational efficiency, trajectory quality, and mission success rates. The results highlight the framework's capability to handle complex mission requirements, ensuring adherence to predefined specifications while navigating challenging environments effectively.

In the final contribution, Torrejón et al. present the design and development of Shadow, a cost-effective mobile social robot intended for human-following applications. The study emphasizes the use of 3D printing technology for rapid prototyping and customization, allowing for a highly agile and adaptable robot. Key features include omnidirectional movement, advanced sensors such as 360° cameras and 3D LiDAR, and a flexible power electronics system. Extensive testing demonstrated Shadow's stability, agility, and ability to operate autonomously for at least seven hours, successfully advancing from technology readiness level (TRL) 2 to TRL 7 within a year. The results highlight Shadow's potential as a versatile, low-cost solution for various human–robot interaction scenarios.

3. Further Directions

As the fields of HMI, AI, and robotics continue to evolve, several key areas warrant further exploration. First, the development of more sophisticated AI models that can understand and predict human intentions will be crucial for advancing HMI. Future research should focus on creating transparent AI systems that provide justifiable decisions, particularly in applications where safety and ethical considerations are paramount.

Significant challenges remain in making XR technologies accessible and user-friendly. One critical issue is designing interaction models that reduce cognitive load, making it easier for users to control and collaborate with robots. In medical robotics, for example, surgeons use VR-based training systems to practice complex procedures, reducing the risk of errors in actual operations. Such applications demonstrate the potential of immersive technologies to improve skills and safety, yet also highlight the need for continuous refinement to ensure that these systems are both effective and intuitive.

Ethical considerations are also at the forefront of HMI research. As robots and AI systems become more autonomous, questions arise about accountability, transparency, and user trust. There is an urgent need for frameworks that ensure AI-driven decisions are interpretable and align with human values, particularly in high-stakes areas like healthcare and autonomous driving. Public acceptance of robots will depend not only on technological advancements but also on the perceived fairness, safety, and reliability of these systems.

Additionally, the role of AR, VR, and XR in enhancing HMI will expand, with future work needed to improve the usability and integration of these technologies in everyday robotic applications. This includes optimizing interfaces to reduce cognitive load and developing standards for safe and ethical interactions in virtual environments. There is also significant potential in leveraging these technologies for education and training, particularly in fields like healthcare, where realistic simulations can greatly enhance learning outcomes.

Finally, as robots become more autonomous, it will be essential to develop regulatory frameworks that address the ethical implications of HMI. This includes ensuring that AI systems are free from biases, respect user privacy, and operate transparently. Collaborative efforts between technologists, ethicists, and policymakers will be necessary to guide the responsible development of these technologies and ensure they are deployed in ways that benefit society.

By addressing these future directions, the research community can continue to push the boundaries of what is possible in HMI, AI, and robotics, paving the way for a future where intelligent machines work seamlessly and safely alongside humans.

Funding: This research was founded by the Generalitat Valenciana (Grant GV/2021/181) and by the Spanish Government (Grant PID2020-117421RB-C21 funded by MCIN/AEI/10.13039/501100011033).

Acknowledgments: We express our gratitude to all the researchers who contributed their work to this Special Issue. We extend our congratulations to the authors whose papers were featured, and appreciate their willingness to share their significant findings with us. Thanks also to the diligent reviewers whose insightful feedback helped curate the high-quality content of this issue. We are thankful for the Editorial Board of Electronics for allowing us the privilege to serve as Guest Editors, and to the Editorial Office for their meticulous oversight and management, ensuring the prompt release of this issue.

Conflicts of Interest: The authors declare no conflicts of interest.

List of Contributions

1. Al-Yacoub, A.; Flanagan, M.; Buerkle, A.; Bamber, T.; Ferreira, P.; Hubbard, E.-M.; Lohse, N. Data-Driven Modelling of Human-Human Co-Manipulation Using Force and Muscle Surface Electromyogram Activities. *Electronics* **2021**, *10*, 1509. https://doi.org/10.3390/electronics10131509.
2. Martí-Testón, A.; Muñoz, A.; Solanes, J.E.; Gracia, L.; Tornero, J. A Methodology to Produce Augmented-Reality Guided Tours in Museums for Mixed-Reality Headsets. *Electronics* **2021**, *10*, 2956. https://doi.org/10.3390/electronics10232956.

3. Kim, H.; Hwang, S.; Kim, J.; Lee, Z. Toward Smart Communication Components: Recent Advances in Human and AI Speaker Interaction. *Electronics* **2022**, *11*, 1533. https://doi.org/10.3390/electronics11101533.
4. Castillo-Vergara, M.; Álvarez-Marín, A.; Villavicencio Pinto, E.; Valdez-Juárez, L.E. Technological Acceptance of Industry 4.0 by Students from Rural Areas. *Electronics* **2022**, *11*, 2109. https://doi.org/10.3390/electronics11142109.
5. Xie, X.; Shen, X. Convolutional Network Research for Defect Identification of Productor Appearance Surface. *Electronics* **2022**, *11*, 4218. https://doi.org/10.3390/electronics11244218.
6. Castiblanco Jimenez, I.A.; Gomez Acevedo, J.S.; Olivetti, E.C.; Marcolin, F.; Ulrich, L.; Moos, S.; Vezzetti, E. User Engagement Comparison between Advergames and Traditional Advertising Using EEG: Does the User's Engagement Influence Purchase Intention? *Electronics* **2023**, *12*, 122. https://doi.org/10.3390/electronics12010122.
7. Mandischer, N.; Gürtler, M.; Weidemann, C.; Hüsing, E.; Bezrucav, S.-O.; Gossen, D.; Brünjes, V.; Hüsing, M.; Corves, B. Toward Adaptive Human–Robot Collaboration for the Inclusion of People with Disabilities in Manual Labor Tasks. *Electronics* **2023**, *12*, 1118. https://doi.org/10.3390/electronics12051118.
8. Mourtzis, D.; Tsoubou, S.; Angelopoulos, J. Robotic Cell Reliability Optimization Based on Digital Twin and Predictive Maintenance. *Electronics* **2023**, *12*, 1999. https://doi.org/10.3390/electronics12091999.
9. Burčiar, F.; Važan, P.; Juhásová, B.; Juhás, M. Methodical Approach to Proactivity Using a Digital Twin of Production Process. *Electronics* **2023**, *12*, 3335. https://doi.org/10.3390/electronics12153335.
10. Lee, K.; Im, E.; Cho, K. Mission-Conditioned Path Planning with Transformer Variational Autoencoder. *Electronics* **2024**, *13*, 2437. https://doi.org/10.3390/electronics13132437.
11. Torrejón, A.; Zapata, N.; Bonilla, L.; Bustos, P.; Núñez, P. Design and Development of Shadow: A Cost-Effective Mobile Social Robot for Human-Following Applications. *Electronics* **2024**, *13*, 3444. https://doi.org/10.3390/electronics13173444.

References

1. Sandini, G.; Sciutti, A.; Morasso, P. Artificial cognition vs. artificial intelligence for next-generation autonomous robotic agents. *Front. Comput. Neurosci.* **2024**, *18*, 1349408. [CrossRef] [PubMed]
2. Ferreira, J.F.; Portugal, D.; Andrada, M.E.; Machado, P.; Rocha, R.P.; Peixoto, P. Sensing and Artificial Perception for Robots in Precision Forestry: A Survey. *Robotics* **2023**, *12*, 139. [CrossRef]
3. Ong, S.; Yew, A.; Thanigaivel, N.; Nee, A. Augmented reality-assisted robot programming system for industrial applications. *Robot. Comput. Manuf.* **2020**, *61*, 101820. [CrossRef]
4. Solanes, J.E.; Muñoz, A.; Gracia, L.; Martí, A.; Girbés-Juan, V.; Tornero, J. Teleoperation of industrial robot manipulators based on augmented reality. *Int. J. Adv. Manuf. Technol.* **2020**, *111*, 1077–1097. [CrossRef]
5. Tram, M.Q.; Cloud, J.M.; Beksi, W.J. Intuitive Robot Integration via Virtual Reality Workspaces. In Proceedings of the 2023 IEEE International Conference on Robotics and Automation (ICRA), London, UK, 29 May–2 June 2023; pp. 11654–11660.
6. Malik, A.A.; Masood, T.; Bilberg, A. Virtual reality in manufacturing: Immersive and collaborative artificial-reality in design of human-robot workspace. *Int. J. Comput. Integr. Manuf.* **2019**, *33*, 22–37. [CrossRef]
7. Hoebert, T.; Seibel, S.; Amersdorfer, M.; Vincze, M.; Lepuschitz, W.; Merdan, M. A Framework for Enhanced Human–Robot Collaboration during Disassembly Using Digital Twin and Virtual Reality. *Robotics* **2024**, *13*, 104. [CrossRef]
8. Mugisha, S.; Guda, V.K.; Chevallereau, C.; Chablat, D.; Zoppi, M. Motion Prediction With Gaussian Processes for Safe Human–Robot Interaction in Virtual Environments. *IEEE Access* **2024**, *12*, 67470–67485. [CrossRef]

electronics

MDPI

Article

Data-Driven Modelling of Human-Human Co-Manipulation Using Force and Muscle Surface Electromyogram Activities

Ali Al-Yacoub *, Myles Flanagan, Achim Buerkle, Thomas Bamber, Pedro Ferreira, Ella-Mae Hubbard and Niels Lohse

Intelligent Automation Centre, Wolfson School of Mechanical, Electrical, and Manufacturing Engineering, Loughborough University, Loughborough LE11 3TU, UK; m.flanagan@lboro.ac.uk (M.F.); a.buerkle@lboro.ac.uk (A.B.); t.bamber@lboro.ac.uk (T.B.); p.ferreira@lboro.ac.uk (P.F.); e.hubbard@lboro.ac.uk (E.-M.H.); N.Lohse@lboro.ac.uk (N.L.)

* Correspondence: a.al-yacoub@lboro.ac.uk

Citation: Al-Yacoub, A.; Flanagan, M.; Buerkle, A.; Bamber, T.; Ferreira, P.; Hubbard, E.-M.; Lohse, N. Data-Driven Modelling of Human-Human Co-Manipulation Using Force and Muscle Surface Electromyogram Activities. *Electronics* **2021**, *10*, 1509. https://doi.org/10.3390/electronics10131509

Academic Editors: Juan Ernesto Solanes Galbis, Luis Gracia and Jaime Valls Miro

Received: 29 April 2021
Accepted: 17 June 2021
Published: 22 June 2021

Abstract: With collaborative robots and the recent developments in manufacturing technologies, physical interactions between humans and robots represent a vital role in performing collaborative tasks. Most previous studies have focused on robot motion planning and control during the execution of the task. However, further research is required for direct physical contact for human-robot or robot-robot interactions, such as co-manipulation. In co-manipulation, a human operator manipulates a shared load with a robot through a semi-structured environment. In such scenarios, a multi-contact point with the environment during the task execution results in a convoluted force/toque signature that is difficult to interpret. Therefore, in this paper, a muscle activity sensor in the form of an electromyograph (EMG) is employed to improve the mapping between force/torque and displacements in co-manipulation tasks. A suitable mapping was identified by comparing the root mean square error amongst data-driven models, mathematical models, and hybrid models. Thus, a robot was shown to effectively and naturally perform the required co-manipulation with a human. This paper's proposed hypotheses were validated using an unseen test dataset and a simulated co-manipulation experiment, which showed that the EMG and data-driven model improved the mapping of the force/torque features into displacements.

Keywords: human-robot collaboration; human-human co-manipulation; data-driven modelling; mathematical modelling; object manipulation; impedance control

1. Introduction

Robots in the industry are starting to transfer from confined spaces into areas that are shared with humans, which reduces the operational cost for several industrial applications [1]. The co-existence of the human and the robot, however, raises many critical challenges regarding the safety of the human, tasks scheduling, and system evaluations [2]. To tackle these challenges, researchers in human-robot collaboration (HRC) focus on improving the production efficiency, safety, and collaboration quality between humans and robots.

Until now, the human often remains in a superior guidance role, which is due to human perception, cognition, and dexterity exceeding the capability of robots [3]. Robots, on the other hand, cope well with high payloads and repetitive tasks, while delivering high precision. Henceforth, several approaches established a combination of both human cognitive and perceptual abilities with the robot's endurance to perform a collaborative task. This included intended physical contact between humans and robots during actions, such as hand-overs, co-manipulation, co-drilling, and many other applications [4,5].

To ensure human health and safety in such scenarios, robots operate at limited speeds and torque settings and perform a full stop in the case of a collision [6]. According to [5], however, these collisions are permissible when limiting the impact forces. Therefore, another group of researchers proposed to control unavoidable collision by limiting the impact forces, such as the work presented by [7]. These methods rely on the kinematic and dynamic behaviour of the robot and human during the task. Such approaches require accurate models of the given setup [7–9]. Thus, there is a growing interest in measuring physical interactions between humans and robots [10]. Moreover, these interfaces have been utilised to establish intuitive human-robot interactions.

This paper presents a novel approach based on human-human co-manipulation to teach an industrial robot how to react to a human leader in a co-manipulation task. The main benefit of such an approach is the intuitive modelling that allows the robot to have similar behaviour to the human. This also allows the robot to isolate human haptic input. Hence, it is possible to estimate the force originating from the human guidance and the forces caused by contact with the environment (third contact point).

This paper's proposed approach is based on two hypotheses investigated and validated on unseen test datasets. The first hypothesis includes adding a muscle activity sensor, namely an electromyograph (EMG), to improve the data-driven model quality. The second hypothesis is that data-driven approaches can achieve higher accuracy compared with mathematical modelling and hybrid modelling approaches, despite adding the complexity of human data processing. In order to validate the hypotheses, a simple leader–follower demonstration scenario was conducted. It provided the required data to model the follower behaviour and, thus, allowed teaching the robot to react similarly.

The paper is structured as follows: a brief literature review is presented in Section 2, Section 3 describes the co-manipulation problem from a mathematical point of view. Then, Section 4 details the equipment utilised during the human-human demonstration and data collection. The adopted research methodology in this research is outlined in Section 5, followed by the simulation setup and control-loop scheme in Section 6. Section 7 presents the results and discussion of the obtained outcome from the conducted experiment. Finally, the conclusions and future work are drawn in Section 8.

2. Literature Review

HRC is widely considered a critical concept to advance the quality and performance in several domains [9]. However, despite intensive research in this field, there are still many unsolved challenges that must be tackled to fully establish a safe and effective collaboration [11]. This includes vital questions such as: How can a robot predict human intentions? What role should the robot perform? At what time? Finally, how can a HRC setup be evaluated [12]? Whereas some companies have invested in HRC and have collaborative robots (cobots) on their manufacturing lines; many others are still waiting for more mature solutions.

The authors in [13] claimed that the reason behind this is the lack of knowledge when integrating cobots into manufacturing and business. Therefore, Ref. [13] examined current training programs that inform manufacturers about finances and tools that support decision makers to analyse assembly workstations and determine whether HRC would be beneficial to their applications. The study concluded with the fact that there is a lack of knowledge about the integration of cobots into the manufacturing processes. This could also be due to several definitions of HRC being available. In some cases, HRC is treated as a synonym for human-robot interaction in general.

In order to distinguish different kinds of human-robot interactions, Ref. [14] established criteria, such as a workplace, working time, aim, and contact. At the lowest level, human-robot coexistence includes a shared working environment, where tasks of the human and the robot do not interfere [15]. In addition to a shared working environment and working time, human-robot cooperation also includes a shared aim of the overall task [14]. On the highest level in HRC, physical contact between humans and robots is also permitted, which makes it the most challenging method of interaction among the three [15]. Hence, human-robot mutual awareness is required, as well as the exact timing of tasks and activities [11].

To understand the required mutual awareness, Ref. [16] introduced a generic definition of several types of human-human and human-robot interactions, in which interaction was considered as a function of physical distances between the human and the robot. Therefore, these interactions were categorised into avoiding, passing, following, approaching, and touching. Hence, the parties in a co-manipulation context can be two humans, a human and a robot, or two robots who manipulate a shared object from point A in the workspace to point B. According to [16], this concept can be extended to multiple humans with a single robot (multiple–single) or multiple humans with multiple robots (multiple–multiple).

Using this analogy, therefore, human-human co-manipulation can provide useful insights on how humans perform a task and consequently teach robots to perform such tasks with humans. Subsequently, various controllers have been designed to allow multiple robots to work together when manipulating an object [17]. Other researchers proposed controllers that are inspired by human anatomy and behaviour, and such research takes the damping and impedance characteristics of human movement into consideration [18]. The authors in [19] stated that human-friendly robot cooperation requires an adaptive impedance control that adjusts the robot impedance based on human characteristics. Hence, motion data from a human-human co-manipulation experiment was conducted.

Using dynamic model identification techniques, damping and stiffness factors have been estimated based on a simplified mathematical model (MM). The method mentioned above, however, requires an accurate MM to be conceived, which is often complicated and time-consuming. The collected data only contains position, speed, and acceleration, while the forces are estimated accordingly. Another approach to model human-human co-manipulation, similar to [18,19], can be found in [20]. An analysis was performed on the leader and follower human, in which one human provided the haptic guidance and the other human followed the haptic clues. The study concluded that most forces originated from the leader, while the follower focused on tracking the co-manipulated object.

A control scheme that enables a humanoid robot to perform a co-manipulation task with a human partner was proposed by [21]. The proposed control scheme consisted of three phases. At first, the robot predicted the human's intentions to move based on a Force/Torque (F/T) sensor attached to the robot. In a second phase, the human and the robot switched roles, where the robot provided guidance and the human followed. In the third phase, the robot was controlled remotely with a joystick. The main problem with this work that it ha a discrete nature, and it required initiation through a joystick.

Since HRC requires the human and the robot to be co-existing in the same workspace, the design and development of a suitable HRC space is still an open challenge [22]. The authors in [23] examined the HRC shared workspace requirements based on a case study of disassembling press fitted components using collaborative robots. The study concluded that the compliance behaviour of a collaborative robot enabled the operator to work closely with the robot, which means lower installation costs and increasing efficiency as the robot and the human can work simultaneously.

However, many challenges need to be addressed regarding the performance evaluation, task assignments, and role management. Researchers proposed to equip the workspace with sensors that can improve the communication between the human and the robot to address the workspace challenges. These sensors can be classified as contextual sensors, such as cameras, motion trackers, biomechanical and psychological sensors, and motion sensors. These combined sensors are believed to improve human-robot communication as they can be used to infer the physical and psychological states of the human during the execution of the HRC task.

In more recent years, approaches have utilised Machine Learning (ML), including advanced classifiers such as Artificial Neural Networks (ANNs), to process sensory data [24]. In [25], an ANN was employed in human-human co-manipulation to predict the required motion based on the F/T input from the leader. The controllers used in this approach followed the desired trajectory to some degree of accuracy. However, the predicted trajectory was described as jerky, and the maximum error reached was 0.1–0.2 m. In further research,

Ref. [26] investigated human-human co-manipulation and proposed the use of a Deep Neural Network (DNN) to accurately estimate the velocity and acceleration of the human over 50 time steps of 0.25 s. The trained model showed higher accuracy in comparison with the work presented in [25], although it was prone to noise interference.

In addition to haptic interfaces and F/T sensors, a growing interest in wearable sensors can be observed, which is intended to improve communication between humans and robots [27]. These approaches also aim to improve the mutual awareness of both parties in HRC [28]. Combining wearable sensors with existing technologies is believed to significantly improve HRC, as they can be used to infer the physical and psychological states of the human during the execution task [29,30].

However, processing signals originating from wearable sensors is considered challenging due to large amounts of subject-specific noise within the data. For example EMG signal depends on the individual internal structure, such as skin temperature, blood flow rate, muscle structure, and many other factors [31]. Moreover, signals can even vary during different recording sessions for the same individual [32]. Nevertheless, advanced ML classifiers can be deployed to demonstrate their characteristic strengths of coping well with noise [33].

A common wearable sensor for detecting muscular fatigue, as well as applied muscular contraction, can be found in EMGs. The EMG signal directly correlates with the forces applied [34]. For instance, Ref. [35] proposed the use of EMG to estimate the required stiffness during HRC tasks since stiffness is an essential component in cooperative leader–follower tasks. The estimated stiffness was employed in a hybrid force/impedance controller. EMG signals in conjunction with an Online Random Forest were used to detect muscular fatigue/or a human operator struggling with a high payload in order to trigger an assistance request for a cobot [27].

Additionally, Brain-Computer Interfaces (BCIs) have gained research interest in HRC. In one approach, a BCI was utilised for communicating human movement intentions to a robot [36]. A DNN was deployed to process electroencephalogram (EEG) signals, which allowed for measuring and classifying human upper-limb movements up to 0.5 s prior to the actual movements. A similar result have also been reported in [37]. Another approach based on a DNN to predict human intentions to move a limb was presented by [38]. In this paper, the human limb position was estimated based on torque readings collected from a F/T sensor attached to the robot end-effector. In general, estimating human-intention-based different sensors is still at an early stage, and further research is required.

Overall, there is an eminent research interest in HRC, of which co-manipulation can be viewed as a small building block. Strategies for classical co-manipulation control vary between force-based and motion-based; however, almost all are limited as they require accurate mathematical modelling pre-knowledge about the desired trajectory. Nevertheless, based on the literature, promising potential towards more accurate models can be found in ML, including ANNs.

Advanced ML algorithms enable the classification of bio-sensory data, such as EMGs. Utilising EMGs, in conjunction with F/T data to predict human motions for co-manipulation tasks is still at an early stage. This would allow the collaborative robot to learn a behaviour, based on human-human co-manipulation within different data-driven models. Moreover, the performance of such data-driven models can be compared with previous mathematical models and hybrid models. This paper provides a comprehensive study on human-human co-manipulation, including a data-driven model, which also considers EMG signals.

3. Problem Definition

The human-human co-manipulation problem can be defined as transporting an object by at least two humans through unstructured/structured environments. In such a task, the human (leader) uses his/her perception to navigate the surroundings while communicating with others (followers) using haptic forces and verbal and gesture clues. The main focus of this paper is the haptic communication between the leader and the follower. Figure

1 depicts the fundamental concept of the co-manipulation task, in which two human operators are carrying out a co-manipulation task of handling a shared weight. The influential factors in such a scenario are the muscle stiffness, resultant forces, object mass, and object displacements in the 3D space.

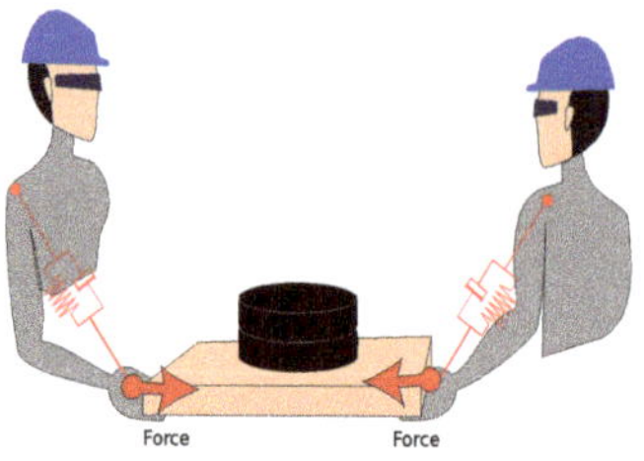

Figure 1. Human-human co-manipulation problem.

The problem at hand can be described as a one-to-one mapping that aims to map follower displacement, and directions with the muscle EMG signal in response to the leader F/T input. Formally, the input data are the F/T data and follower EMG signal, while the output is the displacement of the load in the 3D space. Equations (1) and (2) depict the mathematical definition of the mapping problem.

$$\text{Input} = \begin{cases} F, & F \in \mathbb{R}^{6\times m} \\ emg, & emg \in \mathbb{R}^{2\times m} \end{cases} \tag{1}$$

$$\text{Output} = \begin{cases} x_d, & x_d \in \mathbb{R}^{1\times m} \\ y_d & y_d \in \mathbb{R}^{1\times m} \\ z_d, & z_d \in \mathbb{R}^{1\times m} \end{cases} \tag{2}$$

Henceforth, the problem can be mathematically defined as finding the mapping between the input (Equation (1)) and the output (Equation (2)) as shown in Equation (3).

$$M(F, emg) = \text{Input} \rightarrow \text{Output} \tag{3}$$

Such a problem can be considered as a regression problem [39] that can be solved using ML approaches to identify suitable mapping while minimising the error.

4. Experimental Setup and Data Collection

To test the proposed hypotheses in this paper, an instrumented load was used to collect data during the co-manipulation task, as shown in Figure 2. Two sEMG sensors were utilised, which were fitted on the arm and the forearm as illustrated in Figure 3. For the biceps muscle, the electrodes of the sensors must be aligned with the muscle axial, which was identified as shown in Figure 3a, while the reference electrode must be shifted away from the muscle axial.

Similarly, the sensor electrodes on the forearm muscle must be fitted on the forearm muscle, specifically on the brachioradialis muscle [40], while the reference electrode placed on the outside of the forearm close the bone side; as illustrated in Figure 3b. The Myoware sensor used in this paper has on-board functionality that permitted the reading of the rectified signal, making the signal suitable to be integrated with the presented setup. The signals were sampled using a 12-bit Analogue-To-Digital Converter with a ~85 Hz sampling frequency. The instrumented load is a wooden board with a 5.0 kg weight attached to it in the centre. The following sensors were utilised:

1. A six-axis F/T (F/T) sensor [41].
2. Surface electromyography (sEMG). [42], which is worn by the follower human
3. Motion tracker markers: eight cameras—VICON Vantage 5, https://www.vicon.com/hardware/cameras/vantage/.

The F/T, VICON, and sEMG sensors were sampled at different frequencies; therefore, these sensory data were synchronised using an adaptive algorithm implemented in the *messageFilter-ApproximateTime* tool (http://wiki.ros.org/message_filters/ApproximateTime). The bottleneck of this tool is the slowest signal, the sEMG. Thus, the synchronised data will almost have the same frequency as the sEMG, which is around (∼85 Hz).

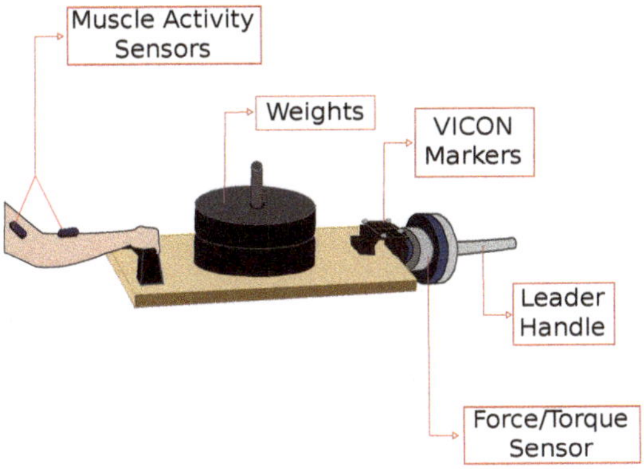

Figure 2. Experimental setup.

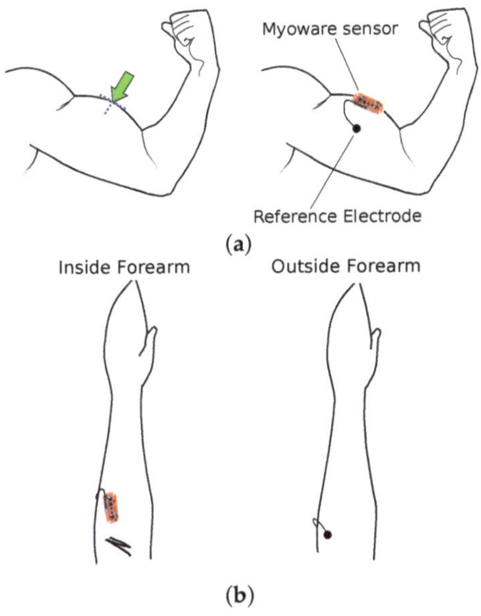

Figure 3. Fitting sEMG (Surface electromyography) sensors on (**a**) biceps and (**b**) forearm.

For the experiment presented in this paper, two participants were asked to co-manipulate the load described above while avoiding an obstacle within the workspace. Figure 4 depicts the floor plan for the experiment and the path that the leader and the follower had to follow. The participants were assigned a leader or follower role and were not allowed to communicate during the experiment. This prevents the participants from verbally sharing their intention. The follower was equipped with muscle activity sensors, which were integrated with the Robot Operating System (ROS) network [43].

The 5.0 kg load, in this scenario, provided some resistance while manipulating the object to emulate a realistic scenario. Additionally, each participant was only permitted to use one arm whilst carrying the object. This enabled the F/T readings to be mapped to a single local reference point. The leader guided the manipulation within the workspace while avoiding the obstacle and towards the endpoint. At the same time, the follower reacted to the leader's movements and mimicked his/her motions until the endpoint was reached. The experiment was designed in this way to replicate human-robot co-manipulation.

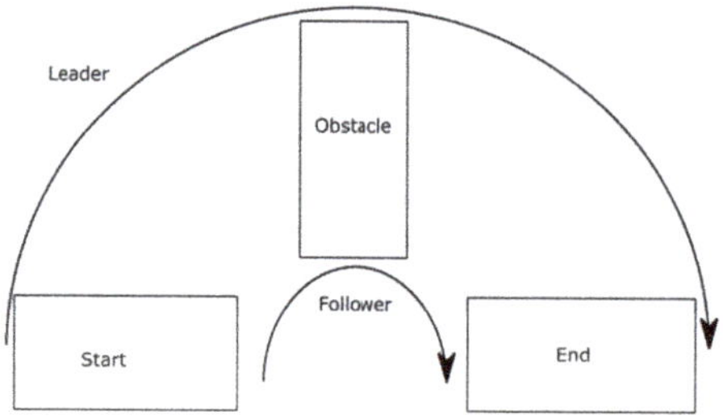

Figure 4. Floor plan, human-human.

Sensor Placement

The F/T sensor was placed on the follower side in the centre of the object. The correct EMG sensor placement is essential as the quality of the signal can be affected. As such, the sensor must be placed over the centre of the muscle as shown in Figure 3 [42]. Finally, the motion capture reference point was placed on the leader's side in the object's centre, while the F/T sensor was located between the leader's handle and the load. Hence, a transformation between the F/T coordinate into the workspace coordinate is required. Figure 5 illustrates the required transformation; also, it can be noticed that the coordinate system of the F/T sensor in which the Z-axis is aligned with the handle axial and XY plane was parallel to the surface of the sensor.

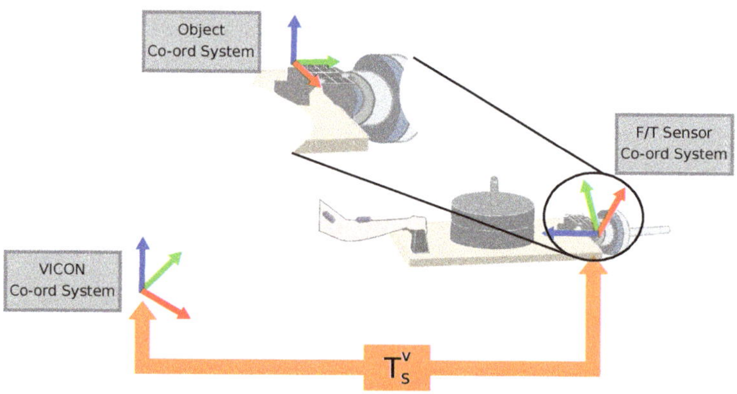

Figure 5. Coordinate system transformations: F/T sensors into VICON system.

5. Methodology

Four different sets of features were used to predict the required displacements based on leader guidance to validate the proposed hypotheses. The fitted models were evaluated based on unseen test datasets using the root mean square error (RMSE). An overall displacement error (overall RMSE) was calculated to determine the resultant error ($\sqrt{\text{RMSE}_x^2 + \text{RMSE}_y^2 + \text{RMSE}_z^2}$). The employed feature sets are shown in Table 1.

Table 1. Feature sets utilised to fit data-driven models.

Feature Set	Features	Set Dimension
Features 1 (F1)	normalised F/T, normalised EMG (arm/forearm), previous 3D displacements	$\mathbb{R}^{11}$
Features 2 (F2)	F/T, previous 3D displacements	$\mathbb{R}^9$
Features 3 (F3)	F/T, EMG (arm/forearm), previous 3D displacements	$\mathbb{R}^{11}$
Features 4 (F4)	normalised F/T, EMG (arm/forearm), previous 3D displacements	$\mathbb{R}^9$

The F/T features were the F/T data ($\mathbf{F} = \{F_x, F_y, F_z, T_x, T_y, T_z\} \in \mathbb{R}^6$), EMG arm and forearm ($\mathbf{EMG} = \{emg_{arm}, emg_{forearm}\} \in \mathbb{R}^2$, respectively) and previous 3D displacement, which is the displacement from thge previous timestamp ($\mathbf{\Delta} = \{\delta x, \delta y, \delta z\} \in \mathbb{R}^3$). Then, the performance of the fitted models on the unseen test dataset was calculated using RMSE. This allows **for** testing the impact of including EMG sensory data in such a context. Finally, the performance of the best data-driven model was compared against the performance of the MM and the hybrid model. Another important feature in the co-manipulation tasks is the time, in which the human intention to move the shared object at time point t not only depends on the F/T and EMG at the same point but also depends on the displacements at the previous timestamp ($t-1$), as summarised in Equation (4).

$$\mathbf{\Delta}(t) = \mathbf{M}(\mathbf{F}(t), \mathbf{EMG}(t), \mathbf{\Delta}(t-1)) \tag{4}$$

where $\mathbf{M}(-)$ is the mapping function of the given features to the intended displacement $\mathbf{\Delta}$. The displacement $\mathbf{\Delta}(t-1)$ is measured using the VICON system by comparing the Cartesian position at t with the Cartesian position at $t-1$.

5.1. Mathematical Modelling

The problem described in Section 3, can be simplified as a mass–spring–damper system, as shown in Figure 6. The human arms can be simplified as a spring–damper on both sides of the transported object in 3D space.

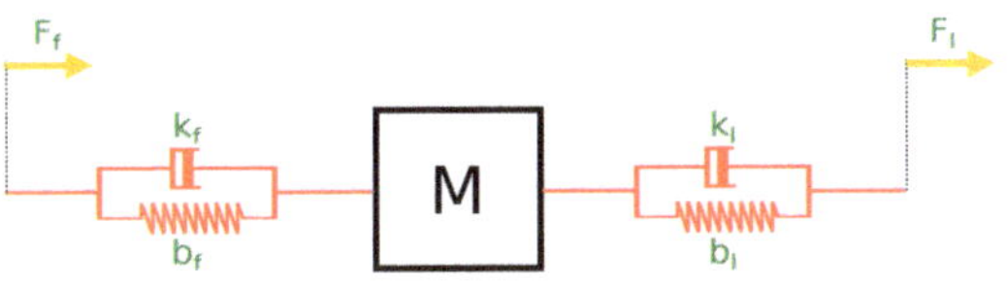

Figure 6. Simplified mathematical system, where F_f, F_l are the follower and leader forces, respectively; K_f, K_l are the follower and leader muscle stiffness, respectively; b_f, b_l are the follower and leader damping factor, respectively; and M is the mass of the shared load.

Using Newton's second law ($\sum F = m\,a$), the problem in Figure 6 can be described as shown in Equation (5).

$$m\Delta a(t) + (b_f + b_l)\Delta v(t) + (k_f + k_l)\Delta X = 0 \tag{5}$$

The superposition concept can be used for further simplification, as the 3D space system can be split into three separated equations (vector form), as shown in Equation (6). Based on the experimental setup and the problem at hand, the resultant force is measured using the F/T sensor. Furthermore, the total mass of the moving object is known; thus, the model described in Equation (5) can be simplified by omitting the muscle stiffness and damping effect as shown in Equations (5) and (6). To determine the displacements based on the measured forces, Equation (6) can be rewritten as in Equation (7).

$$\begin{bmatrix} f_x \\ f_y \\ f_z \end{bmatrix} = m \begin{bmatrix} a_{xs} \\ a_{ys} \\ a_{zs} \end{bmatrix} \tag{6}$$

$$\begin{bmatrix} \Delta x_s \\ \Delta y_s \\ \Delta z_s \end{bmatrix} = \iint \begin{bmatrix} \frac{f_x}{m} \\ \frac{f_y}{m} \\ \frac{f_z}{m} \end{bmatrix} \partial^2 t \tag{7}$$

In Equation (7), Δx_s, Δy_s, and Δz_s are the displacements in the F/T sensors. Therefore, they must be transformed into the VICON coordinate system using a transformation matrix that was calculated based on the alignment of the F/T sensor with respect to the VICON markers (Figure 2). The final MM is shown in Equation (8), where T_s^v is the transformation matrix from the F/T sensor into the VICON coordinate system.

$$\begin{bmatrix} \Delta x_v \\ \Delta y_v \\ \Delta z_v \end{bmatrix} = T_s^v \begin{bmatrix} x_v \\ y_v \\ z_v \end{bmatrix} = T_s^v \iint \begin{bmatrix} \frac{f_x}{m} \\ \frac{f_y}{m} \\ \frac{f_z}{m} \end{bmatrix} \partial^2 t \tag{8}$$

5.2. Model-Free Approaches: Data-Driven Models

Modern manufacturing systems are complicated since they integrate a wide variety of equipment that extends from machinery and automation equipment on the shopfloor up to cloud systems and data-acquisition tools. In addition, the complexity on the shopfloor level due to the fast development of communication is exponentially increasing, which means higher data flows between different elements on the shopfloor. Consequently, equipment has higher nonlinearities, disturbances, and uncertainties. Therefore, it is almost impossible to describe these complicated systems using conventional mathematical models, such as differential equations or statistical models, in real applications. Nonetheless, with the fast advancement of sensing technology and data collection technologies, data-driven modelling (DDM) becomes more feasible in comparison with mathematical modelling [44].

Based on the regression problem explained in Section 3, we propose the use of Linear Regression (LR), Random Forest (RF) regression, Boosted-Trees (BT), and Recurrent Neural Networks (RNN) as these methods represent state-of-the-art approaches [45]. LR is well-known for simplicity and its ease of use. In contrast, BT and RF are ensemble ML approaches that are powerful and have shown high performance on several datasets. Finally, an RNN as part of a Deep Learning Neural Network is utilised. Hence, in this paper, we compared the performance of each ML algorithm and the performance of the data-driven approaches with the mathematical and hybrid models. In the following subsection, the data-driven approaches are explained in the co-manipulation context.

5.3. Hybrid Modelling Approach (HM)

As described in the mathematical modelling section, mathematical models are often derived from the fundamental laws of physics, such as Newton's laws of motion. Physical models extrapolate well by design and, therefore, are preferred for model-based control approaches. In realistic scenarios, however, modelling errors exist due to omitted dynamics, modelling approximations, lack of suitable friction models, backlash, or unmodelled elasticity in the mechanism. Classically, these problems can be tackled with assumptions, linearisation around an operation point, and enhancing the model parameters based on theoretical or experimental methods. In the case of a very complex mechanism, however, these solutions might not be feasible.

On the contrary, data-driven modelling approaches utilise the behavioural response of the system for different inputs and then extract a set of generic rules that describe the correlations amongst the inputs and outputs without omitting or simplifying the system. The main drawback of such systems is that they are not always interpretable as in physical/mathematical modelling. The quality of the data-driven model depends on the size and quality of the collected data.

Furthermore, data can barely ever deplete all possible configurations. Thus, a hybrid model can be used that combines simplified MM with a data-driven error model [46]. The target is to capture the main physical attributes of the given system (e.g., the robot) while substituting for model approximations and inaccuracies. Hence, the hybrid model has a grey-box character due to the mixture of a physical and data-driven (black-box) error model. In this paper, we decided to model the error within a mathematical model, Section 5.1, using the best data-driven approach from the previous section. Then, the problem description can be now rewritten, as shown in Equation (9).

$$\begin{bmatrix} \Delta x_s \\ \Delta y_s \\ \Delta z_s \end{bmatrix} = \iint \begin{bmatrix} \frac{f_x}{m} \\ \frac{f_y}{m} \\ \frac{f_z}{m} \end{bmatrix} \partial^2 t + E(\text{emg}, F) \tag{9}$$

where $E(\text{emg}, F)$ is the error between the real displacement measured using VICON and the estimated displacement using the mathematical models. The error function $E(-)$ can be seen as a regression problem that can be tackled using the best data-driven approach. Consequently, the final model is a combination of MM and data-driven models. For evaluation purposes, the hybrid model was compared with all the approaches above on unseen test data.

6. Simulation Setup

A simulated UR10 robot with a 5.0 kg load was exploited to evaluate the different methods mentioned above. Hence, the output from these methods was used with a Proportional–Integral–Derivative (PID) controller, as depicted in Figure 7. In this control scheme, the output disp(t) can be seen as a feedforward control scheme, in which the prediction of error (disp(t)) can be added to the error from the previous action (feedback-loop).

The inner loop is also a position control loop that attempts to maintain a precise position given the prediction from the data-driven models combined with the position error. The outer loop can be seen as a force-based control loop in which the robot must react to human EMG and forces in a spring–damper manner. Therefore, this control scheme is an Impedance Controller.

The simulation setup composed of a Workstation that runs Ubuntu 18.04 (developed by Canonical Ltd.), ROS-Indigo (Developed by Willow Garage, Menlo Park, CA, USA) with 100 Hz simulation frequency and the models developed earlier. The PID parameters were experimentally chosen, and similar settings were implemented to test the methods highlighted earlier.

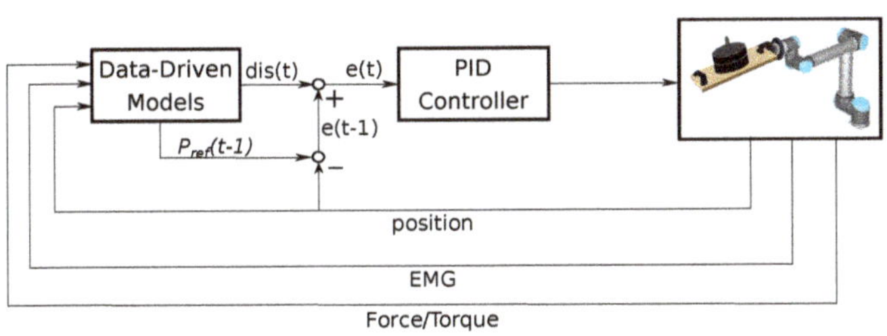

Figure 7. UR10 Position Control-Loop.

7. Results and Discussion

7.1. Results

During the human-human demonstration, two participants performed the co-manipulation task, while data, from the F/T sensor, EMG sensor, and VICON, were collected, filtered, and synchronised. The total number of collected data points was 5125. The EMG signal was collected only from the follower; one could argue that the sEMG data are insufficient to draw a generalised solution. However, studies revealed that the pattern of sEMG was comparable amongst different individuals; and hence, magnitude normalisation allows us to generalise the findings of this paper [47].

Out of the 5125 data points, 4212 data points were used for training and validation and 513 data points were used for testing. The synchronised data frequency was ~80 Hz, in which sensory data were synchronised using an approximation time tool developed for ROS. The F/T sensory data were filtered using a low-pass filter with a cut-off frequency at 50 Hz. The VICON data were filtered using moving-window-average and the manual removal of anomaly data that occurred due to flip [48]. The collected data included the F/T signal, the Cartesian position of the co-manipulated object, and the sEMG muscle activity signal of the follower's right arm. As highlighted in the problem definition section, the goal is to find the mapping between relevant features and the displacements on the Cartesian space.

For training the models, four different sets of features were used as illustrated in Table 1, and these sets can be summarised as follows: normalised F/T signals and normalised EMG signals (F1), F/T signals (F2), F/T signals and EMG signals (F3), and normalised F/T signals (F4). The main reason behind this choice of features was to test the proposed hypotheses that the use of EMG signals can improve the accuracy of the data-driven models.

Figure 8 shows the accuracy of each predicted displacement in the X, Y, and Z directions for the data-driven models. The best model shown in Figure 8d was the RNN model based on feature set F1, which had the lowest RMSE with about 0.025 m on all axes and about 0.045 m overall error. The remaining data-driven approaches did not show the same impact of including the EMG data as illustrated in Figure 8a–c.

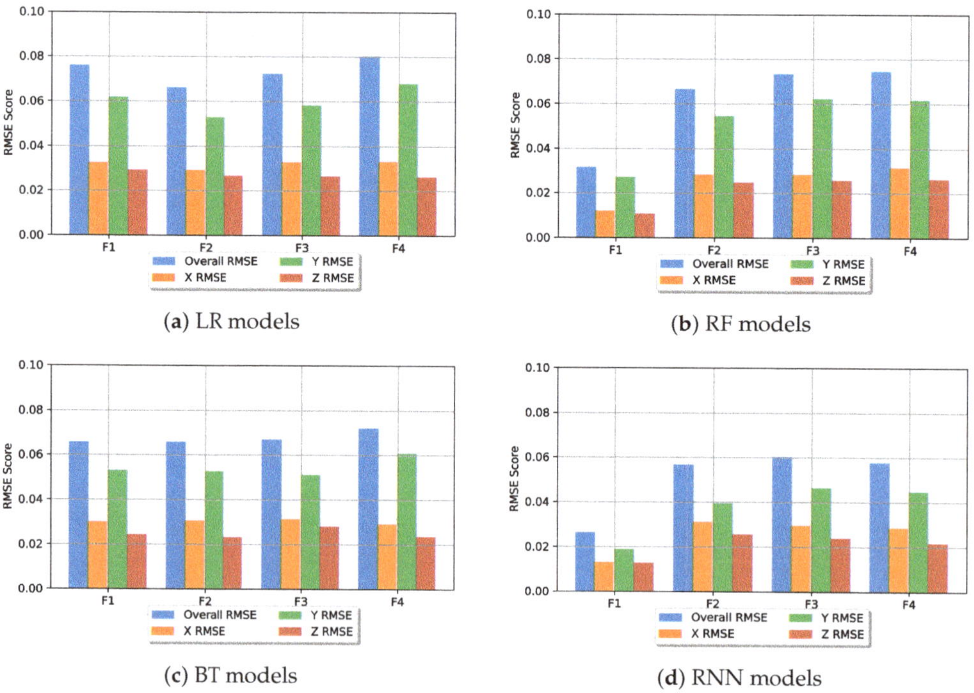

(**a**) LR models (**b**) RF models

(**c**) BT models (**d**) RNN models

Figure 8. RMSE (root mean square error) scores of different models using the sets of features F1, F2, F3, and F4.

In terms of accuracy, however, the RF models showed tangent accuracy to the RNN models with an overall RMSE of around 0.05 m. Finally, the BT and LR models had similar performance with an overall RMSE of around 0.07 m as depicted in Figure 8a–c. Another significant result is that sEMG features did not necessarily improve the quality of the data-driven models, especially in the LR and BT models, in which the performance was almost constant regardless of the feature set.

The general trend regarding the accuracy in the $X - Y - Z$ direction is that the RMSE in the Y direction was higher than the RMSE in X and Z across all models and feature sets, as illustrated in Table 2. The Z axis models had the lowest RMSE but were still very close to the X axis RMSE values. This performance variation on the $X - Y - Z$ models is believed to be due to the quality of the VICON data, which could be degraded due to reflective objects, obstacles, and light variations.

Table 2. Accuracy (m) in $X - Y - Z$ directions.

Model	X	Y
LR	0.032	0.060
RF	0.030	0.060
BT	0.030	0.054
RNN	0.026	0.037

Models with the lowest RMSE were chosen and compared with the MM and HM, as shown in Figure 9. This figure shows that the RMSE values for the MM were (0.75, 1.34, 1.0)m. The HM (Figure 10) RMSE values were (0.051, 0.056, 0.051)m, which is comparable to the data-driven approach. We propose that these results occur due to the unknown dynamics naturally originating from the human body that allow for an adaptive non-linear change of stiffness and compliance, which is not captured in the simplified MM.

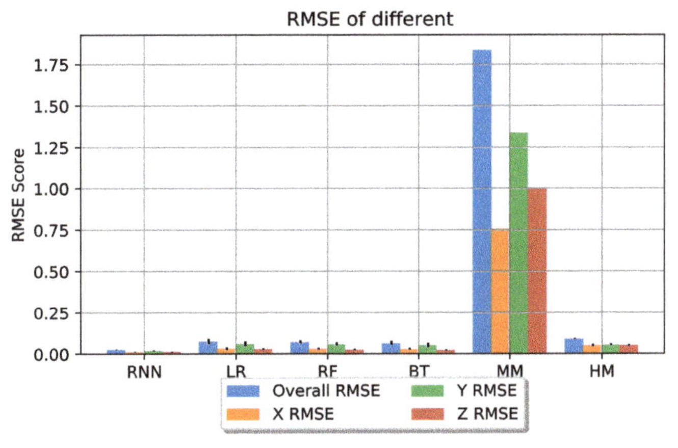

Figure 9. The best RMSE scores for data-driven models vs. the mathematical models.

As the RMSE scores for the MM were very large, it is not easy to compare amongst different models in Figure 9. Therefore, Figure 10 illustrates the accuracy of the data-driven models in comparison with HM, where it is clear that the RNN models had the lowest error (overall error 0.025 m) while the rest of the data-driven models had an error range between (∼0.065 m for BT models) and (∼0.075 m for LR models). The RNN models had the lowest variations on all axes variations in comparison with other methods.

This result is of tremendous importance, as in human-robot co-manipulation, movement variation (fluctuation) might result in jerky movements that represent a safety issue, especially if the human is physically interacting with the robot. By a closer look at how the models behave in $X - Y - Z$ directions, all models had relatively larger error along the Y directions. This indicates the lack of variation along the Y axis in the captured data. Another possible explanation is that the participants blocked the VICON cameras' field, which reduced the quality of the data in a certain direction.

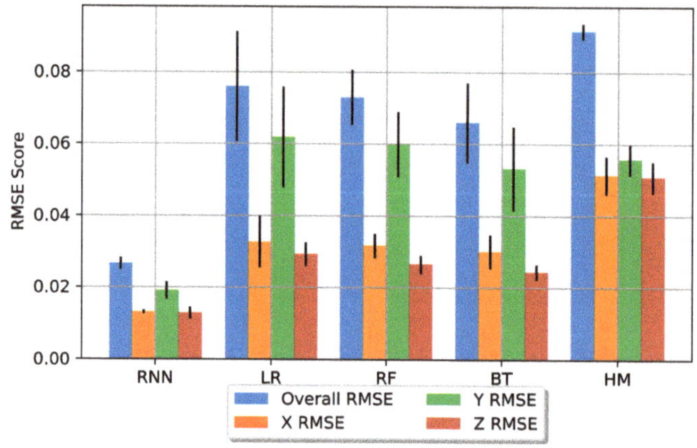

Figure 10. Data-driven models and hybrid-modelling (HM).

7.1.1. Simulation Results

The first 50 sampled points from the fourth trial were used to control a simulated setup as described in Section 6. The overall displacements of these 50 points were ~3.5 m, and the predicted displacements were used as a set point for a PID controller as illustrated in Figure 7. The displacement error per-sampling point of the best data-driven models in comparison with MM and HM is depicted in Figure 11. It is obvious from this figure that the data-driven models had an error less than (~6%), the HM model had an error of (~7.8%), and the MM had an error of ~11.9%.

This shows that data-driven models had higher accuracy in comparison with HM and MM. The error of data-driven models, however, appeared to be tangibly similar (on average ~4%), in which LR and BT had the lowest error followed by RF and RNN, respectively. Since the co-manipulation and force control, in general, is a non-linear problem, these results come as a surprise given the results in the previous section. The explanation for these results could be that the non-linear behaviour was achieved through the control scheme (a feedforward–feedback loop).

Another essential aspect in the human-robot co-manipulation task is the interaction forces during the execution [49]. Hence, during the simulation, interaction forces based on a dynamical model of the load (5.0 kg) were estimated, and then physical metrics, such as the work and kinetic energy, were calculated as shown in Figure 12. The results show that the force, work, and kinetic energy of MM and HM were very high (relatively) compared to the data-driven approach.

This not only means that it is challenging to do co-manipulation based on these approaches but also that it is not safe to do such a task due to the speed variation ($acc \neq 0$). Jerky movements with some impact force can cause injuries to the human during co-manipulation tasks. On the other hand, the data-driven approaches appeared to have much smoother movements as illustrated by the lower interaction force, work, and kinetic energy, which indicates that movements occurred at a constant speed ($acc = 0$) with less jerky movements.

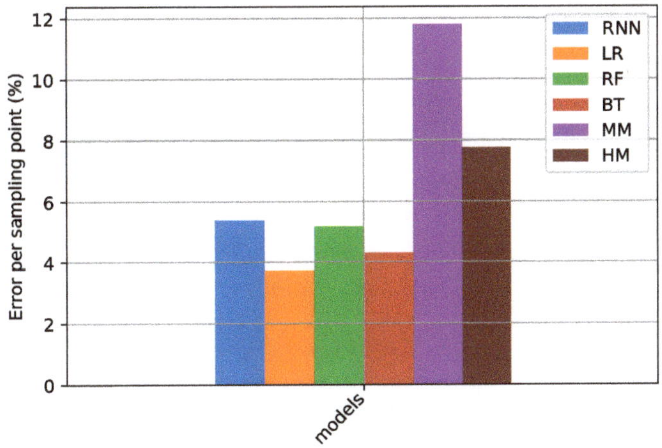

Figure 11. Model accuracy per sampling point in (%).

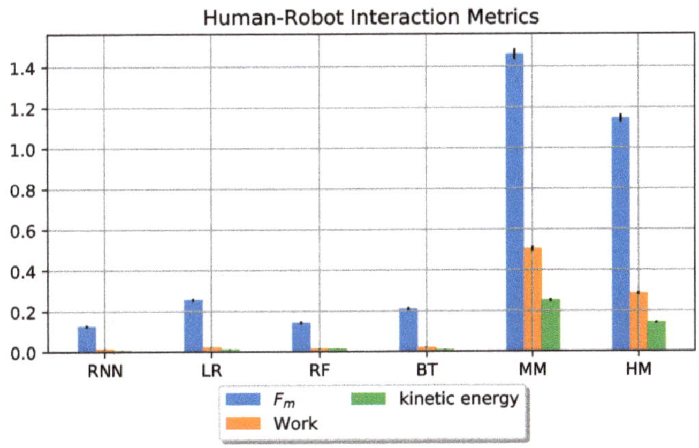

Figure 12. Interaction force (N), work (N·m), and kinetic energy (kg·m·s^{-1}) of the simulated setup.

7.2. Discussion

The results revealed that the RNN models with feature set F1 were the most accurate, followed by the RF, BT, and LR models, respectively. However, the RNN and the RF models had tangible results. This is particularly important when a data-driven approach is adopted for a HRC system with limited computational resources. In that case, the RF models can give very accurate results with much lower computational requirements. Another important observation is that the RNN and RF models trained on normalised F/T and EMG (F1) had the best performance amongst other models. However, RF does not require normalised features, and the performance of RF models must be the same with and without normalisation. We speculate that this is due to the combination of the features within the F1 set, which resulted in better performance.

The second outcome in this paper is that data-driven models had higher accuracy in capturing the human-human co-manipulation. Hence, it is expected to be more accurate in the human-robot scenario. This points towards being correct since mathematical models require an accurate dynamical description of humans and robots to build such a system. Assuming that an accurate model is available of a given robot, building such a system will be feasible without a data-driven model. The counterargument to this is that, even if it is possible to obtain a very accurate mathematical model of the robotics system, this solution is not generic enough and can only be applied on one robot and one type of load. In other words, the model does not guarantee resilience to variations in the system.

The simulation results unexpectedly revealed that LR had the lowest displacement error, due to the combination of LR models with a feedforward control scheme as shown in Figure 7. Nonetheless, displacement accuracy is not the only aspect that needs to be considered. Once the human is physically in contact with the robot, the robot's responses must not cause any injuries to the human. In other words, for movements that require high forces, jerkiness should be prohibited. Hence, even though LR models achieved the most accurate displacements, they had the highest interaction forces between humans and robots. This means that the human must do more work to co-manipulate an object with the robot. Hence, it will be more exhausting for the human to perform the required task.

8. Conclusions and Future Work

This paper utilised a data-driven approach to extract and model a human-human (demonstration) co-manipulation skill, which can be utilised to teach an industrial robot a human-like behaviour. The collected experimental data included F/T data, the manipulated object's Cartesian position, and the EMG signal from the human muscles (follower). The collected data were then used to fit an RNN, an RF, an LR, and BT using four sets of features (F1, F2, F3, and F4). The accuracy of the fitted models was tested using unseen, randomly split test data, which illustrated that the sequential RNN trained on F1 features had the lowest RMSE compared to other ML models.

Moreover, this showed that the use of EMG sensory data positively impacted such a model's accuracy. After that, the best data-driven model was compared with a simplified mathematical model. The results illustrated that the RNN outperformed the mathematical model; in fact, all data-driven approaches outperformed the mathematical models. Finally, the best data-driven models were validated in a simulated environment with an impedance controller to evaluate these approaches compared to MM and HM in a more realistic scenario. The results exhibited that data-driven models had higher accuracy and smoother trajectories in comparison with HM and MM.

In order to extend the work completed in this paper, it is essential first to outline the vision for the work. This project's desired outcome was to create a controller that allowed co-manipulation tasks, including multiple robots following a human leader. However, substantial work needs to be completed until this vision can be established. The data-driven approach offers promising potential for more intuitive interfaces in HRC and, thus, more effective collaboration between humans and robots. Hence, testing the model experimentally in a human-robot manipulation scenario will be conducted in the future.

Author Contributions: Conceptualization, A.A.-Y., M.F. and A.B.; methodology, A.A.-Y. and M.F.; software, A.A.-Y.; validation, A.A.-Y., M.F. and A.B.; formal analysis, A.A.-Y.; investigation, A.A.-Y., M.F. and A.B.; resources, Intelligent Automation Centre lab; data curation, A.A.-Y., M.F.; writing—original draft preparation, A.A.-Y., M.F. and A.B.; writing—review and editing, A.A.-Y., M.F., A.B., T.B., P.F., E.-M.H. and N.L.; supervision, E.-M.H. and N.L.; project administration, E.-M.H. and N.L.; funding acquisition, E.-M.H. and N.L. All authors have read and agreed to the published version of the manuscript.

Funding: This project was funded by EPSRC:project (DigiTOP; EP/R032718/1).

Institutional Review Board Statement: The study was conducted according to the guidelines of the Declaration of Helsinki, and approved by the Ethics Approval Sub-Committee of Wolfson School, Loughborough University (25 November 2019).

Informed Consent Statement: Written informed consent has been obtained from the participant(s) to publish this paper.

Data Availability Statement: The data presented in this study are openly available in Loughborough University Resporitory at https://doi.org/10.17028/rd.lboro.12942122.v1.

Conflicts of Interest: The authors declare no conflict of interest.

References

1. Tsarouchi, P.; Makris, S.; Chryssolouris, G. Human-robot interaction review and challenges on task planning and programming. *Int. J. Comput. Integr. Manuf.* **2016**, *29*, 916–931. [CrossRef]
2. Kroemer, O.; Niekum, S.; Konidaris, G. A review of robot learning for manipulation: Challenges, representations, and algorithms. *arXiv* **2019**, arXiv:1907.03146.
3. Zou, F. Standard for human-robot Collaboration and its Application Trend. *Aeronaut. Manuf. Technol.* **2016**, *58–63, 76.*
4. Hentout, A.; Aouache, M.; Maoudj, A.; Akli, I. Human–robot interaction in industrial collaborative robotics: A literature review of the decade 2008–2017. *Adv. Robot.* **2019**, *33*, 764–799. [CrossRef]
5. ISO/TS 15066. *Robots and Robotic Devices Collaborative Robots*; ISO: Geneva, Switzerland, 2016.
6. Haddadin, S.; Haddadin, S.; Khoury, A.; Rokahr, T.; Parusel, S.; Burgkart, R.; Bicchi, A.; Albu-Schäffer, A. On making robots understand safety: Embedding injury knowledge into control. *Int. J. Robot. Res.* **2012**, *31*, 1578–1602. [CrossRef]
7. Kaneko, K.; Harada, K.; Kanehiro, F.; Miyamori, G.; Akachi, K. September. Humanoid robot HRP-3. In Proceedings of the 2008 IEEE/RSJ International Conference on Intelligent Robots and Systems, Nice, France, 22–26 September, 2008; pp. 2471–2478.
8. Robla-Gomez, S.; Becerra, V.M.; Llata, J.R.; Gonzalez-Sarabia, E.; Torre-Ferrero, C.; Perez-Oria, J. Working Together: A Review on Safe human-robot Collaboration in Industrial Environments. *IEEE Access.* **2017**, *5*, 26754–26773. [CrossRef]
9. Pratt, J.E.; Krupp, B.T.; Morse, C.J.; Collins, S.H. The RoboKnee: An exoskeleton for enhancing strength andendurance during walking. In Proceedings of the Robotics and Automation (ICRA), 2004 IEEE International Conferenceon, New Orleans, LA, USA, 26 April–1 May 2004; Volume 3, pp. 2430–2435. [CrossRef]
10. Peternel, L.; Noda, T.; Petrič, T.; Ude, A.; Morimoto, J.; Babič, J. Adaptive control of exoskeleton robots for periodic assistive behaviours based on EMG feedback minimisation. *PLoS ONE* **2016**, *11*, e0148942. [CrossRef] [PubMed]
11. Dalle Mura, M.; Dini, G. Designing assembly lines with humans and collaborative robots: A genetic approach. *CIRP Ann.* **2019**, *68*, 1–4. [CrossRef]
12. Hayes, B.; Scassellati, B. Challenges in shared-environment human-robot collaboration. *Learning* **2013**, *8*, 1–6.
13. Oberc, H.; Prinz, C.; Glogowski, P.; Lemmerz, K.; Kuhlenkötter, B. Human Robot Interaction-learning how to integrate collaborative robots into manual assembly lines. *Procedia Manuf.* **2019**, *31*, 26–31. [CrossRef]
14. Schmidtler, J.; Knott, V.; Hölzel, C.; Bengler, K. Human Centered Assistance Applications for the working environment of the future. *Occup. Ergon.* **2015**, *12*, 83–95. [CrossRef]
15. Weichhart, G.; Åkerman, M.; Akkaladevi, S.C.; Plasch, M.; Fast-Berglund, Å.; Pichler, A. Models for Interoperable Human Robot Collaboration. *IFAC-PapersOnLine* **2018**, *51*, 36–41. [CrossRef]
16. Yanco, H.A.; Drury, J. October. Classifying human-robot interaction: An updated taxonomy. In Proceedings of the 2004 IEEE International Conference on Systems, Man and Cybernetics (IEEE Cat. No. 04CH37583), The Hague, The Netherlands, 10–13 October 2004; Volume 3, pp. 2841–2846.
17. Sieber, D.; Deroo, F.; Hirche, S. November. Formation-based approach for multi-robot cooperative manipulation based on optimal control design. In Proceedings of the 2013 IEEE/RSJ International Conference on Intelligent Robots and Systems, Tokyo, Japan, 3–7 November 2013; pp. 5227–5233.
18. Ikeura, R.; Inooka, H. Variable impedance control of a robot for cooperation with a human. *Proc. IEEE Int. Conf. Robot. Autom.* **1995**, *3*, 3097–3102.
19. Ikeura, R.; Morita, A.; Mizutani, K. Variable damping characteristics in carrying an object by two humans. In Proceedings of the 6th IEEE International Workshop on Robot and Human Communication. RO-MAN'97 SENDAI, Sendai, Japan, 29 September–1 October 1997.
20. Rahman, M.M.; Ikeura, R.; Mizutani, K. Control characteristics of two humans in cooperative task and its application to robot Control. *IECON Proc. Ind. Electron. Conf.* **2000**, *1*, 1773–1778.
21. Bussy, A.; Gergondet, P.; Kheddar, A.; Keith, F.; Crosnier, A. Proactive behavior of a humanoid robot in a haptic transportation task with a human partner. In Proceedings of the 2012 IEEE RO-MAN: The 21st IEEE International Symposium on Robot and Human Interactive Communication, Paris, France, 9–13 September 2012.
22. Galin, R.; Meshcheryakov, R. Review on human-robot Interaction During Collaboration in a Shared Workspace. In *International Conference on Interactive Collaborative Robotics*; Springer: Cham, Switzerland, 2019; pp. 63–74.
23. Huang, J.; Pham, D.T.; Wang, Y.; Qu, M.; Ji, C.; Su, S.; Xu, W.; Liu, Q.; Zhou, Z. A case study in human–robot collaboration in the disassembly of press-fitted components. *Proc. Inst. Mech. Eng. Part B J. Eng. Manuf.* **2020**, *234*, 654–664. [CrossRef]
24. Hakonen, M.; Piitulainen, H.; Visala, A. Current state of digital signal processing in myoelectric interfaces and related applications. *Biomed. Signal Process. Control* **2015**, *18*, 334–359. [CrossRef]
25. Mielke, E.; Townsend, E.; Wingate, D.; Killpack, M.D. human-robot co-manipulation of extended objects: Data-driven models and control from analysis of human-human dyads. *arXiv* **2020**, arXiv:2001.00991.
26. Townsend, E.C.; Mielke, E.A.; Wingate, D.; Killpack, M.D. Estimating Human Intent for Physical human-robot Co-Manipulation. *arXiv* **2017**, arXiv:1705.10851.
27. Buerkle, A.; Lohse, N.; Ferreira, P. Towards Symbiotic human-robot Collaboration: Human Movement Intention Recognition with an EEG. In Proceedings of the UK-RAS19 Conference: "Embedded Intelligence: Enabling & Supporting RAS Technologies" Proceedings, Loughborough, UK, 27 January 2019; pp. 52–55.

28. Wang, P.; Liu, H.; Wang, L.; Gao, R.X. Deep learning-based human motion recognition for predictive context-aware human-robot collaboration. *CIRP Ann.* **2018**, *67*, 17–20. [CrossRef]
29. Mukhopadhyay, S.C. Wearable sensors for human activity monitoring: A review. *IEEE Sens. J.* **2014**, *15*, 1321–1330. [CrossRef]
30. Peternel, L.; Fang, C.; Tsagarakis, N.; Ajoudani, A. A selective muscle fatigue management approach to ergonomic human-robot co-manipulation. *Robot. Comput. Integr. Manuf.* **2019**, *58*, 69–79. [CrossRef]
31. Chowdhury, R.H.; Reaz, M.B.; Ali, M.A.B.M.; Bakar, A.A.; Chellappan, K.; Chang, T.G. Surface electromyography signal processing and classification techniques. *Sensors* **2013**, *13*, 12431–12466 [CrossRef] [PubMed]
32. Lazar, J.; Feng, J.H.; Hochheiser, H. Measuring the human. In *Research Methods in Human-Computer Interaction*, 2nd ed.; Hochheiser, E., Ed.; Morgan Kaufmann: Boston, MA, USA, 2017; pp. 369–409.
33. Géron, A. *Hands-on Machine Learning with Scikit-Learn, Keras, and TensorFlow: Concepts, Tools, and Techniques to Build Intelligent Systems;* O'Reilly Media: Sebastopol, CA, USA, 2019.
34. Naufel, S.; Glaser, J.I.; Kording, K.P.; Perreault, E.J.; Miller, L.E. A muscle-activity-dependent gain between motor cortex and EMG. *J. Neurophysiol.* **2019**, *121*, 61–73. [CrossRef] [PubMed]
35. Peternel, L.; Tsagarakis, N.; Ajoudani, A. A human–robot co-manipulation approach based on human sensorimotor information. *IEEE Trans. Neural Syst. Rehabil. Eng.* **2017**, *25*, 811–822. [CrossRef] [PubMed]
36. Buerkle, A.; Al-Yacoub, A.; Ferreira, P. An Incremental Learning Approach for Physical human-robot Collaboration. In Proceedings of the 3rd UK Robotics and Autonomous Systems Conference (UKRAS 2020), Lincoln, UK, 17 April 2020.
37. Buerkle, A.; Eaton, W.; Lohse, N.; Bamber, T.; Ferreira, P. EEG based arm movement intention recognition towards enhanced safety in symbiotic Human-Robot Collaboration. *Robot. Comput. Integr. Manuf.* **2021**, *70*, 102137. [CrossRef]
38. Li, Y.; Ge, S.S. Human–robot collaboration based on motion intention estimation. *IEEE/ASME Trans. Mech.* **2013**, *19*, 1007–1014. [CrossRef]
39. Herbrich, R.; Graepel, T.; Obermayer, K. Support vector learning for ordinal regression. In *IET Conference Proceedings;* Institution of Engineering and Technology: London, UK, 1999
40. Lieber, R.L.; Jacobson, M.D.; Fazeli, B.M.; Abrams, R.A.; Botte, M.J. Architecture of selected muscles of the arm and forearm: Anatomy and implications for tendon transfer. *J. Hand Surg.* **1992**, *17*, 787–798. [CrossRef]
41. ATI Industrial Automation. Force/Torque Sensor Delta Datasheet. Available online: https://www.ati-ia.com/products/ft/ft_models.aspx?id=Delta (accessed on 18 February 2020).
42. Myoware. EMG Sensor Datasheet. Available online: https://cdn.sparkfun.com/datasheets/Sensors/Biometric/MyowareUserManualAT-04-001.pdf (accessed on 11 February 2020).
43. Al-Yacoub, A.; Buerkle, A.; Flanagan, M.; Ferreira, P.; Hubbard, E.M.; Lohse, N. Effective human-robot collaboration through wearable sensors. In Proceedings of the 2020 25th IEEE International Conference on Emerging Technologies and Factory Automation (ETFA), Cranfield, UK, 3–4 November 2020; Volume 1, pp. 651–658.
44. Brunton, S.L.; Kutz, J.N. *Data-Driven Science and Engineering: Machine Learning, Dynamical Systems, and Control*; Cambridge University Press: Cambridge, UK, 2019.
45. He, T.; Xie, C.; Liu, Q.; Guan, S.; Liu, G. Evaluation and comparison of random forest and A-LSTM networks for large-scale winter wheat identification. *Remote Sens.* **2019**, *11*, 1665. [CrossRef]
46. Reinhart, R.F.; Shareef, Z.; Steil, J.J. Hybrid analytical and data-driven modeling for feed-forward robot control. *Sensors* **2017**, *17*, 311. [CrossRef]
47. Naik, G.R. *Computational Intelligence in Electromyography Analysis: A Perspective on Current Applications and Future Challenges*; InTech: Rijeka, Croatia, 2012.
48. Wyeld, T.; Hobbs, D. Visualising Human Motion: A First Principles Approach using Vicon data in Maya. In Proceedings of the 2016 20th International Conference Information Visualisation (IV), Lisbon, Portugal, 19–22 July 2016; pp. 216–222.
49. Al-Yacoub, A.; Zhao, Y.C.; Eaton, W.; Goh, Y.M.; Lohse, N. Improving human robot collaboration through Force/Torque based learning for object manipulation. *Robot. Comput. Integr. Manuf.* **2021**, *69*, 102111. [CrossRef]

electronics

MDPI

Article

A Methodology to Produce Augmented-Reality Guided Tours in Museums for Mixed-Reality Headsets

Ana Martí-Testón †, Adolfo Muñoz †, J. Ernesto Solanes *,†, Luis Gracia † and Josep Tornero †

Instituto de Diseño y Fabricación, Universitat Politècnica de València, 46022 València, Spain; anmartes@upvnet.upv.es (A.M.-T.); amunyoz@idf.upv.es (A.M.); luigraca@isa.upv.es (L.G.); jtornero@idf.upv.es (J.T.)
* Correspondence: esolanes@idf.upv.es
† All authors contributed equally to this work.

Abstract: In recent years, the use of technology in the museum context has changed radically. It has switched from the display of information to offering emotive, immersive, and rich experiences with heritage. Virtual interactive media have the potential to put museums back into a relevant place in our increasingly digital society. The emergence of augmented-reality glasses offers the possibility to test and implement new methodologies compatible with this aim. However, most of the first examples developed in recent years did not take advantage of the possibilities of this new medium. This paper presents a novel methodology for producing mixed-reality applications for museums and heritage sites, with an intuitive, immersive, and natural way of operating. An experimental prototype designed for the archaeological museum of the Almoina is shown in the paper to demonstrate the benefits of the proposed system and methodology of production. In addition, the paper shows the results of several tests.

Keywords: augmente-reality interface; interactive design; archaeology; UX; holograms; storytelling

Citation: Martí-Testón, A.; Muñoz, A.; Solanes, J.E.; Gracia, L.; Tornero, J. A Methodology to Produce Augmented-Reality Guided Tours in Museums for Mixed-Reality Headsets. *Electronics* **2021**, *10*, 2956. https://doi.org/10.3390/electronics10232956

Academic Editor: George A. Tsihrintzis

Received: 3 November 2021
Accepted: 26 November 2021
Published: 27 November 2021

1. Introduction

The last two decades have seen a remarkable increase in the use of Information and Communication Technology (ICT) in Museum and Heritage sites. They have provided fertile ground where ICT has raised more accessible connections to social and cultural audiences, personalizing the visitor experience and enhancing communication [1,2]. Technology has proved to be an essential tool to reinvent the role and relevance of museums and heritage institutions, facilitating new and wider audiences [3–5].

The recent museological practice has started the use of online digital resources as a means of enhancing technological interfaces between artifacts and audiences. Economic and cultural pressures have made the reinvention of the role and relevance of museums and heritage institutions an imperative in the search for new and wider audiences, especially for young audiences who are normally detached from museums. Technology has proved to be an essential tool in making that happen.

Many cultural institutions have increased their spending on digitizing collections to improve archiving, conservation, presentation, and accessibility. Whilst this reduced some of the audience's logistical barriers such as time and cost to travel to the museums site, it did little to break down more complex and intransigent barriers such as cultural and educational barriers in order to widen audiences [6]. Hence, something else has to be done if it is essential to achieve audience engagement with culture.

New and more interactive museology is required to improve linear exhibitions that utilize classical narratives in order to motivate wider audience exploration and understanding. Consequently, new methodologies for presentation are emerging, creating novel sensitive narratives that use and engage with the practice of storytelling, making for a more socially inclusive interaction [7].

Engaging audiences through tablets and smartphones has boosted new storytelling techniques, making information more accessible. Nevertheless, recent developments are fueling museums practice with innovative storytelling based on virtual reality (VR), augmented reality (AR), Big Data (BD), and Artificial Intelligence (AI).

1.1. Motivation

Traditionally, museums have used printed drawings, labels, models, or digital infographics to add information about the exhibits or ruins; however, in the last decade, different virtual and augmented-reality devices have appeared that are radically changing this phenomenon. Commercial investment has transformed VR and AR from science fiction to life, making smart headsets an everyday object in information technology (IT) culture and society. In particular, the use of 3D stereoscopic visual systems, utilized to track user movements of the head, hands, and eyes in space and accompanied by fully immersive sound environments, has been greatly successful in creating unreal or virtual worlds [8].

AR systems, which incorporate digital data in the real environment, allow users to perceive digital recreations without losing their perception of the physical world. The AR approach offers a more familiar way to better interact with data for the less well-travelled IT users since it allows information to be included in layers. In this way, information is modified to fit into real space/time without overloading users while maintaining the integrity of the original work in the context of a more natural presentation of related data.

The first version of the Microsoft *HoloLens glasses*, which were introduced in 2016, has been used in different contexts, including education, tourism, entertainment, medicine, architecture, or manufacturing. This head-mounted display (HMD) can combine tangible physical aspects with virtual elements while scanning space, thus allowing for free movement while maintaining the virtual objects correctly placed in the real space. They are portable, relatively light, and self-sufficient, since they do not need a PC connected to them. The device has two key features: one the one hand, they can track the space and the hands of the user to enable the placement and interaction of the virtual contents by making just some gestures; on the other hand, the stereoscopic images are generated in the central part of the transparent headsets to blend the user's natural vision with digital objects. In addition to gestures, the system can be controlled with voice commands and indirectly by the location of the user in space.

In 2019, the second generation of Microsoft *HoloLens glasses* appeared, and news about new AR devices and prototypes are continuously appearing in the media, from small and big companies such as Apple, Google, Facebook, Magic Leap, and Nreal, demonstrating that the competition for AR has just begun. The challenge of these companies is to offer more affordable devices for a broader audience while maintaining the same capacity of Microsoft *HoloLens glasses* to anchor digital contents to our natural visual perception.

Superimposing information in the real world stimulates museological practice to develop a more accessible interface with audiences, encouraging visitors to achieve a better understanding of archives, objects, places, and their history and making the real world more enchanted [9].

As pointed out before, there is a need for museums to engage new audiences, especially young generations. Technology can help to this purpose but is not enough per se. There is a need to include an emotional component, applying scenography and theatrical techniques, interactivity, and empathy, to create an experience as a whole. With this, museums and heritage sites could offer a new manner of showing and presenting their findings, giving to the visitor a reason not only to repeat the experience but also to recommend their experience with heritage.

In order to mitigate this need, this works presents a new methodology to design new visitor museum interfaces based on augmented-reality devices and scenography and theatrical techniques.

In particular, this article explains the challenges gathered while designing and implementing the experience and creating the scenarios and dynamics to amaze visitors and engage them with complex concepts of our history. Results of the research study indicate that the application is especially effective in involving audiences with the museum's contents. A novel manner of storytelling related to heritage has been specified, testing different mechanics of interactivity that allow content to be customized according to the visitor's profile and their interests while taking a trip back in time. A natural interaction with contents has also been developed by adding some gamification techniques to encourage visitors to make relations between the real and the virtual.

1.2. Related Work

One of the first museums to incorporate VR technology into its educational program was the British Museum. It offered the possibility of exploring a reconstruction of the Bronze Age from 3D-scanned pieces in their collection [10]. In 2017, VR was ready to be implemented in the physical and real museum. An example is the experience developed at London's Tate Modern, focused on Modigliani's studio [11].

Similarly, AR has been used successfully in conjunction with tablets and smartphones in projects that demonstrate how museums can benefit from this technology. The use of the Microsoft *HoloLens glasses* to increase visitor experiences has begun to flourish in museum presentations and heritage centers. For instance, Leiden's Rijksmuseum collaborated with the University of Delft to exhibit the Egyptian Temple of Teffeh [12,13]. Bovington's UK Tank Museum showed a mixture of missing and actual conserved German tanks from the Second World War [14].

Smart headsets are appropriate to be used in science museums since they can help to explain some complex processes and techniques. They are of interest in historical and archaeological museums because they are able to reconstruct the contexts. Recently, a few articles about this topic have been published; an interesting example is the experience designed for the Egyptian Museum in Cairo [15,16]. This research is focused on the idea of substituting the museum guide, analyzing technical issues to display contents and interact with digital data when using Head Mounted Displays such as Microsoft *HoloLens glasses*. Other similar articles are just focused on reproducing the museum classical visit with the new media, for example, presenting a prototype that is just focused on the display of information for one object, without benefiting from the possibilities of this new media [17–20].

The continuous evolution of technology will enable museums to steadily develop further improvements with their interface between audience and artifact. If museums can develop a multimedia approach that exploits the new generation's familiarity with IT devices, it could create an evolutionary leap in the way museums reach out to new audiences. With augmented-reality headsets, you can take advantage of the ruins of buildings to build digital information about them. Normally, in excavations, a series of data are obtained from which the interpretations are made. Consequently, in most cases, an "approximate" and provisional reconstruction of the buildings is carried out, which allows one to get an idea of what it was like [21]. This is the reason why an archaeological museum was selected, so an immersive storytelling was created for the smart headsets that took the user on an emotional journey, taking advantage of all the capabilities of the device.

1.3. Aims and Contributions

The main objective of this work is to present a novel methodology based on augmented-reality techniques combined with stage and theatrical techniques to produce a more emotive, intuitive, and natural manner to explore heritage. Although the proposed methodology is general and can be applied to other areas, it is specifically designed to enhance the museum visit experience.

Without loss of generality, the proposed methodology is applied to a particular case study: the Almoina archaeological museum https://cultural.valencia.es/es/museu/la-almoina-centro-arqueologico/, accessed on 25 November 2021. The Almoina museum is located at the city center of Valencia, Spain, holding different archaeological findings of great value dating from the Roman period to the Middle Ages. This paper fully describes the human machine interface designed for the Almoina museum following the proposed methodology and using the Microsoft *HoloLens glasses* 1st generation as the augmented-reality device. The effectiveness of the proposed approach is shown with several usability tests as well as observational studies carried out for visitors of the Almoina museum.

The main contributions of this work are:

- To determine what type of storytelling can meet the requirements of the Museology 4.0, whcih are that it has to be immersive, experiential, naturalized, narrative, interactive, intelligent, gamified, transmedia, and social.
- To design a general methodology to produce a more emotive, intuitive, and natural manner to explore heritage.
- To develop a methodology to present contents with augmented-reality HMD and integrate virtual and physical information of objects in a user-friendly environment.
- To present all the steps followed to develop a functional prototype for the Almoina archaeological museum based on the proposed methodology.
- To study the usability and effectiveness of the developed prototype based on the opinion of the museum's visitors.

1.4. Content of the Article

This paper is organized as follows: Section 2 fully describes the augmented-reality-based user interface and methodology used to develop the proposed application. Next, the feasibility of the proposal is proved in Section 3 with usability tests. Finally, Section 4 presents a discussion about the results obtained, and Section 5 presents the conclusion of this work.

2. Proposed Approach

This works presents a novel methodology based on augmented-reality techniques combined with stage and theatrical techniques to produce an emotive, intuitive and natural way to explore heritage. The interface is specially designed to enhance the museum visit experience. The methodology combines digital audiovisual production pipeline to generate an emotional reaction on visitors who can engage with a virtual guide close to a human presence in space.

The proposed methodology is applied to develop a novel human machine interface (HMI) for the Almoina archaeological museum placed in Valencia (Spain). However, this methodology is extensible to other types of museums such as science museums, history museums or natural history museums, among others.

Next, a complete description of the methodology and the developed HMI is given.

2.1. Methodology

From the beginning it was important to find out what AR headsets can contribute to the museum visit those previous devices could not provide, such as augmented reality through mobile devices, or a simple poster placed on the museum wall. Therefore, it was important to design an application that went further, to be sensitive and impressive while incorporating digital data in a natural manner.

"Immersive design" was used to fit storytelling requirements, such as media convergence, or a more natural way of relating to digital data. Immersive design is a process that has been normally used in environments such as architecture, video games, art or education [22] and was adopted it to the museum context.

The original idea was to implement a non-linear immersive experience in a real museum. The design had to be adjusted to the museological requirements, so it was important to determine what those qualities could be which has been named Museography 4.0. [23]. Museography 4.0 is the set of techniques and practices relative to the functioning of the museum, which have evolved from the analogical museography towards the natural, immersive, and intuitive integration of the digital data in the expositional context. It can be immersive, experiential, naturalized, narrative, interactive, intelligent, gamified, transmedia, and social.

It must be connected to a fully immersive and natural experience facilitated by augmented-reality devices. Narrative can be used to create innovative storytelling, allowing interactivity and the personalization of information. It can use artificial intelligence to anticipate user's needs and gamification techniques to initiate and sustain user motivation for deeper exploration of information and contents of presentations.

In our analysis, the Museography 4.0 can benefit from the use of transmedia where the main narrative is articulated and adapted to different media in changing situations. It can also be social and culturally responsive.

2.1.1. Production Scheme

Based on the proposed objectives, several blocks were created in the phases of the project: analysis, design, development, and implementation, as seen in the following diagram in Figure 1.

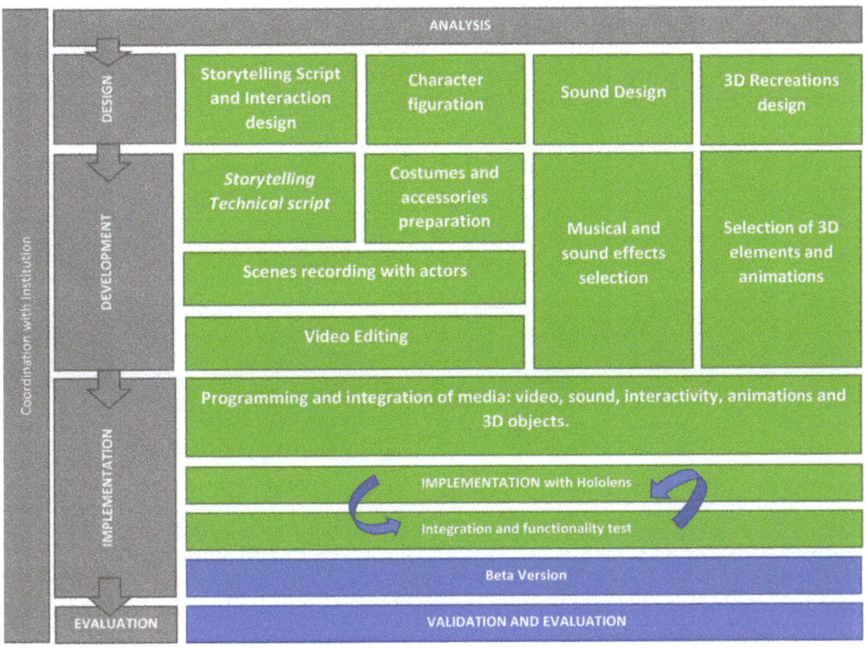

Figure 1. Almoina AR Production Scheme.

In this scheme, sections that were completed are marked in green, and actions related to the future official implementation are colored in blue.

Following the production scheme outlined above, the resulting actions are listed:

- **Analysis:** Analyze the contents to be represented and determine how it will be presented.
- **Design:** Design a narrative script that contains museography 4.0 requirements, with the appropriate interactivity. Design the environmental sound and architectural elements and objects to be recreated in 3D and 2D, as well as the figuration of human characters.
- **Development:** Create a technical script that develops the storytelling. Create the 3D assets, images, and videos. Choose and prepare an actress to act as a guide. Record the scripts on a chrome set. Post-produce the videos to be integrated into the computer program. Choose the music and sound effects.

- **Implementation:** Coordinate and guide the programming of the application with the programmer. Run the first integration and functionality tests. Draw conclusions and analyze the results.

2.1.2. Storytelling Requirements

After several meetings with the museum's director, it was decided to bring the virtual city to life in the republican period and the first settlement of a city in the 2nd century BC. This allowed to focus the discourse on the first civilizations, their religious rites, commerce, etc.

Most of the representations seen of cities reconstructions are focused on an architectural representation, in which the volumes of the buildings are shown without attending to the life and people. For this reason, it was agreed to show what the city was like at that time, what people inhabited it, and what kind of life they led, in order to try to reproduce the feeling of having traveled through time.

2.1.3. Contents and Interaction Design

The application was focused on the visitor's interaction. For this reason, each user could decide what content they were interested in and could go deeper into it, according to their interest. Different narratives were presented related to each building to expand the information on the chosen topics. The main topics were: the city foundation, the Horreum and Commerce, the sanctuary and religious life, and the Terms and the social life (see Figure 2).

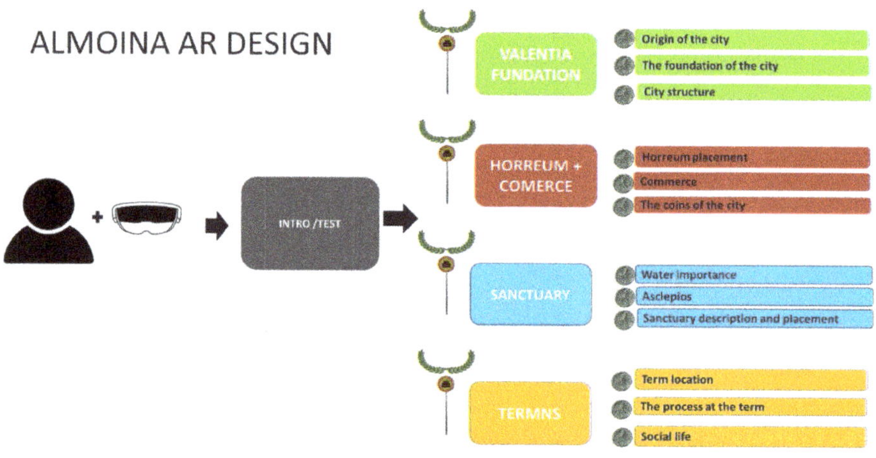

Figure 2. Content scheme.

2.2. Augmented-Reality-Based Interface

It was determined that each scene of the tour should have a brief introduction conducted by a human guide in the form of a video-hologram, complemented with some small audible messages of information of less than a minute each and some visual extra images (photographic images and illustrations) that help visitors to understand the concepts explained by the guide. All the contents were corrected and confirmed by the director of the museum.

The interaction of the application follows the principles of natural interaction to avoid problems derived from the use of computers, such as pressing buttons or choosing items from menus. The application for the AR headsets were designed with a short introduction to teach the way to operate the device during the experience. At the beginning of the experience, a life-size video image of a person—the virtual guide—was the first thing the user could watch and hear when they were wearing the headsets. Our guide invited the visitor to come closer from a specific location in the museum to continue the teaching. After that, the program measured the approach distance till the user was close enough, and then it activated another part of the multimedia sequence, welcoming the visitor, presenting the historical visit, and teaching them how to activate the virtual objects to discover each one of the sequences of the tour.

In previous experients, it was noticed that some users had difficulty commanding the headsets by gestures with a finger snap in the air or "Air tap" [23]. Implementation of the voice commands were also problematic in the museum because of noise, so it was decided that an interaction be designed that was exclusively dependent on the visitor's position and the place where they looked. This way of operating, already common in many virtual-reality systems, works with a timer that counts the seconds an object is marked by the gaze and triggers the animation of a circle of light to show the visitor the progression of the activation. In this sense, it was decided that there would only be two activators: one was in the form of a medallion/banner to activate each one of the four sequences into which the tour was divided, and the other one was a coin that opened specific pieces of information for each sequence.

The diagram shown in Figure 3 presents the flow of the interaction, divided into a first part where the application is presented and where the user is trained to activate banners and coins, and a second part, free movement, where the visitor is given freedom to move through space to discover the sequences marked in space.

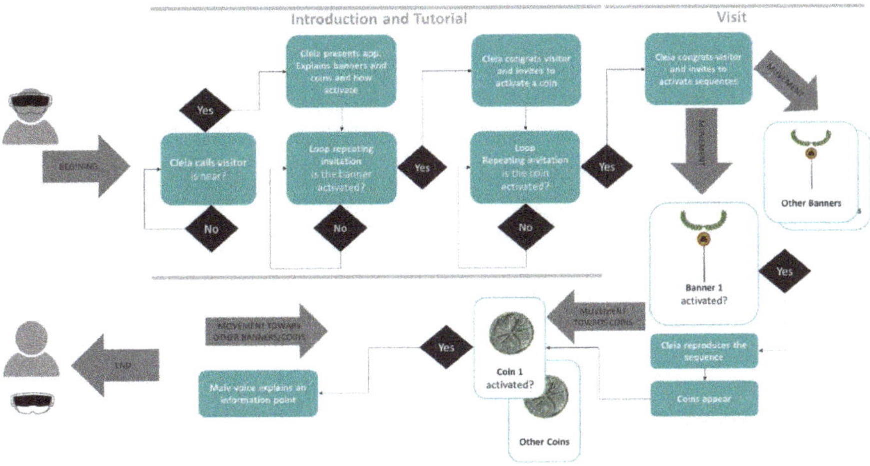

Figure 3. Interaction design.

2.2.1. Characters and Voices

It was decided that the guide character be based on the myth of Clelia (Latin Cloelia), who was one of the most recognized heroines of Rome during the Republic. Storytelling was conducted by a real actress playing the role of Clelia using highly effective theatrical techniques to humanize the virtual experience. Thus, the Roman woman invited the user to begin the visit by approaching her, and then she began to teach within 3 min how to activate the holographic contents arranged in the space.

Clelia was the presenter for the four scenes and the main narrative, and a male voiceover appeared when an informative coin was activated to complete the presentation (see Figure 4).

Figure 4. Insignia of Clelia "Promptuarii Iconum Insigniorum". Guillaume Rouille 1553.

2.2.2. Emplacement

The storytelling was linked to the different areas of the museum already discussed related to the republican roman ruins: the foundation of Valentia, the Horreum and the commerce, the sanctuary and the water, and the thermal baths and social life, marked in blue in the museum map; see Figure 5.

Figure 5. Museum map.

Each of the information points, shaped as coins, were built as a synchronized animations that two minutes long, composed of 3D figures, pictures, and diagrams that appeared during the voice explanation exactly in the proper place of the museum to understand the value of the ruins.

2.2.3. Display Banners and Associated Narratives

To differentiate content levels, different types of interactive labels were designed. On the one hand, four roman banners indicated each of the scenes in the museum: the Crossroads, with a tale of the origin of the city; the Sanctuary of Asclepios, telling the religious traditions of the Romans; The Horreum, introducing the way of trading of this period; and the baths, with a story about the social life in this building. Clelia briefly explained the related contents of each area marked by banners, accompanied synchronously by a multimedia sequence that showed the digital reconstruction of that area as it was in the Roman period (see example in Figure 6a).

(a) (b)

Figure 6. Examples of banners and Valentian coins used in the interface. (**a**) Main banner. (**b**) Valentian coins.

Once the contents of each banner had been activated and the reconstruction of the building was finished, the user could continue enjoying the scene by discovering some coins spread in the area (see Figure 6b). These coins, based on the coin minted in the city of Valentia during the republic, marked different points of interest that could be triggered by the user by staring in front of them. For example, in the case of the Sanctuary, after listening to Clelia's introduction and watching the reconstruction of the building, the visitor had the chance to activate each of the three coins suspended in the space, one at a time. The small stories of each coin helped to explain the importance and symbology of the god Asclepios in Roman times.

2.2.4. Video Production and Postproduction

The videos of Clelia were produced on a chroma set at the Polytechnic University of Valencia. After a casting process, which lasted several days, it was decided that the role of Clelia be played by a young local actress. The costumes and jewels were purchased for the occasion based on the characteristics described in the history books and expert advice (see Figure 7).

During filming, a teletypewriter was enabled to facilitate the reading of the texts for the actress. The camera used was a Lumix 4G, and it was recorded in 4K resolution to maximize the possibilities to re-frame and zoom the character in post-production. The audio capture system was performed using a Sennheiser professional lapel wireless microphone concealed in the actress's neckline.

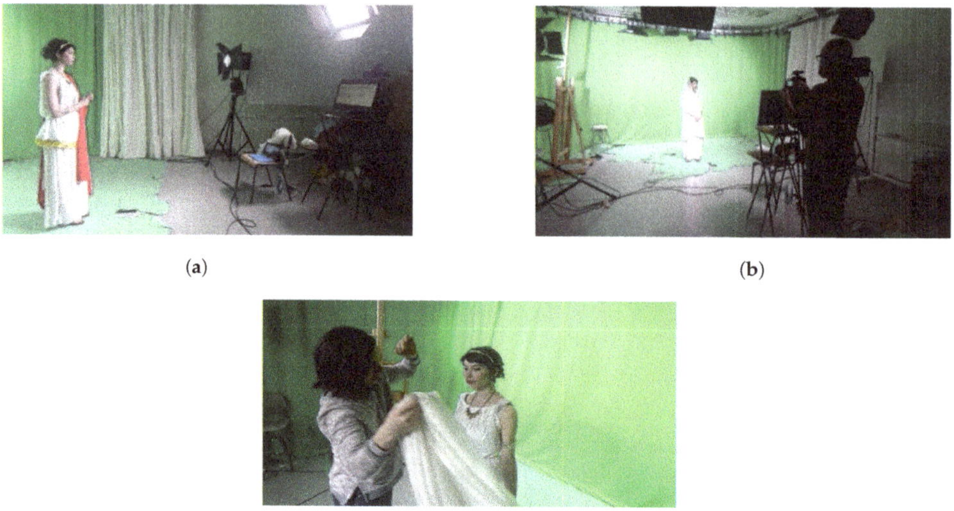

(a) (b) (c)

Figure 7. Recording studio: (**a**–**c**) images show different moments of the recording process.

Post-production was carried out with Adobe After Effects CC 2017, where the figure was isolated from the environment to be inserted into the program (see Figure 8). The presentation sequence was especially complex, since it had to be divided into six moments in which Clelia instructs the visitor, where three of these are character loops enabled the ability to await the visitor's reaction. In the image below, you can see the sections defined as loops marked in pink and those of a single reproduction in green.

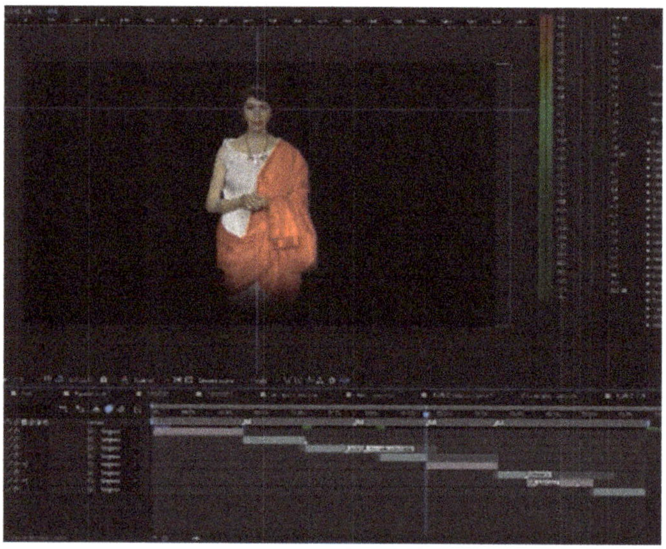

Figure 8. Post-production: adding effects with Adobe After Effects CC 2017.

The videos were exported with a square resolution of 1000 × 1000 pixels and in a special format, called webm, which was the only one able to preserve a transparency channel when the figure was integrated in the video game engine. We discovered that transparency is a very necessary feature of the video to create a credible integration of

Clelia with the 3D virtual objects that appear around her; otherwise, she would look like a cut square like a TV screen without a natural relation with the rest of the virtual set.

2.3. Application Development

2.3.1. Application Programming

Programming was done with Unity video game engine, an author tool for creating programs for the Microsoft *HoloLens glasses*. With this program, all the materials and assets such as photos, videos, music, 3D objects, and animations were integrated to create the interactive scenes. The programming language used was C-Sharp, and some specialized libraries for AR applications, such as Microsoft Mixed-Reality Toolkit, were used to accelerate the production, making it easy to handle the input of the sensors to detect the interactions of the user and to react in consequence (see Figure 9).

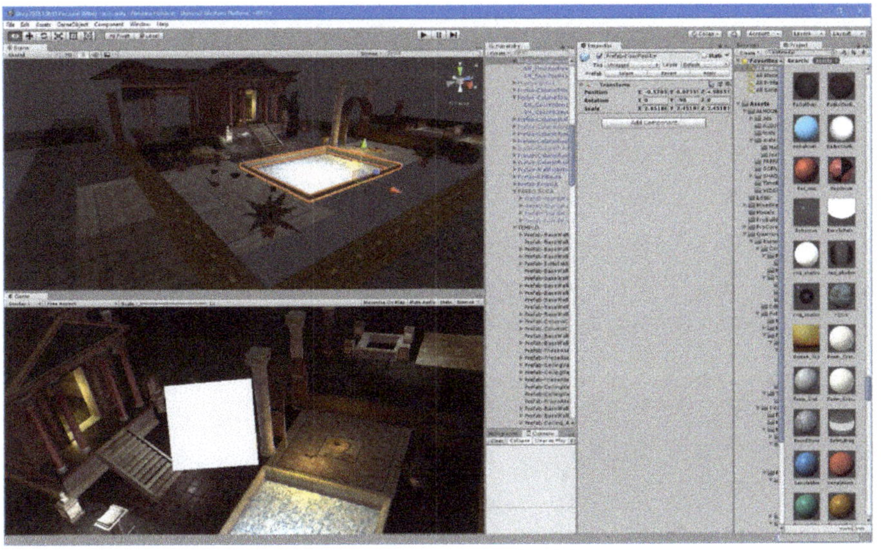

Figure 9. Unity3D video game engine.

During this phase, the integration of the audio-visual elements in the computer program was coordinated, and many graphic development questions could only be solved from experimentation with the video game engine with which these types of applications are programmed.

After integrating all the elements and programming their behavior, the program was uploaded into the Microsoft *HoloLens glasses* to carry out the functional tests in the real space.

2.3.2. Asset Development

For the design of the buildings and stages it was decided that the the existing images from the virtual reproductions made by the Almoina museum be used, to which some three-dimensional elements were added to give the feeling of life in the buildings, such as the inclusion of plants or mosaics on the walls.

The programming of the appearance of the three-dimensional elements on the museum space was carried out gradually, so that they were composed as Clelia commented on the contents associated with that building while listening to background music. In this sense, it was decided that materials be created that could be shown as dissolutions of matter in space, instead of simply appearing, since the introduction of virtual elements must appear organically to enhance the magic of the moment of their appearance as if rebuilt by traveling back in time. The materials were created from a special shader programmed with a variable that can be animated to make the objects appear or disappear when necessary, following an organic pattern that helped to gradually perceive the correspondence of the position of the virtual objects with the ruins.

2.3.3. Integration and Functionality Tests

To check the feasibility of the application, different tests were carried out. Specifically, three formal sessions were conducted. First was the development of two Integration tests to check the proper functioning of the program (see Figure 10). These types of tests are normally used in the design of computer applications. After some adjustments were made, a usability test was applied to check the validation of the first alpha version of the application in the museum. In addition, an observational study was used to complement the necessary data to check the feasibility of the application.

The Integration tests were developed with five people each. In both sessions, the objectives were clearly defined to be analyzed. Likewise, in both tests, it was determined that focus be placed on assessing whether it was a natural environment for the user that validates it, as if it were an experience like any visit to a museum.

The first session focused on testing the interactive possibilities when executing the contents through the gaze. For this reason, a first test was carried out before definitively adjusting the interactivity mode. The second session focused on analyzing the functionality offered by the narrative and the audio according to the spatial location in the space of the Almoina. Subsequently, pertinent improvements were made so that the buildings were adjusted to the plan of the ruins and the contents were in the corresponding space.

The first integration test was carried out with a set of non-definitive materials to speed up the verification of functionality in the headsets. For this task, the necessary shots were recorded to assemble the introduction and the tutorial without the help of the actress. The banners and coins—created with a 3D modeling program for this test—were integrated in Unity, and the materials of these objects were assembled with images previously treated with Adobe Photoshop. These functional tests were first tested within the video game editor itself, in simulation mode, with a joystick connected to the development PC with which the the eyeglass wearer can simulate the movement and direction of their gaze.

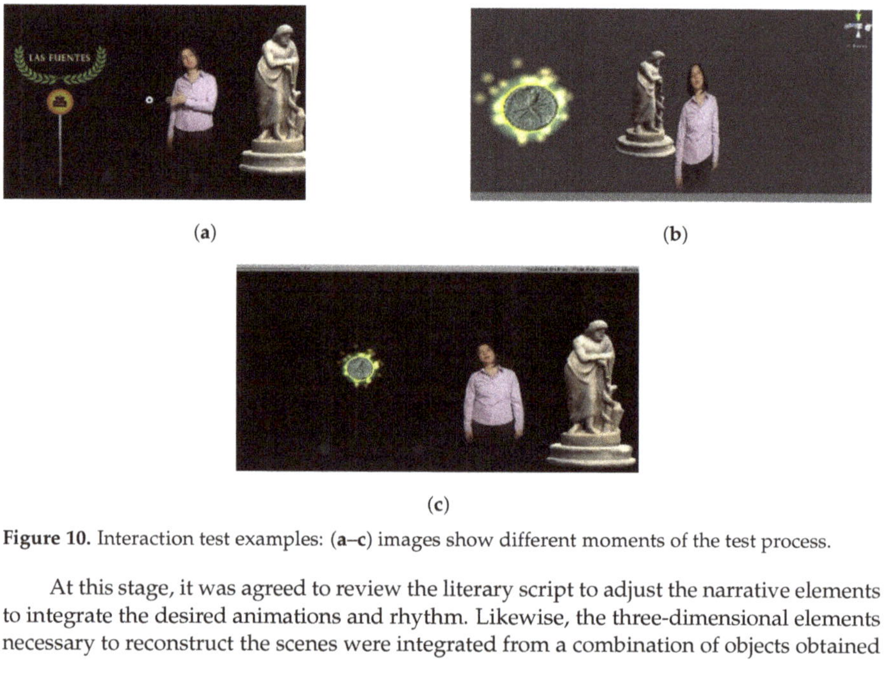

(a) (b) (c)

Figure 10. Interaction test examples: (**a**–**c**) images show different moments of the test process.

At this stage, it was agreed to review the literary script to adjust the narrative elements to integrate the desired animations and rhythm. Likewise, the three-dimensional elements necessary to reconstruct the scenes were integrated from a combination of objects obtained from free-use libraries and models created by ourselves, all adapted to follow the plan of physical reconstruction and historically consistent with the guidelines of the Museum.

Finally, a functional alpha version was generated on Microsoft *HoloLens glasses*, with the final footage shot with the actress. The animations and the reconstructions of the presentation and tutorial were then developed (see Figure 11).

(a)

(b)

(c)

(d)

(e)

(f)

Figure 11. Alpha version of the AR-based interface developed: (**a**–**f**) images show different moments of the Almoina museum visit using the proposed AR interface.

3. Experimental Results

The developed application is an example of an efficient interface to explore museum collections and ruins. A video of the experience can be seen in at the following link: https://media.upv.es/player/?id=7574fcb0-3c89-11ec-af84-dfb8313cf291, accessed on 25 November 2021.

In accordance with [24–26], different methodologies such as usability tests of applications, which are commonly used in the verification of hardware and software, along with presence questionnaires, surveys, and in-depth interviews, were used to evaluate and validate the effectiveness of the proposed AR-based interface for guided tours in museums.

Ten people were invited to visit the museum and check the application on site. They had different profiles (5 women and 5 men with different ages, from 18 to 58 years old). Additionally, they were given the opportunity to explain comments and suggestions in order to obtain some extra information apart from the usability and presence questionnaires.

Specifically, the System Usability Scale (SUS) questionnaire was carried out to check the usability of the application (see Table 1) [27]. This test took an average of 50 min, including the training with the virtual guide Clelia (approx. 8 min), the visit to the content (approx. 30 min), and finally some time to respond to the questionnaire and interview (8 to 10 min).

Table 1. Questions of the SUS questionnaire [27].

Q1	I think that I would like to use this system frequently
Q2	I found the system unnecessarily complex
Q3	I thought the system was easy to use
Q4	I think that I would need the support of a technical person to be able to use this system
Q5	I found the various functions in this system were well integrated
Q6	I thought there was too much inconsistency in this system
Q7	I would imagine that most people would learn to use this system very quickly
Q8	I found the system very cumbersome to use
Q9	I felt very confident using the system
Q10	I needed to learn a lot of things before I could get going with this system

As a result, the overall perceived usability was 84.67 out of 100 (min: 79.9; max: 100; SD: 17.41) for $n = 10$. This result means that the proposed interface reached a high level of usability. In addition, Figure 12 shows the results obtained for each question of the SUS questionnaire. It is remarkable that most of the participants indicated that they would use this interface frequently and found the interface easy to use. The participants also indicated that all the interface functionalities were well integrated and that the proposed interface was consistent. Moreover, participants felt confident with the interface. An initial tutorial might be needed to learn the interactivity, but once it is explained, the system is easy to use.

In addition, the presence questionnaire (PQ) was filled by visitors [28–33]. PQ contained 24 items in the form of closed-ended questions on a scale of 1 ("not at all") to 7 ("completely"). Figure 13 shows the results of the PQ. Specifically, the "realism" score obtained a mean of 6.60 out of 7 with a standard deviation of 0.44, while the "possibility to act" score obtained a mean of 6.15 out of 7 with a standard deviation of 0.55. The "quality of interface" score obtained a mean of 6 out of 7 with a standard deviation of 0.95, while the "possibility to examine" score obtained a mean of 6.47 out of 7 with a standard deviation of 0.12. The "self-evaluation performance" score obtained a mean of 6.25 out of 7 with a standard deviation of 0.07, while the "sounds" score obtained a mean of 6.73 out of 7 with a standard deviation of 0.25. These results demonstrate that the objectives presented in the preparation of the methodology were achieved. All users demonstrated engagement with the digital avatar together with the holograms that recreated the scenarios, with music and effects.

Moreover, the Igroup Presence Questionnaire (IPQ), based on 14 questions on a scale of 1 ("not at all") to 7 ("completely"), was used [34]. This questionnaire is normally used for testing virtual-reality-based interfaces, and some of the questions included in the original version are not appropriate for augmented-reality-based interfaces (see [35] for more details about the differences between augmented-reality and virtual-reality interfaces). For this reason, only five questions from the IPQ were used in this study (see Table 2).

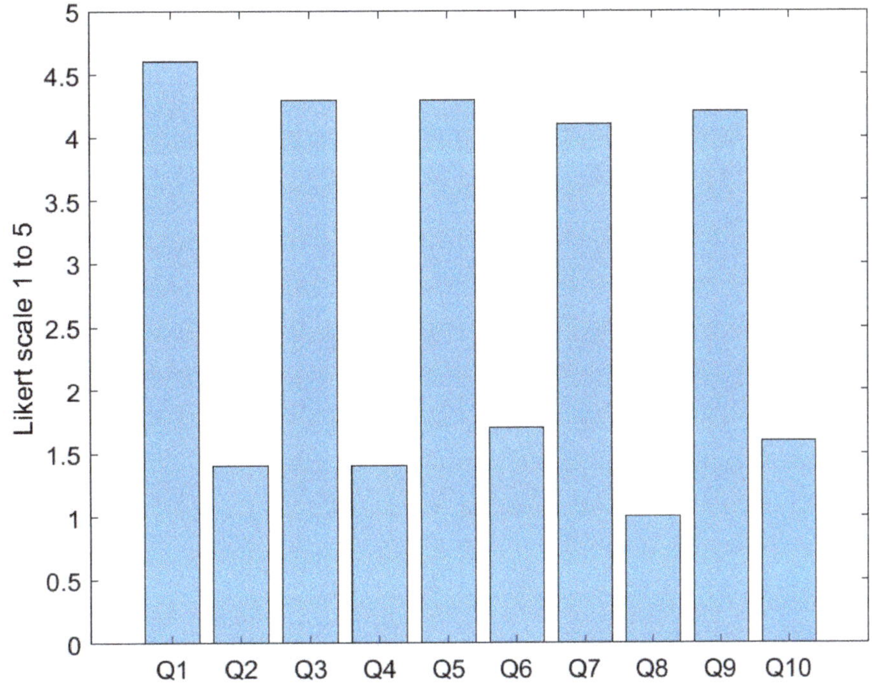

Figure 12. SUS questionnaire results per question. 1 = strongly disagree, 5 = strongly agree.

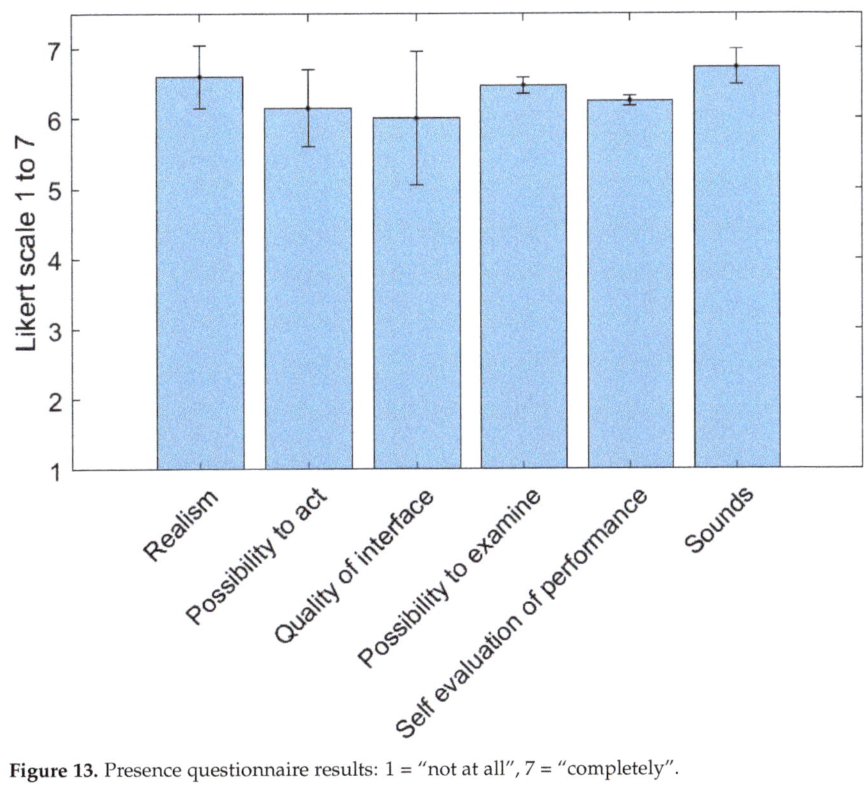

Figure 13. Presence questionnaire results: 1 = "not at all", 7 = "completely".

Table 2. Selected questions from the IPQ questionnaire [34].

Q11	How aware were you of the real world surrounding while navigating in the augmented reality world?
Q12	I felt present in the virtual space
Q13	Somehow, I felt that the holograms surrounded me
Q14	I still paid attention to the real environment
Q15	I was completely captivated by the holograms

Figure 14 shows the results of this study. The majority of the users indicated in Q11 that they were extremely aware of the surroundings, which is characteristic of AR HMD experiences (mean: 6.90 out of 7; standard deviation: 0.32). However, the results shown in Q12 indicate that users were also aware of the virtual elements and felt surrounded by them (mean: 6.90 out of 7; standard deviation: 0.32). This kind of results are typical in augmented-reality applications and indicate that users are interacting with the virtual world without losing contact with reality. Another important result was that the majority of the users indicated that they felt surrounded by the holograms (mean: 6.50 out of 7; standard deviation: 1.27, in Q13). This was precisely the effect that all augmented-reality interfaces look for to engage the user and transmit the required information in a natural manner. The users also indicated that the holograms did not interfere in the moments they wanted to pay attention to the real elements (mean: 6.60 out of 7; standard deviation: 0.97, in Q14). However, they were captivated by the holograms when needed, paying attention to them, and receiving the information in a natural manner (mean: 6.20 out of 7; standard deviation: 0.79, in Q15).

The above results sustained the effectiveness of the developed augmented-reality interface based on the proposed methodology in terms of usability and visitor perception.

In addition to these results, the observational study showed that users took an average of 55 min using the application, and 93% executed the training correctly. Ninety percent entered the application via the Roman Banner, and one user directly entered a coin first. Most of them stood in front of the holograms and did not move around them. Most of them tried to touch the holograms.

The users understood very well how to run the tutorial that explained how to activate the contents with their eyes. Neither needed help, and they moved naturally around the room.

Several of the users complained that there were large differences between the guide's audio volume (Clelia) and the other narrator. Some of the dialogues could be improved to make them shorter and more open to questions.

In general, most of the users were very surprised, enjoyed the experience, and understood the associated content.

The team was satisfied with the results of these usability tests; they helped to verify that the proposed methodologies are functional and that they meet the proposed requirements. The methodology is viable, as demonstrated by the experiments.

In the interview, most of the participants explained that the field of view was small. Some of them had problems fixing the Microsoft *HoloLens glasses* when wearing other headsets and felt uncomfortable after 30 min.

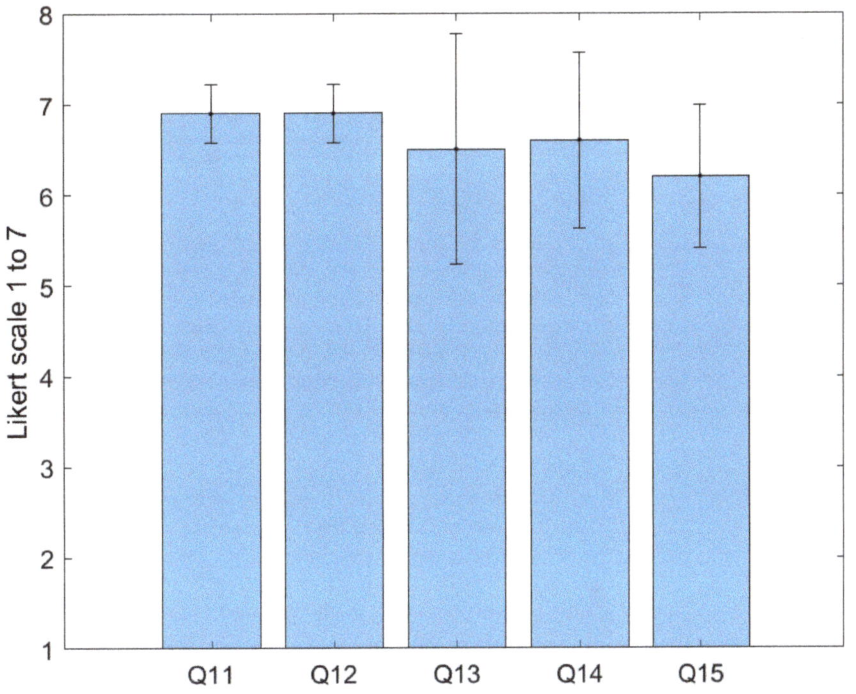

Figure 14. Selected questions from the Igroup Presence Questionnaire results: 1 = "not at all", 7 = "completely".

4. Discussion

Results of previous section show a success in terms of the user experience when exploring the exhibition with the holographic contents activated with the interface. However, some comments made by the users should be considered when developing future versions of the proposed interface, as discussed below.

Users highlighted the attractiveness of the application due to the novelty of the media. They also pointed out that it was very useful to understand the origins of the ruins and what they belonged to. Moreover, they highlighted the ease of interaction with the virtual guide, the banners, and labels with the coins. One user suggested adding more voices to make the storytelling more inclusive. The authors consider that this is a good suggestion and should be contemplated.

Arguably, the main complaint of participants was that the field of view (FoV) of the device was too small. In particular, the FoV of the Microsoft *HoloLens glasses* used in the tests is a 34-degree angle. Therefore, participants could see digital objects interacting with the real world while looking straight ahead, but if they turned their head a little, digital objects disappeared or got cut off. It is important to reveal that users explained that once they were involved in the visit, they forgot about the problem of the field of view and instead became involved in the storytelling. Nevertheless, the second version of the Microsoft *HoloLens glasses* has improved this issue, and now the FoV is a 52-degree angle.

Some visitors also expressed their worries about the fatigue produced by the weight of the headset. Moreover, they pointed out the difficulty of wearing them with other headsets. The Microsoft *HoloLens glasses generation 2* has changed and has the weight at the back, which is made with the purpose of improving this problem.

However, users indicated that they finally understood the history of the ruins and their origin and that they had enjoyed the experience enough to repeat it, pay for it, and even recommend it to friends.

Currently, the market of AR headsets is growing with companies such as Nreal, which are are developing AR headsets that promise similar features to the Microsoft *HoloLens glasses* for a much less cost [36] as a periphery device that can be connected to any Android phone to work. There are still many problems that will need to be resolved in the future, but with devices of this type and the knowledge reached with this research, we consider the integration of AR solutions in museums to be in the near future.

5. Conclusions

It can be concluded that specific methodologies are feasible to be used by current museums. The article has provided a fertile space to tell stories, fostering a magical, emotional, and spiritual environment where the user becomes more open, active, and sensitive to stimuli. Therefore, specific methodologies are feasible for use by current museums. The article has provided a fertile space to tell stories, fostering a magical, emotional, and spiritual environment where the user becomes more open, active, and sensitive to stimuli.

As result of applying the principles of museography 4.0 on the Almoina experience, it can be concluded that

- A storytelling methodology was design hat was adapted to the wishes and profiles of visitors, placing them at the center of the experience and creating views with a marked experiential character.
- The intuitive manner of operating with augmented-reality media "view-through" allows one to eliminate the barriers that many individuals have when facing digital media.
- A novel way of approaching stories was specified related to heritage, testing a type of interactivity that allows the personalization of content according to the profile of the visitor and their interests.
- The use of audio, video, and animated 3D recreations that surround the visitor helped to make the experience much more immersive, bringing the user closer to the feeling of taking a trip back in time.

The development of the 4.0 museography that understands the synthesis between traditional exhibition forms and their fusion with digital media can help museums to effectively use new technologies with the aim of successfully incorporating new audiences.

It has been proved how augmented-reality devices introduce new means of communication capable of containing unique immersive experiences that will have a huge impact on society and museums. Although these technologies are still in a very early stage of development, and it is difficult to fully assess their potential, it is nevertheless possible to foresee that their mere appearance is having a significant impact in the context of museums. In this sense, more and more publications appear around museums and AR, and the number of experiences carried out by different museums is increasing.

Nevertheless, the introduction of augmented-reality smart headsets in the museum context offers some challenges to be analyzed:

- In terms of production, the need for professional with hybrid profiles and the need for scientific 3D reconstructions will involve some additional media production costs.
- Regarding design, the dependency must be mentioned between the design of the interaction rules and the specific storytelling that need to be told.
- The model of exploitation must consider the high costs and maintenance of devices.

The use of certain strategies, such as interactive languages from the world of videogames or the development of narratives from staging or theater, can help to generate valid experiences in the context of museums. Through the development of our experience, it has been verified how these types of mechanics are very effective in involving audiences with the museum's contents. Proposing the discovery of information through an exploration and activation of coins distributed in space in Almoina AR helped to generate a non-linear guided tour. Other ideas brought from the world of video games, such as the use of a virtual guide, can encourage visitors to learn how to interact with the holographic content effortlessly, following a non-technical narrative thread from the beginning. Likewise, it was verified that the creation of reactive scenes due to the proximity to the visitor has enormous potential, especially when linking this body position in space to animations that are automatically triggered, giving the visitor the feeling of receiving a reward for it.

An experimental case has been presented that brings about innovation with respect to these type of devices and narratives. It is a new medium, and this experience has only confirmed that it has still much to discover. As for future research, in the short term, carrying out part of the implementation of the Almoina AR with the second version of the Microsoft *HoloLens glasses* is expected, to create the opportunity to validate the system with different types of users and museum visitors.

Precisely the ability of these devices to present digital information linked to the physical in a perceptively non-aggressive way can allows visitors to relate to each other and experience the visit in a natural and social way. Likewise, in the examples that have been developed, it was verified that the different narratives associated with the museum's contents take force when they are presented in the room in a holographic way, creating a binding dialogue between the real and virtual elements that participate in the same perceptual space, that is, the museum room.

Museography 4.0 will allow museums and their objects to have a central role, as they did in traditional museography, making the experience of the visit attractive, interactive, and motivating.

In addition, further potential work includes a comparative study between different methodologies and technologies currently used in museums with the one proposed in this work. This study will need a significant number of visitors to test each proposal in order to highlight the advantages and drawbacks of each one of them. Based on the results of this study, it is expected that the proposed methodology will keep improving in order to develop more natural, intuitive, and emotive interfaces to enhance the museum visit experience.

Author Contributions: Conceptualization, A.M. and A.M.-T.; methodology, A.M.-T.; software, A.M.; validation, A.M.-T., A.M., J.E.S. and L.G.; formal analysis, L.G. and J.E.S.; writing—original draft preparation, A.M.-T.; writing-review and editing, L.G. and J.E.S.; supervision, L.G. and J.T.; project administration, L.G. and J.T.; funding acquisition, L.G., J.T. and J.E.S. All authors have read and agreed to the published version of the manuscript.

Funding: This research was founded by the Generalitat Valenciana (Grant GV/2021/181) and by the Spanish Government (Grant PID2020-117421RB-C21 funded by MCIN/AEI/10.13039/501100011033).

Conflicts of Interest: The authors declare no conflict of interest.

References

1. Tallon, L.; Walker, K. Digital Technologies and the Museum Experience: Handheld Guides and Other Media. Available online: http://www.tate.org.uk/whats-on/tate-modern/exhibition/modigliani/modigliani-vr-ochre-atelier (accessed on 2 November 2021).
2. Wang, Y.; Stash, N.; Aroyo, L.; Gorgels, P.; Rutledge, L.; Schreiber, G. Recommendations based on semantically enriched museum collections. *J. Web Semant.* **2008**, *6*, 283–290. [CrossRef]
3. Horwitz-Bennett, B. High-Tech Museums: The Future Is Now. Available online: https://www.buildings.com/articles/33370/multimedia-transforms-high-tech-museums (accessed on 2 November 2021).
4. MacDonald, G. The Digital Museum. In *The Wired Museum: Emerging Technology and Changing Paradigms*; American Association of Museums: Washington, DC, USA, 1997.
5. Panagiotis, Z.; Despina, M.-G.; Chrysanthou, Y. Learning through Multi-touch Interfaces in Museum Exhibits: An Empirical Investigation. *Educ. Technol. Soc.* **2013**, *16*, 374–384.
6. Bourdieu, P.; Darbel, A.; Schnapper, D. *The Love of Art: European Art Museums and Their Public*; Polity Press: Cambridge, UK, 1991.
7. Gillam. Spotlight VR/AR: Innovation in Transformative Storytelling. Available online: https://mw17.mwconf.org/paper/spotlight-vrar-innovation-in-transformative-storytelling/ (accessed on 2 November 2021).
8. Billinghurst, M.; Thoma, B. Introduction to Virtual Reality. Available online: https://es.slideshare.net/marknb00/comp-4010-lecture-1-introduction-to-virtual-reality (accessed on 2 November 2021).

9. Osterhout, R. AWE Annual AR Versus VR Debate. Available online: https://www.youtube.com/watch?v=7P-rQXiyyrQ&t=1733s (accessed on 2 November 2021).
10. Rae, J.; Edwards, L. Virtual Reality at the British Museum: What Is the Value of Virtual Reality Environments for Learning by Children and Young People, Schools, and Families? Available online: https://mw2016.museumsandtheweb.com/paper/virtual-reality-at-the-british-museum-what-is-the-value-of-virtual-reality-environments-for-learning-by-children-and-young-people-schools-and-families/ (accessed on 2 November 2021).
11. Tate. DModigliani VR The Ochre Atelier. Available online: https://doi.org/10.1002/sce.20355 (accessed on 2 November 2021).
12. Eric Bele. Available online: http://erikbele.com/portfolio/hololens-museum-tour/ (accessed on 2 November 2021).
13. Reuters. HoloLens to Help Improve Museum Experience. Available online: https://www.reuters.com/video/2016/10/25/hololens-to-help-improve-museum-experien?videoId=370256067 (accessed on 2 November 2021).
14. Malley, J.O. Tanks for the Memories: How Augmented Reality Is Bringing an Iconic German Tank Back to Life. Available online: http://www.gizmodo.co.uk/2017/08/tanks-for-the-memories-how-augmented-reality-is-bringing-an-iconic-nazi-tank-back-to-life/ (accessed on 2 November 2021).
15. Hammady, R.; Ma, M.; Strathern, C.; Mohamad, M. Design and development of a spatial mixed reality touring guide to the Egyptian museum. *Multimed. Tools Appl.* **2019**, *79*, 3465–3494. [CrossRef]
16. Hammady, R.; Ma, M.; Strathern, C. User experience design for mixed reality: A case study of HoloLens in museum. *Int. J. Technol. Mark.* **2020**, *13*, 354–375. [CrossRef]
17. Pollalis, C.; Minor, E.J.; Westendorf, L.; Fahnbulleh, W.; Virgilio, I.; Kun, A.L.; Shaer, O. Evaluating Learning with Tangible and Virtual Representations of Archaeological Artifacts. *Assoc. Comput. Mach.* **2018**, *1*, 626–637. [CrossRef]
18. Gao, T.H.; Tian, Q.Y.; Zhou, S. The Virtual Museum Based on HoloLens and Vuforia. In Proceedings of the 4th Annual International Conference on Network and Information Systems for Computers, Wuhan, China, 19–21 April 2018; pp. 382–386.
19. Glinka, K.; Fischer, P.T.; Muller-Birn, C.; Krohn, S. Investigating Modes of Activity and Guidance for Mediating Museum Exhibits in Mixed Reality. *arXiv* **2020**, arXiv:2106.13494.
20. Hunsucker, A.J.; Baumgartner, E.; McClinton, K. Evaluating an Ar-Based Museum Experience. Available online: https://interactions.acm.org/archive/view/july-august-2018/evaluating-an-ar-based-museum-experience (accessed on 2 November 2021).
21. Hernández, F. Los Museos Arqueológicos y su Museografía. Available online: https://www.culturaydeporte.gob.es/dam/jcr:51cd3de8-12ca-4d96-ab4f-08925caf5c89/museos-arqueologicos-museografia.pdf (accessed on 2 November 2021).
22. Marketwired. Unity Technologies Lands $12 Million in Series B Funding Led by WestSummit Capital and iGlobe Partners. Available online: http://www.marketwired.com/press-release/unity-technologies-lands-12-million-series-b-funding-led-westsummit-capital-iglobe-partners-1540593.htm (accessed on 2 November 2021).
23. Muñoz, A.; Martí, A. Holomuseum: A hololens application for creating extensible and customizable holographic exhibitions. In Proceedings of the 10th International Conference on Education and New Learning Technologies, Palma de Mallorca, Spain, 2–4 July 2018; pp. 2303–2310.
24. Attig, C.; Wessel, D.; Franke, T. Assessing Personality Differences in Human-Technology Interaction: An Overview of Key Self-report Scales to Predict Successful Interaction. In Proceedings of the 10th International Conference on PErvasive Technologies Related to Assistive Environments, Island of Rhodes, Greece, 21–23 June 2017; pp. 75–82.
25. Blattgerste, J.; Strenge, B.; Renner, P.; Pfeiffer, T.; Essig, K. Comparing Conventional and Augmented Reality Instructions for Manual Assembly Tasks. In Proceedings of the HCI International 2017–Posters' Extended Abstracts, Island of Rhodes, Greece, 21–23 June 2017; pp. 19–29.
26. Franke, T.; Attig, C.; Wessel, D. TA Personal Resource for Technology Interaction: Development and Validation of the Affinity for Technology Interaction (ATI) Scale. *Int. J. Hum. Comput. Interact.* **2018**, *35*, 456–467. [CrossRef]
27. Brooke, J. SUS-A quick and dirty usability scale. In *Usability Evaluation in Industr*; CRC Press: Boca Raton, FL, USA, 1996. Available online: https://www.crcpress.com/product/isbn/9780748404605 (accessed on 25 November 2021).
28. Brunnström, K.; Dima, E.; Qureshi, T.; Johanson, M.; Andersson, M. Latency impact on Quality of Experience in a virtual reality simulator for remote control of machines. *Signal Process. Image Commun.* **2020**, *89*, 116005. [CrossRef]
29. Ding, S.; ShiruQu, Y.; Wan, S. A long video caption generation algorithm for big video data retrieval. *Future Gener. Comput. Syst.* **2018**, *93*, 583–595. [CrossRef]
30. Gao, Z.; Xuan, H.-Z.; Zhang, H.; Wan, S.; Choo, K.-K.R. Adaptive Fusion and Category-Level Dictionary Learning Model for Multiview Human Action Recognition. *IEEE Internet Things J.* **2019**, *6*, 9280–9293. [CrossRef]
31. Liang, H.N.; Lu, F.; Shi, Y.; Nanjappan, V.; Papangelis, K. Evaluating the effects of collaboration and competition in navigation tasks and spatial knowledge acquisition withual reality environments. *Future Gener. Comput. Syst.* **2019**, *95*, 855–866. [CrossRef]
32. Witmer, B.G.; Singer, M.J. Measuring Presence in Virtual Environments: A Presence Questionnaire. *Presence Teleoperators Virtual Environ.* **1998**, *7*, 225–240. [CrossRef]
33. Wu, Y.; Ma, Y.; Wan, S. Multi-scale relation reasoning for multi-modal Visual Question Answering. *Signal Process. Image Commun.* **2021**, *96*, 116319. [CrossRef]
34. Brown, S.; Ladeira, I.; Winterbottom, C.; Blake, E. The effects of mediation in a storytelling virtual environment. In *Virtual Storytelling: Using Virtual Reality Technologies for Storytelling, Proceedings of the 2nd International Conference ICVS, Toulouse, France, 20–21 November 2003*; Springer: Berlin/Heidelberg, Germany, 2003; pp. 102–111. Available online: https://citeseerx.ist.psu.edu/viewdoc/summary?doi=10.1.1.99.7163 (accessed on 25 November 2021).

35. Milgram, P.; Takemura, A.; Utsumi, C.; Kishino, F. Augmented reality: A class of displays on the reality-virtuality continuum. *Telemanipulator Telepresence Technol.* **1995**, *2351*, 282–292.
36. Robertson, A. Nreal's Augmented Reality Glasses Are Shipping This Month in Korea. Available online: https://www.theverge.com/2020/8/10/21362407/nreal-light-ar-glasses-lg-uplus-samsung-galaxy-note-retail-launch-availability-price (accessed on 2 November 2021).

electronics

MDPI

Article

Toward Smart Communication Components: Recent Advances in Human and AI Speaker Interaction

Hyejoo Kim [1], Sewoong Hwang [1], Jonghyuk Kim [2] and Zoonky Lee [1,*]

1 Graduate School of Information, Yonsei University, Seoul 03722, Korea; hyejoo.kim@yonsei.ac.kr (H.K.); indimoa@gmail.com (S.H.)
2 Division of Computer Science and Engineering, Sunmoon University, Asan-si 31460, Korea; jonghyuk@sunmoon.ac.kr
* Correspondence: zlee@yonsei.ac.kr; Tel.: +82-02-2123-4528

Abstract: This study aims to investigate how humans and artificial intelligence (AI) speakers interact and to examine the interactions based on three types of communication failures: system, semantic, and effectiveness. We divided service failures using AI speaker user data provided by the top telecommunication service providers in South Korea and investigated the means to increase the continuity of product use for each type. We proved the occurrence of failure due to system error (H1) and negative results on sustainable use of the AI speaker due to not understanding the meaning (H2). It was observed that the number of users increases as the effectiveness failure rate increases. For single-person households constituted by persons in their 30s and 70s or older, the continued use of AI speakers was significant. We found that it alleviated loneliness and that human-machine interaction using AI speaker could reach a high level through a high degree of meaning transfer. We also expect AI speakers to play a positive role in single-person households, especially in cases of the elderly, which has become a tough challenge in the recent times.

Keywords: AI speaker; speech recognition; system and semantic failure; effectiveness communication; expectancy disconfirmation; single-person households; human-machine interaction

Citation: Kim, H.; Hwang, S.; Kim, J.; Lee, Z. Toward Smart Communication Components: Recent Advances in Human and AI Speaker Interaction. *Electronics* **2022**, *11*, 1533. https://doi.org/10.3390/electronics11101533

Academic Editors: Juan Ernesto Solanes Galbis, Luis Gracia and Jaime Valls Miro

Received: 10 April 2022
Accepted: 9 May 2022
Published: 11 May 2022

1. Introduction

According to the Market Insights Reports 2022, the global artificial intelligence (AI) speaker market has achieved continuous growth, reaching 5.08 billion dollars in 2021 and is expected to reach 8.71 billion dollars by 2022, as shown in Table 1. The report projects the market to reach 21.94 billion dollars by 2027, at a compound annual growth rate of 26.10% from 2022 to 2027. The supply of AI speakers surpassed 100 million in 2018, and is predicted to go beyond 200 million by 2022. This is a remarkable achievement only eight years after Amazon's Echo with Alexa was released in November 2014. The forecast for the future demand for AI speakers is reassuring—that they will become as important as smartphones.

Table 1. Global AI speaker market by vendor (shipments in millions of units).

Vendors	Market Share (2021)	Shipments (2020)	Shipments (2021)	Growth Rate
Amazon	26.6%	33.6	42.4	8.8%
Google	17.3%	23.8	27.6	3.8%
Baidu	15.6%	19.4	24.8	5.4%
Alibaba	12.6%	17.1	20.0	2.9%
Apple	9.6%	7.3	15.2	7.9%
Xiaomi	6.3%	10.6	10.0	−0.6%
Others	12.0%	18.9	19.1	0.2%
Total	100.0%	130.7	159.1	28.4%

AI speaker is a service platform designed to communicate and process user commands by combining speech recognition and text analysis technologies [1]. In 1954, when the speech recognition technology was first studied, it could not be commercialized owing to its poor recognition rate. AI speakers based on speech recognition technology began to be commercialized when Siri was installed in iPhone 4S in 2011. This has grown into a service provided in most IT products and mobile devices [2]. The mechanism of AI speaker is shown in Figure 1. The AI speaker transmits commands from the speech of the user and voice transmission through speech to text (STT) and conversation recognition stages [3]. Conversely, services are delivered to users through text to speech (TTS) and voice transmission [4].

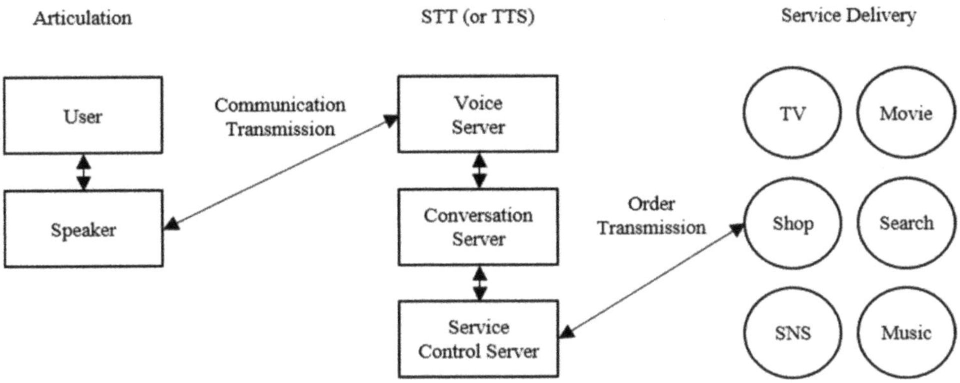

Figure 1. Operating process of AI speaker.

As extended technology and processing stages are required, the completion of the service is still lacking. Despite the lack of the technology readiness level, the services provided by AI speakers are expanding, and various companies are attempting to replace the existing services with new services [5]. As shown in Figure 2, the report published by voicebot.ai suggests that the most frequently used monthly services by the US consumers are music, searching the web, weather checking, and timer and alarm services [6].

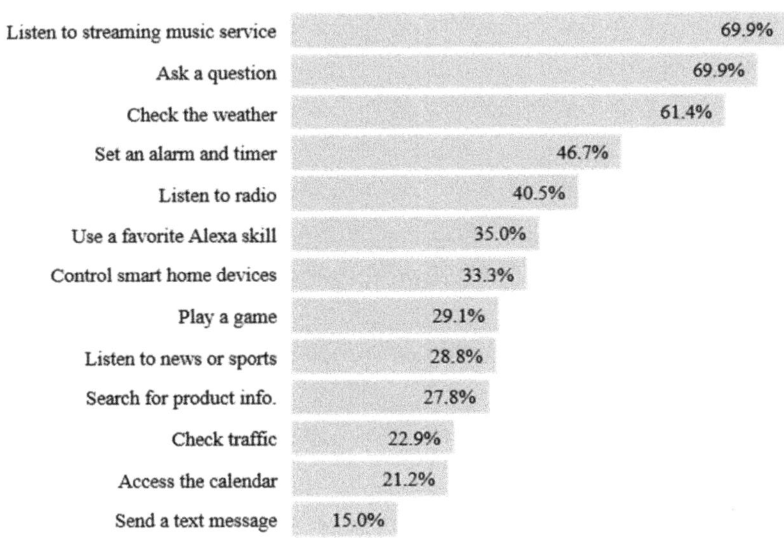

Figure 2. AI speaker use case frequency.

This paper comprises four chapters. Section 2 covers the mathematical theory of communication, which deals with the technical (or system) and semantic communication issues required for the interaction between humans and AI speakers and detects the issues of communication effectiveness. In addition, we examine the expectation of the customers and disconfirmation with the acceptance and non-use of specific technologies. Finally, we investigate the mechanism and current status of AI speaker development. In Section 3 we perform statistical analysis based on the user of AI speaker services. We conduct quantitative analysis using statistical techniques and descriptive statistics to establish and verify the hypotheses on which this study is based, according to prior studies. In Section 4, we present the expected effects of using the results of our study. Finally, in Section 5, we discuss the implications and limitations of the study and propose a future study that builds upon our findings.

2. Background

2.1. Shannon–Weaver Model of Communication: A Mathematical Theory of Communication

Shannon and Weaver provided rigorous and formal solutions to technical problems on which the information theory is based. Initially, Shannon and Weaver focused only on technical communication, intentionally excluding all accessible accidents related to semantic and effectiveness communication [7]. However, as communication develops into Internet of things (IoT) that connect humans and machines across various levels of intelligence and enables new services, semantic and effectiveness communication has become a core concept that can no longer be ignored [8]. The model proposed by Shannon and Weaver is an approach that views communication as a simple linear process, transmits as much information as possible in each path, and evaluates the information. Furthermore, this model quantifies the degree of complexity of information delivery by linking the information concept to the total amount of information and the amount of selectable information. That is, noise may occur in the communication process, apart from the issues of redundancy and optimality [9]. This may be engineering noise or semantic noise that may occur in the information interpretation process [10]. Shannon and Weaver divided the problems in communication into technical problems and semantic problems along with effectiveness problems according to the problem level [11]. The technical problem involves how accurately the signal is transmitted, the semantic problem involves whether the symbol conveys the meaning intended, and the effectiveness problem is whether the received meaning is performed as expected [12].

First, in terms of technical problems, noise must be eliminated or minimized because the noise generated in a limited channel reduces the efficiency of overall information transfer [13]. Furthermore, the noise in the information design of the print media includes decorations that make it difficult to read data, unnecessary visual devices, complex patterns that cause optical errors, vocabularies that make it difficult to convey meaning, and inappropriate images [14].

Second, according to the semantic problem, communication between humans involves the exchange of information, in which the word information is associated with meaning. The information conveyed when passing a concept from a source to a destination is a relevant aspect, not how the message is delivered to the destination [15]. An accurate semantic communication occurs when the concepts associated with the message sent by the source are correctly interpreted by the destination. This does not necessarily mean that the entire bit sequence used to transmit the message is decoded without errors. In other words, one of the main reasons that semantic levels offer significant performance gains relative to purely descriptive levels is that they leverage the sharing of prior knowledge between source and destination [16]. This knowledge can be human language or a formal language (at a more general level) consisting of a set of logical rules that enable entities and receivers to correct errors that occur at the symbol level. An interesting aspect of the semantic problem is that it arises from interactions between different languages. In the semantic problem, the noise serves as a clue to infer and predict the meaning of the message delivered to the receiver. The number of selection conditions of the recipient is reduced when the amount of information is small in the information delivery process, such that the probability of the message being selected is high [17]. Conversely, if the amount of information is large, the number of message selection conditions increases. This makes it less likely that the recipient will select a particular message, and it is difficult to predict the meaning conveyed by the message.

Third, the effectiveness or goal-oriented problem is performed to achieve a common goal through communication between interacting entities. The basic system specification uses a number of resources (e.g., energy and computation) to precisely achieve the desired goal within a given time constraint. A communication system that enables interaction between goals and related entities should be defined to focus on goal-related specifications and constraints [18]. For example, any information that is not strictly related to attaining a goal can be ignored. The efficiency level is the level responsible for the efficient management of goal-oriented communication. The effectiveness problem is undoubtedly the most important virtue in any information design, regardless of the nature and purpose of information. However, if this is overemphasized, the role of information design may be limited only to solving technical problems of communication. Early research on the effectiveness problem mainly focused on how to visualize data, and qualitative aspects of information such as images and narratives were mainly studied [19]. Appropriate expression of entropy and redundancy in information design can achieve information delivery by arousing interest and increasing the level of involvement to actively interpret information [20]. Various studies have suggested the possibility of actively utilizing noise in information design by interpreting the noise in the communication process as "noise as an interest factor" and "surplus as a persuasion factor" from the audience perspective. Particularly, play, storytelling, and interaction with information surplus are more effective because information design requires user participation and interrelationship in a multimedia environment.

Shannon and Weaver proposed that communication is composed of three levels as follows [21]:

Low level of the stack (The technical problem): How accurately can the communication symbols be transmitted.

Middle level of the stack (The semantic problem): How precise the transmitted symbols convey the desired meaning.

High level of the stack (The effectiveness problem): How effective the received meaning affects conduct in the desired way.

2.2. Expectation Disconfirmation Theory

Generally, people react differently in terms of satisfaction even when they use the same product or service, implying that product performance (i.e., quality perceived by consumers) is determined by the expectation of the consumers in addition to the objective function of the product. In other words, consumers do not determine their level of satisfaction with a product based only on the performance level of the product but compare the product performance with their initial expectations to determine their satisfaction [22]. In the expectancy disconfirmation paradigm, the most studied concept as a comparative criterion is expectation. However, there is no clear conceptual consensus on what expectations mean. Several researchers have conceptualized expectations as "perceptions of the likelihood of some event" or "perceptions of the probability of occurrence of some event". By contrast, other researchers view expectations as a concept that includes the "estimation of the likelihood of a specific event" and "evaluation of the good or bad of that event" [23].

Expectations include predictive expectation, desired expectation, and normative expectation. Predictive expectation is wherein the performance is up to a certain extent whereas desires expectation is that it is desirable to have a certain level of performance [24]. Normative expectations imply that performance should be up to some extent. There are four types of expectations: ideal, predictive, natural, and minimum acceptable expectations. There are studies that divide consumer expectations into predictive and normative expectations. Predictive expectation is the prediction of the consumer regarding the expected frequency of problem occurrence, and normative expectation is defined as the normative evaluation of how often problems occur [25,26]. As shown in Figure 3, the initial interest in expectancy disconfirmation research in marketing investigated how expectations, rather than expectations and satisfaction, affect perceived consumer performance. These studies were primarily concerned with whether the effect of expectations on the perceived performance is based on the assimilation theory or contrast theory. At the beginning of the studies, contradictory research results were obtained. However, in later studies, it was reported that consumer expectations generally have a positive effect on product perception [27].

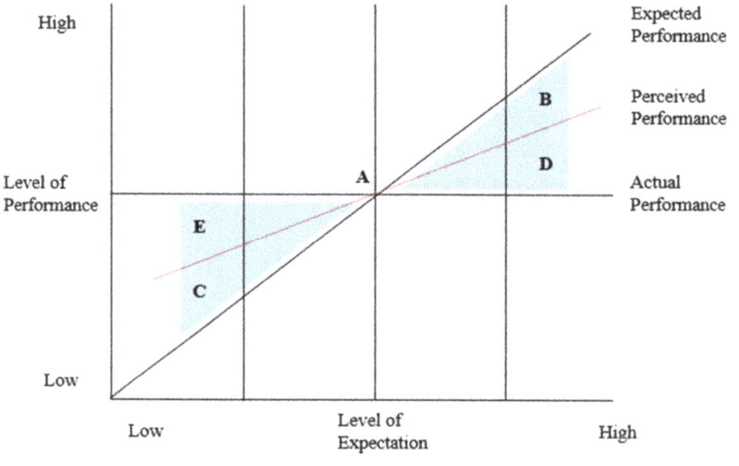

Figure 3. Schematic of the expectancy disconfirmation theory.

Early research on consumer satisfaction mainly focused on analyzing how expectations affect user satisfaction rather than the effect of expectancy disconfirmation on the performance. Most of these studies have attempted to explain the effect of expectation as an assimilation effect based on the cognitive dissonance theory of Festinger [28]. For example, a consumer who purchases a product with high expectations will feel psychologically uncomfortable when the performance of the product fails to meet the expectations. As it is impossible to increase the performance of the product, to solve the psychological discomfort (cognitive dissonance), they try to satisfy themselves based on their high expectations, thereby increasing the level of satisfaction [29].

Expectancy disconfirmation is based on product expectations and perceived performance. Therefore, this theory can accurately explain how expectations and perceived performance affect consumer satisfaction. This theory is generally known as the main theory that explains consumer satisfaction based on expectations [30]. If the product performance is higher than the expectations of the consumer, the level of satisfaction rises, and the consumer becomes dissatisfied if the product performance is lower than the expectation owing to the disappointment effect. When product performance is judged to be lower than expected, better than expected, or equal to expectation, it is called negative disconfirmation, positive disconfirmation, or simple confirmation, respectively. Therefore, in the case of simple confirmation and positive confirmation, the consumer is satisfied whereas the consumer is dissatisfied in the case of negative confirmation [31].

The expectancy disconfirmation theory hypothesizes expectations tied to perceived performance, leading to post-purchase satisfaction. This effect is mediated through positive or negative disconfirmation between expectation and satisfaction; satisfaction occurs when the service expectation is exceeded whereas the customer is dissatisfied if the expectation is not met. As shown in Figure 4, the expectation of the present time point (t) is connected with the disconfirmation of the future time point (t + 1) and affects the choice of the consumer [32].

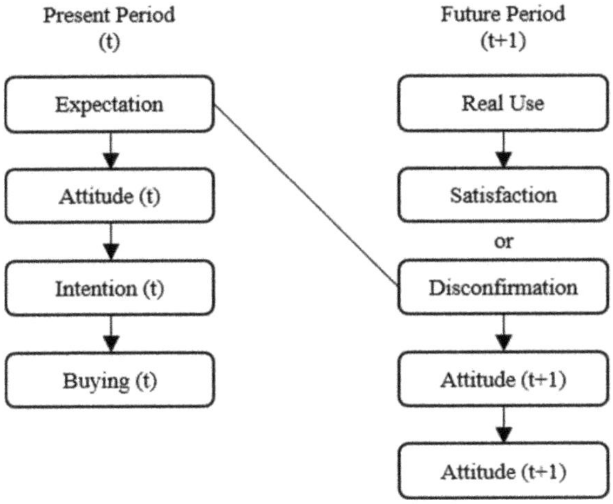

Figure 4. Consumer satisfaction process by time series.

If a good reputation is created by appropriately responding to changes in the demands and expectations of major stakeholder groups and maintaining harmony, then building consumer trust and confidence will naturally follow. Therefore, it is necessary for any company to pay sufficient attention to its key stakeholders and strive to meet their expectations [33]. By meeting stakeholder expectations, a company can anticipate and respond to potential crises in advance, build trust in the organization, and have the results of the company confirmed by stakeholders. The expectations and interests of stakeholders are constantly evolving; therefore, companies should conduct regular stakeholder monitoring and dialogue to keep pace with these developments, and thus, the stakeholder feedback can be obtained [34,35].

2.3. Technical Background of AI Speaker

IoT is one of the representative information technologies leading the fourth industrial revolution. The core technology of IoT consists of the collection, processing, and management of data coming through sensors, wired or wireless communication and network infrastructure, security technology to prevent information leakage, and software that can connect various technologies [36]. Therefore, although IoT is a service industry related to individual consumption, it has a complex structure in which large industries in various fields are complementary to each other. AI speakers focus on convenience functions in general life based on IoT [37,38]. Companies that design AI speakers focus on content businesses that consider human accessibility and intimacy as well as the functional aspects of devices. They have even started to formulate the name of AI assistant service. The AI speaker is a voice command device with a built-in virtual assistant, which provides interactive work and hands-free activation [39]. The core of the virtual assistant service is human–machine interaction through question answering (QA). All AI speakers are equipped with voice recognition technology by default, but a special wake word is required to link the device so that it can communicate with the server [40]. AI collects and analyzes user commands to provide information and services tailored to the situation. In other words, the AI speaker collects the command, compares it with other commands stored in the cloud, and recognizes it when a user inputs a command to the AI speaker. The service is operated in such a way that the suitable data are retrieved from the big data and appropriate information is provided to the user through the recognized command [41,42].

This enables the industry to launch AI services that can satisfy accessibility and interactivity. Furthermore, an AI speaker is composed of a speech recognition technology that converts human voice into text data that can be recognized by a computer and a natural language processing technology that can process the converted data [43,44]. The convergence of these two speech-language processing technologies is not only used in the AI speaker industry, but also in the wearable device and artificial intelligence industry (which is based on human intimacy). AI speakers are based on voice assistants or voice user interfaces (VUIs), such as Google Assistant and Amazon Alexa. VUIs receive language as input information through a speech recognizer and output voice information through speech synthesis or pre-recorded audio. There is a growing interest in integrating the voice assistant with various devices, such as AI speakers, smartphones, and smart TVs, to improve the voice recognition rate. The error rate is 5% when a person hears and transcribes the conversation over the phone. In 2017, the interactive agent recognition error rate reached 5%, a level similar to that of humans [45]. Figure 5 shows the basic model of acoustic echo cancellation. When a user tries a voice command while the music is playing on the speaker, the AI speaker removes the music signal by applying acoustic echo cancellation technology and only accepts the voice command signal without distortion. For the acoustic echo cancellation technology to work ideally, the reference signal (R) for signal processing and the signal (R^) reproduced through the AI speaker and input back to the microphone must exactly match. In this case, even if the reproduced music signal is much larger than the voice command, the AI speaker accurately recognizes only the voice command signal [46].

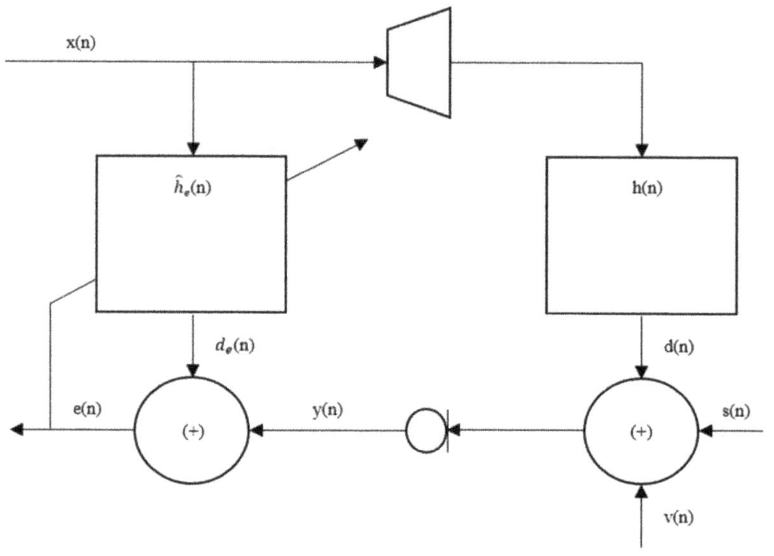

Figure 5. Block diagram of the acoustic echo cancellation system.

The most basic principle for acoustic echo cancellation is to estimate the characteristics of the acoustic path, which should be modeled as accurately as possible to implement a pattern similar to the actual echo. An adaptive filter should be used as the characteristics of the acoustic path generally vary according to time and surrounding conditions [47,48]. The situation of the music interference seriously affects the voice recognition performance. The quality of acoustic echo cancellation depends on the speed of convergence and the accuracy of the adaptive filter. The echo signal is typically modeled as a convolution of the musical signal and the impulse response of the audio path [49].

3. Methodology

3.1. Research Methods

IT corporations, which develop and sell AI speakers, have been persistently making colossal investments in marketing to survive in the competitive market. This emphasizes the importance of understanding consumer behavior in developing and expanding the services that enable the consumers to lock-in the company product. Therefore, we focus on discussing and analyzing the following two issues: (1) How the initial experience of the user affects the continued use of the speaker and (2) how the individual characteristics of the user affect consumption. We seek to provide insight into what customer behavior characteristics companies should consider to increase sustainability in the future.

In this study, we used real consumer data on AI speaker obtained from Korea Telecom (KT), which is one of the most representative broadband companies in South Korea. The company launched an AI speaker service, Giga-Genie, which is installed in all-in-one set-up box to control Internet Protocol Television (IPTV). The content of the communication appears on the TV screen which improves the function by helping consumers know how their words are recognized. As the service comes along with the IPTV registration, there are consumers who unwillingly registered with the AI speaker, and this could provide a meaningful consequence because we specifically used three months' data of the customers registered in December 2017.

To analyze the initial user experience, we started with the section that is highlighted by the users. Tracing back to the resource above, voicebot.ai, the most important function that consumers focus on is the understandability of the communication between the AI speaker and users. To improve this, failure to maintain communication should be reviewed. The three aspects of the success in communication consist of technical (or system), semantic, and effectiveness aspects as defined by the mathematical theory of communication in Section 2. As shown in Table 2, we analyzed communication failure between AI speakers and users in these three aspects.

Table 2. Classification of the typical failure experiences of AI speaker users.

Type	Request Message (By Customer)	System Message	Results
System Comm. Failure	Do "something."	The network connection failed to cancel the service. Please try again later.	Cancellation of service
	How is the weather in Kangnam, Seoul?	I cannot access the weather information. Please try again later.	A sudden service failure
	Turn on the Netflix service.	A subscription to the service is required.	Requirement to sign-in to additional service
Semantic Comm. Failure	How is the weather in Kangnam, Seoul?	I cannot find the name of the location. Please ask another location.	Rejection to unavailable service request or incomprehensible request
	Play the music of "ABBA".	I will turn on the music of "Bach".	Searching for other results with similar pronunciation.
	Search for the movie 'Smile'.	I'll smile with you too, ha-ha-ha.	error in recognizing the meaning of words
Effectiveness Comm. Failure	Search for the movie "Squid Game".	Should I search contents related to "Squid Game" in TV or in web browser?	Inducement of the user's choice amongst possible actions
	Call Mr. Smith.	Do you want to call Mr. Smith?	Confirmation of the user's will
	I want to make a call.	Let me know the contact number you would like to make a call.	Request for the additional information

We observed and analyzed the log data of 27,308 AI speaker users for three months from December 2017 to February 2018. We used variables that consider individual attributes to quantify the exposure level of the user environment along with basic demographic information. We defined exposure level as the TV viewing time as the IPTV and set-up box are all-in-one service. The gender and age of the subscribers were used for personal profile information. The failure in each field was measured by the failed percentage of the request attempt. We classified independent variables (Xs) as the percentage of three types of failures with the moderating variables considering the first day, accumulated three days, one week, and two and more weeks. We used two more types of independent variables: exposure level of the user environment and demographic information such as age and gender. Finally, we defined two types of dependent variables (Ys) to display continuous usage of the speaker as shown in Table 3. We considered a discrete dependent variable (Y1) and a continuous dependent variable (Y2), both of which indicate continuous use as a dependent variable, simultaneously. We defined the continuous use of discrete Y1 as 1 for more than five days and 0 for less than five days. In the case of continuous Y2, the date and number of use cases were quantitatively constructed.

Table 3. Operational definition of variables.

Variables		Definition
Independent Vars. (Xs)		Percentage of three types of failures with system, semantic, and effectiveness. the exposure level of the user environment, and demographic information (ex. age and gender)
Moderating Vars.		Period of customer failure with first-day, accumulated three-days, one-week, and two and more weeks.
Dependent Var.	Discrete Var. (Y1)	Sustainable use of AI speaker, with one for more than five days, and 0 for less than five days
	Continuous Var. (Y2)	Sustainable use of AI speaker, with the date of use, and the number of use cases

3.2. *Hypothesis*

We discovered that systematic (or technical) service error that occurs in the verbal request owing to the circumstances where the service is not ready, the user should sign-in to the additional service, or voice recognition technology is not working, leads to a decline in the customers' trust in the voice service. This eventually hinders customers from purchasing further subscription to the AI speaker. Thus, we assumed hypothesis 1 as a system failure.

Hypothesis 1 (H1). *If no service is technically provided in response to consumer request, the continued use of AI speakers will be negatively affected.*

The provision of the wrong service refers to the incident where the result of the verbal request of the user is dissatisfying, leading to another request within 5 s. This refers to unrelated emotional chat or some other reason due to the absurdness of the situation. The circumstance where a different type of service from what the consumer requested is provided can be explained, for example, as in not providing music service when the consumer has requested for it. We argued that the disharmony in the service during the initial experience within the first day, first three days, first week, and first two weeks or more, leads to the absence of consumer needs. Therefore, we assumed the second hypothesis as a semantic failure.

Hypothesis 2 (H2). *Providing a kind of service that is different from the one ordered by the consumer will have a negative impact on the continued use of the AI speaker.*

If the AI speaker cannot recognize the verbal request at once, or requires additional information on the verbal request, the impression on its continued use is negative. For example, when the user commands, "turn on Beatles", and the speaker replies, "If you want to listen to the music of Beatles, say 'Turn on the music of Beatles'". This is a typical example of the circumstance requesting a change in the method of verbal request or additional information. Replying with sentences such as "I couldn't understand" or

"Repeat your request" lowers the likelihood of continuing the subscription. Therefore, we assumed a third hypothesis as an effectiveness failure.

Hypothesis 3 (H3). *If the consumer does not recognize the commands at once or has requested for additional information, the continued use of the AI speaker is negatively affected.*

In addition to the three hypotheses, we hypothesized that the degree of continued use of AI speakers varies according to the degree of exposure to the usage environment and demographic information. Accordingly, we established two more hypotheses.

Hypothesis 4 (H4). *The continuity of usage depends on the mechanical time the users stay at home.*

Hypothesis 5 (H5). *The continuity of the usage differs based on the age, range, and gender of the users.*

Figure 6 schematically illustrates the causal relationships for the above five hypotheses, and each independent variable is classified according to the customer failure period, which is a moderator variable.

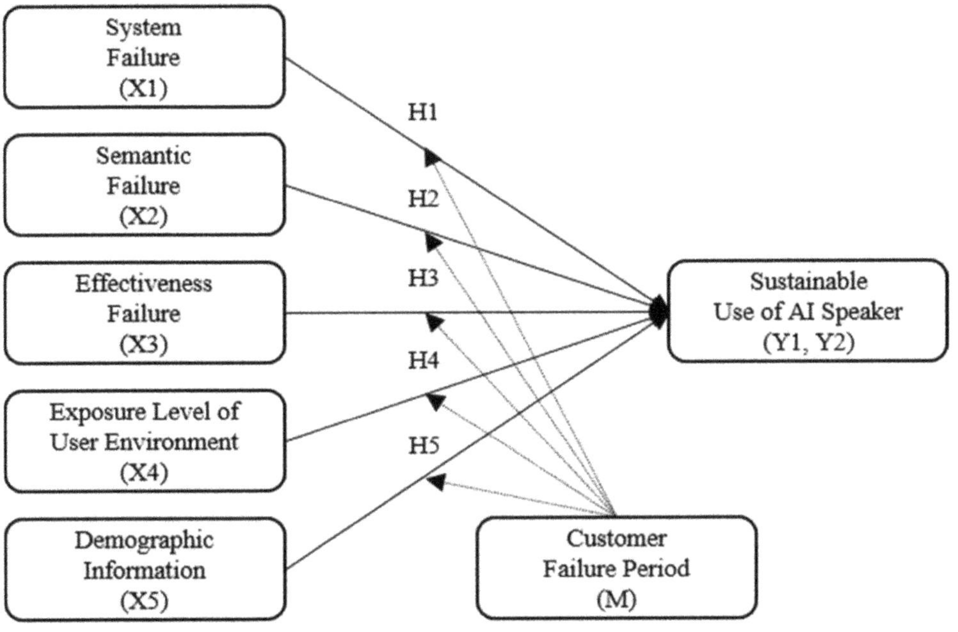

Figure 6. Causality of the hypotheses.

4. Results

To test the first hypothesis, as shown in Figure 7, we explored the continuous use of the AI speaker for each customer failure period related to system failure. We found that the sustained use was negatively affected if a system failure occurred in any period and that the most significant difference in sustained use was for users with a period of two weeks or more.

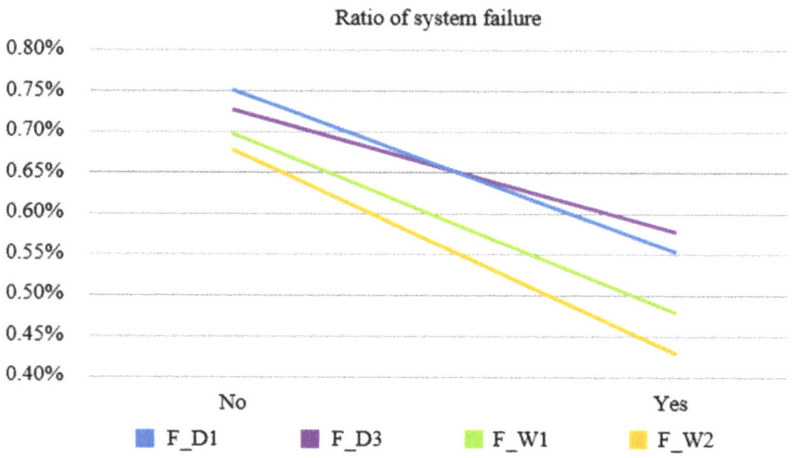

Figure 7. Ratio of system failure.

We explored the continuous use of AI speakers for each failure period of semantic failure-related customers to test the second hypothesis. As shown in Figure 8, we found that the occurrence of semantic failure across all periods had a negative effect on sustained use. The largest difference in continued use was the users over a period of two weeks.

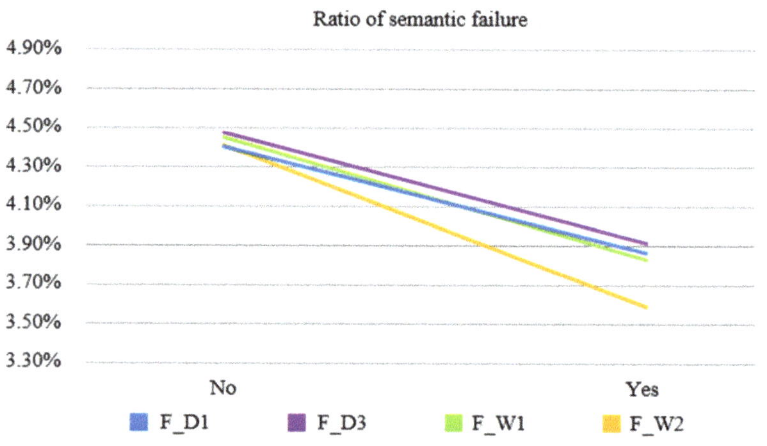

Figure 8. Ratio of semantic failure.

Finally, to test of the third hypothesis, we explored the continuous use of the AI speaker for each failure period related to the effectiveness failure. We reached conclusions that were contrary to the results of the previous hypotheses. That is, the negative effect on continuous use did not increase even if the effectiveness failure occurred in almost all periods, as shown in Figure 9. Rather, most of the cumulative users, except for 1-day users, showed a positive will to use despite the failure. Moreover, we discovered that, as with the previous hypotheses, the biggest difference in sustained use was for users over a period of two weeks.

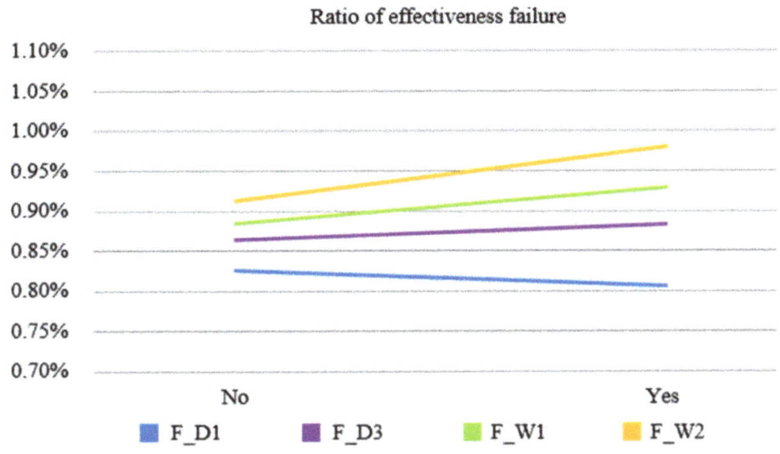

Figure 9. Ratio of effectiveness failure.

We searched for each failure variable by date for customers using the AI speaker for more than five days a week for three consecutive months. Based on all graphs, we found that the period that showed the greatest difference was the failure rate over two weeks. Therefore, we performed a logistic regression analysis for Y1 and regression analysis for Y2 with reference to the failure rate of two weeks to test each hypothesis. Tables 4 and 5 lists the results.

Table 4. Result of analysis 1.

Hypothesis	Y1	Y2
H1	0.0007 **	0.0096 **
H2	<0.0001 **	<0.0001 **
H3	0.721 (N.S.)	0.0575
H4	<0.0001 **	0.0042 **

(Significant Level: * $p < 0.1$, ** $p < 0.05$, *** $p < 0.01$).

Table 5. Result of analysis 2.

Components of H6		Case of Y1 = 1	Y2 (Days)
Gender	F	9.23%	10.2
	M	9.37%	10.0
	Diff.	N.S.	N.S.
Age	Under 20	5.05%	7.6
	20s	8.07%	9.9
	30s	12.31%	11.2
	40s	5.79%	8.7
	50s	4.21%	7.5
	60s	9.45%	9.1
	>70s	12.31%	10.8
	Diff.	<0.0001 **	<0.0001 **

(Significant Level: * $p < 0.1$, ** $p < 0.05$, *** $p < 0.01$).

We statistically proved that the failure due to system error (H1) and not understanding the meaning (H2) resulted in negative results on continued use of the AI speaker when two dependent variables were applied. However, in the case of H3, contrary to H1 and H2, the higher the failure rate, the greater the number of cases used. We proved that the additional queries and re-words of H3 provide a positive experience for people to continue the conversations.

We found no statistically significant differences between sexes. However, found a difference in usage according to age. We found that sustained use was significantly higher for those in their 30s and 70s or older. The common tendency between the two age groups is that there are mainly single-person household; therefore, the lack of a conversation partner could increase conversation with the AI speaker, which explains the positive result of continued use.

5. Conclusions

From the results of this study, unlike the system and semantic communication failure, effectiveness failure has a positive effect on the continuous use of AI speakers. This proves that human–machine interaction can reach a high level through a high degree of meaning transfer. AI speakers are expected to play a positive role in the case of single-person households, especially the elderly; such cases are ubiquitous. This study improves the continued customer use of products based on data from the top telecommunication service companies in South Korea and proves the three types of communication functions academically. However, short-term data may cause a problem in that the failure type is simple. To address these problems, we plan to include type diversification along with customer groups in future research.

Author Contributions: Data curation, H.K.; formal analysis, H.K., S.H. and J.K.; investigation, J.K.; methodology, J.K.; project administration, H.K., S.H. and Z.L.; resources, H.K.; supervision, Z.L.; validation, S.H. and Z.L.; visualization, J.K.; writing—original draft, H.K. and S.H.; writing—review and editing, J.K. All authors have read and agreed to the published version of the manuscript.

Funding: This research received no external funding.

Conflicts of Interest: The authors declare no conflict of interest.

References

1. Shalini, A.; Jayasuruthi, L.; VinothKumar, V. Voice recognition robot control using android device. *J. Comput. Nanosci.* **2018**, *15*, 2197–2201. [CrossRef]
2. Lee, W.; Seong, J.J.; Ozlu, B.; Shim, B.S.; Marakhimov, A.; Lee, S. Biosignal sensors and deep learning-based speech recognition: A review. *Sensors* **2021**, *21*, 1399. [CrossRef] [PubMed]
3. Yadav, S.; Kaushik, A. Do You Ever Get Off Track in a Conversation? The Conversational System's Anatomy and Evaluation Metrics. *Knowledge* **2022**, *2*, 55–87. [CrossRef]
4. Jeong, H.D.J.; Ye, S.K.; Lim, J.; You, I.; Hyun, W. A computer remote control system based on speech recognition technologies of mobile devices and wireless communication technologies. *Comput. Sci. Inf. Syst.* **2014**, *11*, 1001–1016. [CrossRef]
5. Xie, Y.; Li, F.; Wu, Y.; Wang, Y. HearFit: Fitness monitoring on smart speakers via active acoustic sensing. In Proceedings of the IEEE INFOCOM 2021-IEEE Conference on Computer Communications, Vancouver, BC, Canada, 10–13 May 2021; pp. 1–10. [CrossRef]
6. Youn, M.A.; Lim, Y.; Seo, K.; Chung, H.; Lee, S. Forensic analysis for AI speaker with display Echo Show 2nd generation as a case study. *Forensic Sci. Int. Digit. Investig.* **2021**, *38*, 301130. [CrossRef]
7. Strandberg, P.E. Automated system-level software testing of industrial networked embedded systems. *arXiv* **2021**, arXiv:2111.08312.
8. Yang, W.; Liew, Z.Q.; Lim, W.Y.B.; Xiong, Z.; Niyato, D.; Chi, X.; Cao, X.; Letaief, K.B. Semantic communication meets edge intelligence. *arXiv* **2022**, arXiv:2202.06471.
9. Semrau, D.; Lavery, D.; Galdino, L.; Killey, R.I.; Bayvel, P. The impact of transceiver noise on digital nonlinearity compensation. *J. Light Technol.* **2018**, *36*, 695–702. [CrossRef]
10. Dušek, O.; Howcroft, D.M.; Rieser, V. Semantic noise matters for neural natural language generation. *arXiv* **2019**, arXiv:1911.03905. [CrossRef]
11. Gillespie, D.J.; Schiffman, R. A critique of the Shannon-Weaver theory of communication and its implications for nursing. *Res. Theory Nurs. Pract.* **2018**, *32*, 216–225. [CrossRef]
12. Weng, Z.; Qin, Z. Semantic communication systems for speech transmission. *IEEE J. Sel. Areas Commun.* **2021**, *39*, 2434–2444. [CrossRef]
13. Lippi, G.L.; Mørk, J.; Puccioni, G.P. Numerical solutions to the laser rate equations with noise: Technical issues, implementation and pitfalls. In *Nanophotonics*; SPIE: Bellingham, WA, USA, 2018; Volume 10672, pp. 82–95. [CrossRef]
14. Bergemann, D.; Morris, S. Information design: A unified perspective. *J. Econ. Lit.* **2019**, *57*, 44–95. [CrossRef]

15. Fedushko, S.; Benova, E. Semantic analysis for information and communication threats detection of online service users. *Procedia Comput. Sci.* **2019**, *160*, 254–259. [CrossRef]
16. Strinati, E.C.; Barbarossa, S. 6G networks: Beyond Shannon towards semantic and goal-oriented communications. *Comput. Netw.* **2021**, *190*, 107930. [CrossRef]
17. Maulud, D.H.; Zeebaree, S.R.; Jacksi, K.; Sadeeq, M.A.M.; Sharif, K.H. State of art for semantic analysis of natural language processing. *Qubahan Acad. J.* **2021**, *1*, 21–28. [CrossRef]
18. Michael, J.; Rumpe, B.; Zimmermann, L.T. Goal modeling and mdse for behavior assistance. In Proceedings of the 2021 ACM/IEEE International Conference on Model Driven Engineering Languages and Systems Companion (MODELS-C), Fukuoka, Japan, 10–15 October 2021; pp. 370–379. [CrossRef]
19. Li, G.; Kou, G.; Peng, Y. A group decision making model for integrating heterogeneous information. *IEEE Trans. Syst. Man Cybern. Syst.* **2016**, *48*, 982–992. [CrossRef]
20. Lopez-Caudana, E.; Ramirez-Montoya, M.S.; Martínez-Pérez, S.; Rodríguez-Abitia, G. Using robotics to enhance active learning in mathematics: A multi-scenario study. *Mathematics* **2020**, *8*, 2163. [CrossRef]
21. Grech, N.; Brent, L.; Scholz, B.; Smaragdakis, Y. Gigahorse: Thorough, declarative decompilation of smart contracts. In Proceedings of the 2019 IEEE/ACM 41st International Conference on Software Engineering, Montreal, QC, Canada, 25–31 May 2019; pp. 1176–1186. [CrossRef]
22. Lee, C.P.; Hung, M.J.; Chen, D.Y. Factors affecting citizen satisfaction: Examining from the perspective of the expectancy disconfirmation theory and individual differences. *Asian J. Political Sci.* **2022**, 1–26. [CrossRef]
23. Nuradiana, S.; Sobari, N. Expectancy disconfirmation theory on millenials consumer behaviour in retail store. *ICORE* **2021**, *5*, 116–125.
24. Liu, F.; Lim, E.T.; Li, H.; Tan, C.W.; Cyr, D. Disentangling utilitarian and hedonic consumption behavior in online shopping: An expectation disconfirmation perspective. *Inf. Manag.* **2020**, *57*, 103199. [CrossRef]
25. Wang, X.; Zhou, R.; Zhang, R. The impact of expectation and disconfirmation on user experience and behavior intention. In *International Conference on Human-Computer Interaction*; Springer: Cham, Switzerland, 2020; pp. 464–475. [CrossRef]
26. Zhang, X.; Chen, Y. Admissibility and robust stabilization of continuous linear singular fractional order systems with the fractional order α: The $0 < \alpha < 1$ case. *ISA Trans.* **2018**, *82*, 42–50. [PubMed]
27. Ugaddan, R.G. Does performance management effectiveness matter? Testing the expanded expectations disconfirmation model of local disaster risk reduction. *Asia-Pac. Soc. Sci. Rev.* **2021**, *21*, 220–235.
28. Delly, M.C.; Kealesitse, B.; Moeti-Lysson, J.; Nametsegang, A. An Expectation Disconfirmation Analysis of Undergraduate Research Supervision: Opinions of Business Students at the University of Botswana. *Botsw. J. Bus.* **2021**, *13*. Available online: https://journals.ub.bw/index.php/bjb/article/view/1964 (accessed on 6 April 2022).
29. Fadel, K.J.; Meservy, T.O.; Kirwan, C.B. Information filtering in electronic networks of practice: An fMRI investigation of expectation (dis) confirmation. *J. Assoc. Inf. Syst.* **2022**, *23*, 491–520. [CrossRef]
30. Wang, C.; Liu, J.; Zhang, T. 'What if my experience was not what I expected?': Examining expectation-experience (dis) confirmation effects in China's rural destinations. *J. Vacat. Mark.* **2021**, *27*, 365–384. [CrossRef]
31. Dos Santos, M.A.; Baeza, S.; Lizama, J.C. The intention of attending a sporting event through expectation disconfirmation and the effect of emotions. In *Integrated Marketing Communications, Strategies, and Tactical Operations in Sports Organizations*; IGI Global: Hershey, PA, USA, 2019; pp. 223–240. [CrossRef]
32. Liu, J.; Shah, C. Investigating the impacts of expectation disconfirmation on web search. In Proceedings of the 2019 Conference on Human Information Interaction and Retrieval, Glasgow, UK, 10–14 March 2019; pp. 319–323. [CrossRef]
33. Evangelidis, I.; Van Osselaer, S.M. Points of (dis) parity: Expectation disconfirmation from common attributes in consumer choice. *J. Mark. Res.* **2018**, *55*, 1–13. [CrossRef]
34. Matikiti, R.; Mpinganjira, M.; Roberts-Lombard, M. Antecedents and outcomes of positive disconfirmation after service failure and recovery. *J. Glob. Bus. Technol.* **2018**, *14*, 43–57.
35. Kaushik, A.; Loir, N.; Jones, G.J. Multi-view conversational search interface using a dialogue-based agent. In *European Conference on Information Retrieval*; Springer: Cham, Switzerland, 2021; pp. 520–524.
36. Bentley, F.; Luvogt, C.; Silverman, M.; Wirasinghe, R.; White, B.; Lottridge, D. Understanding the long-term use of smart speaker assistants. *Proc. ACM Interact. Mob. Wearable Ubiquitous Technol.* **2018**, *2*, 1–24. [CrossRef]
37. Ling, H.C.; Chen, H.R.; Ho, K.K.; Hsiao, K.L. Exploring the factors affecting customers' intention to purchase a smart speaker. *J. Retail. Consum. Serv.* **2021**, *59*, 102331. [CrossRef]
38. Wang, J.S. Exploring biometric identification in FinTech applications based on the modified TAM. *Financ. Innov.* **2021**, *7*, 1–24. [CrossRef]
39. Ashfaq, M.; Yun, J.; Yu, S. My smart speaker is cool! perceived coolness, perceived values, and users' attitude toward smart speakers. *Int. J. Hum.–Comput. Interact.* **2021**, *37*, 560–573. [CrossRef]
40. Kim, S.; Choudhury, A. Exploring older adults' perception and use of smart speaker-based voice assistants: A longitudinal study. *Comput. Hum. Behav.* **2021**, *124*, 106914. [CrossRef]
41. Smith, E.; Sumner, P.; Hedge, C.; Powell, G. Smart-speaker technology and intellectual disabilities: Agency and wellbeing. *Disabil. Rehabil. Assist. Technol.* **2020**, 1–11. [CrossRef] [PubMed]
42. Hu, K.H.; Hsu, M.F.; Chen, F.H.; Liu, M.Z. Identifying the key factors of subsidiary supervision and management using an innovative hybrid architecture in a big data environment. *Financ. Innov.* **2021**, *7*, 10. [CrossRef] [PubMed]

43. Hashemi, S.H.; Williams, K.; El Kholy, A.; Zitouni, I.; Crook, P.A. Measuring user satisfaction on smart speaker intelligent assistants using intent sensitive query embeddings. In Proceedings of the 27th ACM International Conference on Information and Knowledge Management, Turin, Italy, 22–26 October 2018; pp. 1183–1192. [CrossRef]
44. Zhang, J.X.; Yang, G.H. Low-complexity tracking control of strict-feedback systems with unknown control directions. *IEEE Trans. Autom. Control.* **2019**, *64*, 5175–5182. [CrossRef]
45. Brause, S.R.; Blank, G. Externalized domestication: Smart speaker assistants, networks, and domestication theory. *Inf. Commun. Soc.* **2020**, *23*, 751–763. [CrossRef]
46. Choi, Y.; Demiris, G.; Thompson, H. Feasibility of smart speaker use to support aging in place. *Innov. Aging* **2018**, *2* (Suppl. S1), 560. [CrossRef]
47. Jung, H.; Oh, C.; Hwang, G.; Oh, C.Y.; Lee, J.; Suh, B. Tell me more: Understanding user interaction of smart speaker news powered by conversational search. In Proceedings of the Extended Abstracts of the 2019 chi Conference on Human Factors in Computing Systems, Glasgow, UK, 4–9 May 2019; pp. 1–6. [CrossRef]
48. Kaushik, A.; Jones, G.J. A Conceptual Framework for Implicit Evaluation of Conversational Search Interfaces. *arXiv* **2021**, arXiv:2104.03940.
49. Ito, T.; Oyama, T.; Watanabe, T. Smart speaker interaction through ARM-COMS for health monitoring platform. In *International Conference on Human-Computer Interaction*; Springer: Cham, Switzerland, 2021; pp. 396–405. [CrossRef]

electronics

MDPI

Article

Technological Acceptance of Industry 4.0 by Students from Rural Areas

Mauricio Castillo-Vergara [1,*], Alejandro Álvarez-Marín [2], Eduardo Villavicencio Pinto [3,4] and Luis Enrique Valdez-Juárez [5]

1 Facultad de Economía y Negocios, Universidad Alberto Hurtado, Santiago 8320000, Chile
2 Departamento de Ingeniería Industrial, Universidad de La Serena, La Serena 1720170, Chile; aalvarez@userena.cl
3 PROCASUR NGO, Heriberto Covarrubias 21, Oficina 705 Ñuñoa, Santiago 7750000, Chile; eavillavicencio@uc.cl
4 Dirección de Formación Continua, Universidad SEK, Fernando Manterola 0789, Santiago 7520317, Chile
5 Department of Business and Economics Sciences, Technological Institute of Sonora Mexico, Obgregon 85000, Mexico; levaldez@itson.edu.mx
* Correspondence: mhcastillo@uahurtado.cl

Abstract: In this study, our objective was to identify the factors that explain the acceptance of Industry 4.0 technologies by technical students. Industry 4.0 is made up of a series of technologies, such as the Internet of Things; cyber-physical systems; big data, data analytics, or data mining; cloud computing or the cloud; augmented reality or mixed reality; additive manufacturing or 3D printing; cybersecurity; collaborative robots; artificial intelligence; 3D simulation; digital twin or digital twin; drones. We designed a theoretical model based on the technology acceptance model to explain the acceptance of these technologies. The study was carried out on a sample of 326 technical professional students. Students are considered ideal samples to test theoretical predictions regarding the relationships between variables in emerging technologies. The results show the positive effect of technological optimism on perceived usefulness and ease of use. However, there was not a direct effect on the attitude towards the use. A mediating effect was established. In addition, the facilitating conditions influence optimism and the ease of using the technology. These elements influence the attitude and intention to use, which is consistent with previous studies on technology acceptance. The results will guide the design of public policies to incorporate technologies into education.

Keywords: Industry 4.0; technology; technology acceptance model; emerging technologies

Citation: Castillo-Vergara, M.; Álvarez-Marín, A.; Villavicencio Pinto, E.; Valdez-Juárez, L.E. Technological Acceptance of Industry 4.0 by Students from Rural Areas. *Electronics* **2022**, *11*, 2109. https://doi.org/10.3390/electronics11142109

Academic Editors: Juan Ernesto Solanes Galbis, Luis Gracia and Jaime Valls Miro

Received: 21 May 2022
Accepted: 16 June 2022
Published: 6 July 2022

1. Introduction

The future of rural development has aroused the interest of broad and diverse academic communities, which is due, among other things, to its relevance when facing the effects of massive shocks, such as the COVID-19 pandemic or the sustained increase in food prices [1–3]. An essential point on the global research agenda has been the inclusion of 4.0 technologies in agriculture, looking at both their social and environmental impacts [4], the effects on transition patterns [5], and the types of challenges they may face [6], such as the construction of territorial indicators [7], or their practical implementation in production [8]. However, there does not seem to be a sufficient approximation regarding the degree of acceptance between this technological phenomenon and a whole social group for the future of agricultural development, such as rural youth.

With regard to this group, in particular, the literature discusses, at a theoretical level, the possibility of sharing a definition that addresses the diversity of conditions and characteristics that rural youth represent [9–11], the factors that influence the development of their economic activities [12,13], and the elements that affect national and international mobility practices [14,15].

Although during the last decade of the 20th century, there was little theoretical evolution in the study of rural youth [14,16], some factors made it possible for this context to markedly change, intensifying structural analysis within the framework of public policy design. Thus, during the last five years, the difficulties, challenges, and opportunities faced by rural youth have been at the center of the concerns of both governments and international organizations linked to rural development. The International Fund for Agricultural Development (IFAD), in its 2019 annual report, highlights the depth of the economic and technological transformations that this group is experiencing worldwide. This preoccupation has generated high expectations and uncertainty about which methods would be more efficient in improving their living conditions [17].

The report states that there are three essential elements for the development of rural youth. Increased productivity is associated with the challenge of improving educational conditions to facilitate interaction with technological schemes that have a positive impact on the efficiency of economic processes; connectivity has the potential to create more opportunities to generate business [18]; finally, agency refers to rural youth's ability to make autonomous and empowered decisions about their life strategies. In turn, access to better information and education has increased financial and labor expectations, which has strained the ecosystem of opportunities offered by rural areas, which are characterized by a diversity of structural conditions [19].

In addition to the above, rural young people's aspirations or ways of perceiving the future have played a central role in their interaction with technology and the type of strategic decisions that they make. This trajectory could be mediated by global factors, such as the climate crisis, but also by the local adaptive capacity of agriculture in the face of economic phenomena, which are dominated by growing and dominant corporate and industrial participation, for example, in the area of food production [20].

Following the criteria used by the National Youth Institute of Chile and the Ibero-American Youth Organization, rural youth are defined as the population between 15 and 29 years of age who live in rural areas, which represents 13% of people at the national level. Regarding their socio-labor characteristics, the essential occupational sectors are agriculture (37%), commerce (17%), and services (16%). This group's education level is significantly higher than that of their parents due to the universalization and increased territorial coverage of the Chilean educational system, which has allowed them to become, among other things, stable and recurrent users of technologies. Although rural youth, in general, have access to low-skilled jobs, there is an essential group of young people with expectations linked to agricultural innovation. They believe that access to technologies, investments, and credit systems is necessary for this [14].

Industry 4.0 (I4.0) represents a recent technology trend [21,22]. This is a significant revolution that is changing industry, as well as social and economic life [23]. It is based on the adoption of digital technologies [24–26] for the collection of data in real time, which provide helpful information to systems [27,28]. I4.0 is based on several technological pillars (big data, cloud, industrial internet, horizontal and vertical integration, simulation, augmented reality, additive manufacturing, cybersecurity, and advanced manufacturing) [29,30]. The key benefits of I4.0 reported in the literature include: cost reduction; improvements in quality, efficiency, flexibility, and productivity; and a competitive advantage [31]. What could be used as a springboard for the development of rural youth?

With the advancement of this technology and its incorporation into both professional and private user environments, whether it is accepted or rejected is critical. Leveraging I4.0 technologies is far from trivial, and user acceptance is key to successfully implementing the technology [32]. Since I4.0 relies heavily on interactions between individuals, technologies, organizations, and people, it is critical to investigate the causal factors for adopting and using the technology [33]. The Technology Acceptance Model (TAM) has evolved to become the crucial model in understanding the predictors of human behavior towards potential technology acceptance or rejection [34], has been widely used to recognize the factors that affect technology acceptance in a variety of contexts [35,36], and is considered an influential model that is commonly applied in the field of information systems [37]. Therefore, given that the TAM model is among the most widely used for modeling behaviors, we find it helpful when modeling the intention to adopt Industry 4.0 technologies by technical professional students from rural areas.

The I4.0 acceptance study has been addressed in other contexts, such as small and medium enterprises [31], manufacturing companies [38], managers [32], and governments [39]. However, to the best of our knowledge, it has not been addressed from the students' perspectives. This situation is serious because investments in any new technology are costly and require a lot of time and effort [40], and future professionals could affect the success of these initiatives.

Therefore, this study aimed to measure the acceptance of Industry 4.0 technology in vocational–technical studies and, additionally, to address the call to extend the original TAM by incorporating new variables to improve its applicability and validity [33,34,41]. We have introduced subjective norms, enabling conditions, and technological optimism as the factors that could explain technology acceptance.

The remainder of the paper is structured as follows. The theoretical foundations and hypotheses are presented. Then, the methodology and results are presented. Finally, a discussion of the results and the conclusions of the study are presented.

2. Theoretical Background and Hypotheses

In 1985, Davis [42] proposed the technology acceptance model (TAM) as an adaptation of the theory of reasoned action (TRA), which was initially proposed by [43] to specifically explain computer-usage behavior. The TRA demonstrates the intention to use through attitudes towards using and subjective norms. However, the TAM suggests that the subjective criteria do not directly influence attitudes towards use. Attitudes towards using and use could be explained by perceived ease of use and perceived usefulness. Two additional extensions to the models have also been proposed: TAM2 [44] and TAM3 [45], both of which include other factors, such as subjective norms, that contribute to a better explanation of the intention of use [46].

Parasuraman [47] proposed the construct of technology readiness (TR) to explain technological acceptance. This is composed of four dimensions: optimism and innovativeness, as drivers of technology readiness, as well as discomfort and insecurity, which are inhibitors. However, previous studies suggest that optimism and innovativeness are stable individual dimensions used to measure TR [48].

Venkatesh et al. proposed [49] the unified theory of acceptance and use of technology (UTAUT), and, in 2012, an extension of this (UTAUT2) [50], with the purpose of integrating various existing models. In both cases, social influence is proposed as one of the constructs that helps to explain the behavioral intention to use.

Lin, Shih, and Sheren proposed the TRAM model [51], which uses TR as a construct in the TAM model, thus explaining its influence on perceived ease of use and perceived usefulness, as well as behavioral intention to use.

However, the TAM model proposed by Davis is widely used to study the adoption of new technologies [52]. This model explains the factors that could lead a user to adopt a certain technology [53], and it considers the impact of these factors on the attitude towards use and, finally, on the intention to use [54]. This model comprises several variables that directly or indirectly explain behavioral intentions and technology use (i.e., perceived usefulness, perceived ease of use, attitudes towards technology) and it can be extended with external variables, such as self-efficacy, subjective norms, and the facilitating conditions of technology use [40].

Numerous studies confirm the robustness of the model, emphasizing its broad applicability to a diverse set of technologies and users [30]. It has been used in recent years to study the adoption of new technologies, such as wearables [55], Google Glass [56], augmented reality [57], Smart Home systems [58], IoT-based systems [24], and digital transformation strategies [59].

Based on the above, a theoretical model was developed using the TAM to understand Industry 4.0 acceptance.

Facilitating Conditions

Enabling conditions are defined as the degree to which an individual perceives that an organizational and technical infrastructure exists to support the use of a technology [60]. Individuals who are unfamiliar with new technologies may have difficulty using them. However, if they have sufficient contextual support, they can easily accept the technology [61]. Then, the facilitating conditions consist of modifying objective factors that support the easy use of the technology [62]. The presence of favorable conditions, such as internet availability, technological support, organizational/managerial support, motivation, etc., can enhance people's willingness to try new technologies [63]. Facilitating conditions are the perceived enablers or barriers in the environment that influence a person's perception of the ease or difficulty of performing a task [64]. These serve as a critical indicator for the promotion of new technology because they help users learn to use the technology within a shorter period, and minimize the problems that they may encounter when using it [65]. In addition, facilitating conditions regarding the use of software have been related to technological optimism [66]. Based on these antecedents, we propose the following hypotheses:

Hypothesis 1 (H1). *Facilitating conditions will be significantly associated with technological optimism.*

Hypothesis 2 (H2). *Facilitating conditions will be significantly associated with ease of use.*

Subjective Norms

The subjective norm refers to the perception of people importance to an individual regarding a specific behavior [43]. The importance of people's opinions to an individual can influence the use of technologies [67].

In a systematic review of 142 studies in the banking sector, the influence of subjective norms on the perceived usefulness of using banking-service applications was determined [68]. Industry 4.0 is characterized by an increase in the digitization of its operations [69]. One of the technologies that led the digitization processes in this industry is augmented reality. The influence of subjective norms on the intention to use AR applications has been studied [70] with regard to their perceived usefulness [71,72]. Therefore, we formulated the following hypothesis:

Hypothesis 3 (H3). *Subjective norms will be significantly associated with perceived usefulness.*

Technological Optimism

Technological optimism is defined as "a positive view of technology and the belief that it offers people increased control, flexibility, and efficiency in their lives" [47]. It is associated with a positive view of technology and with the belief that it can increase control, flexibility, and efficiency in life [73]. Therefore, people who are optimistic about using new technologies are believed to have positive intentions to use them. They consider technology helpful and are not concerned about its negative outcomes [74]. As a result, optimists are more willing to use new technologies and knowledge [75]. Today's students are considered digital natives, and most of them have favorable views towards the use of technology [76]. Technological optimism is a strong predictor of technology choice in some young people compared with adults [77] (for example, in new learning methods [73], the adoption of mobile banking [74], or cryptocurrencies [78]). This view shows their tendency to be pioneers in using technology as a motivational behavior [79], and a positive relationship between technological optimism and perceived ease of use and perceived usefulness [80]. With these arguments, we put forward the following hypotheses:

Hypothesis 4 (H4). *Technological optimism will be significantly associated with perceived usefulness.*

Hypothesis 5 (H5). *Technological optimism will be significantly associated with attitude towards use.*

Hypothesis 6 (H6). *Technological optimism will be significantly associated with perceived ease of use.*

Technology Acceptance Model

There is sufficient support [41,42,57,81,82] for the role of perceived usefulness (PU), which is understood as "the degree to which a person believes that using a particular system would improve performance." Perceived ease of use (PEOU) is defined as "the degree to which a person believes that using a particular system would be effortless", which is a significant factor in predicting variations in the attitude towards technology use. Davis [42] defines attitudes towards new system use (ATU) as "an individual's general effective reaction to the use of the system," and perceived ease of use (PEOU) has been explained as "the degree to which an individual believes that he or she will continue to use the system." Considering the TAM model, we consider the following hypotheses:

Hypothesis 7 (H7). *Perceived usefulness will be significantly associated with attitude towards use.*

Hypothesis 8 (H8). *Perceived ease of use will be significantly associated with attitude towards use.*

Hypothesis 9 (H9). *A positive attitude towards technology use will be significantly associated with intention to use.*

Figure 1 presents the proposed research model.

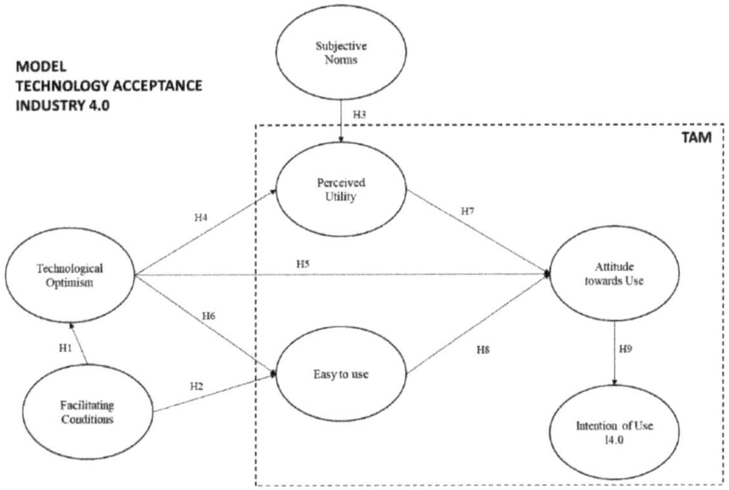

Figure 1. Research model.

3. Methodology

Data were analyzed using structural equation modeling (SEM), based on variance, taking advantage of the partial-least-squares (PLS) technique, which is suitable for information processing in social science research and has advantages over SEM and traditional multivariate analysis [83]. Structural equation modeling is implemented in research that seeks to test complex models [84]. Two models have been calculated using this technique: the measurement model (or external), which relates the observed variables to the latent variables, and the structural model (or internal), which calculates the strength and direction of the relationships between the variables [85]. The steps differ depending on whether the measurement model is reflective or formative. In this case, for reflective measurement models, the steps are as follows: (1) estimate the item loads and assess the importance; (2) assess the reliability of the indicator; (3) assess the overall reliability constructs; (4) examine the average variance extracted (AVE); (5) confirm the discriminant validity using the HTMT method; (6) assess the nomological validity [86].

Empirical Context and Data Sources

The sample comprised 326 students within technical–professional education. Students are considered ideal samples for testing theoretical predictions regarding variable relationships [87], which is in line with this study. Student samples have frequently been used in exploratory technology-adoption studies [29]. Information was obtained from a self-administered questionnaire following participation in a workshop on Industry 4.0. Indications were given that there were no right or wrong answers, and the anonymity and strict confidentiality of the data were guaranteed.

The survey was applied between the months of May and June 2021. A total of 37% of the interviewees were women, and 63% were men. The average age was 19 years, and the median was 18 years, with a minimum age of 15 years and a maximum of 30 years.

Measures

The scale was elaborated from the literature review and previous studies. Table 1 presents the indicators associated with the model constructs.

Table 1. Studies and indicators used.

Construct	Study	Indicator
Subjective norms	[88]	People whose opinions I value encourage me to use new Industry 4.0 technologies. People who are important to me help me use the new Industry 4.0 technologies.
Technology optimism	[89]	The products and services that use the newest technologies are much more convenient. I prefer to use the most advanced technology available. Technology makes my work more efficient.
Facilitating conditions	[90]	I can easily access information on how to use Industry 4.0 technology. Industry 4.0 technology is compatible with other technologies I use (tablet, notebook, smartphone). I can easily get guidance and instruction if I have difficulties in using Industry 4.0 technologies.
Perceived ease of use	[91]	The use of Industry 4.0 technologies is easy for me. The use of Industry 4.0 technologies is understandable and clear to me. It will not be difficult for me to be proficient in the use of Industry 4.0 technologies.
Perceived usefulness	[92]	Industry 4.0 technology can help me to be more efficient. Industry 4.0 technology is useful. The use of Industry 4.0 technologies benefits me
Attitude towards using	[91]	The use of Industry 4.0 technologies is a good idea. The use of Industry 4.0 technologies is a wise idea. I like to develop my activities using Industry 4.0 technologies.
Behavioral intention to use	[93]	I intend to use Industry 4.0 technologies in the coming months. I will continuously use Industry 4.0 technologies in my activities. In general, I am willing to use Industry 4.0 technologies for the development of my activities. I would recommend others to incorporate Industry 4.0 technologies in their activities.

Data Analysis

The hypotheses were tested using the Smart PLS 3.3.9 © package [94] and partial least squares. The technique consists of different steps and has been previously used in this type of exploration [95]. First, the model fitting is performed by applying a bootstrapping process (5000 subsamples). Second, the measurement model is evaluated [96], which is followed by an evaluation of the structural model [97].

4. Results

The study had 326 participants, of whom 63% were male and 37% were female. The average age was 19 years, and the students were in their third or fourth academic year. Of those interviewed, 27% were studying and working, 67% were only studying, and the rest shared their studies with unpaid work. Regarding technical specialization, the sample showed that 16% were students of automotive mechanics, 20% were agricultural technical students, 56% were agricultural technical students, and 8% were technical students in agroindustrial and agricultural administration.

The loading (λ) of each item is more significant than 0.707, which verifies the reliability of the indicator [98]. The reliability of the construct was satisfied if it had values greater than 0.7 for the Cronbach's alpha coefficients, composite reliability, and Dijkstra–Henseler indicator (RhoA) [99], as presented in Table 2. The convergent validity is presented in Table 3, of which the values are higher than 0.5 [100]. Table 4 also shows the heterotrait–monotrait ratios (HTMT) with values below 1, which provide discriminant validity evidence [97].

Table 2. Evaluation of the measurement model.

Construct/Indicator	Loads	Cronbach's Alpha	Dijkstra–Henseler's Rho	Composite Reliabilities	Average Variance Extracted
Subjective norm (SN)		0.8391	1.201	0.9168	0.8468
SN1	0.8657				
SN2	0.9716				
Technology optimism (TO)		0.9029	1.116	0.9283	0.8126
TO1	0.9619				
TO2	0.9244				
TO3	0.8113				
Facilitating conditions (FC)		0.8994	1.056	0.9324	0.8217
FC1	0.9300				
FC2	0.9352				
FC3	0.8518				
Perceived ease of use (PEOU)		0.8971	0.913	0.9353	0.8282
PEOU1	0.8958				
PEOU2	0.9371				
PEOU3	0.8966				
Perceived usefulness (PU)		0.9321	1.558	0.9474	0.8574
PU1	0.9048				
PU2	0.9721				
PU3	0.8992				
Attitude towards using (ATU)		0.9305	1.185	0.952	0.8688
ATU1	0.8948				
ATU2	0.9758				
ATU3	0.9239				
Behavioral intention to use (BIU)		0.9177	1.034	0.9354	0.7838
BIU1	0.8976				
BIU2	0.8124				
BIU3	0.9017				
BIU4	0.9255				

Table 3. Fornell–Larcker criterion.

	ATU	BIU	PEOU	PU	SN	FC	TO
ATU	0.9321						
BIU	0.8731	0.8853					
PEOU	0.8220	0.8055	0.9100				
PU	0.8501	0.8204	0.7256	0.9260			
SN	0.7463	0.7364	0.7405	0.6510	0.9202		
FC	0.7204	0.7427	0.7675	0.6417	0.7036	0.9065	
TO	0.7477	0.7449	0.7390	0,.3910	0.6629	0.7570	0.9015

Note: ATU: attitude towards using; BIU: behavioral intention to use; PEOU: perceived ease of use; PU: perceived usefulness; S.N.: subjective norm; FC: is facilitating conditions; TO: technology optimism.

Table 4. Heterotrait–Monotrait ratios.

	ATU	BIU	PEOU	PU	SN	FC	TO
ATU							
BIU	0.9223						
PEOU	0.8961	0.9032					
PU	0.8933	0.8804	0.7947				
SN	0.8231	0.8244	0.8585	0.7261			
FC	0.7736	0.8041	0.8632	0.6772	0.8039		
TO	0.7875	0.8072	0.7891	0.8038	0.7377	0.7976	

Note: ATU: attitude towards using; BIU: behavioral intention to use; PEOU: perceived ease of use; PU: perceived usefulness; SN: subjective norm; FC: facilitating conditions; TO: technology optimism.

The results obtained for the model are presented in Table 5 and illustrated in Figure 2. Eight hypotheses are accepted, and one is rejected. The results are consistent with those of other studies that capture the predictive power of the TAM in the educational environment. The R2 values represented in the figure are significant at 0.01%; all values meet the minimum requirements [101,102].

Table 5. Results from the structural model.

Hypothesis	Path	*t*-Value	*p*-Value	Supported
H1: *Facilitating Conditions (FC)→Technology optimism (TO)*	0.7570	12.519	0.0000	Yes
H2: *Facilitating Conditions (FC)→Perceived ease of use (PEOU)*	0.4873	4.229	0.0000	Yes
H3: *Subjective norm (SN)→Perceived usefulness (PU)*	0.2874	2.563	0.0052	Yes
H4: *Technology optimism (TO)→Perceived usefulness* (PU)	0.5486	4.378	0.0000	Yes
H5: *Technology optimism (TO)→Attitude towards using (ATU)*	0.0860	0.793	0.2139	No
H6: *Technology optimism (TO)→Perceived ease of use (PEOU)*	0.3703	3.071	0.0011	Yes
H7: *Perceived usefulness* (PU)*→Attitude towards using (ATU)*	0.4989	4.072	0.0000	Yes
H8: *Perceived ease of use (PEOU)→Attitude towards using (ATU)*	0.3965	3.327	0.0004	Yes
H9: *Attitude towards using (ATU)→Behavioral intention to use (BIU)*	0.8731	32.785	0.0000	Yes

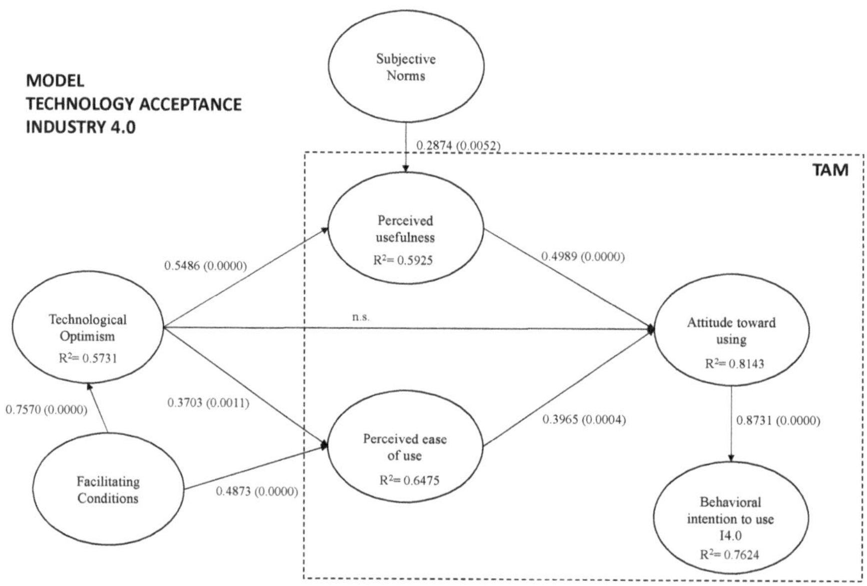

Figure 2. Resulting research model. Dashed arrow shows nonsignificant paths.

5. Discussion

This section discusses the study's main findings in the order in which the model hypotheses are presented. A theoretical model was developed, using the TAM, to understand

Industry 4.0 acceptance, based on previous research. The results show that the acceptance of H1 and H2, and the enabling conditions, which are defined as the degree to which an individual perceives that an organizational and technical infrastructure exists to support the use of the system, will positively affect technological optimism and perceived ease of use [60]. Regarding technological optimism, favorable conditions generate a propensity to try new technologies and are established as an indicator to promote the use of new technology [63], helping users use the technology sooner and reducing problems in its use [65]. If there is sufficient support, even people who may have difficulties using the technology may perceive greater ease. Recently, countries with emerging economies in rural areas of Latin America are betting on investment in technological infrastructure to trigger innovation and thereby reinforce the resilience of societies and sustain the economy in the face of global megatrends, such as demographic, technological, and environmental changes during the current global crisis caused by the COVID-19 pandemic [103].

Subjective norms have been widely considered in many models that have traditionally been used to assess technology adoption, and they refer to the "perceived pressures on a person to perform a given behavior and the person's motivation to comply with those pressures" [104]. H3 is accepted, showing that subjective norms influence how the student is affected by the perceptions of some significant referents (family, friends, teachers) regarding the perceived usefulness of I4.0. The results are in line with other studies and technologies [105], and it is suggested that subjective norms have an indirect effect on the intention to use through perceived usefulness, as is the case in this study [106]. Starting from the perspective of the TAM model developed by Davis in 1989, subjective norms are not the most determining factor for the use of technologies and their adaptability. Therefore, people's intrinsic and extrinsic behavioral factors are complementary and influence technology adoption [107]. These manifestations occur in individuals in educational and business contexts.

Technological optimism does not directly affect the decision to use or reject H5. Its effect is mediated by the variable's usefulness and ease of use, meaning that H4 and H6 are accepted. When people are more innovative, they can withstand a higher degree of uncertainty and have more positive intentions to use the innovation. In other words, they are less likely to perceive risks and are more receptive to technological innovation [108], thus perceiving greater usefulness and ease of use. This optimistic view of technology makes them more inclined to see the positives of the adoption process. However, technological optimism is often clouded by external factors from the social, economic, and cultural environments. During the COVID-19 pandemic, people (young people and adults) experienced unprecedented emotional impacts, which led to stress and high resistance to the use of unfamiliar digital platforms [109]. Therefore, mistrust in technologies increased in urban communities and was more accentuated in rural populations [110].

Our results for H7, H8, and H9 are in line with previous research on the roles of perceived usefulness (PU), which is understood as "the degree to which a person believes that using a particular system would improve his or her performance", and perceived ease of use (PEOU), which is defined as "the degree to which a person believes that using a particular system would be effortless", as significant factors in predicting variations in the attitude towards using I4.0 technologies. In addition, the more favorable the students' attitudes towards I4.0 use, the greater their intentions to use the technology [42]. Although there is a significant digital divide between urban and rural areas in the Latin American region, the adoption of Industry 4.0 is becoming more pervasive in different economic sectors. In education, new technologies have promoted new forms of learning through digital platforms, which can educate at a distance and in real time [111]. Therefore, the academic society shows high perceived usefulness and a positive attitude regarding the use of increasingly intelligent and autonomous technology [112].

Regarding the R^2 values, the results of attitude towards use (81.43%) and intention to use (76.24%) are sufficiently high to explain the endogenous variables. For the other variables, the result is considered moderate [96,102].

6. Conclusions

In this study, we proposed an extended TAM model to explore the factors that may influence technical education students' intention to use Industry 4.0 technology. Several studies have addressed the acceptance of these technologies. However, none have considered the educational field that we have addressed in this study. Therefore, our study has high theoretical value and contributes to the development and strengthening of the TAM model by exploring the internal and external factors that affect the behavior and use of new technologies through Industry 4.0.

We have also introduced an external variable to the model, which is referred to as technological optimism, to understand its influence on attitudes towards using technology, considering that this population is regarded as digital natives. Considering this condition, educational institutions and public policymakers should consider this characteristic as a strength. Students can be introduced to technology and challenged to incorporate it into their educational processes. Agile methodologies of entrepreneurship and innovation should be introduced so that students use technology to solve problems. This strengthens students' creative abilities. Indeed, future work activities will require these capabilities with the imminent arrival of I4.0. The rural regions of Latin American countries face more significant challenges than these communities or areas in countries with more stable economies. Therefore, our study makes an empirical contribution of high value by exploring the particularities that make up the TAM model when applied to behavior and application in student communities.

The inclusion of subjective norms is also fascinating, as it helps us to understand how the environment can influence the usefulness of this technology. We believe that teachers' perceptions of these technologies can affect the students' perceived usefulness. Previous studies in this segment show the importance of the teacher's role in the professional expectations of students, and mainly in lower-income groups [96]. In addition, student communities have been making greater use of new technologies in the current hectic times caused by the COVID-19 pandemic. This has converted the regions into digital and virtual communities to improve education and culture and strengthen the economy [110,113].

Training can be supplied to address the integration of technology into the educational process to support this outcome. For example, augmented-reality or virtual-reality applications allow for integrating teaching. Alternatively, programs can be promoted that support the creation of technology startups that develop technology for incorporation into the classroom. Given the importance of the subjective norms, it is recommended that educational institutions support these processes and do not leave this task to the trainers.

These recommendations are intended to strengthen the virtual educational models applied in rural communities through the use of Industry 4.0 [114]. During the COVID-19 pandemic, most citizens from different regions, including students, showed greater resilience when adapting to new technological changes, as well as the actions that helped them in terms of struggles and survival [115].

In addition to the practical implications described above, the present study has several theoretical implications. First, we propose an extended TAM model to explore the factors that influence students to use technologies associated with I4.0. The proposed model adds value because, although many studies have addressed technological acceptance in education, we have not found studies that relate it to the field addressed. However, several studies analyze I4.0 in education. Still, the focus is on the skills required by students, the integration of I4.0 into curricula, and the effectiveness of teaching technologies. However, the acceptance of the technology by the users is critical; otherwise, the institutions' efforts may be unsuccessful. Secondly, we incorporate factors that have not been studied in this context, such as technological optimism and facilitating conditions. With this, we hope to understand the behavior of students exposed to new technologies that are incorporated into the world of work. Finally, this study validates the results generated from the TAM model for technology acceptance and use. In doing so, we extend the theoretical model to a field that has not been addressed.

The work is not free of limitations, which may lead to future lines of research. First, the sample refers to technical students, and so the results cannot be generalized. Future work could include other students or professionals. Secondly, the information is cross-sectional; future research could consider longitudinal studies that allow for a longer-term view or other techniques [116,117]. Other lines of research that could be addressed from our study include models that explain which factors facilitate I4.0 adoption in emerging-market SMEs, what kinds of resources and capabilities affect the implementation of I4.0, or the impact of I4.0 on performance and innovation. Finally, innovation ecosystems could be developed to boost startups using I4.0 as a value proposition.

Author Contributions: M.C.-V. is the author of the manuscript and is responsible for the design and execution of the model; writing the hypotheses, discussion, and conclusions; and coordinating with co-authors. A.Á.-M. collaborated on a general review of the document and constructing the theories. E.V.P. collaborated on the general review of the document, the survey application, and the redaction of the manuscript's introduction. L.E.V.-J. collaborated on the general examination and edition of the paper. All authors have read and agreed to the published version of the manuscript.

Funding: This paper received funding for its development and publication from Gobierno de Chile: Proyecto FIC Gobierno Regional de O'Higgins 40027680-0.

Informed Consent Statement: Informed consent was obtained from all subjects involved in the study.

Data Availability Statement: The data and the questionnaire used in the study are available to other authors who require access to this material.

Acknowledgments: The authors would like to thank the Faculty of Economics and Business of the Universidad Alberto Hurtado for their support in developing the research.

Conflicts of Interest: The authors declare no conflict of interest.

References

1. De Luca, C.; Tondelli, S.; Åberg, H.E. The Covid-19 pandemic effects in rural areas. *TeMA J. Land Use Mobil. Environ.* **2020**, 119–132. [CrossRef]
2. Luo, R.-F.; Liu, C.-F.; Gao, J.-J.; Wang, T.-Y.; Zhi, H.-Y.; Shi, P.-F.; Huang, J.-K. Impacts of the COVID-19 pandemic on rural poverty and policy responses in China. *J. Integr. Agric.* **2020**, *19*, 2946–2964. [CrossRef]
3. Mastronardi, L.; Cavallo, A.; Romagnoli, L. Diversified farms facing the COVID-19 pandemic: First signals from Italian case studies. *Sustainability* **2020**, *12*, 5709. [CrossRef]
4. Rose, D.C.; Wheeler, R.; Winter, M.; Lobley, M.; Chivers, C.A. Agriculture 4.0: Making it work for people, production, and the planet. *Land Use Policy* **2021**, *100*, 104933. [CrossRef]
5. Klerkx, L.; Rose, D. Dealing with the game-changing technologies of Agriculture 4.0: How do we manage diversity and responsibility in food system transition pathways? *Glob. Food Sec.* **2020**, *24*, 100347. [CrossRef]
6. Zhai, Z.; Martínez, J.F.; Beltran, V.; Martínez, N.L. Decision support systems for agriculture 4.0: Survey and challenges. *Comput. Electron. Agric.* **2020**, *170*, 105256. [CrossRef]
7. Maja, P.W.; Meyer, J.; Von Solms, S. Development of smart rural village indicators in line with industry 4.0. *IEEE Access* **2020**, *8*, 152017–152033. [CrossRef]
8. Lima, G.C.; Figueiredo, F.L.; Barbieri, A.E.; Seki, J. Agro 4.0: Habilitando a transformação digital da agricultura por meio da IoT. *Rev. Ciência Agronômica* **2021**, *51*, 119–132. [CrossRef]
9. Caggiani, M.E. Heterogeneidad en la condición juvenil rural. In Proceedings of the VI Congreso de la Asociación Latinoamericana de Sociología Rural, Porto Alegre, Brazil, 25–29 November 2002.
10. Dirven, M. *Nueva Definición de lo Rural en América Latina y el Caribe*; FAO: Santiago, Chile, 2019.
11. Cangas, G.Y. Juventud rural: Trayectorias teóricas y dilemas identitarios. *Nueva Antropol.* **2003**, *19*, 153–175.
12. Dirven, M. Expectativas de la juventud y el desarrollo rural. *Rev. CEPAL* **1995**, *55*, 123–137. [CrossRef]
13. Sili, M.; Fachelli, S.; Meiller, A. Juventud rural: Factores que influyen en el desarrollo de la actividad agropecuaria. Reflexiones sobre el caso argentino. *Rev. Econ. Sociol. Rural* **2016**, *54*, 635–652. [CrossRef]
14. Durston, J. Juventud rural y desarrollo en América Latina. *J. Adolesc. Juv.* **2001**, *99*, 1–7.
15. Orozco, M.; Jewers, M. *IFAD Research Series 56 The Impact of Migrants' Remittances and Investment on Rural Youth*; IFAD Research Series 56; IFAD: Rome, Italy, 2019; SSRN 3532468.
16. Durston, J. Juventud y desarrollo rural: Marco conceptual y contextual. *Ser. Políticas Soc.* **1998**, *1*, 1–41.
17. Fondo Internacional de Desarrollo Agrícola (FIDA). Crear Oportunidades Para Los Jóvenes del Medio Rural. 2019, pp. 1–44. Available online: https://www.ifad.org/ruraldevelopmentreport/es/download/ (accessed on 20 May 2022).

18. Arslan, A.; Tschirley, D.E.; Egger, E.-M. Rural Youth Welfare along the rural-urban gradient: An empirical Analysis across the Developing World. *J. Dev. Stud.* **2021**, *57*, 544–570. [CrossRef]
19. Sumberg, J.; Chamberlin, J.; Flynn, J.; Glover, D.; Johnson, V. IFAD Research Series 47 Landscapes of Rural Youth Opportunity. Papers of the 2019 Rural Development Report. 2019. Available online: https://papers.ssrn.com/sol3/papers.cfm?abstract_id=3521380 (accessed on 20 May 2022).
20. White, B. *Agriculture and the Generation Problem*; Fernwood Publishing: New Scotland, NY, USA, 2020; ISBN 1773631675.
21. Sony, M. Industry 4.0 and lean management: A proposed integration model and research propositions. *Prod. Manuf. Res.* **2018**, *6*, 416–432. [CrossRef]
22. Xu, L.D.; Xu, E.L.; Li, L. Industry 4.0: State of the art and future trends. *Int. J. Prod. Res.* **2018**, *56*, 2941–2962. [CrossRef]
23. Reischauer, G. Industry 4.0 as policy-driven discourse to institutionalize innovation systems in manufacturing. *Technol. Forecast. Soc. Chang.* **2018**, *132*, 26–33. [CrossRef]
24. Brar, P.S.; Shah, B.; Singh, J.; Ali, F.; Kwak, D. Using modified technology acceptance model to evaluate the adoption of a proposed IoT-based indoor disaster management software tool by rescue workers. *Sensors* **2022**, *22*, 1866. [CrossRef]
25. Zhong, R.Y.; Xu, X.; Klotz, E.; Newman, S.T. Intelligent manufacturing in the context of industry 4.0: A review. *Engineering* **2017**, *3*, 616–630. [CrossRef]
26. Liao, Y.; Deschamps, F.; Loures, E.F.R.; Ramos, L.F.P. Past, present and future of Industry 4.0—A systematic literature review and research agenda proposal. *Int. J. Prod. Res.* **2017**, *55*, 3609–3629. [CrossRef]
27. Frank, A.G.; Dalenogare, L.; Ayala, N. Industry 4.0 technologies: Implementation patterns in manufacturing companies. *Int. J. Prod. Econ.* **2019**, *210*, 15–26. [CrossRef]
28. Lu, Y. Industry 4.0: A survey on technologies, applications and open research issues. *J. Ind. Inf. Integr.* **2017**, *6*, 1–10. [CrossRef]
29. Hizam-Hanafiah, M.; Soomro, M.A.; Abdullah, N.L. Industry 4.0 readiness models: A systematic literature review of model dimensions. *Information* **2020**, *11*, 364. [CrossRef]
30. Mittal, S.; Khan, M.A.; Romero, D.; Wuest, T. A critical review of smart manufacturing & industry 4.0 maturity models: Implications for small and medium-sized enterprises (SMEs). *J. Manuf. Syst.* **2018**, *49*, 194–214. [CrossRef]
31. Masood, T.; Sonntag, P. Industry 4.0: Adoption challenges and benefits for SMEs. *Comput. Ind.* **2020**, *121*, 103261. [CrossRef]
32. Rodríguez-Espíndola, O.; Chowdhury, S.; Dey, P.K.; Albores, P.; Emrouznejad, A. Analysis of the adoption of emergent technologies for risk management in the era of digital manufacturing. *Technol. Forecast. Soc. Chang.* **2022**, *178*, 121562. [CrossRef]
33. Kang, Y.; Choi, N.; Kim, S. Searching for new model of digital informatics for human-computer interaction: Testing the Institution-Based Technology Acceptance Model (ITAM). *Int. J. Environ. Res. Public Health* **2021**, *18*, 5593. [CrossRef]
34. Granić, A.; Marangunić, N. Technology acceptance model in educational context: A systematic literature review. *Br. J. Educ. Technol.* **2019**, *50*, 2572–2593. [CrossRef]
35. Rafique, H.; Omran, A.; Shamim, A.; Anwar, F. Investigating the acceptance of mobile library applications with an extended technology acceptance model (TAM). *Comput. Educ.* **2020**, *145*, 103732. [CrossRef]
36. Na, S.; Heo, S.; Han, S.; Shin, Y.; Roh, Y. Acceptance model of artificial intelligence (AI)-based technologies in construction firms: Applying the Technology Acceptance Model (TAM) in combination with the Technology–Organisation–Environment (TOE) framework. *Buildings* **2022**, *12*, 90. [CrossRef]
37. Chatterjee, S.; Rana, N.P.; Dwivedi, Y.K.; Baabdullah, A.M. Understanding AI adoption in manufacturing and production firms using an integrated TAM-TOE model. *Technol. Forecast. Soc. Chang.* **2021**, *170*, 120880. [CrossRef]
38. Khin, S.; Kee, D.M.H. Factors influencing industry 4.0 adoption. *J. Manuf. Technol. Manag.* **2022**, *33*, 448–467. [CrossRef]
39. Molino, M.; Cortese, C.G.; Ghislieri, C. The promotion of technology acceptance and work engagement in industry 4.0: From personal resources to information and training. *Int. J. Environ. Res. Public Health* **2020**, *17*, 2438. [CrossRef] [PubMed]
40. Al-Emran, M.; Mezhuyev, V.; Kamaludin, A. Technology acceptance model in m-learning context: A systematic review. *Comput. Educ.* **2018**, *125*, 389–412. [CrossRef]
41. Al-Qaysi, N.; Mohamad-Nordin, N.; Al-Emran, M. Employing the technology acceptance model in social media: A systematic review. *Educ. Inf. Technol.* **2020**, *25*, 4961–5002. [CrossRef]
42. Davis, F.D. Perceived usefulness, perceived ease of use, and user acceptance of information technology. *MIS Q.* **1989**, 319–340. [CrossRef]
43. Fishbein, M.; Ajzen, I. Belief, attitude, intention, and behavior: An introduction to theory and research. *Philos. Rhetor.* **1977**, *10*, 177–188.
44. Venkatesh, V.; Davis, F. A Theoretical extension of the technology acceptance model: Four longitudinal field studies. *Manag. Sci.* **2000**, *46*, 186–204. [CrossRef]
45. Venkatesh, V.; Bala, H. Technology acceptance model 3 and a research agenda on interventions. *Decis. Sci.* **2008**, *39*, 273–315. [CrossRef]
46. Davis, F.D.; Bagozzi, R.P.; Warshaw, P.R. User acceptance of computer technology: A comparison of two theoretical models. *Manag. Sci.* **1989**, *35*, 982–1003. [CrossRef]
47. Parasuraman, A. Technology Readiness Index (TRI) a multiple-item scale to measure readiness to embrace new technologies. *J. Serv. Res.* **2000**, *2*, 307–320. [CrossRef]
48. Berger, S.C. Self-service technology for sales purposes in branch banking: The impact of personality and relationship on customer adoption. *Int. J. Bank Mark.* **2009**, *27*, 488–505. [CrossRef]

49. Venkatesh, V.; Morris, M.G.; Davis, G.B.; Davis, F.D. User acceptance of information technology: Toward a unified view. *MIS Q.* **2003**, *27*, 425–478. [CrossRef]
50. Venkatesh, V.; Thong, J.; Xu, X. Consumer acceptance and use of information technology: Extending the unified theory of acceptance and use of technology. *MIS Q.* **2012**, *36*, 157–178. [CrossRef]
51. Lin, C.-H.; Shih, H.-Y.; Sher, P.J. Integrating technology readiness into technology acceptance: The TRAM model. *Psychol. Mark.* **2007**, *24*, 641–657. [CrossRef]
52. Yalcin, E.M.; Kutlu, B. Examination of students' acceptance of and intention to use learning management systems using extended TAM. *Br. J. Educ. Technol.* **2019**, *50*, 2414–2432. [CrossRef]
53. Cabero-Almenara, J.; Fernández-Batanero, J.M.; Barroso-Osuna, J. Adoption of augmented reality technology by university students. *Heliyon* **2019**, *5*, e01597. [CrossRef]
54. Esteban-Millat, I.; Martínez-López, F.J.; Pujol-Jover, M.; Gázquez-Abad, J.C.; Alegret, A. An extension of the technology acceptance model for online learning environments. *Interact. Learn. Environ.* **2018**, *26*, 895–910. [CrossRef]
55. Al-Emran, M.; Al-Maroof, R.; Al-Sharafi, M.A.; Arpaci, I. What impacts learning with wearables? An integrated theoretical model. *Interact. Learn. Environ.* **2020**, 1–21. [CrossRef]
56. Al-Maroof, R.S.; Alfaisal, A.M.; Salloum, S.A. Google glass adoption in the educational environment: A case study in the Gulf area. *Educ. Inf. Technol.* **2020**, *26*, 2477–2500. [CrossRef]
57. Álvarez-Marín, A.; Velázquez-Iturbide, J.Á.; Castillo-Vergara, M. Technology acceptance of an interactive augmented reality app on resistive circuits for engineering students. *Electronics* **2021**, *10*, 1286. [CrossRef]
58. Song, Y.; Yang, Y.; Cheng, P. The investigation of adoption of voice-user interface (VUI) in smart home systems among chinese older adults. *Sensors* **2022**, *22*, 1614. [CrossRef] [PubMed]
59. Moumtzidis, I.; Kamariotou, M. Digital transformation strategies enabled by internet of things and big data analytics: The use-case of telecommunication companies in Greece. *Information* **2022**, *13*, 196. [CrossRef]
60. Nyesiga, C.; Mayoka, K.G.; Musa, B.M.; Grace, A. Effort expectancy, performance expectancy, social influence and facilitating conditions as predictors of behavioural intentions to use ATMS with fingerprint authentication in Ugandan banks. *Glob. J. Comput. Sci. Technol. Netw. Web Secur.* **2017**, *17*, 5–23.
61. Park, I.; Kim, D.; Moon, J.; Kim, S.; Kang, Y.; Bae, S. Searching for New Technology acceptance model under social context: Analyzing the determinants of acceptance of intelligent information technology in digital transformation and implications for the requisites of digital sustainability. *Sustainability* **2022**, *14*, 579. [CrossRef]
62. Thompson, R.L.; Higgins, C.A.; Howell, J.M. Personal computing: Toward a conceptual model of utilization. *MIS Q. Manag. Inf. Syst.* **1991**, *15*, 125–142. [CrossRef]
63. Bervell, B.; Arkorful, V. LMS-enabled blended learning utilization in distance tertiary education: Establishing the relationships among facilitating conditions, voluntariness of use and use behaviour. *Int. J. Educ. Technol. High. Educ.* **2020**, *17*, 6. [CrossRef]
64. Teo, T. Examining the influence of subjective norm and facilitating conditions on the intention to use technology among pre-service teachers: A structural equation modeling of an extended technology acceptance model. *Asia Pac. Educ. Rev.* **2010**, *11*, 253–262. [CrossRef]
65. Wang, C.-S.; Jeng, Y.-L.; Huang, Y.-M. What influences teachers to continue using cloud services? *Electron. Libr.* **2017**, *35*, 520–533. [CrossRef]
66. Othman, A.K.; Hamzah, M.I. Modeling the contingent role of technological optimism on customer satisfaction with self-service technologies. A case of cash-recycling ATMs. *J. Enterp. Inf. Manag.* **2020**. [CrossRef]
67. Taneja, A.; Wang, A.; Raja, M.K. Assessing the impact of concern for privacy and innovation characteristics in the adoption of biometric technologies. In Proceedings of the 37th Annual Conference of Decision Sciences Institute, Bricktown, OKC, USA, 2006.
68. Santini, F.; Ladeira, W.J.; Sampaio, C.H.; Perin, M.G.; Dolci, P.C. Propensity for technological adoption: An analysis of effects size in the banking sector. *Behav. Inf. Technol.* **2020**, *39*, 1341–1355. [CrossRef]
69. Fraga-Lamas, P.; Fernández-Caramés, T.M.; Blanco-Novoa, O.; Vilar-Montesinos, M.A. A review on industrial augmented reality systems for the industry 4.0 shipyard. *IEEE Access* **2018**, *6*, 13358–13375. [CrossRef]
70. Jung, T.H.; Lee, H.; Chung, N.; Dieck, T.M.C. Cross-cultural differences in adopting mobile augmented reality at cultural heritage tourism sites. *Int. J. Contemp. Hosp. Manag.* **2018**, *30*, 1621–1645. [CrossRef]
71. Lee, I.-J.; Chen, C.-H.; Su, C.-Y. App based souvenirs and entry tickets: A new means of enhancing post visit memories: A case study from Taiwan. *Tour. Manag. Perspect.* **2017**, *24*, 177–185. [CrossRef]
72. Rese, A.; Baier, D.; Geyer-Schulz, A.; Schreiber, S. How augmented reality apps are accepted by consumers: A comparative analysis using scales and opinions. *Technol. Forecast. Soc. Chang.* **2017**, *124*, 306–319. [CrossRef]
73. Chao, C.M.; Yu, T.K. The moderating effect of technology optimism: How it affects students' weblog learning. *Online Inf. Rev.* **2019**, *43*, 161–180. [CrossRef]
74. Saxena, N.; Gera, N.; Taneja, M. An empirical study on facilitators and inhibitors of adoption of mobile banking in India. *Electron. Commer. Res.* **2022**. [CrossRef]
75. Hung, S.; Cheng, M. Computers & Education Are you ready for knowledge sharing ? An empirical study of virtual communities. *Comput. Educ.* **2013**, *62*, 8–17. [CrossRef]
76. Lewis, J.R.; Mayes, D.K. Development and psychometric evaluation of the emotional metric outcomes (EMO) questionnaire. *Int. J. Hum. Comput. Interact.* **2014**, *30*, 685–702. [CrossRef]

77. Koenigstorfer, J.; Groeppel-Klein, A. Consumer acceptance of the mobile Internet. *Mark. Lett.* **2012**, *23*, 917–928. [CrossRef]
78. Alharbi, A.; Sohaib, O. Technology readiness and cryptocurrency adoption: PLS-SEM and deep learning neural network analysis. *IEEE Access* **2021**, *9*, 21388–21394. [CrossRef]
79. De Melo Pereira, F.A.; Ramos, A.S.M.; Aparecida, M.; da Costa, M.F. Computers in human behavior satisfaction and continuous use intention of e-learning service in brazilian public organizations. *Comput. Hum. Behav.* **2015**, *46*, 139–148. [CrossRef]
80. Álvarez-Marín, A.; Velázquez-Iturbide, J.Á.; Castillo-Vergara, M. The acceptance of augmented reality in engineering education: The role of technology optimism and technology innovativeness the role of technology optimism and technology innovativeness. *Interact. Learn. Environ.* **2021**, 1–13. [CrossRef]
81. Imtiaz, A.; Maarop, N. A Review of technology acceptance studies in the field of education. *J. Technol. Sci. Eng.* **2014**, *69*, 27–32. [CrossRef]
82. Marangunić, N.; Granić, A. Technology acceptance model: A literature review from 1986 to 2013. *Univers. Access Inf. Soc.* **2015**, *14*, 81–95. [CrossRef]
83. Henseler, J. Bridging Design and behavioral research with variance-based structural equation modeling. *J. Advert.* **2017**, *46*, 178–192. [CrossRef]
84. Henseler, J.; Hubona, G.; Ray, P.A. Using PLS path modeling in new technology research: Updated guidelines. *Ind. Manag. Data Syst.* **2016**, *116*, 2–20. [CrossRef]
85. Lamberti, G. Hybrid multigroup partial least squares structural equation modelling: An application to bank employee satisfaction and loyalty. *Qual. Quant.* **2021**. [CrossRef]
86. Hair, J.F.; Hult, G.T.; Ringle, C.M.; Sarstedt, M.; Castillo-Apraiz, J.; Carrion, C.G.; Roldán, J.L. *Manual de Partial Least Squares Structural Equation Modeling (Pls-Sem)*. OmniaScience Scholar. 2019. Available online: https://tore.tuhh.de/handle/11420/5279 (accessed on 20 May 2022).
87. Calder, B.J.; Phillips, L.W.; Tybout, A.M. Designing research for application. *J. Consum. Res.* **1981**, *8*, 197. [CrossRef]
88. Teo, T.; Lee, C.; Chai, C. Understanding pre-service teachers' computer attitudes: Applying and extending the technology acceptance model. *J. Comput. Assist. Learn.* **2007**, *24*, 128–143. [CrossRef]
89. Chung, N.; Han, H.; Joun, Y. Tourists' intention to visit a destination: The role of augmented reality (AR) application for a heritage site. *Comput. Human Behav.* **2015**, *50*, 588–599. [CrossRef]
90. Teo, T.; Noyes, J. An assessment of the influence of perceived enjoyment and attitude on the intention to use technology among pre-service teachers: A structural equation modeling approach. *Comput. Educ.* **2011**, *57*, 1645–1653. [CrossRef]
91. Pantano, E.; Rese, A.; Baier, D. Enhancing the online decision-making process by using augmented reality: A two country comparison of youth markets. *J. Retail. Consum. Serv.* **2017**, *38*, 81–95. [CrossRef]
92. Wojciechowski, R.; Cellary, W. Evaluation of learners' attitude toward learning in ARIES augmented reality environments. *Comput. Educ.* **2013**, *68*, 570–585. [CrossRef]
93. Balog, A.; Pribeanu, C. The role of perceived enjoyment in the students' acceptance of an augmented reality teaching platform: A structural equation modelling approach. *Stud. Inform. Control.* **2010**, *19*, 319–330. [CrossRef]
94. Ringle, C.M.; Wende, S.; Becker, J.-M. SmartPLS 3. Boenningstedt: SmartPLS GmbH. Available online: http://www.smartpls.com (accessed on 20 May 2022).
95. Mustofa, R.H.; Pramudita, D.A.; Atmono, D.; Priyankara, R.; Asmawan, M.C.; Rahmattullah, M.; Mudrikah, S.; Pamungkas, L.N.S. Exploring educational students acceptance of using movies as economics learning media: PLS-SEM analysis. *Int. Rev. Econ. Educ.* **2022**, *39*, 100236. [CrossRef]
96. Hair, F.J., Jr.; Sarstedt, M.; Hopkins, L.; Kuppelwieser, G.V. Partial least squares structural equation modeling (PLS-SEM). *Eur. Bus. Rev.* **2014**, *26*, 106–121. [CrossRef]
97. Henseler, J.; Ringle, C.M.; Sarstedt, M. Testing measurement invariance of composites using partial least squares. *Int. Mark. Rev.* **2016**, *33*, 405–431. [CrossRef]
98. Hair, J.F., Jr.; Sarstedt, M.; Christian, M.; Ringle, S.P.G. *Advanced Issues in Partial Least Squares Structural Equation Modeling*; SAGE: Thousand Oaks, CA, USA, 2017; ISBN 1483377385, 9781483377384.
99. Henseler, J.; Dijkstra, T.K.; Sarstedt, M.; Ringle, C.M.; Diamantopoulos, A.; Straub, D.W.; Ketchen, D.J.; Hair, J.F.; Hult, G.T.M.; Calantone, R.J. Common beliefs and reality about PLS: Comments on Ronkko and Evermann (2013). *Organ. Res. Methods* **2014**, *17*, 182–209. [CrossRef]
100. Fornell, C.; Larcker, D.F. Evaluating structural equation models with unobservable variables and measurement error. *J. Mark. Res.* **1981**, *18*, 39–50. [CrossRef]
101. Frank, F.R.; Miller, N.B. *A Primer for Soft Modeling*; University of Akron Press: Akron, OH, USA, 1992.
102. Chin, W.W. The partial least squares approach to structural equation modeling. *Adv. Hosp. Leis.* **1998**, *295*, 295–336.
103. OECD Organization for Economic Co-operation and Development. Enhancing Innovation in Rural Region. 2022. Available online: https://www.oecd.org/regional/rural-development/rural-innovation.htm (accessed on 20 May 2022).
104. Kim, H.-B.; Kim, T.; Shin, S.W. Modeling roles of subjective norms and eTrust in customers' acceptance of airline B2C eCommerce websites. *Tour. Manag.* **2009**, *30*, 266–277. [CrossRef]
105. Schepers, J.; Wetzels, M. A meta-analysis of the technology acceptance model: Investigating subjective norm and moderation effects. *Inf. Manag.* **2007**, *44*, 90–103. [CrossRef]

106. Rejón-Guardia, F.; Polo-Peña, A.I.; Maraver-Tarifa, G. The acceptance of a personal learning environment based on Google apps: The role of subjective norms and social image. *J. Comput. High. Educ.* **2020**, *32*, 203–233. [CrossRef]
107. Buabeng-Andoh, C. Predicting students' intention to adopt mobile learning: A combination of theory of reasoned action and technology acceptance model. *J. Res. Innov. Teach. Learn.* **2018**, *11*, 178–191. [CrossRef]
108. Hu, Z.; Ding, S.; Li, S.; Chen, L.; Yang, S. Adoption intention of fintech services for bank users: An empirical examination with an extended technology acceptance model. *Symmetry* **2019**, *11*, 340. [CrossRef]
109. Kurian, R.M.; Thomas, S. Perceived stress among information technology professionals in India during the COVID-19 pandemic. *Theor. Issues Ergon. Sci.* **2022**, *23*, 182–198. [CrossRef]
110. Aruleba, K.; Jere, N.; Matarirano, O. Technology adoption readiness in disadvantaged universities during COVID-19 pandemic in South Africa. *Int. J. High. Educ.* **2022**, *11*, 172–180. [CrossRef]
111. Ilmi, Z.; Darma, D.C.; Azis, M. Independence in learning, education management, and industry 4.0: Habitat Indonesia during COVID-19. *J. Anthropol. Sport Phys. Educ.* **2020**, *4*, 63–66.
112. Cyfert, S.; Glabiszewski, W.; Zastempowski, M. Impact of management tools supporting industry 4.0 on the importance of csr during covid-19. generation z. *Energies* **2021**, *14*, 1642. [CrossRef]
113. Asimakopoulos, G.; Hernández, V.; Miguel, J.P. Entrepreneurial intention of engineering students: The role of social norms and entrepreneurial self-efficacy. *Sustainability* **2019**, *11*, 4314. [CrossRef]
114. Lee, Y.; Kozar, K.A.; Larsen, K.R.T.; Lee, Y.; Kozar, K.A.; Lee, Y.; Kozar, K.A.; Larsen, K.R.T. The technology acceptance model: Past, present, and future. *Commun. Assoc. Inf. Syst.* **2003**, *12*, 752–780. [CrossRef]
115. Prasetyo, Y.T.; Ong, A.K.S.; Concepcion, G.K.F.; Navata, F.M.B.; Robles, R.A.V.; Tomagos, I.J.T.; Young, M.N.; Diaz, J.F.T.; Nadlifatin, R.; Redi, A.A.N.P. Determining factors affecting acceptance of e-learning platforms during the COVID-19 pandemic: Integrating extended technology acceptance model and DeLone & Mclean is success model. *Sustainability* **2021**, *13*, 8365.
116. Ding, W.; Wang, Q.G.; Zhang, J.X. Analysis and prediction of COVID-19 epidemic in South Africa. *ISA Trans.* **2021**, *124*, 182–190. [CrossRef]
117. Zhang, X.; Chen, Y.Q. Admissibility and robust stabilization of continuous linear singular fractional order systems with the fractional order α: The $0<\alpha<1$ case. *ISA Trans.* **2018**, *82*, 42–50. [CrossRef]

electronics

MDPI

Article

Convolutional Network Research for Defect Identification of Productor Appearance Surface

Xu Xie and Xizhong Shen *

School of Electrical and Electronic Engineering, Shanghai Institute of Technology, Shanghai 201418, China
* Correspondence: xzshen@yeah.net

Abstract: The accurate and rapid identification of surface defects is an important element of product appearance quality evaluation, and the application of deep learning for surface defect recognition is an ongoing hot topic. In this paper, a lightweight KD-EG-RepVGG network based on structural reparameterization is designed for the identification of surface defects on strip steel as an example. In order to improve the stability and accuracy in the recognition of strip steel surface defects, an efficient attention network was introduced into the network, and then a Gaussian error linear activation function was applied in order to prevent the neurons from being set to zero during neural network training, leaving neuron parameters without being updated. Finally, knowledge distillation is used to transfer the knowledge of the RepVGG-A0 network to give the lightweight model better accuracy and generalization capability. The outcomes of the experiments indicate that the model has a computational and parametric volume of 22.3 M and 0.14 M, respectively, in the inference phase, a defect recognition accuracy of 99.44% on the test set, and a single image detection speed of 2.4 ms, making it more suitable for deployment in real engineering environments.

Keywords: defect detection; structural reparameterization; ECA net; Gaussian error linear units; knowledge distillation; visualization

Citation: Xie, X.; Shen, X. Convolutional Network Research for Defect Identification of Productor Appearance Surface. *Electronics* **2022**, *11*, 4218. https://doi.org/10.3390/electronics11244218

Academic Editors: Juan Ernesto Solanes Galbis, Luis Gracia and Jaime Valls Miro

Received: 15 November 2022
Accepted: 16 December 2022
Published: 18 December 2022

1. Introduction

The detection of defects on a product's surface is important underlying research in the area of intelligent production, and this paper investigates the detection of surface defects in strip steel during industrial production. The surface quality of strip steel is one of the most important indicators of strip steel quality and is linked to the quality of products downstream in areas such as automotive, household appliances and construction. The detection of surface defects in steel has therefore become an extremely significant task in the steel production sector.

The identification of productor surface defects is an important task for enterprise product lines. In the early days, the task was completed by human-eyes checking, and it was limited by the human limitations of the eyes. After the emergence of image processing technology, the task was then completed by the characteristics of the defect image. Zhou [1] et al. applied the SIFT algorithm to the identification of defects on the surface of medium-thick plates and achieved a good accuracy of 95% for defects that occur continuously. Hu [2] et al. extracted four visual features of the target image: geometry, shape, texture and greyscale and used a genetic algorithm to optimize a hybrid chromosome-based classification model for effective identification of image defects. However, the characteristics-based methods made it hard to check for tiny defects or other imperfections. In recent years, deep learning methods, such as the convolutional network, were proposed to be applied in certain fields.

Since the introduction of Alexnet [3] convolutional neural networks in 2012, they have demonstrated high efficiency and accuracy in object recognition. Convolutional neural networks have gradually become an important research direction in detection and recognition, and the accurate, fast and contact-free recognition techniques are continuously investigated. Manzo [4] et al. used some pre-trained convolutional neural networks to detect the COVID-19 disease in CT images and gained an accuracy of 96.5%. Jiang [5] et al. used an improved VGG network to identify rice and wheat leaf disease simultaneously. Tao [6] et al. accurately identified smaller flames using an improved GoogLeNet network. As a new research hotspot, deep convolutional neural networks have been used in a wide range of industries.

Convolutional neural networks have been extensively applied to product surface defect recognition. Vonnocc [7] et al. used traditional machine learning methods and deep learning methods to classify surface defects in hot rolled strip steel, and they found that the deep learning approach worked better. Konovalenko [8] et al. detected surface defects in strip steel based on the ResNet50 framework, with a precision of 96.91% in recognition. Xiang [9] et al. used a small sample dataset to achieve an accurate recognition rate of 97.8% on an improved VGG-19 network. Feng [10] et al. added FcaNet and CMAM modules based on Resnet, achieving an accuracy of 94.11% for the defect identification in hot-rolled strip steel. Tang [11] et al. used multi-scale maximum pooling and an attention mechanism to detect surface defects, where the classification accuracy rate reaches 94.73%. Xing [12] proposes a convolutional classification model with symmetric structure to achieve accurate recognition of surface defects. These studies have focused on accuracy design, ignoring the computational volume, complexity and real-time requirements of the models in real-world applications. Wang [13] et al. designed the VGG-ADB model for defect recognition, which achieved 99.63% classification accuracy and 333 frame/s inference speed. The VGG-ADB model considered the inference speed of the network, but the model was ignored for the parametric design, where the model size reached 72.15 M. This constrained the application of the model on edge devices. In actual production, not only does the network require extremely high detection accuracy, but it also has high requirements for model size, detection speed and real-time detection.

The KD-EG-RepVGG surface defect detection algorithm is designed using structural reparameterization, GELU, ECA networks and knowledge distillation for the task requirement of surface defects identification. Through experimental comparative analysis, the KD-EG-RepVGG network is characterized by a low number of parameters, low computational effort, high speed and high accuracy. The general idea of the method in the paper is illustrated in Figure 1. The teacher network RepVGG-A0 guides the KD-EG-RepVGG network training. The structural re-parameterization technique loads the training weights into the KD-EG-RepVGG inference network to finally obtain the prediction results.

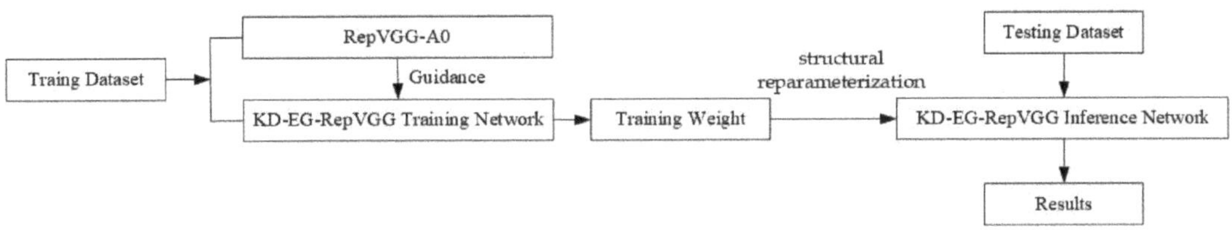

Figure 1. General diagram of defect identification process.

This paper is structured as follows. Section 2 describes in detail the KD-EG-RepVGG network framework. Section 3 verifies the validity of the network from several perspectives, whereas Section 4 is the conclusion of the paper.

2. The KD-EG-RepVGG Network

The EG-RepVGG network is based on structural reparameterization, incorporating a lightweight attention network while using GELU as the activation function in the improved network, stacking the S-RepVGG block module and D-RepVGG block module based on RepVGGBlock. The model is structured as shown in Figure 2. The main function of the D-RepVGG block module is to extract features and adjust the space size and channel number of the feature map, whereas the main purpose of the S-RepVGG block is feature extraction. The S-RepVGG block has an additional directly connected structure compared to the D-RepVGG block, which mimics the residual connection in ResNet [14] and improves the model's ability to extract features. The output of D-RepVGG Block5 is made up of global average pooling and then a softmax classifier is appended. The global average pooling layer is used to downsample the output spatial resolution of the feature map to 1 × 1. The softmax layer is used to output the predicted categories. They together form the classification layer. With the aim of further improving the accuracy and generalization performance of the model, the RepVGG-A0 as a teacher model is used to guide the training of EG RepVGG model using knowledge distillation technology. The final result is a lightweight, fast and highly accurate strip steel surface defect recognition model, the KD-EG RepVGG model. The detailed structural information of the KD-EG-RepVGG model is shown in Table 1.

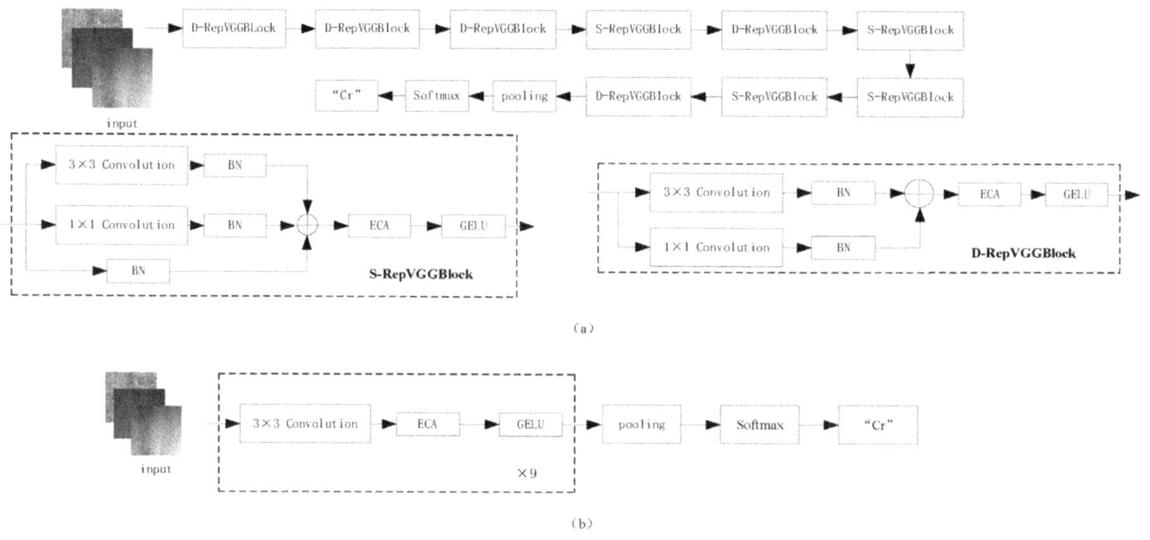

Figure 2. KD-EG-RepVGG Network. (**a**) KD-EG-RepVGG Training Network. (**b**) KD-EG-RepVGG Inference Network.

Table 1. KD-EG-RepVGG Network Structure Details.

Layers	Output Size	Output Channel	Train Parameters	Inference Parameters
input	200 × 200	3		
D-RepVGGBlock1	100 × 100	9	309	252
D-RepVGGBlock2	50 × 50	9	849	738
D-RepVGGBlock3	25 × 25	19	1789	1558
S-RepVGGBlock1	25 × 25	19	3727	3268
D-RepVGGBlock4	13 × 13	38	7375	6536
S-RepVGGBlock2	13 × 13	38	14,671	13,034
S-RepVGGBlock3	13 × 13	38	14,671	13,034
S-RepVGGBlock4	13 × 13	38	14,671	13,034
D-RepVGGBlock5	7 × 7	256	98,307	87,808
Classification	1 × 1	6	1542	1542

2.1. Structural Re-Parameterisation

The structural reparameterization was first proposed in RepVGG networks by Ding XiaoHan [15] et al. The inference network is decoupled from the training network using structural reparameterization techniques. Decoupling the training network and inference network by using structure re-parameterization can not only obtain the full advantage of feature extraction brought by multi branch network training, but also obtain the high speed and low memory consumption of a single path model in inference deployment. The core component of the RepVGG network is the RepVGG Block. Its structure is shown in Figure 3.

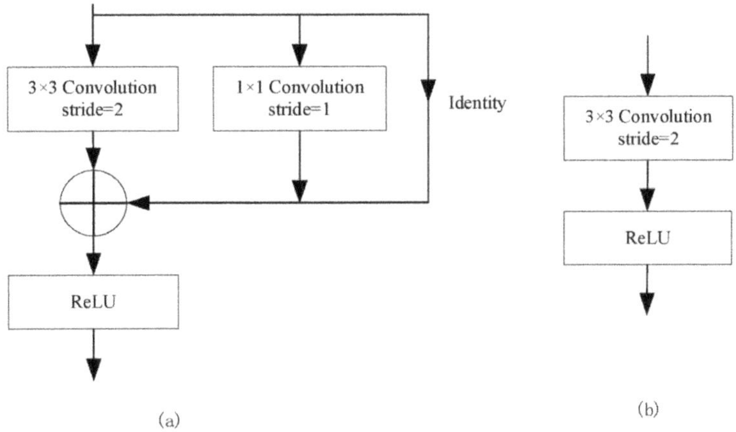

Figure 3. RepVGG Block structure diagram. (**a**) RepVGG Block training. (**b**) RepVGG Block inference.

The structure of the network under training is illustrated in Figure 3a. In the training phase, the RepVGG Block consists mainly of 3 × 3 convolutional kernels, 1 × 1 convolutional kernels and Identity branches. By adding Identities branches and 1 × 1 convolutional branches in parallel, information at different scales of the image can be extracted and fused, increasing the representational power of the model.

In the inference stage, the 1 × 1 convolution and Identity branch from the training are fused into the 3 × 3 convolution, and the inference structure is shown in Figure 3b. RepVGG Block takes the training network and re-parameterizes it structurally, turning the network into a single linear structure consisting mainly of 3 × 3 convolutions without any branches. The inference structure both gains the parameter weights obtained from multi-branch training and allows the use of the single linear structure to speed up the inference of the model during the deployment inference phase. At the same time, deep optimization of the 3 × 3 convolution based on NVIDIA cuDNN's computational library accelerates the model's detection speed in the inference phase.

The structural reparameterization in the inference phase mainly consists of the fusion of the convolution kernel and the Batch Normalization (BN) layer [16], the integration of 1 × 1 convolution into 3 × 3 convolution and the integration of Identity branches into 3 × 3 convolution. The formula for the fusion of the convolution and BN layers in the model is as follows:

$$BN(x) = \frac{x-\mu}{\sqrt{\sigma^2+\varepsilon}}\gamma + \beta \tag{1}$$

where μ denotes the mean of the BN layer and σ^2 denotes the BN layer variance; μ and σ^2 are obtained statistically in the training dataset; ϵ is a constant to prevent the denominator from being zero; γ is the scale factor of the BN layer; β is the offset of the BN layer and the values of both γ and β are obtained in the training.

For convolution, the formula is as it is in (2):

$$Conv(x) = Wx + b \tag{2}$$

where x and $Conv(x)$ are the input and output of the convolution; W denotes the matrix weight of the convolution calculation; and b is the bias of the convolution layer calculation.

The input to the BN layer is the output of the convolution into it. This is equivalent to taking Equation (2) and bringing it into Equation (1), resulting in a calculation such as Equation (3):

$$BN(x) = \frac{(Wx + b)}{\sqrt{\sigma^2 + \varepsilon}}\gamma + \beta \tag{3}$$

The following can be obtained by sorting and simplifying:

$$BN(x) = \frac{\gamma}{\sqrt{\sigma^2 + \varepsilon}}Wx + \left(\frac{\gamma(b - \mu)}{\sqrt{\sigma^2 + \varepsilon}} + \beta\right) \tag{4}$$

From the calculation results, we can obtain a new convolution by incorporating the weight information calculated by Batch Normalization layer into the convolution layer, where the convolution weight is $\frac{\gamma}{\sqrt{\sigma^2+\varepsilon}}W$, and the bias of the convolution is $\frac{\gamma(b-\mu)}{\sqrt{\sigma^2+\varepsilon}} + \beta$.

For the Identity branch in the RepVGG Block, a 1×1 convolution kernel with a weight of 1 is used to construct a 1×1 convolution, and then a 3×3 convolution kernel is set to perform identity mapping on the input features. Keep the output of the Identity layer unchanged before and after the transformation. For a 1×1 convolution branch, a complementary zero operation is performed around the 1×1 convolution kernel so that it becomes a 3×3 convolution. At this point, both the 1×1 convolution and Identity are converted into a 3×3 convolution, and based on the additivity of the convolution operation, the three branches can then be incorporated into a single 3×3 convolution. The process is shown in Figure 4.

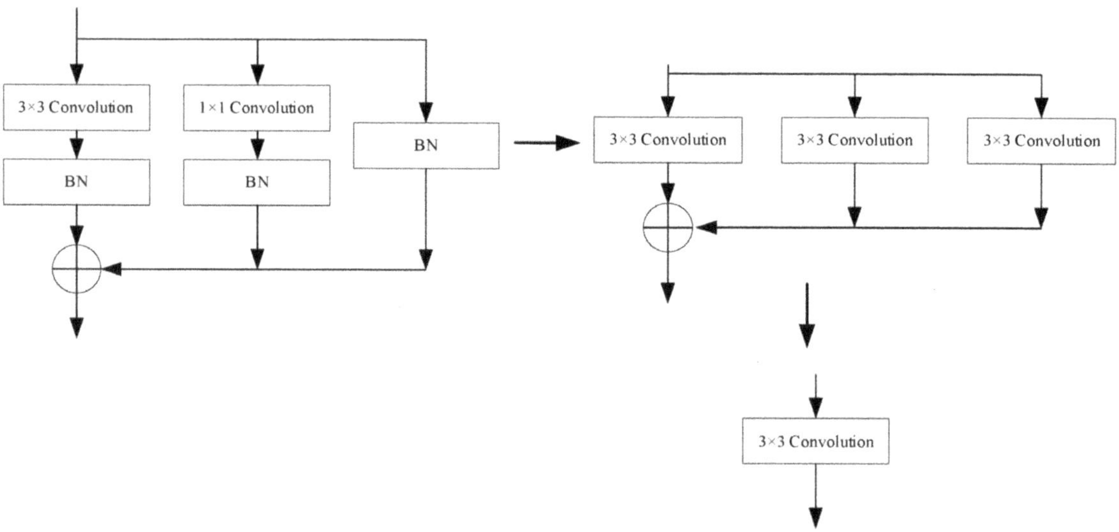

Figure 4. RepVGG Block branched fusion process.

2.2. *Efficient Channel Attention Network*

The Efficient Channel Attention network [17] was added to the RepVGG Block to form the E-RepVGG network. The feature information can be obtained efficiently and without increasing the number of parameters of the model at the same time. The structure of ECA is shown in Figure 5. The feature map $x \in \mathbb{R}^{L\times S\times T}$ output from the convolution is pooled and globally averaged (Global Pooling) over the spatial dimension to output a feature vector y of size $1 \times 1 \times T$, as is shown in Equation (5):

$$y = \frac{1}{WH}\sum_{i=1,j=1}^{W,H} x_{i,j} \tag{5}$$

where L and S are the width and height of the feature map, respectively; and T is the number of channels in the feature map. Channel weighting coefficient obtained after the ECA network can be calculated by the following equation:

$$\Psi = sigmod(\Omega y) \tag{6}$$

where *sigmoid* is the sigmoid activation function; Ψ is the weight of the ECA network on the channel; and Ω is the parameter matrix for calculating the channel attention in ECA networks. The mathematical model is represented as follows:

$$\Omega = \begin{bmatrix} \omega^{1,1} & \cdots & \omega^{1,k} & \cdots & 0 \\ 0 & \omega^{2,2} & \cdots & \cdots & 0 \\ \vdots & \vdots & \vdots & \vdots & \vdots \\ 0 & \cdots & 0 & \cdots & \omega^{T,T} \end{bmatrix} \tag{7}$$

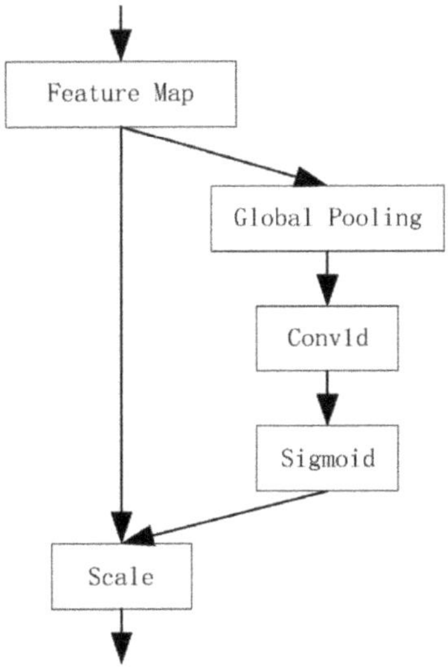

Figure 5. ECA network structure diagram.

It is clear from Ω that the weight value of Ψ is determined only by the k channels in the immediate vicinity of y. This can be expressed as a 1-dimensional convolution ($Conv1d$) with a kernel of size k. Bringing in the simplification yields:

$$\Psi = sigmoid(Conv1d(y)) \tag{8}$$

where $Conv1d$ denotes a 1-dimensional convolution of convolution kernel size k. In this paper, considering the model parameters and inference speed, the size of all 1-dimensional convolution kernels is set to 3.

The weight coefficients of each channel calculated by the efficient attention network are multiplied by the channel weights of the input feature map $x \in \mathbb{R}^{L\times S\times T}$ to obtain the output:

$$\tilde{x} = \Psi x \tag{9}$$

where $\tilde{x} \in \mathbb{R}^{L\times S\times T}$ is the output of the ECA network.

2.3. Gaussian Linear Units

The rectified linear units (ReLU) activation function is used in the RepVGG Block, which effectively solved the problem of disappearing or exploding gradients as the neural network deepens. However, the ReLU activation function also has some problems. When the input is less than zero, the ReLU output will be directly zeroed, and the neuron will be permanently zeroed, which is detrimental to the convergence of the network model and feature extraction. Therefore, Gaussian Error Linear Units [18] (GELU) are selected as the activation function in this paper to form the EG-RepVGG network. The GELU activation function is applied as a non-linear unit after the ECA network. The GELU activation function is differentiable at the origin, and the idea of stochastic regularity is introduced into the function. The activation operation will establish a stochastic connection between the input and output, effectively avoiding the situation where the neurons are set to zero and enhancing the learning speed and stability of the network.

2.4. Knowledge Distillation

The knowledge distillation is a novel technique for model compression proposed by Geoffrey Hinton [19] et al. A complex, highly generalizable large model is used to guide the training of a lightweight small model, allowing the small model to achieve the same accuracy as the large model at a smaller cost. At the heart of the knowledge distillation network is the fact that the different classes of confidence in the output of the teacher network define a rich similarity structure at the data level and can provide more inter- class knowledge for small networks to guide the training of small networks. The characteristic distillation is calculated by:

$$q_i = \frac{e^{\frac{z_i}{T}}}{\sum_i e^{\frac{Z_i}{T}}} \tag{10}$$

The activation operation will establish a stochastic connection between the input and output, effectively avoiding the situation where the neurons are set to zero and enhancing the learning speed and stability of the network. The hyperparameter T softens the output categories of the large and small networks to find the distillation loss of the two networks' outputs and the direct training output loss of the small network. The two losses are weighted and summed to obtain the training losses of the networks. The entire knowledge distillation network training process is shown in Figure 6. In this paper, the KD-EG-RepVGG network was obtained by using RepVGG-A0 as the teacher network and instructing the training of the EG-RepVGG network.

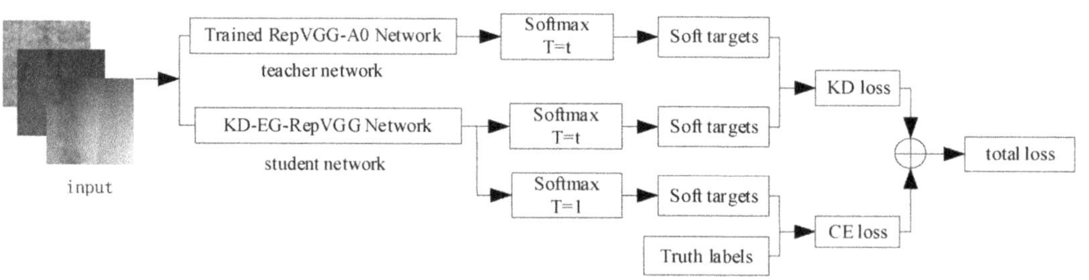

Figure 6. Knowledge distillation procedure.

The loss function used in the training phase is the KL scatter loss and the cross-entropy loss weighted sum is used as the final loss for training and the loss formula is as in (11)

$$Loss = \alpha \cdot L_{kd}(q(u,T), q(z,T)) + (1-\alpha) \cdot L_s(y, q(z,1)) \tag{11}$$

$$L_{kd} = \sum_{i=1}^{N} q_i(u_i,T) \log q_i(u_i,T) - \sum_{i=1}^{N} q_i(u_i,T) \log q_i(z_i,T) \tag{12}$$

$$L_s = -\sum_{i=1}^{N} y_i \log q_i(z_i,1) \tag{13}$$

where N is the number of categories of defects; $q(u, T)$ represents the information about the features of the teacher network after the distillation temperature; $q(z, T)$ represents the information about the features of the student network after the distillation temperature; L_{kd} is the scatter loss, an asymmetry measure of the difference between the probability distributions of $q(u, T)$ and $q(z, T)$. This is shown in Equation (12). L_s is the cross-entropy loss, which indicates how close the predicted output value is to the true sample label, as shown in Equation (13). In this paper, the distillation temperature $T = 7$. α is the default value, which in this paper is 0.3 by default.

3. Experiments and Analysis of Results

3.1. Experimental Paltform

The experimental platform includes: an Intel Core i7-11700F processor, a Nvidia GeForce RTX3060 12 GB graphics card, 32 GB memory; the software is Windows 10 operating system, python 3.8; and the deep learning framework used is pytorch.

3.2. Experimental Data Sets

This paper uses the NEU-CLS dataset [20] of strip surface defects produced and published by Northeastern University for experiments. As shown in Figure 7, the surface defects of the data strip are divided into six categories: Crack (Cr), Inclusion (In), Patch (Pa), Pitted Surface (Ps), Rolled-in Scale (Rs) and Scratch (Sc). Table 2 shows the details of each defective picture. The total 1800 images in the table are divided into training set, validation set and test set at the ratio of 8:1:1. The training set has 1440 images, and the validation set and test set have 180 images each.

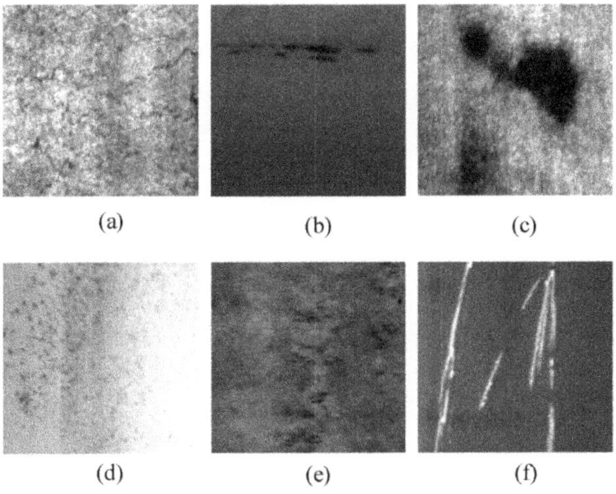

Figure 7. Example of defective image and corresponding label. (**a**) Crack, (**b**) Inclusion, (**c**) Patch, (**d**) Pitted Surface, (**e**) Rolled-in Scale, (**f**) Scratch.

Table 2. Information on the data set.

Defect Category	Pixel	Channel	Amount
Crack	200 × 200	1	300
Inclusion	200 × 200	1	300
Patch	200 × 200	1	300
Pitted Surface	200 × 200	1	300
Rolled-in Scale	200 × 200	1	300
Scratch	200 × 200	1	300

3.3. Experimental Results and Analysis

To analyze and measure the comprehensive performance of the network model in the identification task of strip surface defects, the accuracy, the Matthew's correlation coefficient, FPS, single picture detection time, model parameters and FLOPs were used to evaluate the model.

The accuracy (ACC) rate is the proportion of correctly classified samples to all samples. The higher the accuracy rate, the better the classification effect of the model, and the formula is shown in 14. The Matthews correlation coefficient (MCC) is used to calculate the correlation between the actual classification and the predicted classification, and it is a balanced evaluation index. The value range of MCC is between −1 and 1. When the value of MCC is closer to 1, the result predicted by the classifier is more reliable.

$$TP = \frac{TP + TN}{ALL} \tag{14}$$

where TP is the number of samples correctly predicted by positive samples, TN is the number of negative samples correctly predicted, and ALL is the number of all samples.

3.3.1. Ablation Experiments

The comprehensive performance of KD-EG-RepVGG was evaluated on the NEU-CLS test set and the results are shown in Table 3. The super parameter setting in the teacher network RepVGG-A0 is also applied in the KD-EG-RepVGG network. The network is trained using the stochastic gradient decent (SGD) optimizer with a momentum coefficient of 0.9 and weight decay of 0.0001. The learning rate is set to 0.1. Batch Size and epochs are kept at 64 for 100, respectively.

Table 3. Comparative experimental results of distillation.

Model	Accuracy	MCC	Time	Params	FLOPs
RepVGG-A0	98.83%	97.91%	5.1 ms	7.04 M	1.36 G
EG-RepVGG	97.22%	96.39%	2.4 ms	0.14 M	0.03 G
KD-EG-RepVGG	99.44%	99.02%	2.4 ms	0.14 M	0.03 G

The comparison revealed that the lightweight model KD-EG-RepVGG after knowledge distillation had an accuracy improvement of greater than two percentage points over the EG-RepVGG model. Furthermore, the accuracy of the lightweight KD-EG-RepVGG network after knowledge distillation was improved by 0.6 percentage points over the teacher network RepVGG-A0. The Matthew's correlation coefficient of KD-EG-RepVGG on the test set is 99.02%, which further proves that the model is very accurate in identifying the surface defects of the strip. Figure 8 shows the validation accuracy and loss curve of the network. From the curve change trend, we can find that the KD-EG-RepVGG network converges faster and the model accuracy is higher. The aim of transferring the knowledge of large models to small networks and improving the accuracy and generalizability of the networks is achieved.

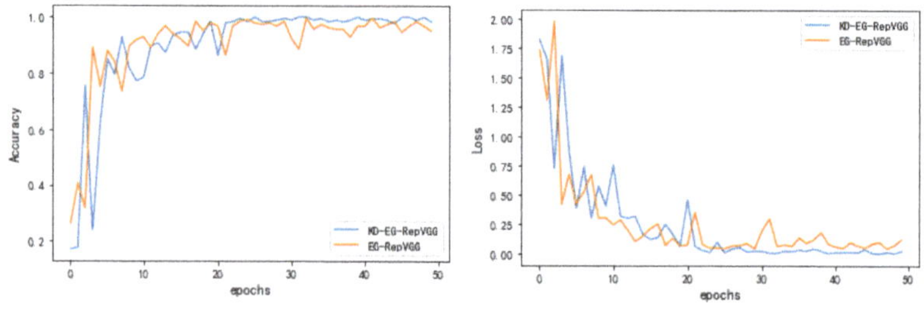

Figure 8. Validation set accuracy curves and loss curves.

Furthermore, to analyze more clearly the capabilities of the model, we calculated the confusion matrix of the model on the test set and the results are shown in Figure 9. From the confusion matrix, it can be obtained that the model had a high recognition rate of defects. The recall rate was calculated according to the confusion matrix, and it was found that only the "In" defect was 97.30%, and the other defects were 100%. The precision was calculated, and it was found that only the "Sc" defect is 97.13%, and the other defects were 100%.

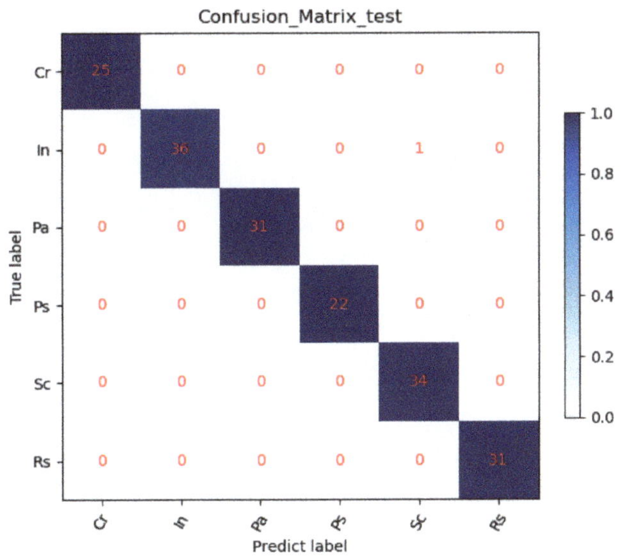

Figure 9. Confusion matrix.

3.3.2. Comparative Experimental Analyses

The KD-EG-RepVGG algorithm was compared with the current mainstream advanced algorithms on the same test set. To demonstrate the validity of the models, the KD-EG-RepVGG is compared with ResNet50, VGG16, ShuffleNetV2 and MobileNetV2 models in the same software and hardware environment. The accuracy, FPS, single picture detection time, calculation amount, parameter amount and other detection indicators of various algorithms are compared and analyzed. The results of the experiment are recorded in Table 4.

Table 4. Comparison of test results for different algorithms.

Model	Accuracy (%)	Time (ms)	FPS (Frame/s)	Params (M)	FLOPs (G)
ResNet50	96.67	6.8	146.9	24.56	4.12
VGG16	95.87	6	143.3	138.3	15.61
ShuffleNetV2	97.25	6	167.4	2.26	0.15
MobileNetV2	96.94	6.2	161.4	3.4	0.33
KD-EG-RepVGG	99.44	2.4	408	0.14	0.03

In comparison, the KD-EG-RepVGG network achieves better classification accuracies than the larger parametric models, VGG16 and ResNet50, outperforming ResNet50 by almost three percentage points. Compared with the lightweight networks shuffleNetV2 and MobileNetV2, the KD-EG-RepVGG network has achieved great advantages in reasoning speed, parameter amount and computation amount. The KD-EG-RepVGG network is more suitable for industrial applications because it achieves an increase in detection efficiency, detection accuracy and detection speed while consuming very little memory and few computing resources.

3.4. Model Visualisation

The features of the middle layer of the convolutional neural network model are visualized in order to gain a clearer understanding of the features learned with the convolutional neural network [21]. A random selection of defective images is fed into the KD-EG-RepVGG inference network, which visualizes the convolutional layers in the network. The visualization results are shown in Figure 10. In the KD-EG-RepVGG network, the shallow convolutional network retains the image information relatively intact, with the main detection being contour information. The deeper convolutional layers focus more on the location features of the target and some abstract information. From the visualization results, it can be observed that important regional features in the image are encoded into the network, indicating that the network is effective for feature learning.

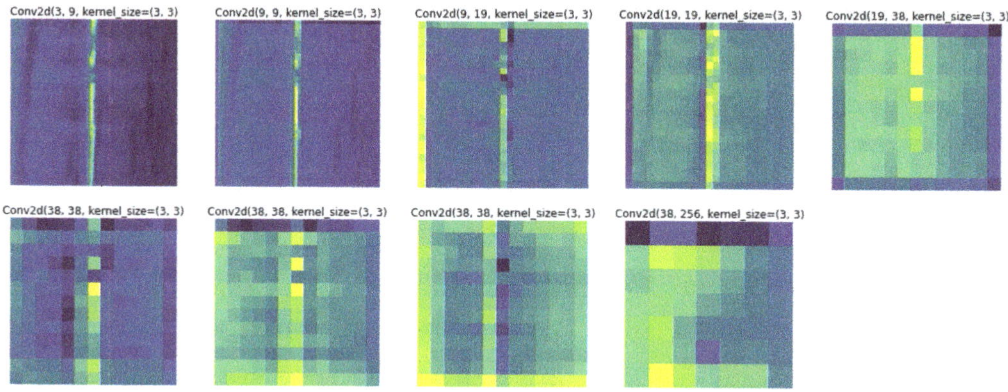

Figure 10. Convolutional layer visualization for RepVGG networks.

The Gradient Weighted Class Activation Mapping algorithm [22] (Grad-CAM) is used to fully demonstrate the ability of the KD-EG-RepVGG network to extract defective features. A heat map was used to show the activated regions in the images, which is more consistent with human vision properties. This is more in line with human visual properties. The final layer of the KD-EG-RepVGG network was chosen for visual representation in this paper. This is because it is a generalized representation of the feature extraction from the previous layer of the network. Images of six types of defects were randomly selected for visualization with darker colors indicating that the network is paying more attention to the point. This is shown in Figure 11.

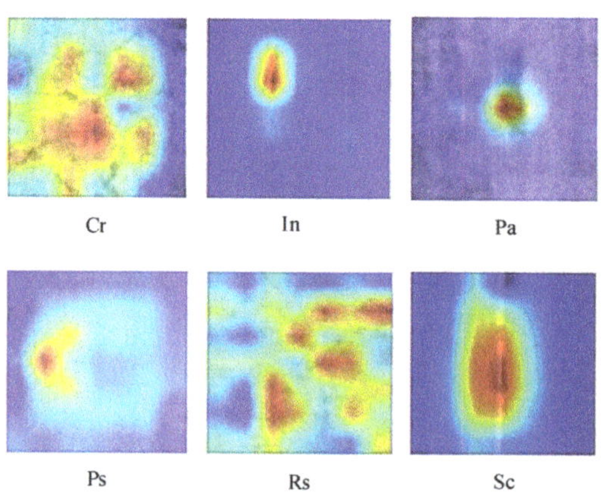

Figure 11. KD-EG-RepVGG network heat map.

As can be viewed in Figure 11, the KD-EG-RepVGG's extraction of defect features is focused on salient feature points, and the KD-EG-RepVGG network demonstrates high efficiency by focusing on only one feature point for the same feature in the case of impurities, spot cracks and pockmark defects. The KD-EG-RepVGG also has the ability to recognize features from multiple angles. The features of cracks at different locations and angles can be fully extracted, demonstrating a strong extraction capability.

4. Conclusions

Aiming at the requirement of strip surface defect detection in actual production, a strip defect recognition method based on a structural re-parameterized KD-EG-RepVGG network is proposed. In RepVGG Block, the ECA network and GELU activation functions are added. Among them, the ECA network improves the accuracy of the KD-EG-RepVGG network while increasing the convergence speed of KD-EG-RepVGG. The GELU activation function avoids neuron necrosis caused by zeroing. Through knowledge distillation technology, the KD-EG-RepVGG model obtains the knowledge of RepVGG-A0, which improves the accuracy and robustness of the model. Through ablation experiments and comparative analysis with other models, it can be seen that the lightweight KD-EG RepVGG network takes up very little memory resources and computing resources without affecting the accuracy, and has a faster detection speed. It is more suitable for deployment and uses in real production.

The future work involves many directions. Firstly, the research in this paper will be used as a basis to study the accurate localization of defects and to analyze the size of defects accurately. Then, the model will be deployed on edge equipment and applied in the production environment within plants.

Author Contributions: Methodology, X.X.; software, X.X.; writing—original draft preparation, X.X.; writing—review and editing, X.S.; All authors have read and agreed to the published version of the manuscript.

Funding: This research received no external funding.

Data Availability Statement: The data presented in this study are available in article.

Conflicts of Interest: The authors declare no conflict of interest.

References

1. Peng, Z.; Ke, X.; Chaolin, Y. Surface defect recognition for moderately thick plates based on a SIFT operator. *J. Tsinghua Univ. (Sci. Technol.)* **2018**, *58*, 881–887.
2. Hu, H.; Liu, Y.; Liu, M.; Nie, L. Surface defect classification in large-scale strip steel image collection via hybrid chromosome genetic algorithm. *Neurocomputing* **2016**, *181*, 86–95. [CrossRef]
3. Krizhevsky, A.; Sutskever, I.; Hinton, G.E. Imagenet classification with deep convolutional neural networks. *Adv. Neural Inf. Process. Syst.* **2012**, *25*, 1097–1105. [CrossRef]
4. Manzo, M.; Pellino, S. Fighting Together against the Pandemic: Learning Multiple Models on Tomography Images for COVID-19 Diagnosis. *AI* **2021**, *2*, 16. [CrossRef]
5. Jiang, Z.; Dong, Z.; Jiang, W.; Yang, Y. Recognition of rice leaf diseases and wheat leaf diseases based on multi-task deep transfer learning. *Comput. Electron. Agric.* **2021**, *186*, 106184. [CrossRef]
6. Tao, L.; Wang, L.; Shen, X.; Liu, C. Research of Fire Identification Method Based on Convolutional Neural Network. In Proceedings of the 2022 7th International Conference on Intelligent Computing and Signal Processing (ICSP), Xi'an, China, 15–17 April 2022; pp. 1656–1659.
7. Vannocci, M.; Ritacco, A.; Castellano, A.; Galli, F.; Vannucci, M.; Iannino, V.; Colla, V. Flatness Defect Detection and Classification in Hot Rolled Steel Strips Using Convolutional Neural Networks. In Proceedings of the 15th International Work-Conference on Artificial Neural Networks (IWANN), Granada, Spain, 12–14 June 2019; pp. 220–234.
8. Konovalenko, I.; Maruschak, P.; Brezinova, J.; Vinas, J.; Brezina, J. Steel Surface Defect Classification Using Deep Residual Neural Network. *Metals* **2020**, *10*, 846. [CrossRef]
9. Wan, X.; Zhang, X.; Liu, L. An improved VGG19 transfer learning strip steel surface defect recognition deep neural network based on few samples and imbalanced datasets. *Appl. Sci.* **2021**, *11*, 2606. [CrossRef]
10. Feng, X.; Gao, X.; Luo, L. A ResNet50-Based Method for Classifying Surface Defects in Hot-Rolled Strip Steel. *Mathematics* **2021**, *9*, 2359. [CrossRef]

11. Tang, M.; Li, Y.; Yao, W.; Hou, L.; Sun, Q.; Chen, J. A strip steel surface defect detection method based on attention mechanism and multi-scale maxpooling. *Meas. Sci. Technol.* **2021**, *32*, 115401. [CrossRef]
12. Xing, J.; Jia, M. A convolutional neural network-based method for workpiece surface defect detection. *Measurement* **2021**, *176*, 109185. [CrossRef]
13. Wang, W.; Lu, K.; Wu, Z.; Long, H.; Zhang, J.; Chen, P.; Wang, B. Surface Defects Classification of Hot Rolled Strip Based on Improved Convolutional Neural Network. *ISIJ Int.* **2021**, *61*, 1579–1583. [CrossRef]
14. He, K.M.; Zhang, X.Y.; Ren, S.Q.; Sun, J.; IEEE. Deep Residual Learning for Image Recognition. In Proceedings of the 2016 IEEE Conference on Computer Vision and Pattern Recognition (CVPR), Las Vegas, NV, USA, 27–30 June 2016; pp. 770–778.
15. Ding, X.H.; Zhang, X.Y.; Ma, N.N.; Han, J.G.; Ding, G.G.; Sun, J.; Ieee Comp, S.O.C. RepVGG: Making VGG-style ConvNets Great Again. In Proceedings of the IEEE/CVF Conference on Computer Vision and Pattern Recognition (CVPR), Electr Network, 19–25 June 2021; pp. 13728–13737.
16. Ioffe, S.; Szegedy, C. Batch Normalization: Accelerating Deep Network Training by Reducing Internal Covariate Shift. In Proceedings of the 32nd International Conference on Machine Learning, Lille, France, 7–9 July 2015; pp. 448–456.
17. Wang, Q.; Wu, B.; Zhu, P.; Li, P.; Zuo, W.; Hu, Q. ECA-Net: Efficient Channel Attention for Deep Convolutional Neural Networks. In Proceedings of the 2020 IEEE/CVF Conference on Computer Vision and Pattern Recognition (CVPR), Seattle, WA, USA, 13–19 June 2020; pp. 11531–11539.
18. Hendrycks, D.; Gimpel, K. Gaussian error linear units (gelus). *arXiv* **2016**, arXiv:1606.08415.
19. Hinton, G.; Vinyals, O.; Dean, J. Distilling the knowledge in a neural network. *arXiv* **2015**, arXiv:1503.02531.
20. Bao, Y.Q.; Song, K.C.; Liu, J.; Wang, Y.Y.; Yan, Y.H.; Yu, H.; Li, X.J. Triplet-Graph Reasoning Network for Few-Shot Metal Generic Surface Defect Segmentation. *Ieee Trans. Instrum. Meas.* **2021**, *70*, 1–11. [CrossRef]
21. Wagner, J.; Kohler, J.M.; Gindele, T.; Hetzel, L.; Wiedemer, J.T.; Behnke, S.; Soc, I.C. Interpretable and Fine-Grained Visual Explanations for Convolutional Neural Networks. In Proceedings of the 32nd IEEE/CVF Conference on Computer Vision and Pattern Recognition (CVPR), Long Beach, CA, USA, 16–20 June 2019; pp. 9089–9099.
22. Selvaraju, R.R.; Cogswell, M.; Das, A.; Vedantam, R.; Parikh, D.; Batra, D. Grad-CAM: Visual Explanations from Deep Networks via Gradient-Based Localization. *Int. J. Comput. Vis.* **2020**, *128*, 336–359. [CrossRef]

electronics

Article

User Engagement Comparison between Advergames and Traditional Advertising Using EEG: Does the User's Engagement Influence Purchase Intention?

Ivonne Angelica Castiblanco Jimenez *, Juan Sebastian Gomez Acevedo, Elena Carlotta Olivetti, Federica Marcolin *, Luca Ulrich, Sandro Moos and Enrico Vezzetti

Department of Management and Production Engineering, Politecnico di Torino, Corso Duca degli Abruzzi 24, 10129 Turin, Italy
* Correspondence: ivonne.castiblanco@polito.it (I.A.C.J.); federica.marcolin@polito.it (F.M.)

Abstract: In the context of human–computer interaction (HCI), understanding user engagement (UE) while interacting with a product or service can provide valuable information for enhancing the design process. UE has been a priority research theme within HCI, as it assesses the user experience by studying the individual's behavioral response to some stimulus. Many studies looking to quantify the UE are available; however, most use self-report methods that rely only on participants' answers. This study aims to explore a non-traditional method, specifically electroencephalography, to analyze users' engagement while interacting with an advergame, an interactive form of advertising in video games. We aim to understand if a more interactive type of advertising will enhance the UE and whether, at the same time, it would influence the user's purchase intention (UPI). To do this, we computed and compared the UE during the interaction with an advergame and a conventional TV commercial while measuring the participants' brain activity. After the interaction with both types of advertising, the UPI was also evaluated. The findings demonstrate that a more interactive advertisement increased the participants' UE and that, in most cases, a UE increment positively influenced the UPI. This study shows an example of the potential of physiological feedback applications to explore the users' perceptions during and after the human–product interaction. The findings show how physiological methods can be used along with traditional ones for enhancing the UE analysis and provide helpful information about the advantages of engagement measurement in HCI applications.

Keywords: user engagement; EEG; purchase intention; advergames

Citation: Castiblanco Jimenez, I.A.; Gomez Acevedo, J.S.; Olivetti, E.C.; Marcolin, F.; Ulrich, L.; Moos, S.; Vezzetti, E. User Engagement Comparison between Advergames and Traditional Advertising Using EEG: Does the User's Engagement Influence Purchase Intention? *Electronics* **2023**, *12*, 122. https://doi.org/10.3390/electronics12010122

Academic Editors: Juan Ernesto Solanes Galbis, Luis Gracia and Jaime Valls Miro

Received: 7 November 2022
Revised: 14 December 2022
Accepted: 22 December 2022
Published: 27 December 2022

1. Introduction

With an increasing number of digital services, HCI studies regarding the analysis of interfaces and approaches to exchange information are a must. In particular, exploring innovative techniques that allow researchers and practitioners to understand users' needs without bias may foster HCI applications in promising consumer–content interaction fields. Affective computing developments have been a matter of interest for interdisciplinary fields due to the practical implications concerning the study and design of systems capable of recognizing and interpreting human emotions. The marketing and video games industries are no exception. Some years ago, video games were a minor activity exclusively earmarked for kids, leaving aside the adult audience. The actual situation of video games is undoubtedly much different: video games ranked first in leisure activities, surpassing the traditional ones such as cinema and music [1]. Additionally, their importance continues to increase, reaching a media resonance and social impact due to the development and implementation of new technologies, especially in an era affected by the COVID-19 pandemic, where technology has taken on a significant role in the entertainment market in terms of popularity and profitability [2]. The impact of the ongoing pandemic, social restrictions, and the recommendation to stay at home have significantly contributed to a rise in the gaming industry's numbers of users.

In an environment where consumers have the choice to pay and get what they desire, advertising can be quickly rejected, and the impact of video games has not gone unnoticed by the publicity market, a sector reinventing itself to find new ways to reach an even more demanding audience. The advergames, a hybrid between advertising and entertainment content in video games, can contribute to a better perception of advertising by developing new possibilities for marketing communication. Advergames have also gained a competitive advantage [3] for attracting and engaging users due to their interactivity and high exposure to a brand or product [4] while offering a non-intrusive experience. The user is the one who addresses the game and interacts with it voluntarily. Additionally, this type of interactive advertising allows easy customization since the brand can include its style and values to create a unique and representative product, thus contributing to the brand's personality and attracting more users who identify with the brand.

This effectiveness is achievable thanks to the capacity of introducing advertising content inside an environment where the users have shown a good perception of the publicity. Furthermore, the value of advergames lies in their ability to provide a compelling advertising message that consumers are more willing to accept [5]. Due to these advantages and the significant impact that video games have worldwide, advertising campaigns should consider advergames, a non-saturated leisure platform [6], as an opportunity to increase user engagement (UE) and contribute to user purchase intention (UPI). In other words, advergames could take advantage of the UE with video games to reach a more demanding audience and increase the willingness to acquire a product.

UE, a typical human–computer interaction parameter, has been described as the degree of focus and immersion in a particular task [7]. Traditionally, this indicator has been measured using almost exclusively self-report measures; however, in order not to rely only on respondents' answers, technological advances have made possible the use of new instruments that can provide physiological outcomes to examine the "ground truth" of the users' perceptions. Among these, electroencephalography (EEG), a non-invasive procedure for measuring and examining the electrical activity of the brain, is becoming a potential instrument for exploring UE. Indeed, by analyzing EEG data collected while participants were exposed to a stimulus, McMahan and Freeman's studies [8,9] have demonstrated that EEG-based metrics can be used to determine whether a user is more or less engaged. The results from the literature would suppose that an advergame will provoke higher engagement than a TV commercial since TV is a passive media; however, it is unclear if a more interactive type of advertising would lead to a higher UPI. The goal of meaningfully quantifying the UE using physiological tools such as EEG will provide additional helpful information that, combined with traditional methods, can enrich this research field.

This empirical study aims to validate the hypothesis that "a more interactive type of advertising impacts the UE, positively influencing the UPI". To do this, we have created an experiment where the users are exposed to two advertisements for the same product whilst their brains' activity is being recorded. In this way, we aim to compare a traditional advertising campaign with an advergame to quantify the UE difference using EEG. A validated questionnaire will be used to determine the UPI before and after the experiment.

This paper is structured as follows: Section 2 presents the research background, including a review of the UE in video games, the EEG as a method for understanding the UE, and the conceptual relation between UE and UPI. Section 3 presents the methodology, the experimental setup, and the data analysis. Section 4 presents the analysis results, and Sections 5 and 6 contain the discussion and conclusions.

2. Research Background

UE has been a matter of interest in different fields, including education, healthcare, and entertainment. The way UE has been evaluated differs from study to study. For the purpose of this research, we will focus our attention on the most common methods to measure the UE during video game interactions and the exploration of EEG as a means to measure this indicator.

2.1. An Overview of User Engagement in Video Games

UE can be defined as the absorption level and willingness to execute a task [7]. In a recent study, Kniestedt et al. [10] delineated the engagement definition in applied games as a concept involving the state of concentrating attention on a task and the involvement with the context where that task occurs. The UE in video games has been a matter of interest in different studies [11–16] under the idea that users can be engaged in activities through meaningful interactions. The interactive possibilities that video game technologies offer can enhance engagement more than other activities. Brockmyer et al. [12] designed the Game Engagement Questionnaire (GEQ) focused on analyzing video games' violence. The study explores the engagement experience in four dimensions: absorption, flow, presence, and immersion. It concludes that it is possible to identify the users' psychological engagement when playing video games and that a higher UE can significantly impact game playing.

On the other hand, Bianchi-Berthouze [14] considered how body movement could affect the UE during gameplay. The movement-based engagement model specifies the relationship between movements and engagement. The model classifies the body movements into five groups and describes their relationships with the engagement. The study concludes that the freedom offered by video games plays an essential role in the UE, allowing a more in-depth immersion in the scenarios presented, attracting users to continue exploring and engaging more and more with the game. This work has been widely appreciated by the scientific community and is an excellent example of the importance of physiological measurements to better understand the UE.

Another significant study is the one carried out by Martey et al. [15], who measured the UE with video games, measuring different characteristics that may influence the users' perception. These characteristics are a player avatar, visual realism, and narrative. In this study, the authors measured five indicators (a self-report survey, the attention to the stimulus, Galvanic skin response (GSR), mouse movements, and game click logs) when playing a video game to measure how these characteristics can influence the capacity of a video game to engage the user. The results indicated that physiological measurements (GSR, mouse movement, and clicks) are highly related to users' expressions and feelings and can provide reliable information for UE identification and analysis.

Abdul Jabbar and Felicia [16] developed a model where emotions and thoughts play an essential role in UE and learning. The study illustrated the impact of some gaming features on cognitive and emotional levels by classifying the engaging elements into four types: motivational, interactive, fun, and multimedia. The study found that some aspects that might influence the UE in the gameplay are related to visuals, role-play, obstacles, virtual environments, control/choice, and rewards.

Likewise, O'Brien and Toms [17] created a survey to test the UE of software applications, named the User Engagement Scale (UES). In this survey, users are asked to answer questions about their experience with the product. This survey was later adapted by Landa-Avila and Cruz [18] for a virtual game to analyze six aspects: endurability, novelty, perceived usability, aesthetics, felt involvement, and focused attention. After data analysis, the authors found that the UES questionnaire can be used to measure the UE in a video games context; however, there were objections about the test's duration and misunderstandings about some items. This situation was later examined by O'Brien et al. [19], who proposed the UES short form.

Other studies on UE analysis in video games are listed in Table 1. Most of these studies, however, relied only on self-report methods, such as questionnaires, interviews, surveys, and scales, in which participants were asked to answer questions or provide responses to prompts that are designed to collect data on a particular topic or construct. The data collected through self-reported methods can be subjective and may be influenced by various factors, such as the participants' memory, motivation, and willingness to reveal personal information. Despite these limitations, self-reports have been widely used as a method for UE analysis, and consequently, this could lead to biased outcomes due to the nature of the responses. In this sense, self-reports could be compared and enhanced with other experimental approaches that do not entirely depend on participants' responses, such as the case of EEG.

Table 1. UE analysis in video games.

Author	Method	Purpose/Outcome
Mayes and Cotton [20]	Questionnaire	Development of an engagement questionnaire (EQ) in video games
Lankoski [21]	Framework	Engagement definition classified as goal-related or empathic.
Schoenau-Fog [22]	Survey	Definition of a player engagement framework based on objectives, activities, accomplish, and affect.
Schonau-Fog and Bjorner [23]	Interview	Method to classify the experience of engagement with video games into six types: sensory, intellectual, physical, social, narrative, and emotional engagement.
Corem et al. [24]	Scale	Proposal of a player-matching system based on the Elo rating system.
Sharek and Wieve [25]	Physiological (haptic) and Survey	Engagement measurement based on how many times a participant clicked a game-clock.
Wieve et al. [26]	Scale	A modified version of the User Engagement Scale (UES) for video game research.
Kirschner and Williams [27]	Interview	Gameplay review method (GRM) for players' engagement using interviews and audiovisual recordings
Pope et al. [28]	Physiological (EEG)	EEG engagement index based on electroencephalographic signals.
McMahan et al. [8]	Physiological (EEG)	Identification and verification of the EEG engagement index developed by Pope et al. [28] as a valid indicator of UE with video games.
Phan et al. [29]	Scale	Game User Experience Satisfaction Scale (GUESS)
Sreejesh and Anusree [30]	Survey	Study on the effects of cognition demand and brand attention.
Sawyer et al. [31]	Scale	Hierarchical Bayesian method to model player engagement.
Nermend and Duda [32]	Physiological (eye tracking, GSR) and Questionnaire	Methodology for choosing the location of advertising in games, using eye tracker and GSR.
Barclay and Bowers [33]	Survey	Use of the Revised Game Engagement Model (R-GEM) to conclude that immersion in an activity may not only be a result of extremely usable systems or particularly receptive users but an effect of the experience itself.

2.2. EEG as a Means for Understanding the Engagement

The literature on the methods, measures, and elements that influence the UE with video games shows a predominance of self-report methods; however, methods based on physiological analysis are becoming more accessible due to the technological advances that have increased the availability and usability of these systems. An example is a study conducted by McMahan et al. [8]. In this research, the authors used EEG to evaluate the player task engagement in video games in two situations, during normal gameplay and player death. The study identified that the engagement corresponds to immersion states, concluding that higher levels of engagement are present during death events compared to general play. Likewise, a recent study [34] used an educational video game created to test medical students' clinical skills and track their engagement using EEG. The results showed a correspondence between the EEG outcomes and the participants' performance.

The evaluation of engagement with EEG has also been explored in the education field. Chaouachi and Frasson [35] analyzed the effect of engagement on the students and found that it strongly influences the response time and can be an indicator of learners' performance. At the same time, the authors used the engagement index, initially proposed by Pope et al. [28] and later validated by Freeman et al. [9]. Similarly, Coelli et al. [36] evaluated the relationship between the level of cognitive engagement and focused attention, concluding that EEG can be used to detect changes in mental state and subjects' reaction times. A recent study [37] proposed a device prototype consisting of an EEG headset and a scarf that provide haptic feedback when a decrease in attention is detected.

Considering the emotional research, Ramirez et al. [38] conducted a study based on EEG to analyze the emotional effect of music in advanced cancer patients, and their findings showed a decrease in anxiety and tiredness. Likewise, in a previous study, Giraldo and Ramirez [39] described an approach to calculate arousal and valence values from EEG activity in real-time. On the other hand, Ramirez and Vamvakousis et al. [39] explored a machine learning approach to detect emotions from EEG signals. In these studies, the authors computed and validated EEG-based indices for obtaining information about the users' emotional states.

A further study [40] explored the engagement analysis with advertising. This study focused on traditional advertising and did not use a validated engagement EEG index, and the EEG data were globally recorded and then correlated with the participant's answers to a questionnaire. However, the results were not conclusive, and the authors recognized the need for more profound research in this field. Likewise, other studies [41] have focused their interest on analyzing players' emotions in VR gaming using EEG data and comparing their results with self-report methods.

The studies on engagement and EEG showed that EEG-based metrics are suitable for studying UE. However, despite the advances in the study of engagement in advertising and video games, these two fields have been explored individually; consequently, there is a research gap regarding the engagement during advergames interactions using EEG.

2.3. Relation between Engagement and User Purchase Intention in Advergames

UPI can be defined as the conscious decision of a user to buy a particular product [42]. This degree of willingness to pay is a variable that depends on several factors, for example, product perception, product price, attitude toward a specific purchase, the interaction experience, engagement with a particular product or brand, and customer service. Survey instruments have been a common choice for assessing these variables and ultimately estimating the UPI.

Goh and Ping [11] developed and validated a post-game questionnaire to measure the UPI and attitude toward the advergame experience, the brand, and ads in general. The study concluded that the attitude toward the brand positively influences the UPI and confirms the advergames' added value in effectively increasing the UPI of the advertised product.

Chen [43] developed a model of the in-game factors influencing the user purchase reaction with an advergame. The study identified that audiences are more likely to develop acquisition desire and positive brand attitudes when they are engaged and attracted during the advergames. On the other hand, Catalan et al. [44] identified a group of elements that could affect user experience and purchase reaction in a mobile advergame. The study defined the following factors that might influence the UPI: skills, challenge, interactivity, focused attention (engagement), and telepresence.

Other studies concluded that advergames lead to a higher purchase desire than TV commercials [45], that UPI and attitude towards a brand increase when there are elements of interactivity [46], and that children who are more involved and have a positive attitude during the game show a higher UPI [47].

Finally, Chang et al. [48] proposed a conceptual framework for exploring the congruity, integration, and prominence as variables persuading the interest and UPI during in-game advertising. The study suggested a survey instrument for measuring the UPI and concluded that user attention/engagement positively affects the purchase interest during gameplay.

Considering the previous findings that highlighted UE as one of the most significant variables that could influence the customer's desire to acquire, in this research, the UE influence on the UPI during an advergame interaction and projection of a tv commercial has also been analyzed.

3. Methods and Tools

The relationship between video games and advertising is complex and multifaceted, with each industry influencing and benefiting from the other in various ways. In the intersection between, there are the advergames (Figure 1), which provide a unique and highly engaging platform for advertisers to reach consumers, with in-game ads and sponsored content offering new and innovative ways for brands to connect with their audience and promote a product or service through the use of interactive and engaging gameplay. This strategy relies on user engagement to be successful, with the level of engagement (UE) influencing the effectiveness of the advertising and the likelihood of a user making a purchase (UPI).

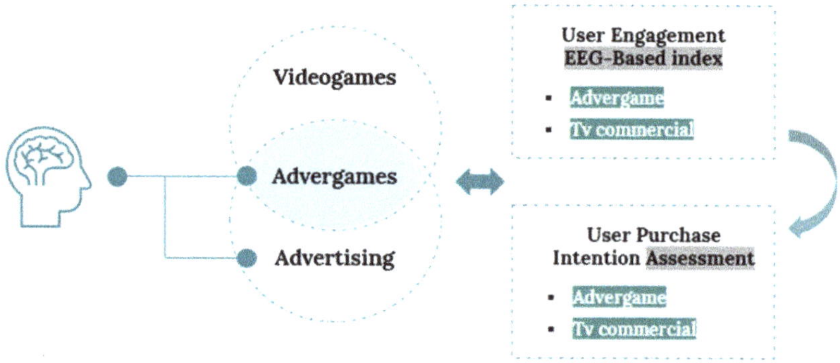

Figure 1. Model of UE influence on UPI.

The interaction between these three contexts (video games, advertising, and advergames) and the UE influence on the UPI frames this research.

This research aims to measure the UE with an advergame and a traditional advertising campaign to analyze if the UE has an incidence on the UPI of a product or brand exposed. To achieve this, we focused the literature background analysis on previous UE and video games research, EEG as a method for UE identification, and the UE influence on the UPI in advergames.

The literature review shows that no study on advergames has been conducted using EEG as a method to measure the UE and its influence on the UPI. Besides, we want to contribute to this field by endorsing previously validated tools employed individually in related areas (games and advertising) to verify the hypothesis: "A more interactive type of advertising impacts the user perception and engagement, positively influencing the purchase intention".

To verify the previous hypothesis, the participants' physiological reactions were measured using EEG to analyze the UE during an advergame and a TV commercial. After both advertising interactions, the UPI was calculated using a questionnaire assessment.

3.1. EEG Engagement Index Data Analysis and Feature Extraction

The neuronal electrical activity is composed of different frequencies that can be obtained through the EEG signal, and these brain waves are grouped into main frequency bands, such as: theta (θ), alpha (α), beta (β), and gamma (γ). Theta waves have a frequency of 4–8 Hz, alpha 8–12 Hz, beta 12–25 Hz, and gamma 25–45 Hz. These different frequency bands are commonly associated with diverse cognitive processes [35].

Beta (β) power is related to system activation and higher mental activity of the brain when a person is aware and cognitively engaged. In contrast, alpha (α) is associated with lower mental vigilance and usually appears in sleep–wake cycles; at the same time, theta (θ) activity occurs most often in sleep or deep meditative states. Pope et al. [28] proposed an EEG-based index to analyze UE; in their research, the authors assessed three possible indices computed using the EEG frequencies' bandwidth and suggested the most accurate UE index (Equation (1)):

$$Engagement\ Index = \frac{\beta}{\alpha + \theta} \quad (1)$$

Following this approach, the UE index (1) considers the ratio between the beta waves (higher mental activity of the brain) and the sum of the theta and alpha waves (both related to lower mental activity of the brain).

This research was carried out employing a mobile EEG headset (Emotiv EPOC+) with 14 wet-EEG electrodes (AF3, AF4, F3, F4, F7, F8, FC5, FC6, P7, P8, T7, T8, O1, O2) placed at standard 10–20 positions (Figure 2). Two additional CMS/DRL reference channels were located at P3 and P4. The sampling rate was 128 Hz, and the bandwidth was between 0.2 and 45 Hz. The band power calculation was performed at 0.125 s intervals (8 Hz). We applied a FFT to the most recent 2 s epoch of EEG data and averaged the FFT-squared magnitude across the frequencies in each band. Before performing the calculation, the EEG stream passed through a 0.18 Hz high-pass FIR filter. To improve the accuracy of the spectral analysis and reduce artifacts from the procedure, a Hanning window was implemented. For the engagement calculation, Equation (1) was employed. Similarly to [49], the engagement index (1) for each participant was computed considering the averaged overall electrodes' measurements.

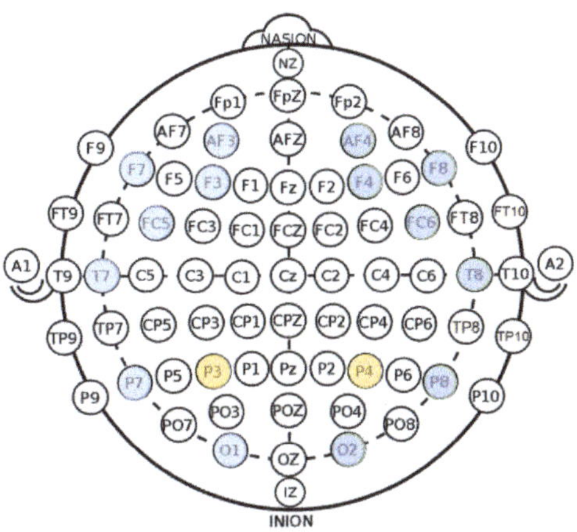

Figure 2. Sensor location. The electrodes' positions employed in this study are highlighted.

Considering that in physiological studies, the initial baseline and the subsequent responses (after stimulus) are highly individual-dependent and differ from participant to participant, there are no absolute (max or min) values for UE. To help reduce errors associated with individual differences, this research employed a "within-subject design" experiment, often used in similar studies [8,9,35,49], to regulate the subjects' measurements by exposing them to all experimental conditions. Users bring their own background and current physical and mental state to the test. Therefore, to minimize the random noise, the EEG data were separated into two phases: The first contains the baseline recording during a relaxed period, useful to identify the primary user's state, and used as a reference point for comparing the brain's activity during different tasks. The second contains the electrical brain data while exposed to a stimulus, in this case, while interacting with the advergame and while watching the traditional advertising. By analyzing and contrasting the brain activity difference between the baseline and the activated engagement during the stimuli, it is possible to identify the activated response and, thus, the increment/decrement of the engagement index; if it increases, this can be interpreted as a higher level of UE (Figure 3).

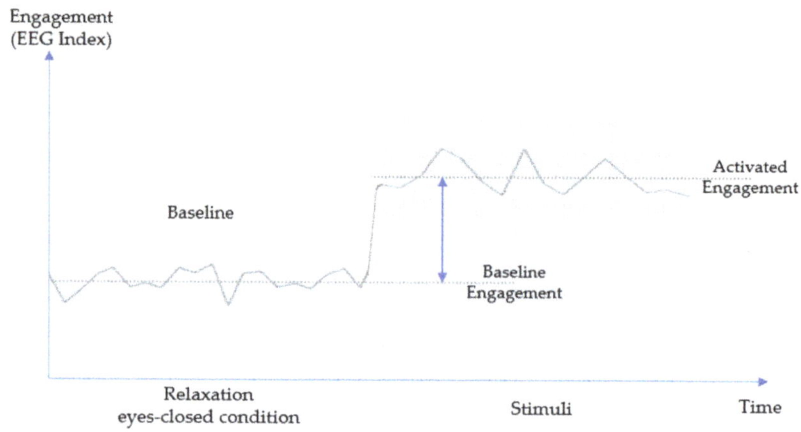

Figure 3. Engagement baseline vs. stimuli activation.

In this way, the participants in a within-subjects design serve as their own control by providing baseline metrics across the different stimuli. After analyzing and normalizing the entire signals, it is possible to generate a general comparable data analysis for all the participants exposed to the same experiment. The goal is to measure the variation resulting from the different stimuli for the engagement outcomes.

3.2. Experiment Setup

A controlled experiment (Figure 4) was conducted in a lab environment with 24 healthy participants, 13 women (55%) and 11 men (45%), aged between 23 and 45, recruited in person. All of them reported computer skills. All participants signed an informed consent after being briefed about the experiment, the use of their data, and its protection. Then, each user was accompanied to perform the test in a controlled environment, a closed room equipped with an adjustable chair, a display monitor, and a gamepad, planned to avoid situations that may influence the results. The experiment was displayed on a 40-inch curved display with an effective viewing area of 884.74 mm (horizontal) and 497.66 mm (vertical) at a 3000 mm radius curvature with a pixel density of 110 per inch. The participants sat approximately 800 mm ($\pm$50 mm) in front of the display. This monitor was selected as studies [50,51] showed that considering a large field of view of a participant can greatly enhance their experience, and with the help of its curvature and high pixel density, it can increase immersion.

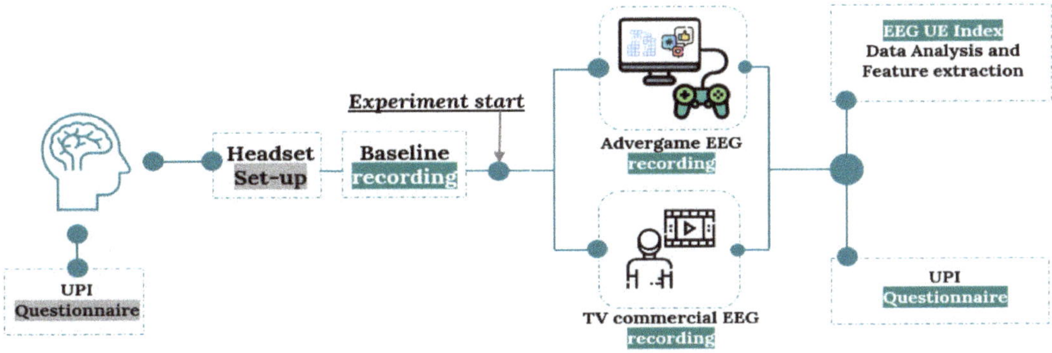

Figure 4. Experiment setup.

First, the users were requested to fill in the UPI questionnaire according to their original perception of the product selected for the study. The EEG headset was positioned on the participant's head, and the correct connection of the electrodes was verified. The participant was invited to relax for 3 min. After the training phase and setting up, to facilitate the immersion and successfully conduct the experiment, the lights were turned off.

A baseline period of 30 s was recorded during the eyes-closed condition. Half of the participants were randomly assigned first to play an advergame and then proceed with a TV commercial, while the other half initially watched the TV commercial and then continued with the advergame activity. In both cases, the participants were asked to play the advergame for 4 min and exposed to a TV commercial for 3 min while measuring their brain activity. Between one activity and the other, the participants were invited to relax for 2 min. At the end of each type of advertising, the participants were requested to fill in the UPI questionnaire again.

To evaluate the UPI, we used the purchase intention evaluation proposed by Chang et al. [48] to assess the consideration, desire, plan, and likelihood of buying the advertised product using a seven-point Likert scale.

The selected product belongs to a well-known brand of carbonated soft drinks. The TV commercial displays an urban scenario with young people singing and dancing in the street while inviting the spectators to join their march, the melody set in the background recalls the brand's iconic music. The advergame is an endless runner third-person perspective game developed to avoid obstacles by running, dashing, and jumping, and the user's role is to save dehydrated people by collecting and delivering them cans of drink. The atmosphere is designed to show branded ads blended with the surroundings throughout the game.

4. Results

The raw EEG data were collected and processed. Artifacts due to body movements and signal noise were removed. Twenty results from the total sample were deemed suitable for the objectives of this study. The EEG data were segmented into the baseline (eyes-closed condition) and activity periods when interacting with the advergame or watching the TV commercial. To determine and contrast the EEG engagement index between periods, the baseline data were compared to the post-stimulus response for both the advergame and the TV commercial; in this way, it was possible to examine the influence of the advertising on the UE.

The EEG engagement index average for each one of the participants is shown in Figure 5, divided into the baseline and activity periods. The results show that during the advergame interaction, the engagement was always higher than the baseline period, indicating increased attention and vigilance while gaming.

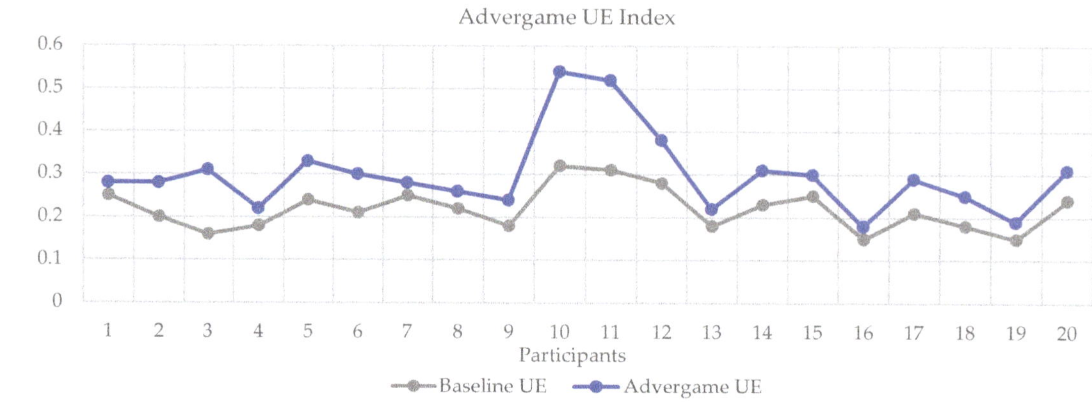

Figure 5. UE index during the advergame interaction.

Regarding the TV commercial, the results show (Figure 6) that in some cases, the EEG engagement index was lower than the baseline period, thus showing a decrease in attention and vigilance, in other words, a lower UE.

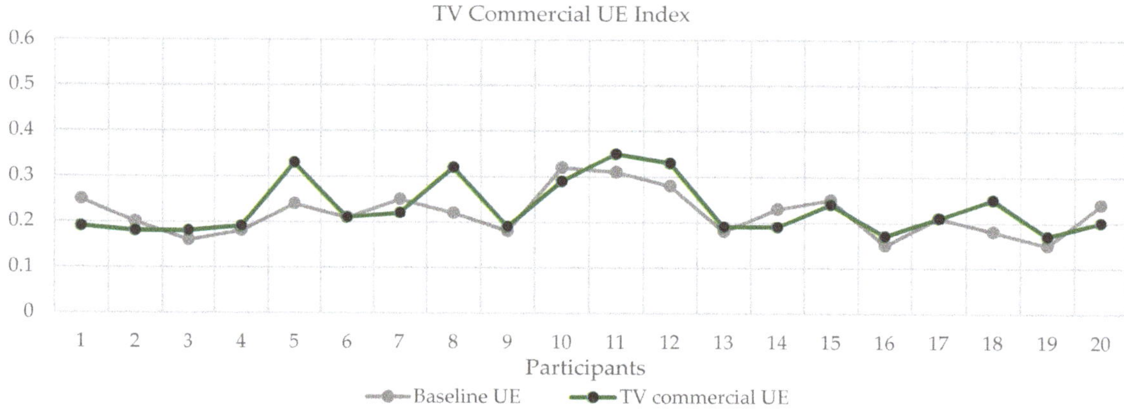

Figure 6. UE index during the TV commercial.

The average UPI for each advertisement and participant is shown in Figure 7. In the case of the TV commercial, the UPI was higher for only 30% of the participants compared to the original UPI reported at the beginning of the experiment. For the advergame, the results show that the UPI was usually higher (70% of the cases) than the original UPI before the advertising interactions. This indicates that advergames generate a post-game response that tends to positively influence the purchase intention/reaction of the participants, encouraging them to consume the product.

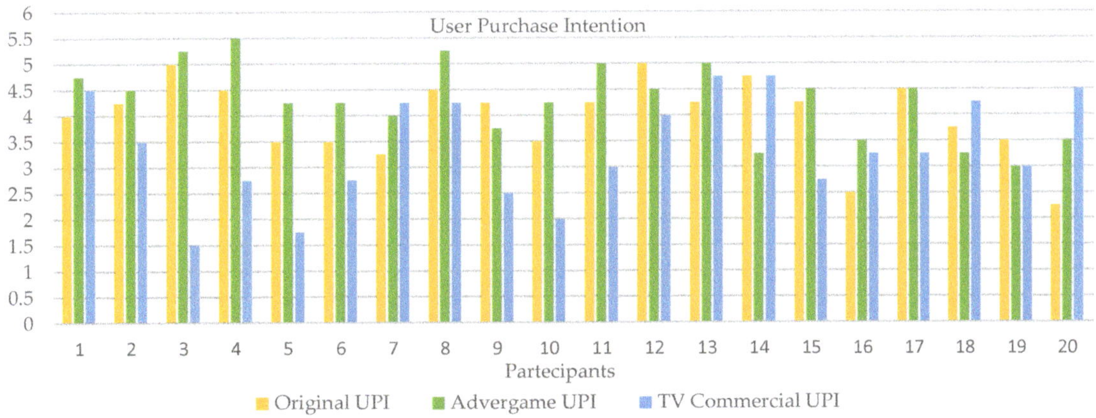

Figure 7. UPI before and after the advertising interactions.

In some cases, however (participants 7, 14, 18, and 20), the UPI was higher after seeing the commercial in contrast to the original UPI and advergame, indicating that for a minority of participants, the traditional advertising has a higher incidence on the UPI. Additionally, it is interesting to notice that for three participants (9, 12, 19), the original UPI was higher than the UPI reported after the advergame and TV commercial activity, representing a negative influence of both advertisements. Thus, considering the total contribution of both advertisements, 25% of the participants reported a positive UPI response for both types (advergame and TV commercial), while 15% reported a negative response. Advergames overall generated the most significant positive responses from the stimulus.

5. Discussion

The results support the initial hypothesis: "A more interactive type of advertising impacts the user perception and engagement, positively influencing the purchase intention". An analysis of variance (ANOVA) on the EEG engagement index was performed to verify the statistical difference between the EEG engagement index while playing an advergame vs. seeing the TV commercial, obtaining: ($F(1,38) = 7.40$, $p < 0.01$). The outcomes show that a more engaging type of advertising significantly influences the UE; in this case, an advergame had a more significant influence on the UE than a traditional TV commercial. This result indicates that the EEG engagement index was statistically significantly higher when the participants interacted with the advergames than when they watched the TV commercial.

Still, the fact that a stimulus produces a more engaging behavior would not necessarily imply that the UE will reflect similarly on the UPI. Hence, to analyze if a more interactive type of advertising generates a more significant influence on purchase intention, an ANOVA was also performed for the average UPI of the participants for both activities, obtaining: ($F(1,38) = 10.75$, $p < 0.01$). The previous result showed that after playing the advergame, the UPI was statistically significantly higher than the UPI after seeing the TV commercial.

The interactions between UE and UPI can be distributed in four clusters according to the participants' responses. For the context of this study, we have developed a four-quadrant model (Figure 8) to show the classification considering the reported UPI and the EEG engagement index variation.

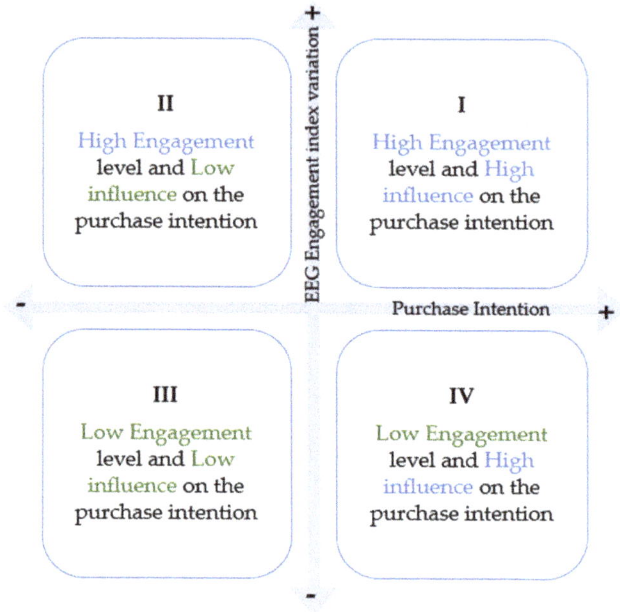

Figure 8. Quadrant model of EEG engagement index variation vs. UPI.

The X-axis refers to the UPI. Number 4 is located at the center since it indicates the neutral response of the participants in the questionnaire. The Y-axis shows the difference between the EEG engagement index during the stimuli and the baseline. By contrasting the difference between the resting period (baseline) and the advertising interaction during the test, it is possible to identify the variation of the index; in other words, if the variation is positive, the stimuli produced an increase in the engagement, and vice versa.

For the advergame (Figure 9), all the participants presented a positive variation in the EEG engagement index, indicating an increase in the UE when interacting with it. In the first quadrant, there were thirteen participants (65%), in the second quadrant, there were seven participants (35%), and in the third and fourth quadrants, there were no participants.

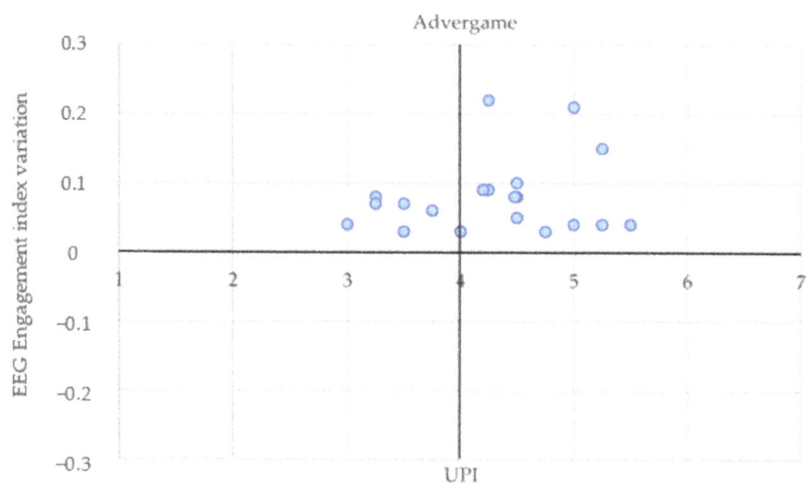

Figure 9. Advergame—Quadrant model of EEG engagement index variation vs. UPI.

For the TV commercial (Figure 10), positive and negative changes in the index were identified, which means that in some cases, there was a negative variation of the EEG engagement index, and in other cases, there was a positive variation. In the first quadrant, there were three participants (15%), in the second quadrant, there were ten participants (50%), in the third quadrant, there were five participants (25%), and in the fourth quadrant, there were four participants (20%).

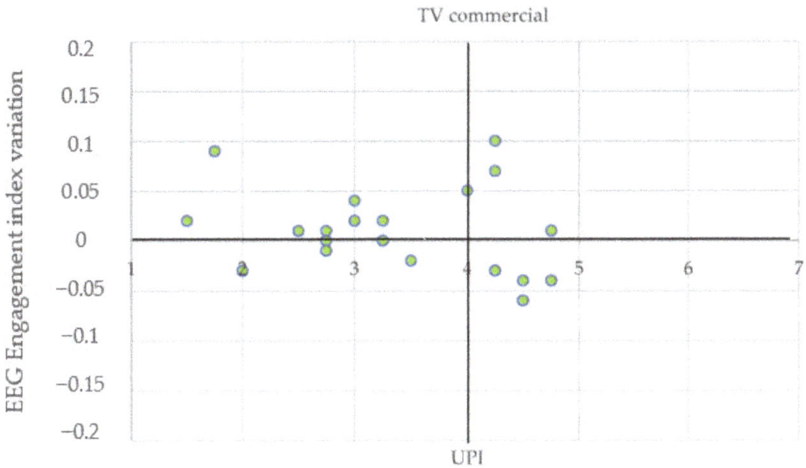

Figure 10. TV commercial—Quadrant model of EEG engagement index variation vs. UPI.

The results in Figure 10 confirm a decrease in the number of participants located in the first quadrant for the TV commercial compared to the results obtained in the advergame (Figure 9), indicating that a lower number of participants presented a high level of engagement and a high UPI while watching the traditional advertisement. In the second quadrant, there was a similarity in the number of participants between the TV commercial and the advergame, indicating a high level of engagement and a low UPI. This result suggests that even if the participant was engaged, the advertising did not affect the UPI of these participants. Only the TV commercial had participants in the third quadrant, showing that traditional advertising is sometimes not attractive. In the fourth quadrant, the TV commercial involved four participants who experienced a decrease in the EEG engagement index but still reported a positive UPI. These persons located in the fourth quadrant reported a positive attitude toward the brand at the start of the test, confirming the study performed by Nelson et al. [52], who indicated that users that have a positive attitude toward the brand or product advertised in games have a higher purchase predisposition.

Finally, the contrast in the total number of points in the rightmost halves of both Figures 9 and 10 shows that the advergame had a positive impact on UPI for thirteen participants (65%), while the TV commercial only for seven (35%). This implies that apart from the UE elicitation, the advergame was most effective at increasing participants' purchasing interest. By playing the advergame, users were exposed to the product in a pleasant and enjoyable way, enhancing their interest in it and increasing their likelihood of considering buying it. Overall, advergames can be an effective marketing strategy to inform customers about the product and its characteristics, improve users' understanding of the product, and boost their desire to purchase it.

6. Conclusions

This study aimed to explore engagement and its influence on purchase intention using a physiological tool, specifically electroencephalography. According to the literature, most studies implemented self-report methods to identify the relationship between video games and UE. Additionally, no previous studies have analyzed the UE during an advergame and its implications on the UPI compared to traditional advertising using EEG.

The study's objective was to verify if a more interactive and engaging type of advertising affects the participants, positively influencing their UPI. In general, by the results obtained through EEG and the EEG engagement index, it was possible to define that a more interactive and engaging type of advertising created a higher UE in the participants. Therefore, it was verified that the advergame increased the level of concentration, surveillance, attention, and engagement of the participants while playing. The graphic correlation between the EEG engagement index variation and the UPI presented in the four-quadrant model showed that most of the time, a more interactive and engaging type of advertising positively influences the UPI. In the case of the advergame, the average UPI was higher than that obtained for the TV commercial (AVG UPI: 4.275 > 3.36), indicating a more substantial influence of the advergame in the post-advertising UPI.

The proposed four-quadrant model is a valid aid for better understanding the relation between the UE and the UPI, allowing to allocate the users in four states: (I) high level of engagement and high UPI, (II) high level of engagement and low UPI, (III) low level of engagement and low UPI, and (IV) low level of engagement and high UPI.

Additionally, the results confirmed some of the advergame advantages identified by Mendiz [4]. Advergames offer high exposure to a brand or product because the participants are in constant contact with them compared to traditional advertising; hence, the participants' levels of engagement are higher when interacting with advergames, maximizing user attention. Similarly, we validated the statement by Goh and Ping [11], proving that users' previous attitudes toward the brand positively influenced the UPI.

We can conclude that it is essential to consider the users' engagement as a parameter to improve advertising campaigns and significantly influence the users, attracting them to a product or brand. Equally important is the right choice of methods (self-report and physiological) implemented to perform this kind of analysis.

Advergames can have both benefits and drawbacks when it comes to user experience and enjoyment. On the positive side, advergames can provide an interactive way for users to engage with a product and enhance their experience. However, the inclusion of ads could also impact the user experience and enjoyment level if the ads are intrusive or irrelevant. For example, if ads are placed in a way that disrupts the gameplay or if they are not pertinent to the player, it can lead to frustration and a negative perception of the overall advergame experience. Thus, the benefits and drawbacks of advergames largely depend on how well the ads are designed and integrated into the game and how they are perceived by the users. In this regard, the analysis of users' perceptions through physiological methods, such as EEG, can offer further considerations to improve the ads' design.

This work presented a use case and validation of EEG-based quantitative indicators in advergames, which can be used alongside self-report methods to minimize biased responses. In this research, the experimental setup included a specific advergame and TV commercial; consequently, the results might differ depending on the advertising to which participants are exposed and the degree of affinity with the product or brand. However, the methodological analysis and the results obtained can be equally considered for similar products; in this sense, there is a research opportunity to explore additional contexts and experimental scenarios to increase the validation value. One potential future research topic could be the EEG analysis of the different design features within the advertising development. Characteristics such as colors, sounds, motion, and forms could be investigated independently to study to which extent these stimuli could influence the users' perceptions. By measuring brain activity, researchers can gain a better understanding of how these factors influence engagement with advertisements. For example, how different colors and musical styles in ads affect attention and memory, or how the use of motion in ads affects the ability to retain information. Likewise, a further research goal is the ecological validity analysis in the real world to understand how well the results of the experiments reflect real-world conditions. In this way, we may be able to develop more effective advertising strategies that better engage audiences and improve the effectiveness of advertisements. Additionally, this research could also have applications in the fields of psychology and neuroscience, providing valuable insights into the workings of the human brain in relation to advertising.

The methodology presented in this research can be replicated in similar studies interested in deepening the UE analysis. This study is expected to provide practical evidence and theoretical foundations for new approaches to user perception analysis.

Author Contributions: Conceptualization, I.A.C.J., F.M. and J.S.G.A.; data curation, I.A.C.J., F.M. and E.C.O.; formal analysis, I.A.C.J. and J.S.G.A.; funding acquisition, F.M. and E.V.; investigation, I.A.C.J., S.M., L.U., F.M. and E.C.O.; methodology, I.A.C.J., S.M., L.U. and J.S.G.A.; supervision, F.M. and E.V.; validation, E.C.O., S.M. and L.U.; visualization, S.M., L.U., F.M. and E.V.; writing—original draft, I.A.C.J. and J.S.G.A.; writing—review and editing, I.A.C.J., E.C.O., L.U. and F.M. All authors have read and agreed to the published version of the manuscript.

Funding: This research received no external funding.

Institutional Review Board Statement: All participants provided written informed consent prior to enrolment in the study, for the correctness, transparency and confidentiality protection, according to art. 13 of the European Regulation n. 679/2016 and Legislative Decree 196/2003, and amended by Legislative Decree 101/2018.

Informed Consent Statement: All participants were informed about the experiment and the protection and use of their data. Informed consent was obtained from all subjects involved in the study.

Data Availability Statement: Supporting data of this study is not publicly available due to sensitive information that could compromise the privacy policy.

Conflicts of Interest: The authors declare no conflict of interest.

References

1. Selva, D. El Videojuego Como Herramienta de Comunicación Publicitaria: Una Aproximación al Concepto de Advergaming. *Comunicacion* **2009**, *1*, 141–166.
2. Tavormina, M.G.M.; Tavormina, R. Video Games and COVID-19: How Do Lockdown And Addiction Interact? *Psychiatr. Danub.* **2021**, *33*, 152–157. [PubMed]
3. Pavel, M.; Martin, M. Application of Knowledge in Advergaming as a Possible Source of Competitive Advantage. *J. Compet.* **2011**, *3*, 108–118.
4. Méndiz Noguero, A. Advergaming. Concepto, Tipología, Estrategia y Evolución Histórica. *Rev. ICONO14 Rev. Científica Comun. Tecnol. Emerg.* **2012**, *8*, 37. [CrossRef]
5. Dahl, S.; Eagle, L.; Báez, C. Analyzing Advergames: Active Diversions or Actually Deception. An Exploratory Study of Online Advergames Content. *Young Consum.* **2009**, *10*, 46–59. [CrossRef]
6. Sebastián Morillas, A.; Núñez Cansado, M.; Muñoz Sastre, D. New Business Models for Advertisers: The Video Games Sector in Spain. Advergaming Vs Ingame Advertising. *Rev. ICONO14 Rev. Científica Comun. Tecnol. Emerg.* **2016**, *14*, 256. [CrossRef]
7. Charland, P.; Léger, P.M.; Sénécal, S.; Courtemanche, F.; Mercier, J.; Skelling, Y.; Labonté-Lemoyne, E. Assessing the Multiple Dimensions of Engagement to Characterize Learning: A Neurophysiological Perspective. *J. Vis. Exp.* **2015**, *2015*, 52627. [CrossRef]
8. McMahan, T.; Parberry, I.; Parsons, T.D. Evaluating Player Task Engagement and Arousal Using Electroencephalography. *Procedia Manuf.* **2015**, *3*, 2303–2310. [CrossRef]
9. Freeman, F.G.; Mikulka, P.J.; Prinzel, L.J.; Scerbo, M.W. Evaluation of an Adaptive Automation System Using Three EEG Indices with a Visual Tracking Task. *Biol. Psychol.* **1999**, *50*, 61–76. [CrossRef]
10. Kniestedt, I.; Lefter, I.; Lukosch, S.; Brazier, F.M. Re-Framing Engagement for Applied Games: A Conceptual Framework. *Entertain. Comput.* **2022**, *41*, 100475. [CrossRef]
11. Goh, K.Y.; Ping, J.W. Engaging Consumers with Advergames: An Experimental Evaluation of Interactivity, Fit and Expectancy. *J. Assoc. Inf. Syst.* **2014**, *15*, 388–421. [CrossRef]
12. Brockmyer, J.H.; Fox, C.M.; Curtiss, K.A.; McBroom, E.; Burkhart, K.M.; Pidruzny, J.N. The Development of the Game Engagement Questionnaire: A Measure of Engagement in Video Game-Playing. *J. Exp. Soc. Psychol.* **2009**, *45*, 624–634. [CrossRef]
13. Fox, C.M.; Brockmyer, J.H. The Development of the Game Engagement Questionnaire: A Measure of Engagement in Video Game Playing: Response to Reviews. *Interact. Comput.* **2013**, *25*, 290–293. [CrossRef]
14. Bianchi-Berthouze, N. Understanding the Role of Body Movement in Player Engagement. *Hum.-Comput. Interact.* **2013**, *28*, 40–75. [CrossRef]
15. Martey, R.M.; Kenski, K.; Folkestad, J.; Feldman, L.; Gordis, E.; Shaw, A.; Stromer-Galley, J.; Clegg, B.; Zhang, H.; Kaufman, N.; et al. Measuring Game Engagement: Multiple Methods and Construct Complexity. *Simul. Gaming* **2014**, *45*, 528–547. [CrossRef]

16. Abdul Jabbar, A.I.; Felicia, P. Gameplay Engagement and Learning in Game-Based Learning: A Systematic Review. *Rev. Educ. Res.* **2015**, *85*, 740–779. [CrossRef]
17. O'Brien, H.L.; Toms, E.G. The Development and Evaluation of a Survey to Measure User Engagement. *J. Am. Soc. Inf. Sci. Technol.* **2009**, *61*, 50–69. [CrossRef]
18. Landa-Avila, I.C.; Cruz, M.L. Engagement in a Virtual Reality Game with Gesture Hand Interface. An Empirical Evaluation of User Engagement Scale (UES). In *Lecture Notes in Computer Science (Including Subseries Lecture Notes in Artificial Intelligence and Lecture Notes in Bioinformatics)*; Springer: Cham, Switzerland, 2017; Volume 10289, pp. 414–427. [CrossRef]
19. O'Brien, H.L.; Cairns, P.; Hall, M. A Practical Approach to Measuring User Engagement with the Refined User Engagement Scale (UES) and New UES Short Form. *Int. J. Hum. Comput. Stud.* **2018**, *112*, 28–39. [CrossRef]
20. Mayes, D.K.; Cotton, J.E. Measuring Engagement in Video Games: A Questionnaire. In *Proceedings of the Human Factors and Ergonomics Society*; SAGE Publications: Los Angeles, CA, USA, 2001; pp. 692–696. [CrossRef]
21. Lankoski, P. Player Character Engagement in Computer Games. *Games Cult.* **2011**, *6*, 291–311. [CrossRef]
22. Schoenau-Fog, H. The Player Engagement Process—An Exploration of Continuation Desire in Digital Games. In Proceedings of the DiGRA 2011 Conference: Think Design Play, Hilversum, The Netherlands, 14–17 September 2011.
23. Schønau-Fog, H.; Bjørner, T. "Sure, I Would Like to Continue": A Method for Mapping the Experience of Engagement in Video Games. *Bull. Sci. Technol. Soc.* **2012**, *32*, 405–412. [CrossRef]
24. Corem, Y.; Brown, N.; Petralia, J. Got Skillz? Player Matching, Mastery, and Engagement in Skill-Based Games. In *ACM International Conference Proceeding Series*; Association for Computing Machinery: New York, NY, USA, 2013; pp. 115–118. [CrossRef]
25. Sharek, D.; Wiebe, E. Measuring Video Game Engagement Through the Cognitive and Affective Dimensions. *Simul. Gaming* **2014**, *45*, 569–592. [CrossRef]
26. Wiebe, E.N.; Lamb, A.; Hardy, M.; Sharek, D. Measuring Engagement in Video Game-Based Environments: Investigation of the User Engagement Scale. *Comput. Hum. Behav.* **2014**, *32*, 123–132. [CrossRef]
27. Kirschner, D.; Williams, J.P. Measuring Video Game Engagement Through Gameplay Reviews. *Simul. Gaming* **2014**, *45*, 593–610. [CrossRef]
28. Pope, A.T.; Bogart, E.H.; Bartolome, D.S. Biocybernetic System Evaluates Indices of Operator Engagement in Automated Task. *Biol. Psychol.* **1995**, *40*, 187–195. [CrossRef] [PubMed]
29. Phan, M.H.; Keebler, J.R.; Chaparro, B.S. The Development and Validation of the Game User Experience Satisfaction Scale (GUESS). *Hum. Factors* **2016**, *58*, 1217–1247. [CrossRef] [PubMed]
30. Sreejesh, S.; Anusree, M.R. Effects of Cognition Demand, Mode of Interactivity and Brand Anthropomorphism on Gamers' Brand Attention and Memory in Advergames. *Comput. Hum. Behav.* **2017**, *70*, 575–588. [CrossRef]
31. Sawyer, R.; Rowe, J.; Azevedo, R.; Lester, J. Modeling Player Engagement with Bayesian Hierarchical Models. In Proceedings of the 14th AAAI Conference on Artificial Intelligence and Interactive Digital Entertainment, AIIDE 2018, Edmonton, AB, Canada, 13–17 November 2018; pp. 215–221.
32. Nermend, K.; Duda, J. Methodology for Choosing the Location for In-Game Advertising Billboards. In *Problems, Methods and Tools in Experimental and Behavioral Economics*; Nermend, K., Latuszynska, M., Eds.; Springer Proceedings in Business and Economics: Cham, Switzerland, 2018; pp. 89–97. ISBN 9783319991863.
33. Barclay, P.A.; Bowers, C. Associations of Subjective Immersion, Immersion Subfactors, and Learning Outcomes in the Revised Game Engagement Model. *Int. J. Game-Based Learn.* **2018**, *8*, 41–51. [CrossRef]
34. Khedher, A.B.; Jraidi, I.; Frasson, C. Tracking Students' Mental Engagement Using EEG Signals during an Interaction with a Virtual Learning Environment. *J. Intell. Learn. Syst. Appl.* **2019**, *11*, 89991. [CrossRef]
35. Chaouachi, M.; Frasson, C. Exploring the Relationship between Learner EEG Mental Engagement and Affect. In *Lecture Notes in Computer Science (Including Subseries Lecture Notes in Artificial Intelligence and Lecture Notes in Bioinformatics)*; Springer: Berlin/Heidelberg, Germany, 2010; Volume 6095, pp. 291–293. [CrossRef]
36. Coelli, S.; Sclocco, R.; Barbieri, R.; Reni, G.; Zucca, C.; Bianchi, A.M. EEG-Based Index for Engagement Level Monitoring during Sustained Attention. In Proceedings of the Annual International Conference of the IEEE Engineering in Medicine and Biology Society, EMBS 2015, 2015-Novem, Milan, Italy, 25–29 August 2015; pp. 1512–1515. [CrossRef]
37. Kosmyna, N.; Maes, P. Attentivu: An EEG-Based Closed-Loop Biofeedback System for Real-Time Monitoring and Improvement of Engagement for Personalized Learning. *Sensors* **2019**, *19*, 5200. [CrossRef] [PubMed]
38. Ramirez, R.; Planas, J.; Escude, N.; Mercade, J.; Farriols, C. EEG-Based Analysis of the Emotional Effect of Music Therapy on Palliative Care Cancer Patients. *Front. Psychol.* **2018**, *9*, 254. [CrossRef]
39. Giraldo, S.; Ramirez, R. Brain-Activity-Driven Real-Time Music Emotive Control. In Proceedings of the ICME3 International Conference on Music and Emotion, Jyväskylä, Finland, 11–15 June 2013; Luck, G., Brabant, O., Eds.; University of Jyväskylä, Department of Music: Jyväskylä, Finland, 2013; pp. 11–15.
40. Balasubramanian, S.; Gullapuram, S.S.; Shukla, A. Engagement Estimation in Advertisement Videos with EEG. *arXiv* **2018**, arXiv:1812.03364.
41. Monteiro, D.; Liang, H.N.; Abel, A.; Bahaei, N.; De Cassia Monteiro, R. Evaluating Engagement of Virtual Reality Games Based on First and Third Person Perspective Using EEG and Subjective Metrics. In Proceedings of the 2018 IEEE International Conference on Artificial Intelligence and Virtual Reality, AIVR 2018, Taichung, Taiwan, 10–12 December 2018; pp. 53–60. [CrossRef]

42. Abdullah, T.; Deraman, S.N.S.; Zainuddin, S.A.; Azmil, N.F.; Abdullah, S.S.; Anuar, N.I.M.; Mohamad, S.R.; Zulkifflii, W.F.W.; Hashim, N.A.A.N.; Abdullah, A.R.; et al. Impact Of Social Media Influencer On Instagram User Purchase Intention Towards The Fashion Products: The Perspectives Of Students. *Eur. J. Mol. Clin. Med.* **2020**, *7*, 2589–2598.
43. Chen, M.J. How Design Factors for Advergames Impact Consumers' Attitudes and Behaviors: The Perspective of Engagement Theory. In Proceedings of the 2017 International Conference on E-Business and Internet, New York, NY, USA, 25–27 May 2017. [CrossRef]
44. Catalán, S.; Martínez, E.; Wallace, E. The Role of Flow for Mobile Advergaming Effectiveness. *Online Inf. Rev.* **2019**, *43*, 1228–1244. [CrossRef]
45. Hudders, L.; Cauberghe, V.; Panic, K. How Advertising Literacy Training Affect Children's Responses to Television Commercials versus Advergames. *Int. J. Advert.* **2016**, *35*, 909–931. [CrossRef]
46. Lee, J.; Park, H.; Wise, K. Brand Interactivity and Its Effects on the Outcomes of Advergame Play. *New Media Soc.* **2014**, *16*, 1268–1286. [CrossRef]
47. Vanwesenbeeck, I.; Walrave, M.; Ponnet, K. Children and Advergames: The Role of Product Involvement, Prior Brand Attitude, Persuasion Knowledge and Game Attitude in Purchase Intentions and Changing Attitudes. *Int. J. Advert.* **2017**, *36*, 520–541. [CrossRef]
48. Chang, Y.; Yan, J.; Zhang, J.; Luo, J. Online In-Game Advertising Effect: Examining the Influence of a Match Between Games and Advertising. *J. Interact. Advert.* **2010**, *11*, 63–73. [CrossRef]
49. Castiblanco Jimenez, I.A.; Marcolin, F.; Ulrich, L.; Moos, S.; Vezzetti, E.; Tornincasa, S. Interpreting Emotions with EEG: An Experimental Study with Chromatic Variation in VR. In *Proceedings of the Advances on Mechanics, Design Engineering and Manufacturing IV*; Gerbino, S., Lanzotti, A., Martorelli, M., Mirálbes Buil, R., Rizzi, C., Roucoules, L., Eds.; Springer International Publishing: Cham, Switzerland, 2023; pp. 318–329.
50. Rooney, K.K.; Condia, R.J.; Loschky, L.C. Focal and Ambient Processing of Built Environments: Intellectual and Atmospheric Experiences of Architecture. *Front. Psychol.* **2017**, *8*, 326. [CrossRef]
51. Schulte-pelkum, J.; Riecke, B.; von der Heyde, M.; Bülthoff, H. Influence of Display Device and Screen Curvature on Perceiving and Controlling Simulated Ego-Rotations from Optic Flow. 2004. Available online: https://www.researchgate.net/publication/216055712_Influence_of_display_device_and_screen_curvature_on_perceiving_and_controlling_simulated_ego-rotations_from_optic_flow (accessed on 23 September 2022).
52. Nelson, M.R.; Keum, H.; Yaros, R.A. Advertainment or Adcreep Game Players' Attitudes toward Advertising and Product Placements in Computer Games. *J. Interact. Advert.* **2004**, *5*, 3–21. [CrossRef]

electronics

MDPI

Article

Toward Adaptive Human–Robot Collaboration for the Inclusion of People with Disabilities in Manual Labor Tasks

Nils Mandischer *,†, Marius Gürtler †, Carlo Weidemann †, Elodie Hüsing †, Stefan-Octavian Bezrucav †, Daniel Gossen †, Vincent Brünjes, Mathias Hüsing and Burkhard Corves

Institute of Mechanism Theory, Machine Dynamics and Robotics, RWTH Aachen University, Eilfschornsteinstr. 18, 52064 Aachen, Germany

* Correspondence: mandischer@igmr.rwth-aachen.de

† These authors contributed equally to this work.

Citation: Mandischer, N.; Gürtler, M.; Weidemann, C.; Hüsing, E.; Bezrucav, S.-O.; Gossen, D.; Brünjes, V.; Hüsing, M.; Corves, B. Toward Adaptive Human–Robot Collaboration for the Inclusion of People with Disabilities in Manual Labor Tasks. *Electronics* **2023**, *12*, 1118. https://doi.org/10.3390/electronics12051118

Academic Editors: Juan Ernesto Solanes Galbis, Luis Gracia and Jaime Valls Miro

Received: 27 January 2023
Revised: 22 February 2023
Accepted: 23 February 2023
Published: 24 February 2023

Abstract: While human–robot collaboration is already integrated in industrial and service robotics applications, it is only used with able-bodied workers. However, collaboration through assistive robots is a major driver toward the inclusion of people with disabilities, which was demonstrated in recent research projects. Currently, inclusive robot workplaces have to be customized toward the work process and the individual needs of the person. Within, robots act along a fixed schedule and are not able to adapt to changes within the process or the needs of the interacting person. Hence, such workplaces are expensive and unappealing for companies of the first labor market, and do not realize the full potential of the technology. In this work, we propose a generalized approach toward the inclusion of people with disabilities with collaborative robots. To this end, we propose a system that analyzes the in situ capabilities of a person using a two-stage reasoning approach. The methodology is based on an ontology that allows the matchmaking of individual capabilities with process requirements. Capabilities are modeled in two time frames, through which fast (e.g., fatigue) and slow effects (e.g., worsening of illness) become distinguishable. The matchmaking is used in task allocation to establish high-level control over the assistive system. By this approach, inclusive workplaces become autonomously adaptive to the in situ capabilities of the individual person, without the need for customization. Therefore, collaborative workplaces become not only inclusive, but a contributor toward a labor market for all.

Keywords: system design; people with disabilities; human–robot collaboration; capabilities

1. Introduction

While human–robot collaboration (HRC) in general is a well-studied field, it is often applied to sectors in which able-bodied workers are supported to reduce strain and increase their ergonomics, besides other benefits. However, those general approaches cannot be used to include people with disabilities (PwD; also used as "person with disabilities" in this work), as their capabilities vastly differ from those of the able-bodied worker. HRC is a tool particularly well suited to assist PwD in the first labor market and manual labor tasks. In Gemany, PwD often work in workshops, which are isolated from the regular labor market and only offer simple tasks. Therefore, workshops essentially establish a parallel labor market, i.e., distinction in the "first labor market" and others.

PwD need to be treated individually, as their type of particular disability is often a combination of different partial disabilities. This results in a highly individual capability profile. If HRC is to be used to include PwD in manual labor tasks, the robot has to adapt to the person's individual needs. However, to keep HRC attractive to the company, customization of workplaces is a non-tolerable socio-economical risk, as this raises the costs and turns inclusion into a financial risk. Therefore, our effort is to design a general approach toward HRC that allows the robot to adapt directly to the observed capability profile of the user rather than to a predefined set of capabilities. The technology is intended for use in manufacturing and implements capabilities required in such applications. In this work, we propose the following:

- A matchmaking ontology that models the collaborative process, including sub-ontologies that model the capability profiles and the process steps, and a sub-ontology that maps sensor observations to capability qualifications.
- A system design that allows reasoning on the evolution of the capability profiles and which interfaces with automated task allocation.

Note that a methodology tailored for PwD is also suitable for other user groups. First, from a modeling viewpoint, able-bodied workers are PwD without limited capabilities. Second, the user group of PwD comprises not only people which are permanently disabled, but also the elderly, temporarily disabled people (e.g., due to illness or injury), or people new to the working process. Hence, every person is characterized by a set of (partially) limited or non-limited capabilities (compare Section 3.2) and may be modeled with the proposed ontologies, and, therefore, be supported by a robot in the HRC process.

This work describes the initial steps taken toward adaptive HRC for PwD. We propose a novel methodology, which is currently in a descriptive state but will be validated over the course of the next years. The paper is structured as follows: First, we discuss related work in Section 2. Section 3 presents the system design and modeling of the capability profiles designed for PwD. Section 4 discusses the composition of the sub-ontologies used in the robotic assistance matchmaking ontology (*RAMO*), including the profile ontology (Section 4.1), the process ontology (Section 4.2), and the observable capability emissions ontology (*OCEO*; Section 4.3). Section 5 describes how the ontologies are embedded in automated task allocation. Section 6 discusses the proposed system design and gives an outlook toward future research. Finally, Section 7 summarizes the work.

2. Related Work

For the design of inclusive workplaces in general, as an initial step, a comparison of the individual capability profile with the process requirements is necessary. The comparison allows to adapt the workplace according to the person's individual needs with the best possible support for the PwD. This section first introduces some concepts to perform capability matchmaking for PwD (Section 2.1). Subsequently, related work in knowledge representation is discussed (Section 2.2), which is later used to model information to assess the PwDs' capabilities.

2.1. Capability Matchmaking for People with Disabilities

IMBA (from German: "Integration von Menschen mit Behinderungen in die Arbeitswelt") is a tool to compare and document the human capabilities and the workplace requirements, established by the German Ministry of Health and Social Security [1,2]. The documented capabilities are elicited by means of an occupational health examination. However, IMBA is not a survey instrument in the sense of a test procedure, but rather a documentation method with general assessment aids. Therefore, IMBA does not allow a clear quantitative survey in the assessment of process requirements. Ranz et al. [3] decompose industrial processes on the basis of a directed graph into a sequence of work processes, which in turn can be described as a sequence of fundamental motions. In industry, the method–time measurement (MTM) [4] approach is a common way to model manual work processes using fundamental motions. The primary method *MTM-1* [5] consists of 19 fundamental motions, which are extended by skills such as *hearing*, *seeing*, *calculating*, and *reading*.

The tool RAMB ("robotic assistance for manufacturing including people with disabilities"), introduced in [6] and elaborated in [7], is used to identify those process steps in which the PwD require individual assistance. This is achieved by combining the process decomposition according to MTM and IMBA such that the process requirements can be evaluated uniformly and compared with the capability profile of a PwD. The profile representation in RAMB is discussed in Section 3.2.

2.2. Knowledge Representation

For advanced AI and HRC applications, often many different sensors have to be used. The vast amount of sensor data has to be evaluated. These evaluations, again, have to be related to each other and thus re-evaluated. Furthermore, the knowledge has to be exchanged between humans and robots or other artificial systems. This requires the development of complex knowledge representation systems that can collect and combine data from different sources and integrate them in a meaningful knowledge base which has a common conceptualization for all users as indicated by Prestes et al. [8].

The term ontology originates from philosophy and denotes a systematic representation of existence. However, in computer science, the term is used as a formal conceptualization of a domain of knowledge. That means describing the universe of discourse ontology by a set of definitions, e.g., classes, relations, constraining axioms, properties, and their instances [9]. Ontologies gained special importance through the approach of the Semantic Web [10], in which the World Wide Web should become computer readable through semantic metadata. Meanwhile, ontologies are used in many applications of robotics as complex and expressive knowledge representation systems to improve the autonomy of robots by enabling fast and convenient reasoning [11].

Projects such as the OpenRobots Ontology (ORO) [12] or KnowRob [13] are examples of specific knowledge base representations for robots. For example, KnowRob and its successor KnowRob2 [14] are knowledge processing systems for autonomous personal robots that are to perform everyday manipulation tasks. Their ontologies consist of encyclopedic knowledge of the task domain and general knowledge about the robot's environment, action models, instances, and computables. Action models describe possible manipulations that can be performed, and computables are used for creating instances or relations between instances. The ORO [12] focuses on human–robot interaction needs and implements a fast, standard-based knowledge storage, where different perception modules, users, or reasoners can pull or push needed or inferred knowledge.

3. Toward Adaptive and Inclusive Human–Robot Collaboration

To allow robots to adapt to the PwDs' needs, we base our approach on the sense–plan–act principle. The robot observes its environment using exteroceptive sensors, e.g., cameras and force–torque sensors. The sensor data are processed to gather information on the human behavior. This information is then used to reason on the human capabilities and perform matchmaking regarding the process requirements. The matchmaking is used in a task scheduler to allocate tasks between the human and the robot. In the following section, we present the system design and capability profiling used to this end. Following definitions are used and detailed accordingly:

Generic

T Task
SP_l Standard process
$\mathbf{g}$ Set of features
g_j Feature, $g_j \in \mathbf{g}$
$\mathbf{p}$ Capability profile
f_i Capability, $f_i \in \mathbf{p}$
$\mathbf{b}_k$ Basic element, $\mathbf{b}_k \subseteq \mathbf{p}$

Qualified

$\mathbf{p}^i$ Capability profile qualified for a person i
f_i^i Capability qualified for a person i, $f_i^i \in \mathbf{p}^i$
$\mathbf{b}_{k,l}$ Basic element $\mathbf{b}_k$ qualified in a standard process SP_l

3.1. System Design

The system consists of sequenced modules interfacing with a database (see Figure 1). Sensor data are processed to generate features g_j on the system state. Such features are, for example, the relation between skeleton joints or the force transmitted into the robot structure. The set of features $\mathbf{g} = \{g_0, g_1, \ldots, g_n\}$ is post-processed in a reasoning module to translate features into the human capability profile $\mathbf{p}$ consisting of individual capabilities f_i. Individual features in the feature set may not be available in situ. Hence, some features may be deactivated for pre-reasoning.

The output of the pre-reasoning is the so-called anytime profile $\mathbf{p}_{any}$ (see Section 3.3.2) that is compared to the process requirements in matchmaking. The decision of whether the human can fulfill the task is then forwarded to the task allocation, which generates a plan of actions on the shared working process. To this end, the task planner manages standard task durations in the database. The task schedule is then forwarded to robot control and the human in an accessible way, e.g., using visual or auditory feedback. The task planning module reasons internally on the success state of the performed actions by incorporating environmental information and the standard task durations. Based on this, new information is gathered that is then used for post-reasoning. The latter is mainly used to update the so-called offline profile $\mathbf{p}_{off}$ (see Section 3.3.1), which represents an ex situ forecast of the person's capabilities throughout the day, and which is used as initialization of $\mathbf{p}_{any}$ at the day's start.

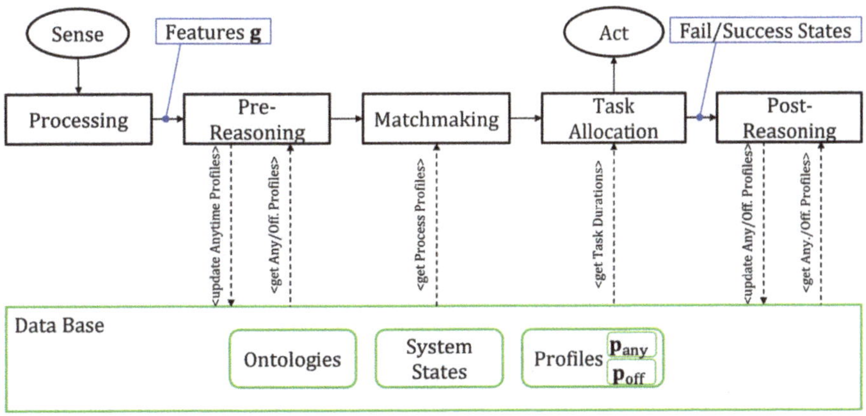

Figure 1. Flowchart of system components consisting of a two-stage reasoning approach, profile matchmaking, task allocation, and sensor processing. The methodology interfaces with a database managing the ontologies, system states and profiles.

3.2. Capability Modeling and Matchmaking for People with Disabilities

In [6], capabilities are defined in relation to a work task T. A task consists of a set of standard processes SP_l, which again define a sequence of basic elements $b_k \subseteq \mathbf{p}$, e.g., *grasp*, *move*. Hereby, index l denotes the standard process and k the specific basic element, which are mutually independent. The qualification of basic elements is set according to a standard process; hence, $b_{k,l}$ denotes the qualification of b_k in SP_l. Further, $\mathbf{p} = \{f_1, f_2, \ldots, f_m\}$ denotes the set of all assessable capabilities ($m = 87$ in RAMB, see Table 1), whereas each capability has a qualification $f_i^i = [-3, 3] \subset \mathbb{Z}$. The qualified capabilities are aggregated in the qualified profile p^i, which is user dependent. After qualification, a regular capability is defined by $f_i^i \geq 0$, and $f_i^i < 0$ denotes a partial disability. While the set of capabilities in each basic element does not change, their qualification $b_{k,l}$ may differ between standard processes containing them, and hence we have the following:

$$||\mathbf{b}_{k,1} - \mathbf{b}_{k,2}|| \geq 0. \tag{1}$$

Hereby, the Manhattan metric is a well-suited choice, as it directly indicates the number of deviations.

Table 1. 87 capabilities defined in RAMB, structured in six main categories: ergonomics, motor functions, perception, cognitive, body motion, and complex capabilities (d.—double sided; s.—single sided).

Cat.	ID	Capability
<ergonomics>		**Posture**
	01	Sitting
	02	Standing
	03	Kneeling
	04	Squatting
		Inclined/Stooped
	05	Sitting, inclined
	06	Sitting, bent
	07	Standing, inclined
	08	Standing, bent
		Arms restrained
	09	Sitting/Standing, arms frontwards
	10	Sitting/Standing, arms overhead
	11	Supine, arms overhead
	12	Lateral, arms frontwards
<motorfunction>		**Head/Neck**
	13	Rotation
	14	Bent, lateral
	15	Bent, sideways
		Torso
	16	Rotation, sit
	17	Rotation, stand
	18	Bent/Erect
		Leg/Foot
	19	Squat
	20	Pedal actuation
		Arm
	21	Reaching, over shoulder, d.
	22	Reaching, over shoulder, s.
	23	Reaching, frontwards, d.
	24	Reaching, frontwards, s.
	25	Reaching, sidewards, d.
	26	Reaching, sidewards, s.
	27	Reaching, backwards, d.
	28	Reaching, backwards, s.
	29	Forearm rotation, d.
	30	Forearm rotation, s.

Cat.	ID	Capability
<motorfunction>		**Hand/Fingers**
	31	Encompassing handle, fist closure, d.
	32	Encompassing handle, fist closure, s.
	33	Encompassing handle, hand closure, d.
	34	Encompassing handle, hand closure, s.
	35	Hand, contact handle, d.
	36	Hand, contact handle, s.
	37	Hand rotation, d.
	38	Hand rotation, s.
	39	Finger, grasping handle, d.
	40	Finger, grasping handle, s.
	41	Finger, contact handle, d.
	42	Finger, contact handle, s.
	43	Thumb, contact handle, d.
	44	Thumb, contact handle, s.
<perception>		**Sight**
	45	Visual acuity, close
	46	Visual acuity, far
	47	Spatial vision
	48	Field of view
	49	Color vision
	50	Mesopic vision
		Hearing
	51	Listening comprehension
	52	Noise/Speech pattern recognition
	53	Frequency
	54	Volume
	55	Direction
<cognitive>		**Basic education**
	56	Vocal output/Speaking
	57	Reading comprehension
	58	Calculating
	59	Writing

Cat.	ID	Capability
<bodymotion>		**Walking/Climbing**
	60	Walking, at level
	61	Walking, on inclined plane
	62	Walking, on loose/uneven ground
	63	Ascending
	64	Climbing
	65	Crawling/Sliding
<complex>		**Lifting**
	66	Horizontal
	67	Floor to waist height
	68	Waist to eye height
	69	Waist to overhead height
		Carrying
	70	Sideways
	71	Front of body
	72	On the back
		Physique
	73	Pushing (objects)
	74	Dragging (objects)
	75	Physical stamina
	76	Balance
		Fine motor skills
	77	Hand dexterity, d.
	78	Hand dexterity, s.
	79	Finger dexterity, d.
	80	Finger dexterity, s.
	81	Hand-arm stability
	82	Control accuracy
	83	Coordination of multiple limbs
	84	Wrist speed
	85	Finger speed
	86	Movement speed, arms
	87	Movement speed, legs

To perform matchmaking, the qualified basic elements are compared to the qualified capabilities of the human $\mathbf{p}^i$, given by

$$\Delta \mathbf{b}^i_{k,l} = \mathbf{b}_{k,l} - (\mathbf{p}^i \cap \mathbf{b}_k). \quad (2)$$

If any entry in $\Delta \mathbf{b}^i_{k,l}$ is positive, the specific basic element in the standard process cannot be performed by the human and, consequently, needs to be allocated to the robot. Note that superscript i denotes the capabilities of a specific human and the derived qualifications, and that a basic element is qualified by the standard process and not by the human. Only the difference in matchmaking is qualified by the human and the standard process; hence, $\Delta \mathbf{b}^i_{k,l}$ carries the corresponding indexes (k: basic element, l: standard process) and the superscript i.

3.3. Dynamics of Capability Profiles

In reality, a capability profile is non-static and changes over time. In [7], this effect is modeled in a Langevin system. The qualified profile can, therefore, be modeled as

$$\mathbf{p}^i(t) = \tilde{\mathbf{p}}^i(t) + \boldsymbol{\epsilon}^i(t), \quad (3)$$

where $\tilde{\mathbf{p}}^i(t)$ are the qualified capabilities originating from the individual disability complex, and where $\boldsymbol{\epsilon}^i(t)$ are small fluctuations in the capabilities. The origin of these capabilities' time dependency is significantly different. While $\tilde{\mathbf{p}}^i(t)$ changes only slowly, it is mostly superimposed by the fast variations in $\boldsymbol{\epsilon}^i(t)$, which is typical in a Langevin system.

To transfer this idea to manual labor tasks, two effects have to be taken into account. First, the worker arrives with a similar capability profile at the start of the day. Second, the capabilities deteriorate over the course of the day. To model this property, two time concepts are introduced: the work time $0 \geq \tau$ (which is delimited by a shift's end) and the global time $t_0 \geq 0$, which is fixated at the start of a day or shift; hence, $t = t_0 + \tau$. Effectively, t_0 becomes constant when observed in the time frame of τ. Therefore, we assume that the influence of the disability changes so slowly that it is assumed constant over the course of the day. Therefore, Equation (3) is rewritten as

$$\mathbf{p}^i(t) := \mathbf{p}^i(t_0, \tau) = \tilde{\mathbf{p}}^i(t_0) + \boldsymbol{\epsilon}^i(\tau). \quad (4)$$

In adaptive HRC, two types of profiles are managed: (1) the offline profile that establishes a baseline to the matchmaking on a per-day basis, and (2) the anytime profile that reflects the in situ capabilities of the person.

3.3.1. Offline Profile

The offline profile is defined as the global time-dependent qualified capability vector

$$\mathbf{p}^i_{off}(t) = \tilde{\mathbf{p}}^i(t_0) + \Delta\tilde{\mathbf{p}}^i(\tau) + \boldsymbol{\nu}(t), \quad (5)$$

where $\Delta\tilde{\mathbf{p}}^i(\tau)$ is the daily fluctuation, and $\boldsymbol{\nu}(t)$ is a noise vector in which entries are independent. The offline profile is initialized with $\Delta\tilde{\mathbf{p}}^i(\tau = 0) = \mathbf{0}$, and $\tilde{\mathbf{p}}^i(t_0 = 0)$ incorporating the data from a medical preliminary examination (MPE) as usually performed in advance of including PwD in work processes. As this—and all sensor data later in the process—is subject to noise or personal bias (medical personnel), $\boldsymbol{\nu}(t)$ is introduced in Equation (5).

With the MPE, $\mathbf{p}^i_{off}(t)$ is constant over the course of a day. To better predict the fluctuations during the day and, therefore, decrease the size of the fluctuations in $\boldsymbol{\nu}(t)$, $\Delta\tilde{\mathbf{p}}^i(\tau)$ is re-evaluated in two ways: (1) continuously by post-reasoning, and (2) by the mining of past profiles and fitting $\Delta\tilde{\mathbf{p}}^i(\tau)$ accordingly. The latter establishes a global optimization problem with the aim of reducing $\boldsymbol{\nu}(t)$ to a minimum, and hence,

$$\lim_{t->\infty} ||\boldsymbol{\nu}(t)|| = 0 \quad (6)$$

In states close to initialization, the values in $\boldsymbol{\nu}(t)$ will superimpose the other factors, particularly $\Delta\tilde{\mathbf{p}}^i(\tau)$ (see Figure 2).

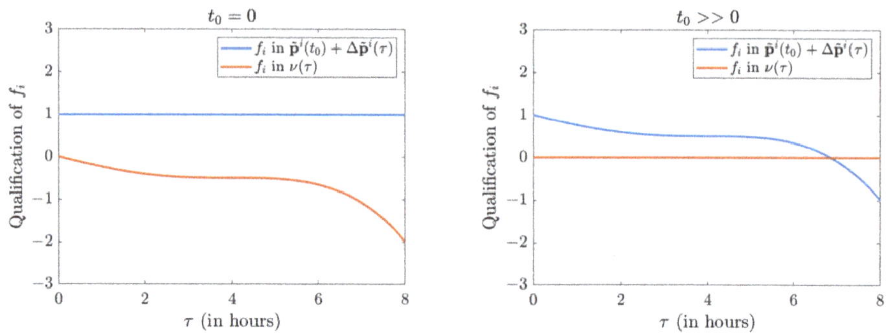

Figure 2. Exemplary evolution of a qualified capability in the offline profile from initialization ($t_0 = 0$) to optimal convergence ($t_0 >> 0$). Note, while the course of the function is continuously displayed, in reality, it is discrete in the range $[-3, 3] \subset \mathbb{Z}$.

3.3.2. Anytime Profile

The anytime profile is defined as the in situ qualified capability vector

$$\mathbf{p}^i_{any}(t) = \mathbf{p}^i_{off}(t) + \boldsymbol{\eta}. \quad (7)$$

The anytime profile is the main output of the reasoning modules and represents the in situ capabilities of the person superimposed by stochastic system noise $\boldsymbol{\eta}$, which is mainly influenced by the following:

- Noise in the sensor signal.
- Uncertainties in feature extraction.
- Propagated uncertainties from hidden Markov model (HMM; see Section 4.3).
- Uncertainties in the modeling approach.

As uncertainties in the model and HMM are Gaussian, and sensor noise is assumed white noise, $\boldsymbol{\eta}$ may be modeled as Gaussian noise.

4. Ontology-Based Reasoning

The next step toward automatic task allocation and scheduling is the estimation of a person's in situ capabilities. As mentioned in Section 3.1, sensor data are processed into features g_j representing certain information on the human behavior, the environment, and the interaction between human and robot. For data processing, typical methods are used, e.g., OpenPose [15] for skeleton tracking or the method by Buondonno and De Luca [16] for interaction force computation. The explicit origin of processed sensor data is not relevant, as the methodology discussed in this section establishes a generalist approach to transform these data into a capability profile estimate.

Equation (2) establishes a common base at the human's capabilities to perform capability matchmaking onto process requirements. There are two ways to reach these capabilities f_i: from the sensors, and from the task defined by the work process. Therefore, there exists an open loop from the processed sensor data to the task. This dependency is modeled in the novel robotic assistance matchmaking ontology (*RAMO*) that is depicted in Figure 3.

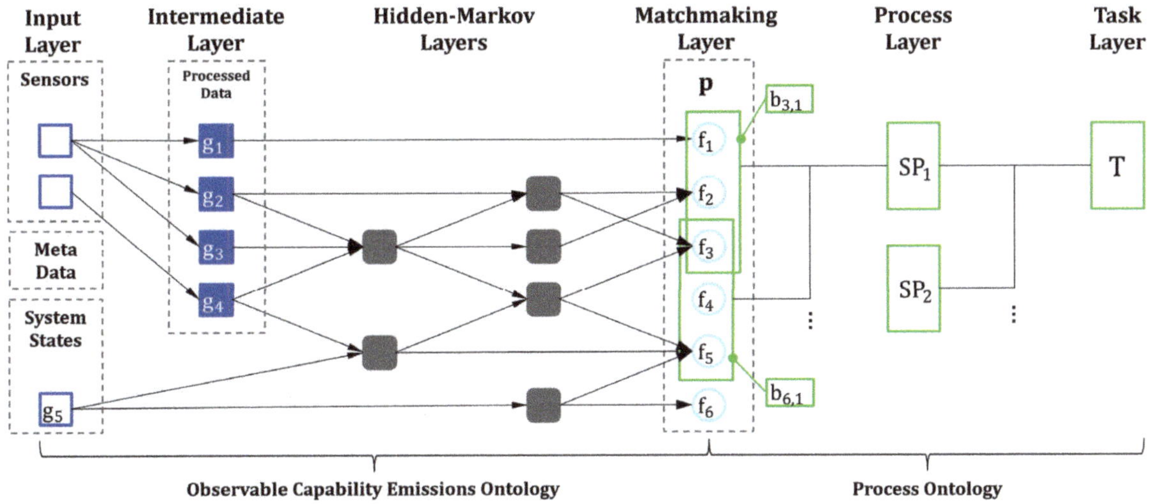

Figure 3. Composition of the robotic assistance matchmaking ontology (*RAMO*) and its system layers. The sub-ontologies observable capability emissions ontology (*OCEO*) and process ontology are connected by the matchmaking layer. The matchmaking layer embeds the profile ontology to model the capability profiles $\mathbf{p}_{any}$ and $\mathbf{p}_{off}$.

RAMO consists of two sub-ontologies. First, the observable capability emissions ontology (*OCEO*) models the emissions of the qualified capabilities measurable by exteroceptive sensors. Second, the process ontology as used in RAMB [7] models the tasks and their structural components. Both sub-ontologies are connected by the profile ontology defined by the capabilities f_i.

4.1. Profile Ontology

The profile ontology models the relations and influences between the capabilities f_i of a human, which are accumulated in the profile $\mathbf{p}$. Capabilities are structured in six main categories: ergonomics, motor functions, perception, cognitive, body motion, and complex capabilities. Usually, human capabilities are not mutually independent, e.g., the capability to perform a *squat* (f_{19}) also influences the capability of *climbing* (f_{64}). Particularly, complex capabilities, e.g., *horizontal lifting* (f_{66}), are highly dependent on basic capabilities, e.g., *reaching sideways* (f_{25}) or *torso rotation* (f_{16} and f_{17}).

Relations between capabilities are modeled directed and may have minor, major, or no influence on the other capabilities. A directed relation is chosen, as some capabilities may be influenced by multiple other capabilities, but the cause of the qualification may be manifold. For example, an impaired capability *reaching sideways* may either come from an impairment in the limbs or the torso, which manifests in different capabilities. Hence, this example is modeled as depicted in Figure 4. Capabilities and their relations are modeled based on *IMBA* [1,2] and according to observations from user tests during the *Next Generation* https://www.nextgeneration-mrk.de/ (accessed on 22 February 2023) project.

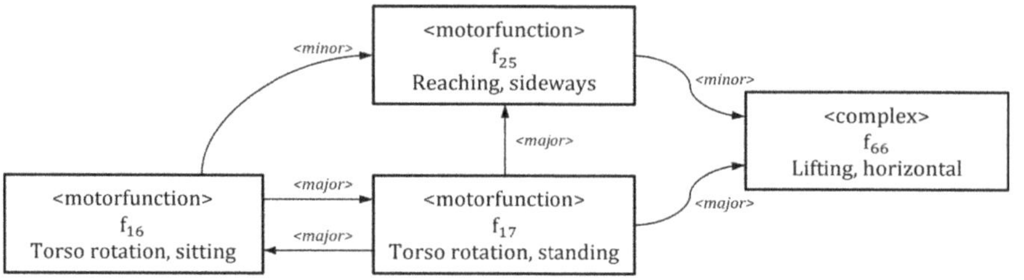

Figure 4. Exemplary modeling of relations in the profile ontology.

4.2. Process Ontology

The process ontology models the structure explained in Section 3.2 (compare right-hand side in Figure 3). A work process is defined as a task T. This task consists of standard processes SP_l. Standard processes are characterized by entry and end states. These are defined with the aim to reduce process dependencies between standard processes, i.e., all sequenced basic elements should be accumulated in one SP_l. Therefore, standard processes are interchangeable if the real system fulfills the requirements of their entry state. A standard process then consists of basic elements $b_{k,l}$ that are sequenced in a fixed manner and must not be interchanged. However, the basic elements can still be inaccessible to the human and, therefore, the robot needs to assist or take them on completely. It is subject to the task planner to assign basic elements to both agents or solely to the robot. There might occur the situation that the human can fulfill only a small margin of basic elements in a SP_l and in which it is more efficient for the robot to take on the complete SP_l.

4.3. Observable Capability Emissions Ontology

The observable capability emissions ontology (*OCEO*) is based on the assumption that qualifications of capabilities manifest in features observable by sensors, system states, and meta information (compare Figure 3). Sensor data are processed into features characterizing the human behavior, the environment, and other agents. System states represent the continuous evaluation of successfully fulfilled actions in the task planner (see Section 5) and meta data are a composition of non-sensor data from outside the system, e.g., the information collected in a medical examination. Sensor, meta, and system data form the *input layer*. The features are then fed into a multilevel hidden Markov model (compare, for example, [17]). In a HMM, non-observable states cause so-called emissions, which are observable and deliver evidence on the origin of the emission's cause, e.g., impaired vision may result in an unsteady gait. The unsteady gait may be measured by a skeleton model and, therefore, may be used as an emission in the HMM. In a multilevel approach, emissions exist that cause emissions themselves, hence obscuring the capability qualifications over multiple layers. Transitions in and between the *hidden Markov layers* are annotated with their uncertainties, which are propagated toward the *matchmaking layer*.

It is to be noted that some features are directly measurable (e.g., f_1 in Figure 3), while others (e.g., f_4 in Figure 3) are not observable at all. Further, features or emissions do not directly qualify a capability. Instead, they map onto a qualification value in the range $[-3,3] \subset \mathbb{Z}$, whereas not all qualification values may be connected to the same emission or feature. Indeed, some qualification values may only manifest in very specific emissions, e.g., a minor vision impairment (f_{46}) may result in unsteady gait, but a major vision impairment may also result in tripping or collisions with the environment. The example is detailed in Figure 5.

In the *matchmaking layer*, the qualified capability profile is compared with the qualified basic elements. Hence, a decision is made as to whether a basic element may be allocated to the human. To this end, the propagated uncertainties are analyzed and reasoned on. While the *matchmaking layer* itself is not part of either the OCEO or the process ontology, both sub-ontologies end in the capability profile. Both sub-ontologies and the *matchmaking layer* generate the robotic assistance matchmaking ontology *RAMO*.

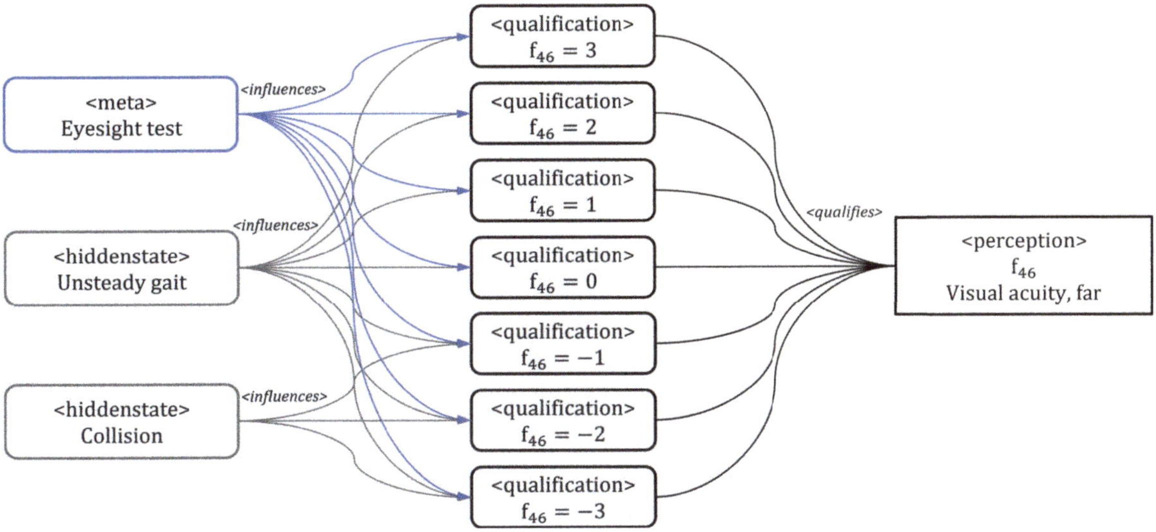

Figure 5. Exemplary modeling of qualification through observation (here through hidden states and meta data) in *OCEO*.

5. AI Task Planning for Human-Robot-Teams

Automated task planning or AI task planning methods compute the actions that must be executed by agents to bring the system to a desired goal state. The goal state of the methodology described in this work is the fulfillment of task T. AI task planning methods (e.g., [18]) perform two steps: (1) select, order, and instantiate abstractly defined actions to specific actions, and (2) optimize the preliminary plan with respect to a set of criteria. The execution of specific actions brings the system from a given initial state to a given goal state, e.g., the generic action *grasp agent object place* can be instantiated to *grasp robot screw table* (read: "the robot grasps the specific screw at the specific table"). This action is assigned to the robot agent. The ordering and instantiation process of actions considers the dependencies between these actions, e.g., a *place* action is selected only when an agent handles an object, and hence, beforehand, a *grasp* action has to be performed. This is also depicted in the standard processes, which define a sequence of basic elements. Note that the task planner may either allocate individual basic elements $\mathbf{b}_{k,l}$ or the whole standard process SP_l to the individual agent. The result of the first solving step is a preliminary plan containing ordered and instantiated actions a_i, whereas a_i is the robot-readable abstraction of the basic elements $\mathbf{b}_{k,l}$. In a second step, AI task planning methods optimize the preliminary plan with respect to a set of criteria (e.g., time). The methods adapt the start times and the order of the planned actions, without violating the dependencies between them, to obtain a plan with minimal makespan (execution time). The final result is the plan

$$\pi =< a_0, \dots, a_n > . \tag{8}$$

The advantages of AI task planning methods are that they require only abstractly defined actions (analogous to $\mathbf{b}_k$), an initial planning state, and a set of goals that must hold in a goal state for solving a planning problem [19]. AI task planning methods can be used as flexible, high-level control strategies. They are able to generate new plans for manifold planning situations, e.g., when new orders arrive or when the characteristics of the agents change. The latter is particularly important when the capabilities of an agent are expected to be dynamically adaptable, which is the case for PwD. For each new planning situation, only the initial and the goal states must be re-set, while the remaining definitions and the planning process itself must not be further adapted. AI task planning approaches were already successfully deployed in several of standard HRC applications using the *ROSPlan* (https://kcl-planning.github.io/ROSPlan/ (accessed on 22 February 2023)) framework [20–22] and may be adapted toward the methodology described in this work.

The capability profiles $\mathbf{p}^{i}_{any}(t)$ are encoded as preconditions for the defined generic actions of a planning problem (see Algorithm 1).

Algorithm 1 Definition of a generic action, of an initial state, and of a goal state.

```
(:action grasp
:parameters (?r - robot ?i - item ?f1, f2 - capability)
:precondition (and (near ?r ?i) (?f1 <= 3) (?f2 > 0))
:effect (and (item_grasped (?r ?i))))
—
(:objects o1 - item r1 - robot)
—
(:init (= f1 -2) (= f2 2))
—
(:goal (and item_grasped(r1, o1)))
```

Further, these profiles are instantiated to specific values as part of the initial state of a planning problem, analogous to the specification in Section 3.2. In Algorithm 1, the *grasp* action has the constraint $f_2 > 0$ as one of its preconditions, i.e., this action can be planned and assigned to a human only if in the initial state of the planning problem, the *standing* capability f^i_2 is instantiated to a value > 0, e.g., to the value $f^i_2 = 3$. The solving process automatically assigns all planned actions to agents by taking into consideration the capability profiles $\mathbf{p}^{i}_{any}(t)$ that are defined in relation to a work task T.

As described in Section 3.3, the capability profiles are dynamic. The allocation of tasks to the agents (robots or PwD) must consider these changes. AI task planning methods enable a seamless integration of these changes for the planning process. Solely the initial state of the planning problems must be adapted, e.g., the considered capability can be modified for a new planning problem from $f^i_2 = 2$ to $f^i_2 = -2$. This is the only modification required by the planning system, such that it can determine new plans that consider the new profiles.

The generated plan π must be executed such that the application reaches the targeted goal state in the real world. The AI task planning framework *ROSPlan* enables a combined planning and execution approach [23]. It uses *action interface* modules to send execution commands to the agents (robots or PwD) and to supervise the execution of the dispatched actions. As part of this work, the existing AI task planning framework is extended with further modules to allow system states as input to the reasoning modules (see g_5 in Figure 3). The new modules translate the execution state (i.e., success or failure) of the actions to features that can be integrated with the reasoning modules. These again transport important knowledge for the assessment of the capability profile $\mathbf{p}^{i}_{any}(t)$ (see transition to post-reasoning in Figure 1). In this way, capability profiles $\mathbf{p}^{i}_{any}(t)$ and $\mathbf{p}^{i}_{off}(t)$, respectively, are additionally updated based on the execution success of the actions and not only based on sensor data. This also closes the control loop from the task execution toward the initial capability assessment.

6. Discussion and Outlook

As mentioned already in Section 1, the proposed methodology is only a system design and ontology description that has not yet been implemented in real work processes. Therefore, this section discusses some aspects that need to be considered when deploying the proposed methodology.

Due to its novel character, there are manifold uncertainties in the later implementation, and particularly the instantiation of the ontologies and the reasoning system likewise.

While the process model, including its process ontology and the central capability profile (compare Section 3.2) are already defined, relations between the capabilities (see Section 4.1), and the transitions and states in *OCEO* (see Section 4.3) are yet to be fully defined. The major challenges in modeling the proposed system are in the design of the *hidden Markov layers*. By Bayesian optimization, it is possible to define the probabilistic dependencies between the emissions and the hidden states, i.e., the capability qualifications. However, emissions have to be modeled manually, which is more complicated than in more modern learning methods, in which features and intermediate states are connected with minimal supervision. On the contrary, in HRC, it is desired to have more explainable AI [24,25], particularly when it comes to direct interaction. Therefore, we expect the HMM to yield more explainability and acceptance in later deployment. However, it remains to be seen how well the emissions can be defined, and how large the uncertainties will be in the final implementation. Note that we assume that there will be fewer features than the total number of qualifications of capabilities, and hence, the instance of the *OCEO* will be under-determined. To this end, of particular importance will be the definition of the relations within the capabilities (e.g., see Figure 4). Well-defined dependencies will reduce the uncertainties propagated from the HMM and the number of degrees of freedom of the whole *OCEO* instance. To this end, we will also reduce the number of capabilities m defined in the capability profile, which again will be performed after a profound modeling of dependencies to assess the influence of the capabilities on the matchmaking decision.

Besides the technical aspects, there are also social and ethical uncertainties. While we assume that such a matchmaking system will raise the efficiency and acceptance of HRC workplaces in manual labor tasks, the opposite may manifest. In particular, when able-bodied workers and PwD share the same work place, and the situation occurs in which the system reallocates certain tasks from the able-bodied worker to the robot (e.g., caused by exhaustion or distraction), the interacting worker may become confused or skeptical. This behavior is expected in the first interactions. However, we assume that over a longer period of working with the HRC workplace, a learning process will take place that lets the worker appreciate the technology and its supportive actions rather than being repelled by it. We further assume that by establishing a work process capable of supporting able-bodied workers and PwD likewise, also the acceptance toward PwD will be increased. This is what makes full inclusion in first labor market processes possible in the first place.

In the following years, we will delve further into the methodology. We aim to implement and evaluate, in particular, the matchmaking ontology *RAMO*. Therefore, we hope to facilitate a discussion on the topic and to use this paper as a vehicle for the improved inclusion of PwD in HRC processes of the first labor market.

7. Conclusions

In this work, we first introduced how capabilities of PwD are modeled and how their dynamics evolve over the course of a workday and over a long time span. To this end, we introduced two time concepts τ and t_0 which eventually manifest in a Langevin system. The emerging capability profile $\mathbf{p}$ states the basis to a two-sided matchmaking ontology consisting of the two sub-ontologies: the process ontology and the observable capability emissions ontology (*OCEO*). While the process ontology models the qualification of sub-sets of capabilities, so-called basic elements $b_k \subset \mathbf{p}$ from the work task T, *OCEO* models how the full capability profile is derived from features g_j, originating from sensors, meta data, and system states. Based on the combined ontology, robotic assistance matchmaking ontology (*RAMO*), people may be observed and matched with process requirements to assess the specific in situ need of assistance. In addition, we showed how the ontology is used in automated task planning to generate dynamic work schedules based on the ontology-based reasoning approach. This results in a system description that allows dynamic and intuitive HRC not only for PwD, but for everyone.

Author Contributions: Conceptualization, N.M., M.G., C.W., E.H., S.-O.B. and D.G.; methodology, N.M., M.G., C.W., E.H., S.-O.B. and D.G.; writing—original draft preparation, N.M., M.G., C.W., E.H., S.-O.B. and D.G.; writing—review and editing, N.M., M.G., C.W., E.H., S.-O.B., D.G., V.B., M.H. and B.C. All authors have read and agreed to the published version of the manuscript.

Funding: This research received no external funding.

Data Availability Statement: No data was generated for this work.

Acknowledgments: We would like to thank Caritas, LVR, and Stiftung Wohlfahrtspflege for funding the predecessor project *Next Generation*, which laid the foundations for our new reflections.

Conflicts of Interest: The authors declare no conflict of interest.

Abbreviations

The following abbreviations are used in this manuscript:

AI	Artificial intelligence
HMM	Hidden Markov model
HRC	Human–robot collaboration
IMBA	Integration von Menschen mit Behinderung in der Arbeitswelt translated: "Integration of people with disabilities in the labor market"
OCEO	Observable capability emissions ontology
ORO	OpenRobots ontology
MPE	Medical preliminary examination
MTM	Method–time measurement
PwD	People/person with disabilities
RAMB	Robotischer Assistenzgrad für Menschen mit Behinderung translated: "Robotic assistance for manufacturing including people with disabilities"
RAMO	Robotic assistance matchmaking ontology

References

1. Greve, J.; Jochheim, K.A.; Schian, H.M.; Kaiser, H. Erhebungsverfahren zur beruflichen Integration behinderter Menschen–vom ERTOMIS-Verfahren zum IMBA-Informations system. *Die Rehabil.* **1997**, *36*, 34–38.
2. Schian, H.M.; Kaiser, H.; Weinmann, S.; Kleffmann, A.; Sturtz, A.; Ramsauer, F.; Rexrodt, C.; Dieckmann, H. IMBA—Introduction: The Instrument for Specialists in Job Rehabilitation and Integration. Available online: http://www.imba.de/documents/einfuehrungenglisch.pdf (accessed on 22 February 2023).
3. Ranz, F.; Hummel, V.; Sihn, W. Capability-based Task Allocation in Human-robot Collaboration. *Procedia Manuf.* **2017**, *9*, 182–189. [CrossRef]
4. Bright Maynard, H.; Stegemerten, G.J.; Schwab, J.L. *Methods-Time Measurement*; McGraw-Hill: New York, NY, USA, 1948.
5. Bokranz, R. *Produktivitätsmanagement von Arbeitssystemen: MTM-Handbuch*, 1st ed.; Schäffer-Poeschel: Stuttgart, Germany, 2006.
6. Hüsing, E.; Weidemann, C.; Lorenz, M.; Corves, B.; Hüsing, M. Determining Robotic Assistance for Inclusive Workplaces for People with Disabilities. *Robotics* **2021**, *10*, 44. [CrossRef]
7. Weidemann, C.; Hüsing, E.; Freischlad, Y.; Mandischer, N.; Corves, B.; Hüsing, M. RAMB: Validation of a Software Tool for Determining Robotic Assistance for People with Disabilities in First Labor Market Manufacturing Applications. In Proceedings of the International Conference on Systems, Man, and Cybernetics, Prague, Czech Republic, 9–12 October 2022.
8. Prestes, E.; Carbonera, J.L.; Rama Fiorini, S.; Jorge, V.A.M.; Abel, M.; Madhavan, R.; Locoro, A.; Goncalves, P.; Barreto, M.E.; Habib, M.; et al. Towards a core ontology for robotics and automation. *Robot. Auton. Syst.* **2013**, *61*, 1193–1204. [CrossRef]
9. Gruber, T.R. A translation approach to portable ontology specifications. *Knowl. Acquis.* **1993**, *5*, 199–220. [CrossRef]
10. Berners-Lee, T.; Hendler, J.; Lassila, O. The Semantic Web: A new form of Web content that is meaningful to computers will unleash a revolution of new possibilities. *Sci. Am.* **2002**, 284, 24–30.
11. Wang, S.; Zhang, Y.; Liao, Z. Review on the Knowledge Graph in Robotics Domain. In Proceedings of the 3rd International Conference on Computer Engineering, Information Science & Application Technology (ICCIA 2019), Sanya, China, 22–24 October 2019; Atlantis Press: Paris, France, 2019. [CrossRef]
12. Lemaignan, S.; Ros, R.; Mösenlechner, L.; Alami, R.; Beetz, M. ORO, a knowledge management platform for cognitive architectures in robotics. In Proceedings of the 2010 IEEE/RSJ International Conference on Intelligent Robots and Systems, Taipei, Taiwan, 18–22 October 2010; pp. 3548–3553. [CrossRef]
13. Tenorth, M.; Beetz, M. KNOWROB—Knowledge processing for autonomous personal robots. In Proceedings of the 2009 IEEE/RSJ International Conference on Intelligent Robots and Systems, St. Louis, MO, USA, 11–15 October 2009; pp. 4261–4266. [CrossRef]

14. Beetz, M.; Bessler, D.; Haidu, A.; Pomarlan, M.; Bozcuoglu, A.K.; Bartels, G. Know Rob 2.0—A 2nd Generation Knowledge Processing Framework for Cognition-Enabled Robotic Agents. In Proceedings of the 2018 IEEE International Conference on Robotics and Automation (ICRA), Brisbane, Australia, 21–25 May 2018; pp. 512–519. [CrossRef]
15. Cao, Z.; Hidalgo, G.; Simon, T.; Wei, S.E.; Sheikh, Y. OpenPose: Realtime Multi-Person 2D Pose Estimation Using Part Affinity Fields. *IEEE Trans. Pattern Anal. Mach. Intell.* **2021**, *43*, 172–186. [CrossRef] [PubMed]
16. Buondonno, G.; de Luca, A. Combining real and virtual sensors for measuring interaction forces and moments acting on a robot. In Proceedings of the 2016 IEEE RSJ International Conference on Intelligent Robots and Systems (IROS), Daejeon, Republic of Korea, 9–14 October 2016; Staff, I., Ed.; IEEE: Piscataway, NJ, USA, 2016; pp. 794–800. [CrossRef]
17. Fine, S.; Singer, Y.; Tishby, N. The Hierarchical Hidden Markov Model: Analysis and Applications. *Mach. Learn.* **1998**, *32*, 41–62. [CrossRef]
18. Coles, A.; Coles, A.; Fox, M.; Long, D. *Forward-Chaining Partial-Order Planning*; AAAI Press: Menlo Park, CA, USA, 2010; pp. 42–49.
19. Ghallab, M.; Dana, N.; Traverso, P. *Automated Planning and Acting*; Cambridge University Press: Cambridge, UK, 2016. [CrossRef]
20. Bezrucav, S.O.; Corves, B. Improved AI Planning for Cooperating Teams of Humans and Robots. In Proceedings of the Planning and Robotics Workshop (PlanRob) at The 30th International Conference on Automated Planning and Scheduling, Online, 22–23 October 2020. [CrossRef]
21. Cashmore, M.; Coles, A.; Cserna, B.; Karpas, E.; Magazzeni, D.; Ruml, W. Replanning for Situated Robots. In Proceedings of the Twenty-Ninth International Conference on Automated Planning and Scheduling, Berkeley, CA, USA, 11–15 July 2019; Benton, J., Lipovetzky, N., Onaindia, E., Smith, D.E., Srivastava, S., Eds.; AAAI Press: Menlo Park, CA, USA, 2019; pp. 665–673.
22. Buksz, D.; Cashmore, M.; Krarup, B.; Magazzeni, D.; Ridder, B. Strategic-Tactical Planning for Autonomous Underwater Vehicles over Long Horizons. In Proceedings of the IEEE/RSJ International Conference on Intelligent Robots and Systems (IROS), Madrid, Spain, 1–5 October 2018; pp. 3565–3572. [CrossRef]
23. Cashmore, M.; Fox, M.; Long, D.; Magazzeni, D.; Ridder, B.; Carrera, A.; Palomeras, N.; Hurtos, N.; Carreras, M. ROSPlan: Planning in the Robot Operating System. In Proceedings of the Twenty-Fifth International Conference on Automated Planning and Scheduling, Jerusalem, Israel, 7–11 June 2015; Brafman, R., Ed.; AAAI Press: Palo Alto, CA, USA, 2015; pp. 333–341.
24. Setchi, R.; Dehkordi, M.B.; Khan, J.S. Explainable Robotics in Human-Robot Interactions. *Procedia Comput. Sci.* **2020**, *176*, 3057–3066. [CrossRef]
25. Paleja, R.; Ghuy, M.; Arachchige, N.R.; Jensen, R.; Gombolay, M. The Utility of Explainable AI in Ad Hoc Human-Machine Teaming. In Proceedings of the 35th Conference on Neural Information Processing Systems (NeurIPS 2021), Online, 6–14 December 2021. [CrossRef]

electronics

Article

Robotic Cell Reliability Optimization Based on Digital Twin and Predictive Maintenance

Dimitris Mourtzis *, Sofia Tsoubou and John Angelopoulos

Laboratory for Manufacturing Systems and Automation, Department of Mechanical Engineering and Aeronautics, University of Patras, 26504 Rio Patras, Greece
* Correspondence: mourtzis@lms.mech.upatras.gr; Tel.: +30-2610-910-160

Abstract: Robotic systems have become a standard tool in modern manufacturing due to their unique characteristics, such as repeatability, precision, and speed, among others. One of the main challenges of robotic manipulators is the low degree of reliability. Low reliability increases the probability of disruption in manufacturing processes, minimizing in this way the productivity and by extension the profit of the company. To address the abovementioned challenges, this research work proposes a robotic cell reliability optimization method based on digital twin and predictive maintenance. Concretely, the simulation of the robot is provided, and emphasis is given to the reliability optimization of the robotic cell's critical component. A supervised machine learning model is trained, aiming to detect and classify the faulty behavior of the critical component. Furthermore, a framework is proposed for the remaining useful life prediction with the aim to improve the reliability of the robotic cell. Thus, following the results of the current research work, appropriate maintenance tasks can be applied, preventing the robotic cell from serious failures and ensuring high reliability.

Keywords: reliability optimization; robotic cell; Industry 4.0; digital twin; predictive maintenance; machine learning; remaining useful life

Citation: Mourtzis, D.; Tsoubou, S.; Angelopoulos, J. Robotic Cell Reliability Optimization Based on Digital Twin and Predictive Maintenance. *Electronics* **2023**, *12*, 1999. https://doi.org/10.3390/electronics12091999

Academic Editors: Juan Ernesto Solanes Galbis, Luis Gracia and Jaime Valls Miro

Received: 6 March 2023
Revised: 22 April 2023
Accepted: 24 April 2023
Published: 25 April 2023

1. Introduction

With the advent of the Industry 4.0 revolution, conventional manufacturing systems have transformed into smart factories. Companies are attempting to integrate Industry 4.0 technologies into their production lines to remain competitive in demanding market needs [1,2]. Robotic systems are essential parts of smart factories since they can perform a wide range of different tasks in volatile environments [3]. Robotic systems are capable of executing multiple tasks, relieving humans from repetitive, tiring, boring, and dangerous work. In the manufacturing domain, robots are used for pick and place applications, materials handling, drilling, palletizing, welding, painting, assembly processes, and more [4]. Since robotic systems are integral parts of industries, high reliability is a prerequisite. However, robot reliability remains a popular topic in the industry since robotic systems are complex and consist of several components. Nowadays, the need for reliable and safe robots is more important than ever since the current generation of robots is collaborative and coexists with humans. For industries equipped with robots, safety is also a critical issue since several accidents have been reported at workstations with robots, and some of them were deadly. However, it should be pointed out that the major cause of these accidents was human error rather than robot malfunction [5]. Additionally, the author in [5] points out that the topic of robot reliability is strongly related to the reliability of its components. Robots suffer from low reliability because their equipment, such as motors, sensors, wiring, and end-effectors, is prone to wear and tear. The configuration of the robots and the type of connection between the components that constitute a robotic system have a huge impact on its reliability. According to studies, DELTA and SCARA robots are more reliable compared to other articulated robots since they consist of fewer links and joints that are connected serially. In reliability modeling, for systems that consist of components that are serially connected, the failure of a component will cause the failure of the whole system. On the other hand, parallel connections demonstrate redundancy, and the failure of one component will not cause the failure of the whole system. The same research work declares that the lifespan of a typical industrial robot is about 10–15 years due to the deterioration of its main mechanical components. As a result, it becomes apparent that by analyzing, assessing, and seeking ways to optimize the reliability of the robotic components, the reliability of the whole robotic system can be improved.

In scientific research, there are plenty of works around the reliability assessment of robots. In addition, different reliability modeling methods for robots are presented in [6]. Detailed fault tree analysis (FTA) and reliability block diagram (RBD) models of a robotic system are provided to analyze and assess the robot's reliability. The authors highlight the capabilities of FTA in finding the root causes of failures and the logical failure path that will lead to the system's failure. The most common traditional reliability assessment techniques are discussed along with their key differences, and a network reduction method of a spot-welding robotic cell's RBD is provided. RBD has widely been used in the literature to analyze and assess the reliability of systems [7].

Engineers are always concerned about the reliability of their machines and are constantly seeking ways to optimize them. This concern has become more significant in recent years due to the high complexity of modern manufacturing systems, which results in an increase in failure modes. Reliability is considered a significant performance indicator of manufacturing systems [8]. The emergence of cutting-edge technologies such as the industrial internet of things (IIoT), smart sensors, big data, digital twin (DT), cyber-physical systems (CPS), cloud computing (CC), artificial intelligence (AI), and so on, has changed the way reliability is assessed. With the DT concept, a twin of the physical system can be constructed, and its condition can be monitored and assessed. DT is considered an optimization tool for the reliability of manufacturing systems. The reliability modeling approaches that have been widely used so far are considered obsolete and ineffective for capturing and analyzing the complexity of today's manufacturing systems. Traditional reliability assessment methods are based on probabilistic theory and expert opinions, which make the reliability assessment less accurate. For complex systems like robotic systems, which consist of several interdependent components with different failure modes, it is challenging to comprehend and extract reliable mathematical models. Additionally, these methods are conducted offline, which does not give the ability to assess the reliability of robots in real time. For this reason, engineers are moving toward data-driven approaches and artificial intelligence (AI) techniques for reliability assessment, leveraging the huge amount of condition monitoring data produced every day [9].

The term "reliability" is highly associated with "maintainability". Proper maintenance will result in higher machine reliability. In an effort to become smarter, engineers are now shifting their focus from failure prevention to failure prediction [10]. PdM is a promising approach that leverages Industry 4.0 tools and technologies with the aim of predicting failures before they occur [11]. The PdM domain is gaining a lot of attention from industries since, according to Reference [12], applying PdM can increase production by 25–35%, reduce maintenance costs by 25–35%, eliminate breakdowns by 70–75%, and reduce breakdown time by 35–45%. Similarly, the author in [5] suggests periodic maintenance to prevent robotic failures and achieve higher reliability of robotic systems. In Reference [13], the authors highlight the importance of PdM since it offers the longest life and highest reliability of equipment. Next, the authors in [14] suggest a data-driven PdM approach for reliability assessment and improvement due to simplifications and assumptions taken into account during the modeling of the robotic cell, such as the selection of the exponential distribution as the reliability function and the constant failure rate.

1.1. Aim of Research Work

The aim of this research work is to improve the reliability of a robot by improving firstly the reliability of its critical component. The bearings of stepper motors are selected as the critical components. This paper presents the predictive maintenance approach that is based on a supervised machine learning algorithm with the aim to detect and classify the faulty behavior of the bearing. The steps that are conducted during a predictive maintenance approach are specific and should be executed with the right sequence. However, most of the steps are executed considering the kind of data in which we are interested. In order to conduct a reliable predictive maintenance approach, the data should be prepared and preprocessed suitably in order to be able to extract features from them. This preparation of data is different every time and depends on the kind of data. After, the feature selection should be performed, which is a challenging issue. It is difficult to know which features are capable of adequately differentiating the data. Time-domain or/and frequency domain features can be used. The feature that will be used is not the same every time, and it depends on the system that is under study and the type of data that has been collected from it. For instance, according to the literature, the selection of the proper ML model is a difficult process. By the time current robotic systems are complex and composed of multiple components with different failure rates, one way to improve the reliability of the whole system is to first improve the reliability of its critical components. This can be accomplished by studying the reliability parameters of the critical components. Specifically, reliability can be optimized by increasing the mean time between failures (MTBF) and/or decreasing the mean time to repair (MTTR) of the critical component. Therefore, it becomes apparent that detecting faulty behavior and predicting the time to failure of the critical component is crucial.

1.2. Contribution of Research Work

The contribution of this research is to present a novel approach based on Industry 4.0 technologies in order to optimize the reliability of industrial robotic manipulators, based on the combination of digital twin (DT), and predictive maintenance (PdM) is presented. Concretely, the DT is proposed as a method to optimize the reliability of a robotic cell by the real-time monitoring of the robot due to embedded sensors and IoT. The starter steps for constructing a DT of the robot are provided. The digital model of the robot is modeled and simulated in MATLAB. This research is based on the principle that the reliability of the robot is based on the reliability of its components. Thus, a PdM approach is presented to detect and classify the faulty behavior of the critical component, and a framework for estimating its remaining useful life (RUL) is presented. With PdM, the right time to conduct maintenance can be determined, saving the company unnecessary maintenance costs. The digital twin (DT) of the robotic cell will be used for monitoring the status of the cell and its components. When coupled with the developed machine learning algorithms, more accurate predictions of the remaining useful life (RUL) of the robots' components are feasible. Concretely, the implementation of the digital twin creates added value for the existing robotic cell in several ways, as explained in the following paragraphs. The digital twin of the robotic cell is accessible remotely, thus enabling engineers to monitor and make any adjustments to the robotic arms' operation remotely. Specifically, the robotic arms, which have been modeled in the case study presented in this manuscript, are installed in a caged robotic cell, which handles heavy and bulky automotive components. Consequently, remote monitoring and control are safer for human operators/engineers. By monitoring the digital twin, it is possible to detect when the robotic arm requires maintenance before it breaks down. This can help to reduce repair costs and minimize unnecessary downtime.

Beyond the key contributions of the digital twin presented in the previous paragraph, additional functionalities are foreseen, such as virtual testing, for simulating and testing changes in the operation of the robotic cell. This can facilitate the identification of potential malfunctions and by extension optimize the cell's performance before making any alterations to the physical installation. In the context of virtual experimentation, the proposed digital twin framework can be utilized for training purposes. Concretely, new human operators and engineers can be trained in a plethora of scenarios, which by extension helps in reducing the risk of accidents. In Figure 1, the primary services of the DT are depicted.

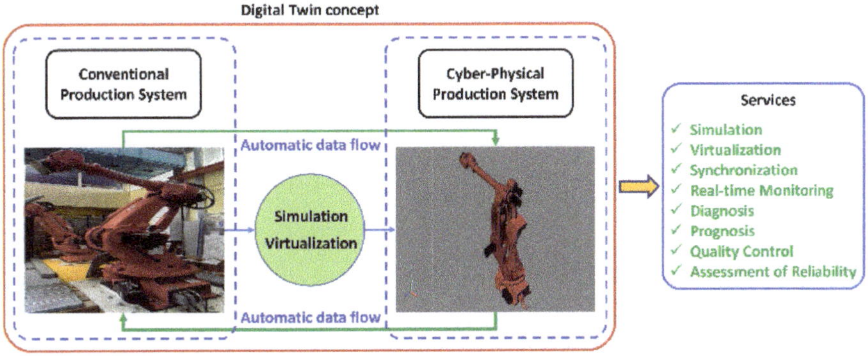

Figure 1. Digital twin services (developed by the authors).

The remainder of the paper is organized as follows. In Section 2, the state of the art is presented. In Section 3, the system architecture and the predictive maintenance flowchart are provided, and in Section 4, the case study is presented. In Section 5, the implementation is made, and in Section 6, the results are discussed. Finally, in Section 7, the research work is concluded, and future work is pinpointed.

2. State of the Art

2.1. Robotic Systems

Today's industries are highly automated and equipped with robots. Industries are widely integrating robotic systems into their production lines with the aim to leverage the benefits of robots and increase their productivity. Industrial revolutions have affected the robotic domain [1]. Indeed, since the first utilization of the industrial robot in the 1960s, considerable advancements in the robotic industry have been made [15]. In the Robotics 1.0 era, which took place between the 1960s and 1980s, the primary role of robots was to relieve humans from monotonous, repetitive, and dangerous tasks. In this era, robots were dangerous, and since they did not have any sense of their environment, they were bounded by fences. During the second generation of robots (Robotics 2.0 era), which occurred between the 1990s and 2000s, collaborative and sensitive robots were introduced, but they were slow when interacting with humans. In 2008, Universal Robotics released the first collaborative (combot) robot in the market. Due to advancements in sensing devices, robots were equipped with sensors where feedback was provided. Currently, we are experiencing the Industry 4.0 and Robotics 3.0 era. This is called the Digital Robotic era, where the robotic industry is leveraging Industry 4.0 technologies such as internet of things (IoT), digital twin (DT), and cyber-physical systems (CPS), to name a few. Furthermore, predictive maintenance on flexible mobile robots [16] or robots with flexible elements [17] involves using data analysis and machine learning algorithms to anticipate potential issues and failures in robots before they occur. This approach can help increase the lifespan of the robot, minimize downtime, and reduce maintenance costs [18]. Path planning and obstacle avoidance are major concerns for mobile robots. In this era, robotic systems are connected to the Internet and can exchange a huge amount of data in real time, ensuring machine-to-machine (M2M) communication. The integration of artificial intelligence (AI) into robots has made them smarter machines. The Robotics 4.0 era is expected to begin in the 2020s and will be characterized by more cognitive, perceptive, and intelligent robots. The human–machine interaction will be more friendly and natural, integrating the artificial intelligence of things (AIoT) [19,20]. Cutting-edge technologies such as 5G, deep learning, reinforcement learning, cloud computing, and big data will give rise to smart robotic systems being capable of adapting to complex unstructured environments and performing intricate manufacturing processes [21]. In Figure 2, the four robotic revolutions are illustrated.

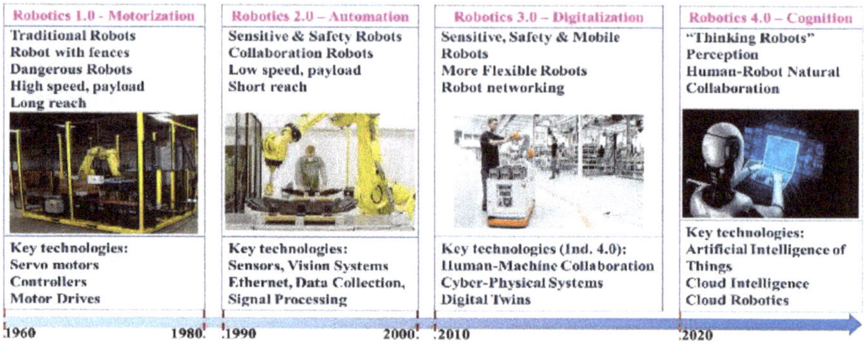

Figure 2. Robotic evolutions from 1960 up to today and key milestones (developed by the authors).

2.2. Reliability in Manufacturing Systems

The aim of each industry is to ensure that its equipment will perform its intended tasks in a predefined time and under certain conditions. From an engineering perspective, reliability is defined as the ability of a system or a component to serve its required functions in a determined period and under certain conditions. Considering the constant failure rate (λ), the reliability of a component is calculated by the following equation:

$$R(t) = e^{-\lambda t} \quad (1)$$

The exponential distribution function is used commonly in reliability formulas due to its efficiency in dealing with constant failure rates. The assumption of the constant failure rate is widely applied in reliability modeling approaches due to the fact that most of the components exhibit a constant failure rate during their useful time [22]. Reliability analysis is an important process in order to ensure that the performance of the equipment is effective when construed in meeting deadlines, satisfying customers, and maintaining the good reputation of the company [6]. The reliability of a system depends on its structure, the flow of materials into it, and the reliability of the machines and components that constitute the system [23], and it can be determined by analyzing and studying its failures [24]. Reliability is closely related to the terms of availability, maintainability, and safety. By improving a system's reliability and maintainability, its availability can be increased [24]. Maintainability is a system's crucial characteristic that indicates how easy and costly it is for a system or a component to be restored to a condition in which it can perform its required functions when maintenance is performed [25]. Today's manufacturing systems should be highly safe since there is a lot of cooperation with humans [26]. However, increased safety in a system can sometimes cause a decline in its reliability.

In practice, the reliability assessment is made by studying the reliability parameters, namely mean time to failure (MTTF), mean time between failures (MTBF), and mean time to repair (MTTR). Reliability assessment is carried out throughout the lifecycle of a component or a system. The traditional reliability assessment includes the reliability modeling of the system, reliability data collection (λ, MTTF, MTBF, MTTR), component reliability assessment, and at the last stage system reliability assessment. The aim of reliability modeling is to extract mathematical models that represent the failure logic relationships between the different system components. From the reliability engineering viewpoint, a complex system is one that consists of many interdependent components with various failure modes, and it is challenging to decompose this into series or/and parallel connections or to recognize the type of connections. The most common reliability modeling approaches are RBD, FTA, failure mode and effect analysis (FMEA), Petri nets

(PNs), and Markov analysis (MA). Each reliability modeling approach examines from a different perspective the reliability of the system that is under study [6]. For instance, RBD is a more representative approach that analyzes the structure of the system and the relationships between its components (series/parallel), while the aim of FTA is to find the root causes of failures and the failure logical paths [22]. The FTA method has been extensively used in industries such as the automotive and aircraft domains [27].

The reliability of complex systems has been thoroughly investigated in recent decades. In our research work, we presented and explicitly discussed the conventional methods. More specifically, traditional reliability modeling approaches such as reliability block diagram (RBD), fault tree analysis (FTA), Petri nets (PNs), and Markov analysis (MA) have been used extensively in the past to study and model the reliability of manufacturing systems. However, these methods present some limitations, which constitute them ineffective for today's complex systems. Firstly, these methods are conducted offline, thus near-real-time health assessment is not feasible. Moreover, these methods are based on modeling the structure of the system seeking the type of connection between the numerous components, which is a challenging process for today's complex systems. On the contrary, modern approaches are mostly based on the acquisition and analysis of data from discrete components (e.g., motors, bearings, etc.), which is an easy and financially viable way of monitoring the health of complex systems. However, such approaches appear to have limited performance in practical complex situations due to various working conditions of the system (i.e., the working environment) and low fault signature signal to noise ratio.

Above all, in this research work, a novel method for the assessment and optimization of robotic manipulators based on the DT and PdM is presented. Concretely, the technology of DT is proposed for the simulation and near-real-time data exchange, which ensures the near-real-time monitoring of the robot along with PdM approaches, aiming at the detection and classification of critical component malfunctions. By using a combinatory method of the DT and PdM approaches, a good estimation of the appropriate time to conduct maintenance can be calculated. By extension, the reliability and performance of the robotic cell can be improved.

Since the maintenance of manufacturing systems has a huge impact on their reliability, the reliability can be assessed by constructing a DT of the investigated system, leveraging the huge amount of operating data that is captured due to sensors. In this way, the faulty behavior of the system can be diagnosed, and the time of failure can be estimated. In Figure 3, the evolution of reliability assessment is presented. Through the synchronization made possible by sensors, data can be updated from the physical system in real time, enhancing in this way the decision making for the maintenance procedures.

Hardware, software reliability, and the impact of human interaction on reliability constitute factors that all should be considered for the assessment of the overall reliability of manufacturing systems. These factors should first be examined separately and after being combined in order to extract a single overall indicator for the reliability of manufacturing systems. The reliability of the hardware components is time-dependent; the failures occur during the operation phase, and the last phase in the bathtub curve is the wear out. RBD, FTA, and MA are some examples of hardware reliability modeling approaches. On the other hand, software reliability is time-independent; most errors occur during the design phase, and the last phase in the bathtub curve is obsolescence where there are no more upgrades that can be performed. Finally, an important factor that should be considered for the reliability of production and manufacturing systems is human interaction. Manual systems are highly affected by human operators' actions. On the contrary, automated systems are less susceptible. Since today's systems are designed in such a way to cooperate and interact with humans, human reliability should be studied. Despite that there is a lot of research regarding hardware and software reliability when it comes to the impact of the human factor in the reliability of manufacturing systems, there is a lack of publications. Primarily, it happens because it is difficult to model and predict human behavior. Humans may be stressed, get tired, make false estimations, and as a result may cause a decline in the reliability of manufacturing systems [8,9,27]. The topic of the impact of humans on the reliability of manufacturing systems should be studied extensively, especially for Industry 5.0 systems, where the core of this era will be the symbiosis and coexistence of humans and machines. In Figure 4, the factors that affect the reliability of manufacturing systems are illustrated.

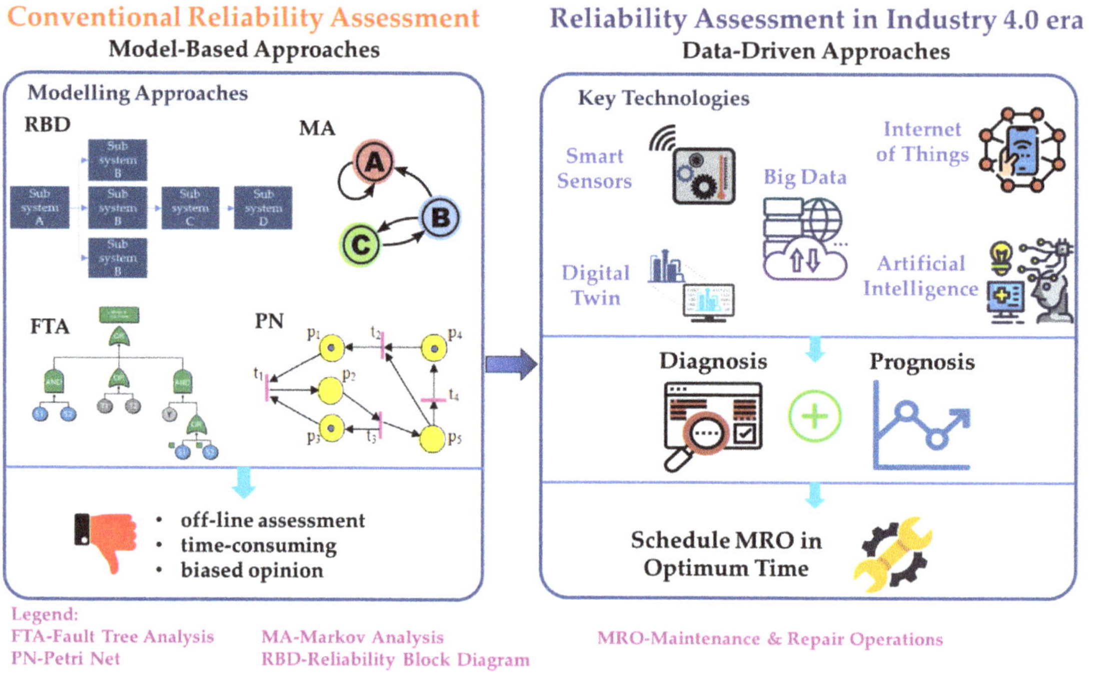

Figure 3. The evolution of reliability assessment in Industry 4.0 era (developed by the authors).

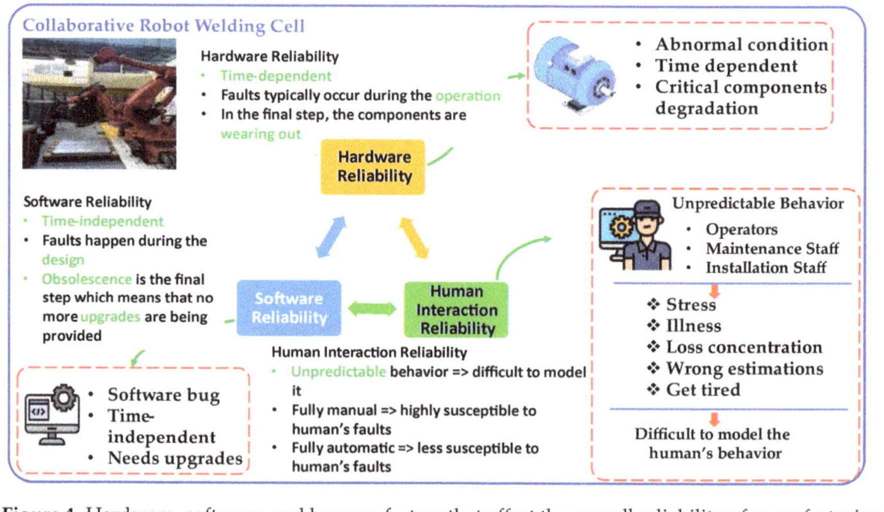

Figure 4. Hardware, software, and human: factors that affect the overall reliability of manufacturing systems (developed by the authors).

In this research, we are focused on hardware reliability and particularly on the assessment and improvement of a robotic cell's reliability. In complex systems, such as robotic cells, the different components that make up the system present different failure rates (λ). All these components should operate correctly in order to achieve high performance of the robotic cell. The failure of a single component may lead to the failure of the whole system. As a result, the failure probability of each component should be studied in order to assess the overall failure probability of the whole system [6]. To gain more knowledge about the failure probability of the main mechanical components of a robotic cell, a literature review was conducted, and their failure rates are presented in Table 1.

Table 1. Failure rates of robotic components in the literature.

Components	Failure Rate λ (Failure/hour)	References
Teach Pendant	4.72×10^{-5}	[28]
Controller	3.79×10^{-5}	[28]
Robotic Manipulator	1.56×10^{-5}	[28]
Wiring Loom	3×10^{-7}	[29]
Motor	1.85×10^{-5} 1.88×10^{-3} 5.01×10^{-5} 2×10^{-6}	[30] [31] [28] [32]
Sensor	2.35×10^{-5} 2.41×10^{-3} 3.42×10^{-6} 1.54×10^{-6} 1.76×10^{-6}	[30] [33] [33] [33] [33]
Break	4.3×10^{-6}	[32]
End Effector	114×10^{-6}	[32]

2.3. Digital Twin

The industrial sector has been affected by digitalization. Today's systems are composed of interconnected intelligent components. Digital twin (DT) is one of the main technologies of the fourth Industrial Revolution [34]. The first definition of DT was provided by Michael Grieves in 2002 during a presentation about product lifecycle management (PLM) [35]. The first deployment of DT was in the aerospace industry. Later in 2011, DT was first defined in relation to Industry 4.0, and in 2013, the first studies of DT in the manufacturing domain emerged [36]. In Reference [35], an analytical definition of the DT in the manufacturing domain is provided. More specifically, it is mentioned that: "The DT consists of a virtual representation of a production system that is able to run on different simulation disciplines that are characterized by the synchronization between the virtual and real system, thanks to sensed data and connected smart devices, mathematical models, and real-time data elaboration. The topical role within Industry 4.0 manufacturing systems is to exploit these features to forecast and optimize the behavior of the production system at each life cycle phase in real time." Thus, it becomes apparent that we are experiencing an era where everything can be digitalized. DT is a virtual or digital representation of physical entities. Physical entities can range from sensors to machines, people, processes, and even whole factories [37]. So, the technology of DTs is not limited to focusing on just one entity but can also be applied to entire systems, creating the idea of digitalized factories [38].

In Reference [35], the key areas of the DT applications in the manufacturing domain are presented, which are the following: (i) Production Planning and Control, (ii) Maintenance, and (iii) Layout Planning. DT can contribute to the maintenance domain. More specifically, the term DT is highly associated with the term predictive maintenance (PdM). By constructing a DT of the physical system, its health status can be monitored, and the best time to arrange maintenance can be found. A topic that is under discussion is the connection between the DT and simulation [39]. Although traditional simulations, such as CAD, are helpful for product design, they are static. Practically, it means that the traditional simulation cannot be simulated for what is currently happening in the under-study system. This challenge can be overcome with the DT. DT is regarded as the most advanced simulation method for modeling, optimization, and simulation. The simulation domain has evolved by leveraging digital technologies. Indeed, with the integration of the industrial internet of things (IIoT), the simulation techniques became more dynamic and more accurate. The key difference is in the real-time data that are captured by embedded smart sensors, enabling engineers to determine if the system is being operated properly or if modifications should be made [39]. Thus, it becomes apparent that the DT technology combines a lot of technologies and tools, such as sensors, historical databases, cloud storage, and so on to achieve real-time monitoring of the production systems [38].

2.4. Maintenance in Manufacturing Systems—Predictive Maintenance in Industry 4.0

Equipment maintenance is a vital process in industries since 60–70% of the total production costs account for industrial equipment maintenance [40]. Maintenance is defined as the repair or replacement of equipment with the aim to increase its original expected operating time. Ineffective maintenance strategies can cause several problems such as unplanned downtime, decreased productivity, and high maintenance costs, minimizing in this way the reliability and the availability of the equipment [41]. In particular, according to [42], ineffective maintenance strategies can reduce a plant's productivity by between 5 and 20%, and unplanned downtime may cost USD 50 billion annually for global producers. The aforementioned results highlight the need for the effective deployment of maintenance strategies in manufacturing systems. In the literature, there are several maintenance strategies, and the most prevailing are Reactive or corrective or run to failure (R2F) maintenance, preventive maintenance (PvM), and predictive maintenance (PdM). In the Industry 4.0 era, the R2F and PvM strategies are considered ineffective. In Figure 5, the evolution of the industrial maintenance strategies is illustrated, highlighting the key differences between them.

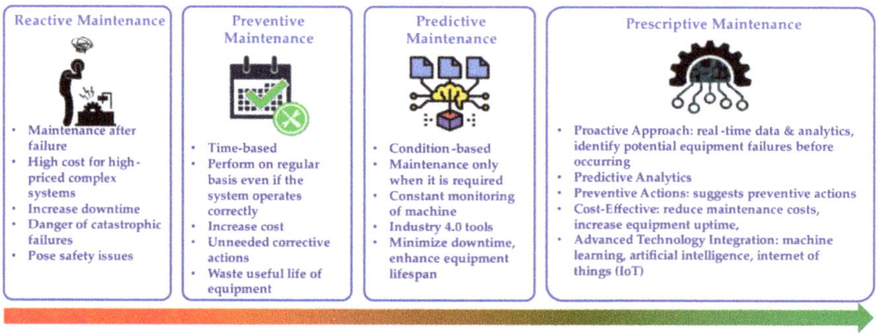

Figure 5. The evolution of industrial maintenance strategies (developed by the authors).

In R2F maintenance, repair, and replacements are conducted only after the machine fails. R2F maintenance may make sense for low-cost systems, i.e., for systems that the repair or replacement will be short and not costly [41]. PvM often known as scheduled maintenance is a type of maintenance that is conducted on a regular basis in order to avoid failures by performing frequent checks on the equipment. This maintenance strategy is applied regularly even if the system operates correctly, and its goal is to maintain the equipment in optimal condition maximizing in this way its availability. However, applying maintenance based on a schedule will lead to repairing or replacing components that still have a significant remaining useful life. Concretely, too early maintenance may lead to a waste of spare parts and resources, and too late maintenance may lead to catastrophic failures [11,41,43]. It becomes apparent that the main challenge of PvM is to find the right time to conduct maintenance. This challenge can be overcome by applying a smart maintenance approach, named predictive maintenance (PdM).

Industry 4.0 gave rise to several concepts and one of them is PdM. PdM is one of the main pillars of Industry 4.0, and it is regarded as the digital type of machine maintenance [13]. PdM utilizes predictive tools such as artificial intelligence algorithms to determine when maintenance is truly necessary to be conducted [11]. In Figure 6, the PdM framework is illustrated. As depicted, PdM is based on the constant monitoring of the equipment, which is achieved by the integrated sensors in the under-study machine. The core of the PdM approach is the data. With the use of sensors and the integration of the IIoT, a huge amount of operation data are produced, which are used to assess the condition and health of the monitored machine. These data may contain alarms and warnings about the abnormal condition of the equipment. Machine learning (ML) methods are widely used in the PdM domain due to their ability to handle high dimensional and multivariate data. ML techniques can be used to detect and classify the faulty behavior of the equipment, as well as predict the time to failure based on intelligent predictive algorithms. The prediction of RUL has become increasingly significant in machine health monitoring. By predicting the RUL of a component, the time of failure can be estimated, and MRO can be arranged at the optimum time. The utilization of historical data is also essential in order to produce more accurate results from a PdM strategy. Consequently, the R2F and PvM strategies must have been already implemented in order to collect data for PdM modeling [11,41,42].

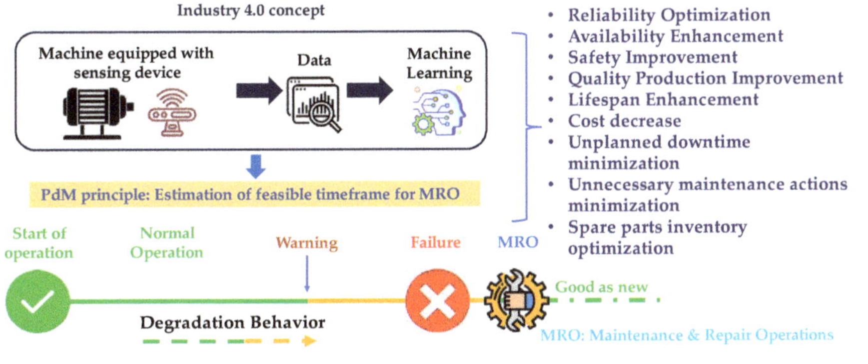

Figure 6. The predictive maintenance framework in Industry 4.0 era (developed by the authors).

2.5. Novelty of Proposed Framework

The key issue identified is that robotic manipulators suffer from low reliability as a consequence of the wearing out of the individual mechanical components. Therefore, based on the principle that the reliability of the robot depends on the reliability of its components, in this manuscript, a framework for the reliability optimization of a robotic cell's critical component is proposed. This framework is based on the predictive maintenance domain, and the aim is to conduct diagnosis and prognosis in the critical component in order to find the optimum time to arrange maintenance. A predictive maintenance approach is proposed with the aim to detect and classify the faulty behavior of the robotic cell's critical component based on a supervised machine learning technique. A PdM approach, which is based on ML techniques, is composed of multiple steps that should be implemented with the right sequence to have a reliable result. The most challenging tasks when conducting machine learning are the selection of the suitable features, as well as the selection of the suitable ML model. The features are the inputs to the ML model. Only useful and distinctive features should be used for faulty behavior classification. For this reason, a supervised ranking technique, named analysis of variance (ANOVA), was used with the aim to use only the useful features, i.e., features that can adequately differentiate the faulty behavior. The selection of the ML model that will be trained is a difficult process. For this reason, we leveraged the capabilities of the Classification Learner App of MATLAB, which gives us the ability to train a variety of well-known supervised ML models, and the ML model with the highest accuracy, i.e., the model that makes the minimum misclassifications, was selected.

3. Proposed System Architecture

3.1. General System Architecture

In the Industry 4.0 era, the interest is focused on data-driven approaches with the aim to assess and optimize the reliability of complex systems, such as robots. In Figure 7, a system architecture for the assessment and optimization of the reliability of a spot-welding robotic cell is presented. Concretely, the system architecture is divided into three steps. In the first step, the robotic cell is discretized into its main modules, and the DT concept of the robot that constitutes the robotic cell is presented; in the second step, the selection of the critical component is made; and in the third step, the component-oriented PdM approach that utilizes an available dataset is implemented. The scope of the PdM is to conduct a diagnosis and prognosis on the monitored equipment in order to determine the optimum time to arrange maintenance.

The discretization of the robotic cell is necessary in order to define the main components of the cell as well as to proceed with the identification of the critical components. The robotic cell that is under study is composed of two robots. A way to improve the reliability of a system is to make a digital counterpart of the real system. The DT concept is proposed in this study as a tool that ensures automatic data flow between the physical and the simulated system. By integrating sensors, automated data flow is achieved between the physical and digital robot. By using expert opinions, publicly available reliability databases, maintenance manuals, and FTA, the selection of the critical component of the robotic cell is made. Depending on the aforementioned tools, the stepper motors of the robotic cell are selected as the critical components. Moreover, the utilization of the failure mode and effect (FMEA) analysis is proposed. The risk criticality assessment in FMEA is made by calculating the risk priority number (RPN) of each component. The procedure for selecting the critical component is depicted in Figure 8. Additionally, this research proposes a component-oriented predictive maintenance approach since the reliability of a robot depends on the reliability of its components. However, the main focus of this paper is the selection of the critical component. The digital twin (DT) technology is proposed as a method to optimize the reliability of a robot due to its ability to capture and monitor the health status of the robot in real time. In order to construct a digital twin, three main parts are needed: (i) physical system, (ii) virtual system, and (iii) type of communication between them. In this research, a start for the development of a digital twin was made. The physical system, SMART NJ-370-3.0 robot, is located in the laboratory, the virtual system is made in the Simulink environment of MATLAB, and our future work will be focused on the connection between the two systems in order to ensure the automated dataflow in real time.

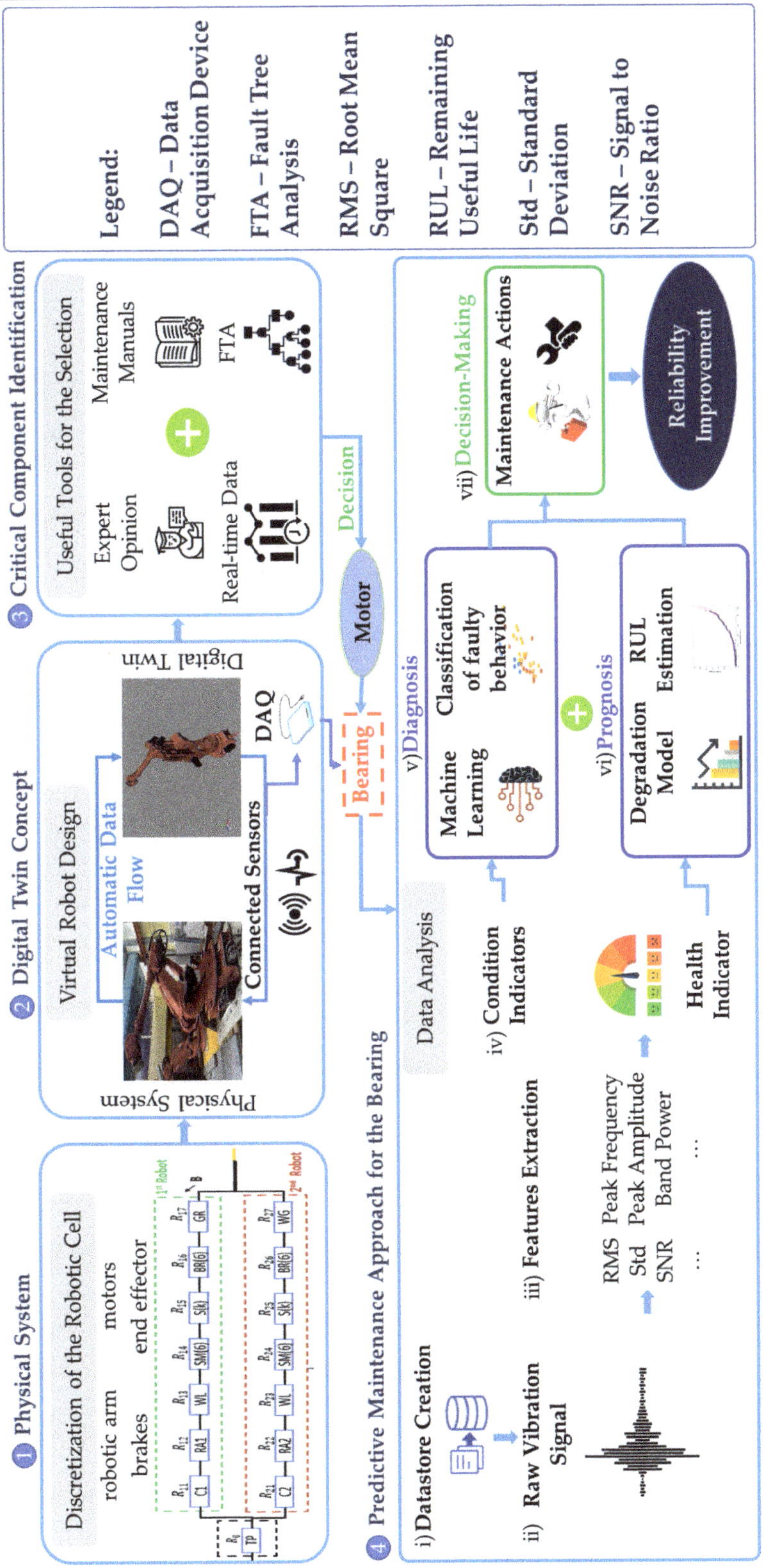

Figure 7. General system architecture (developed by the authors).

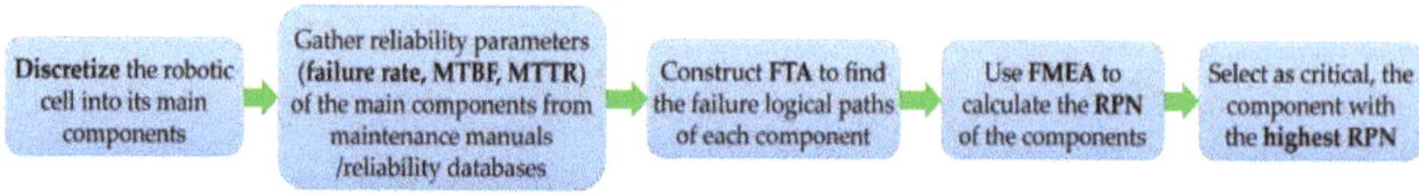

Figure 8. FMEA steps to calculate the risk priority number (developed by the authors).

The operation of robots depends to a large extent on the operation of actuators as they are the equipment that feeds the robot with motion. According to studies, a lot of failures of motors are a result of bearing failure. As a result, the bearing is selected as the critical component. Since the selection of the critical component is made, a DAQ is used to gather data from the real robot. Vibration measurements are used as they are representative of the bearing's degradation. The data are stored in a cloud database through IoT devices. After, a PdM algorithm retrieves vibration data from the bearing that has been stored in the cloud database. The data should be preprocessed in order to extract useful and distinctive features from the raw vibration signal. The raw vibration signals are usually noisy and include outliers and zeros, so time and frequency-domain features are extracted from them. This predictive approach is separated into two main parts, diagnosis, and prognosis. Diagnosis is used to identify patterns in processing data in order to diagnose unanticipated machine malfunctions and classify faulty behavior. The features that are used for faulty detection and classification are named condition indicators (CIs). ML models are fed with CIs with the aim to classify the data. Prognosis is used to estimate the RUL. Health indicators (HI) will be used to train a degradation model. HIs are the features that present a deterioration similar to the deterioration of the raw signal. The decision making is the last step of the PdM. After the implementation of the diagnosis and prognosis approaches, the maintenance staff should be informed in order to implement appropriate maintenance tasks. In this way, the reliability of the bearing can be improved, which will lead to the whole robotic cell's reliability improvement.

3.2. Predictive Maintenance Framework

In complex systems, such as robotic cells, the failure of a single component may lead to the abnormal functionality of the whole system or worse to its breakdown. Therefore, a PdM component-oriented flowchart is presented with the aim to assess and improve the reliability of the critical component and by extension the reliability of the robotic cell. More specifically, in Figure 9, a data-based PdM approach is presented for the detection and classification of the bearing's faulty behavior utilizing a supervised ML algorithm.

Vibration analysis is the most widely used condition monitoring technology in the industry for rotating components, and it is an effective tool for detecting bearing faults [43]. As a result, a large amount of data from an accelerometer, which is located in the bearing, is gathered. Firstly, the data are imported into the workspace. Data preprocessing is necessary in order to prepare the data for feature extraction. Once the data is prepared, we visualize the data to gain more knowledge about the raw vibration signal. Depending on the signal's visualization, edges can be set to label the data. Thus, a supervised ML problem will be developed. Feature extraction is necessary because most of the raw vibration signals have random noise and uncertain interferences. The features that are used to distinguish healthy from faulty conditions are called CIs. CIs can be derived from the raw data by using time domain, frequency domain, and time–frequency domain features. The effectiveness of CIs is quantified with the one way ANOVA (analysis of variance) ranking technique. Feature selection is the process that involves the reduction of the input variables for training ML models in the context of PdM. In some cases, reducing the number of input variables can enhance the performance of the model as the useless features that may harm the model are excluded and also in this way the computational cost of modeling can be minimized [44]. A partition of data is necessary to train the ML algorithm and after to test it. The data split into train (75%) and test (25%) data. Testing of the ML model is needed to see how the model performs in data that has not been "seen" again. To interpret the results of the ML training models, the confusion matrix is used in order to assess the results. The cost matrix can be used as an optimization tool in order to optimize the ML model, setting with high cost the most serious mistakes. If the testing results are inadequate, the performance of the model can be further optimized by fine tuning the hyperparameters. If after the fine tuning of hyperparameters, the testing results are still inadequate, the process should be restarted from the features' selection.

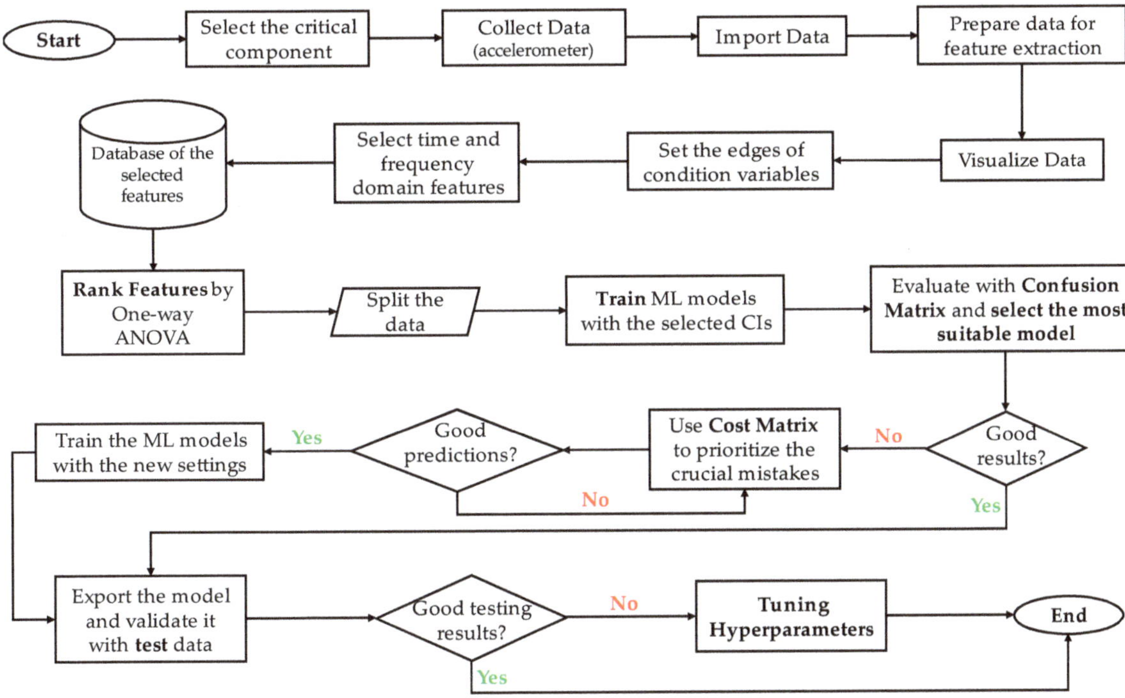

Figure 9. Flowchart for the detection and classification of components' faulty behavior (developed by the authors).

4. Industrial Case Study

The spot-welding robotic cell was discretized into its main modules, and a network reduction method of its RBD is made in order to transform the original complex system into a simple equivalent one and to extract the generalized mathematical equation that describes the reliability of the entire robotic cell. However, assumptions and simplifications in the construction of the robotic cell's RBD make the reliability assessment less accurate. Consequently, a DT concept is proposed along with a component-oriented PdM framework aiming to assess and improve the reliability of the robotic cell. The investigated robotic cell performs spot welding in metal sheets for the automotive industry. Robots are widely used for welding processes due to their accuracy and repeatability. Furthermore, welding operations require more strict security and safety precautions for human welders, thus constituting robotic welders more suitable. The failure of one component may lead to the collapse of an entire system. Therefore, in Figure 10, the discretization of the spot-welding robotic cell is illustrated.

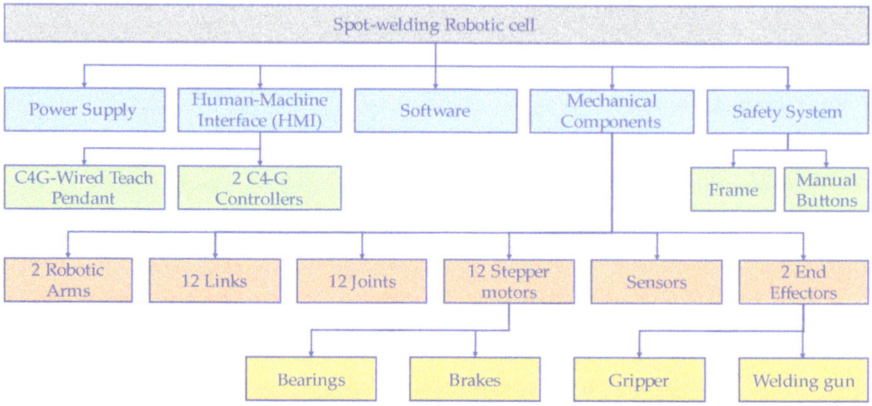

Figure 10. Discretization of the spot-welding robotic cell (developed by the authors).

Power supply, human–machine interface (HMI), software, mechanical components, and safety systems are the main modules comprising the robotic cell. The operator interacts with the robotic cell via the wired C4G teach pendant that communicates the commands to the robots' controllers. The robotic cell consists of 2 identical COMAU NJ-370-3.0 robots. One robot serves as a handler, and the second robot performs the welding operation. The two robots should operate and communicate correctly together in order to perform the welding operation efficiently and up to the quality standard set by the manufacturer. Each robot consists of 6 links, 6 joints, 6 stepper motors, sensors, 1 end effector, and 1 dedicated controller. The robotic cell is bounded by fences, and it is equipped with manual safety buttons for terminating the welding operation. In reliability modeling, the reliability of a system that consists of several components being connected serially or parallel is described by the following generalized reliability equations for series and parallel connections, respectively:

$$R_{total,1}(t) = \prod_{i=1}^{n} R_i \tag{2}$$

$$R_{total,2}(t) = 1 - \prod_{i=1}^{n}(1 - R_i) \tag{3}$$

The development of the FTA of the robotic cell is performed in order to identify the causes of failures and the failure logical paths. Concretely, the factors that may cause a failure event can be examined with the FTA method. Combinations of faults are represented at each tree level with the utilization of logical operators such as "AND", "OR", and "EVENT" [22]. The generalized equations for the FTA modeling for "AND" and "OR" gates, respectively, are as follows:

$$P_{AND}(X) = \prod_{i=1}^{n} P(X_i) \tag{4}$$

$$P_{OR}(X) = 1 - \prod_{i=1}^{n}(1 - P(X_i)) \tag{5}$$

where $P_{AND}(X)$ is the occurrence of the "*AND*" gates output fault event X, n is the number of independent input-fault events, and $P(X_i)$ is the probability of the event X_i. Similarly, $P_{OR}(X)$ is the occurrence of the "*OR*" gates output fault event X. In Figure 11, the FTA of the spot-welding robotic cell is illustrated.

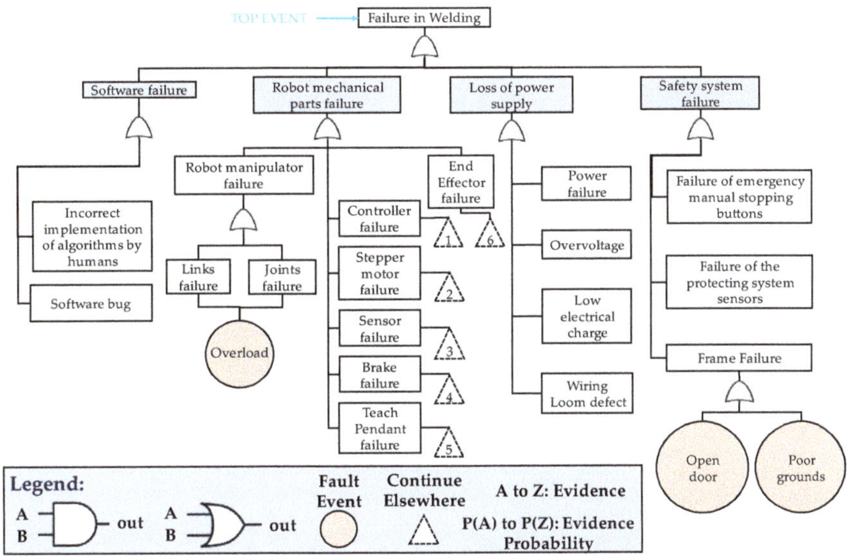

Figure 11. The FTA of the robotic cell along with the modeling equations (developed by the authors).

The top event of the FTA is the failure in welding. The basic fault event corresponds to a fault that does not require any further development, and an intermediate event corresponds to a fault that occurred because of the logical combinations of other events further down the tree [45]. However, FTA is an ineffective reliability modeling approach for modern systems. More specifically, the FTA method is based on domain experts' opinions and on the domain knowledge of the system, which creates a bottleneck as it is challenging to comprehend the root causes of the system's failure. Therefore the robotic cell's digital twin and predictive maintenance framework is implemented in conjunction with the FTA.

One way to improve the reliability of a robotic cell is to constantly monitor and control its health status. This can be accomplished by constructing a digital counterpart of the robotic cell's main module, which is the robot. For this reason, the modeling and simulation of the SMART NJ-370-3.0 robot is made. With simulation, what-if scenarios can be tested without disturbing the physical system.

In order to improve the reliability of the robotic system, we are based on the principle that the reliability of a robot is based on the reliability of its components. Concretely, each robotic arm is considered. For this reason, a component-oriented predictive maintenance approach is developed with the scope to firstly improve the reliability of the critical component and by extension the reliability of the whole robotic system. As mentioned before, we are currently working on the establishment of a connection platform between the physical and the virtual robot. For this reason, a publicly available dataset was used for this paper.

In order to select the critical component, the discretization of the robotic system was made, and the main parts were found. A robotic system is composed of several components that should operate correctly in order to ensure a reliable robotic process. The main mechanical components of a robotic system are the controller, the robotic manipulator, the motors, the sensors, the brakes, and the end-effectors. The motors are essential parts of the robotic systems since they are the equipment that feed with power the joints. For this reason, in order to develop a predictive maintenance approach, the stepper motors are selected as the critical components, and since a lot of malfunctions of the motors are a result of bearings' malfunctions, a publicly available R2F (run-to-failure) experiment of bearings was used. In Figure 12, the construction of the FTA (fault tree analysis) for the main components of the robotic system is presented with the aim to justify the selection of the stepper motors as critical components.

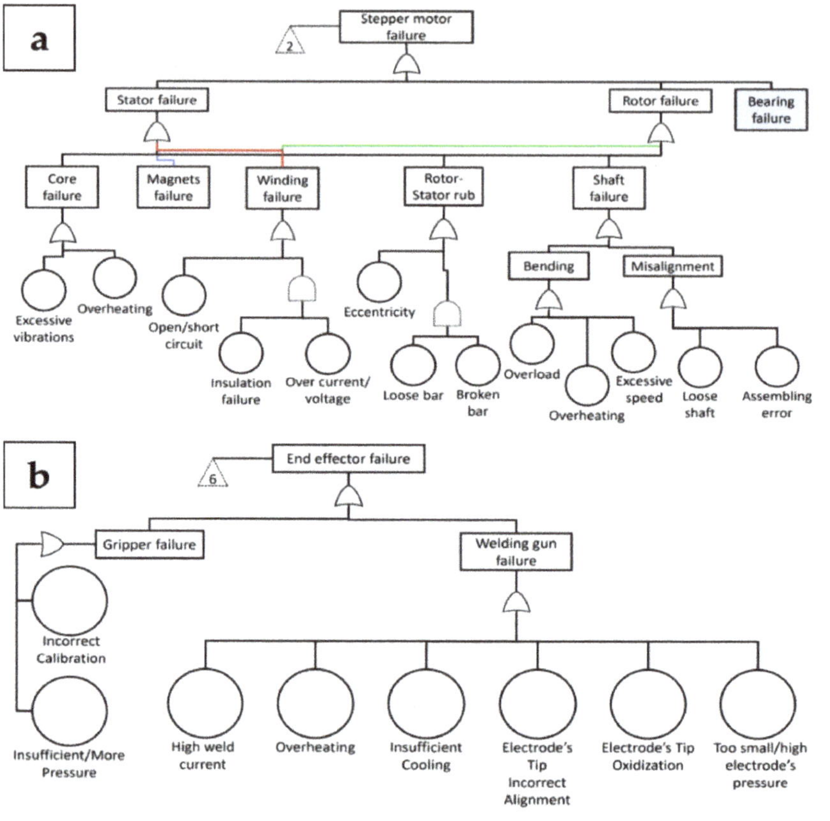

Figure 12. Fault tree analysis: (**a**) stepper motor; (**b**) end effector (developed by the authors).

As depicted, the FTA of the motor is more complicated with different interdependent failure modes. For this reason, the stepper motor is selected as the critical component

From the above figure, it becomes apparent that a motor may fail due to stator failure or rotor failure, or bearing failure. Several publications found that their main focus was the condition monitoring of bearings as they are representative components of any rotating machine, such as motors. For instance, Yang et al. in 2022 [46] highlighted that rolling bearings constitute components that are used extensively in rotating machines, and they are one of the most fault-prone components. In the research work of Lessmeier et al. in 2016 [47], it is mentioned that 40–70% of motor failures are a result of bearing failures that caused increased downtime and financial losses. Similarly, Toma et al. in 2020 [48] highlighted that motor failures can be categorized into four groups: stator, rotor, bearing faults, and other faults. According to research that was conducted by the General Electric Co. and IEEE-IGA, the most common cause of motor failures is bearing failures (more than 40%).

In Figure 13, the blocks of the simulated SMART NJ-370-3.0 robot in the Simscape Multibody environment are depicted. The Simscape Multibody software uses function blocks for the representation of the robot's components. The blocks represent rigid bodies, joints, and transform. The transform block defines a fixed 3-D rigid transformation between two frames. The blocks of the rigid bodies consist of several sub-blocks. Different types of joints are depicted such as cylindrical, revolute, and parallel, which determine the connection and motion between the rigid bodies.

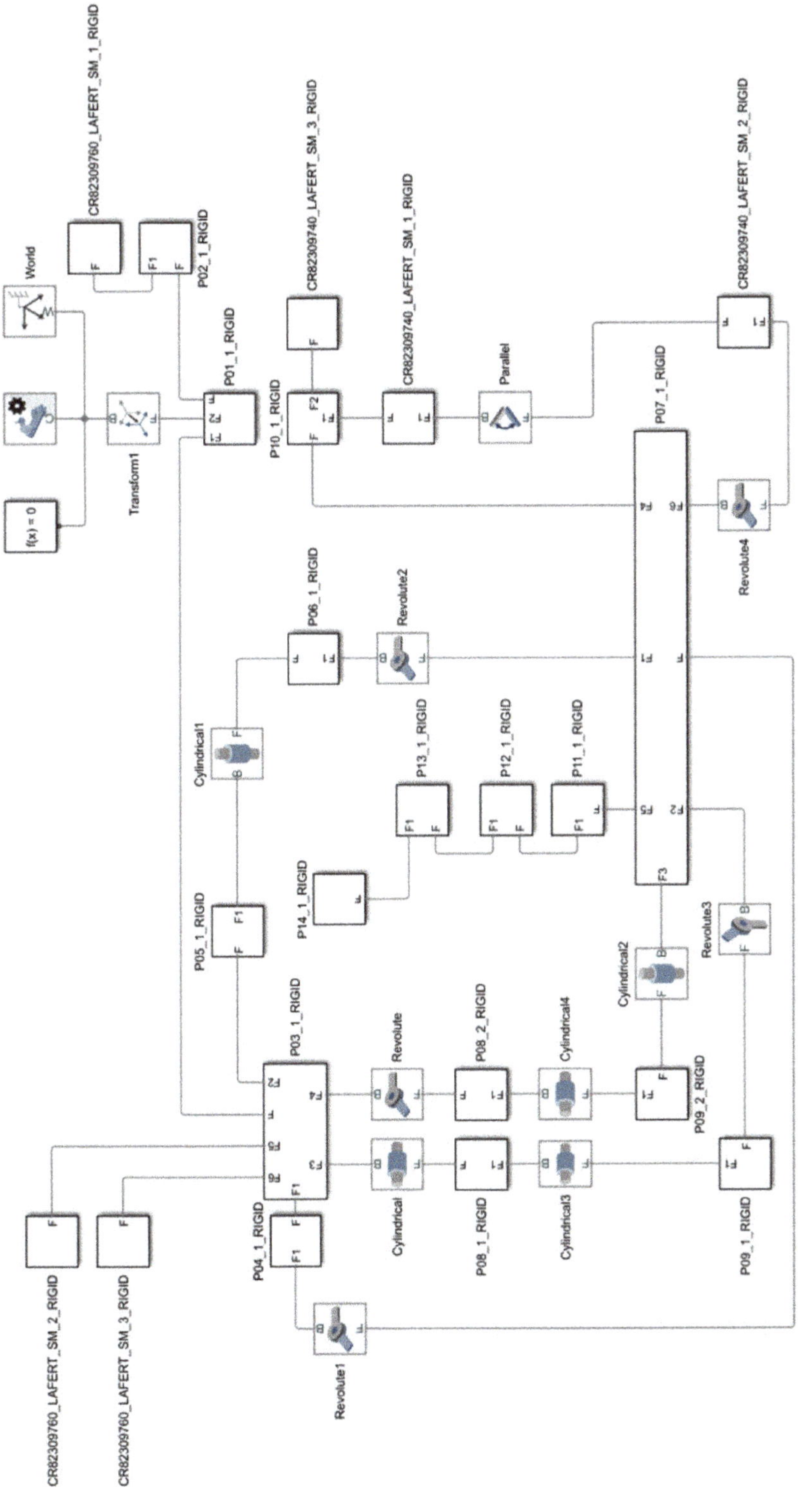

Figure 13. Simscape Multibody block diagram of the robotic cell (developed by the authors).

The next step is to process the dataset that will be used for the component-oriented PdM approach. The NASA Bearing Dataset will be used, which was generated by the NSF I/UCR Center for Intelligent Maintenance Systems. This dataset comprises three sub-datasets with R2F experiments. The dataset includes data for four force-lubricated bearings. The dataset consists of 984 CSV (comma-separated value) files that include vibration signal measurements. The file recording interval was set to 10 min. Each file consists of 20,480 data entries, which corresponds to a sampling rate of 20 kHz. Data were recorded for a time horizon of 7 days. In order to collect the required data, an experimental setup including an AC motor coupled to a shaft via a ribbed belt was used. The AC motor was adjusted to run at a constant angular speed of 2000 RPM (revolutions per minute). Furthermore, a spring mechanism was used in order to apply a radial load of 27 kN to the shaft and bearing. Regarding the sensing equipment, a PCB 353B33 High Sensitivity Quartz ICP accelerometer was installed on the bearing housing in conjunction with a NI DAQCard 6062E.

5. System Implementation

A component-oriented PdM approach focusing on the detection and classification of faulty behavior of the critical components of the robotic cell as presented in the previous paragraphs has been designed and developed. In order to complete the development of the proposed method, the training of an ML algorithm is required. Thus, a supervised ML model will be developed. MATLAB is used for the analysis of the data and for the training of the ML model. In this research work, the Diagnostic Feature Designer and the Classification Learner Apps are used. The corresponding pseudocode for the supervised ML problem is as follows:

SUPERVISED MACHINE LEARNING PSEUDOCODE

```
START
IMPORT VIBRATION DATA
CREATE tabular datastore ds
IMPORT CSV files to ds
ReadSize ds.ReadSize = 'file'
NbrFiles = 984
PREPROCESS AND PREPARE DATA
        Load dataset into a pandas dataframe
        Drop columns not relevant to vibration data
        Create new column and combine X and Y accelerometer readings
        Resample the data at a fixed frequency of 100 ms
        Calculate the rolling_mean = sum(values[-window_size:])/window_size
        Calculate standard deviation rolling_std = values[-window_size:].std()
        Remove rows with missing values
        Export new dataset as a CSV file
END
CALL datetime
Time = datetime(FileNames, "day/month/year hour:minutes:seconds")
CREATE timetable
timetable(Time, dataBearing1)
PLOT (timetable)
FUNCTION Data_Labeling
        SET label edges
        Edges = ["2004.02.12.10.32.39", "2004.02.17.00.00.00", "2004.02.19.00.00.00",
"2004.02.19.06.22.39"]
        CALL datetime
        EdgesDateTime = datetime(Edges, "day/month/year hour:minutes:seconds")
        SET data labels LABELS = {'Good', 'Alert', 'Urgent'}
```

```
            CREATE new column in timetable
            newTimetable = timetable(Time, dataBearing1, HealthStatus)
END
FUNCTION Feature_Extraction
            INPUT data to Diagnostic Designer App
            SELECT time and frequency-domain features
            RANK features with one-way ANOVA
            IMPORT features in datastore
            Features = readall(Features)
END
FUNCTION Data_Split
SPLIT 75% of data TO train & 25% TO test
Float percentageTest = 0.25
CALL randperm
RandomNbrFiles = randperm(984)
GET trainData & testData
ML TRAINING AND TESTING
            Import trainData
            Train all the available ML models
            Select ML model with highest accuracy
            Evaluate the performance of the model with the confusion matrix
            IF training process is adequate THEN
                  Export the model and validate it with the test data
            ELSE
                  use cost matrix to prioritize the serious mistakes
            END_IF
IF (training adequate) THEN
            EXPORT the model and validate it with test data
ELSE
                  use cost matrix with new settings
END
IF testing results are adequate THEN
            END Training process
ELSE
            RETRAIN model with new hyperparameters
END
IF testing results are adequate THEN
            Finish the process
ELSE
            Select new features and REPEAT training
END
END
```

In order to model the virtual robotic cell, the CAD files of the robot have been processed via the educational version of Solidworks 2022 [49]. Further to that, the Simscape Multibody Link Plugin has been enabled within the Solidworks environment, which enables the export of the robot's assembly directly to the Simscape Multibody. Simscape Multibody is a useful tool of MATLAB for modeling multi-object systems [50].

Since there are 984 CSV files of vibration records, the construction of a tabular datastore is necessary to read and process the vibration data that are located on different files on the disk. Each time, specified data files can be retrieved from the datastore. The next step of the PdM approach is the preprocessing and preparation of data for feature extraction. In this step, all the data points of each file, i.e., the 20,480 data points of each file, are positioned into a cell. This process is applied to all 984 files.

The plot of the raw vibration signal is necessary as the visualization of the signal enables the determination of the edges in order to classify the data. The vibration signal was recorded from 12 February 2004 10:32:39 until 19 February 2004 06:22:39, and it includes run-to-failure data. As depicted in Figure 14, a deterioration trend is presented in the vibration data as the bearing reaches close to the failure. Considering the visualization of the signal, the data are classified into three categories: (i) Good data, (ii) Alert data, and (iii) Urgent data. "Good data" are represented with green color, "Alert data" with yellow color, and "Urgent data" with red color.

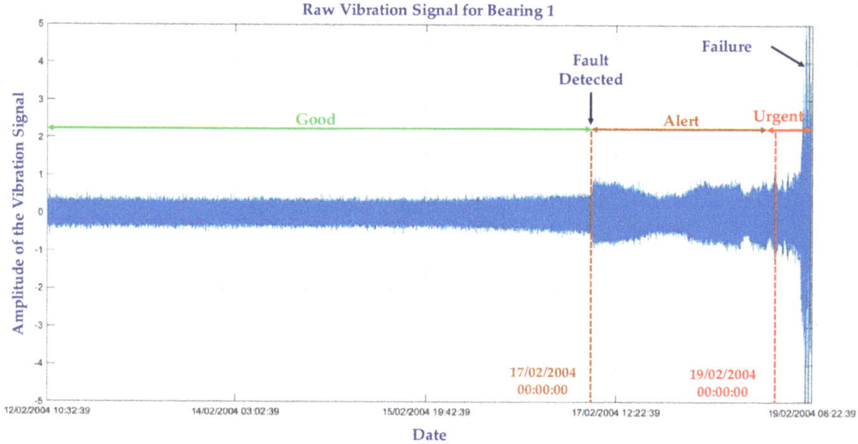

Figure 14. The plot of the vibration signal and the determination of edges for the data classification (developed by the authors).

Depending on the visualization of the signal, a new timetable is constructed with an additional column that represents the components' health status based on the classification of the data. Since the vibration data has been preprocessed, the next step of the PdM approach is the feature extraction. The Diagnostic Feature Designer App is used for this scope. This app provides the necessary automated functionalities for feature extraction from datasets based on three key domains, namely (i) time domain, (ii) frequency domain, and (iii) time/frequency domain. Because the selected critical component is a rotating component and its data are periodic, it is necessary to also extract frequency domain features to give us more insight. In Table 2, the time-domain, and frequency domain features, which are available from this app, are presented.

Table 2. The available time domain and frequency domain features.

Time-Domain Features	Frequency-Domain Features
Clearance Factor	Band Power
Crest Factor	Peak Frequency 1
Impulse Factor	Peak Frequency 2
Kurtosis	Peak Frequency 3
Mean	Peak Frequency 4
Peak Value	Peak Amplitude 1
RMS (Root Mean Square)	Peak Amplitude 2
Shape Factor	Peak Amplitude 3
SINAD	Peak Amplitude 4
Skewness	
SNR (Signal to Noise Ratio)	
Std (Standard Deviation)	
THD (Total Harmonic Distortion)	

Only useful and distinctive features should be used as inputs to the ML algorithms. For this reason, the features should be ranked, and only these features that adequately differentiate the data should be used. In this research, a supervised ranking technique, the one way ANOVA (analysis of variance) will be used as a ranking method for determining which features are suitable for predicting better condition variables. One way ANOVA determines whether the dependent variable, which is the vibration data, changes in relation to the level of the independent variable (time). CIs are the features that can be extracted from the system's data whose behavior changes in a predictable way as the system degrades or operates in different operating modes. A useful CI groups similar data points together and separates those that have different behavior. In Table 3, the ranking process of the time domain and frequency domain features is presented.

Table 3. The ranking process by one way ANOVA method.

Feature	One Way ANOVA
dataBearing1_sigstats/SNR	1.1044×10^3
dataBearing1_sigstats/SINAD	1.1688×10^3
dataBearing1_sigstats/RMS	923.7303
dataBearing1_sigstats/Std	922.8557
dataBearing1_ps_spec/PeakFreq1	712.9482
dataBearing1_sigstats/ShapeFactor	594.9398
dataBearing1_ps_spec/BandPower	396.9077
dataBearing1_ps_spec/PeakFreq3	300.9521
dataBearing1_ps_spec/PeakAmp4	491.0052
dataBearing1_ps_spec/PeakFreq2	259.8081
dataBearing1_sigstats/PeakValue	505.3358
dataBearing1_ps_spec/PeakAmp3	508.8478
dataBearing1_sigstats/Mean	3.8805
dataBearing1_sigstats/Kurtosis	254.5327
dataBearing1_sigstats/THD	74.7677
dataBearing1_sigstats/CrestFactor	1.7973
dataBearing1_sigstats/Skewness	226.9765
dataBearing1_ps_spec/PeakAmp1	500.8816
dataBearing1_ps_spec/PeakAmp2	511.1558
dataBearing1_sigstats/ImpulseFactor	21.0406
dataBearing1_ps_spec/PeakFreq4	102.6391
dataBearing1_sigstats/Clearance	49.9918

There are 984 CSV files of data: 75% of them are used for training and 25% for testing. In addition, to ensure that the data will be selected randomly, the randperm command of MATLAB is utilized. The selection of features is a challenging issue, and it is not an answer to the question of how many features are adequate for ML training. Generally speaking, the more you feed the ML model with features, the more accurate the result will be. However, useless features may harm the response of the model. Considering the results of the one way ANOVA, the best five ranked features will be used. However, because the features SINAD and SNR display similar behavior, only one of them is selected. The same is observed for the RMS and Std features. Selecting features that have similar behavior may harm the ML model. Thus, the selected features that will be the inputs to the ML models are the following: SNR, RMS, Peak Frequency 1, Shape Factor, and Band Power. The Classification Learner app will be used for ML training, and various classifiers will be used as it is impossible to know in advance which model is suitable to classify the data. After the training of the ML models, the medium Gaussian SVM is selected as the best model, since it presents the highest accuracy (98.24%).

The confusion matrix is a visual evaluation tool that is used in supervised ML problems to assess the performance of classifiers [50]. It displays the various ways in which the classification model is confused when making predictions. A confusion matrix has two dimensions: the vertical represents the actual class of the data, and the horizontal represents the class that the classifier predicts [51]. In the main diagonal cells, the percentages of how many times the ML model correctly predicts the class of data are illustrated, whereas in the other cells, the percentages of how many times the ML model makes mistakes when it comes to predicting the class of data are presented. In Figure 15, the confusion matrix of the medium Gaussian SVM model is illustrated along with the statistical measures.

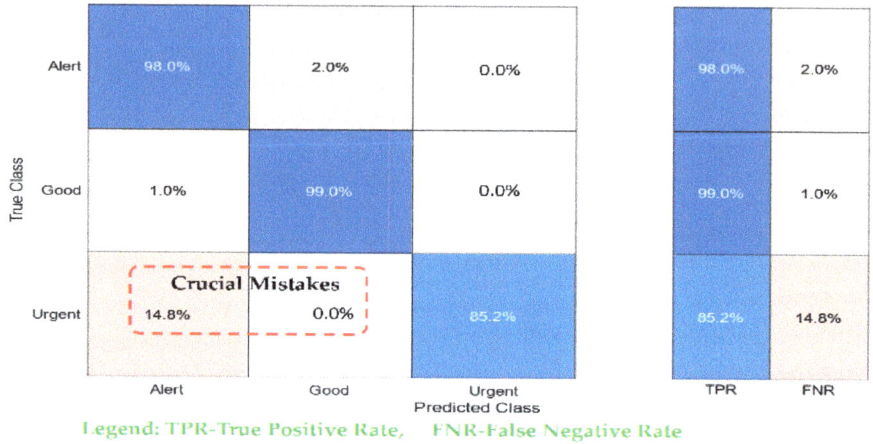

Figure 15. The confusion matrix of the Medium Gaussian SVM ML model (developed by the authors).

It can be observed that the SVM model is capable of correctly predicting "good" data at a rate of 99%, "alert" data at a rate of 98%, and "urgent" data at a rate of 85.2%. Consequently, the rates of wrong predictions are 1.0%, 2.0%, and 14.8%, respectively. The percentages of correct predictions of "good" and "alert" data are adequate. On the other hand, the percentage of the correct prediction of "urgent" data is considered inadequate. It is important to mention that when conducting PdM techniques, some mistakes are more crucial and important than others. The two cells that are highlighted are defined as the most crucial mistakes that the model makes. The most crucial mistake is when the response of the model is that "urgent" data are considered "good" data. It can be observed also that the probability of the SVM predicting "urgent" data as "good" is zero, which is as desired. However, 14.8 times SVM considers "urgent" data as "alert" data. This mistake should be minimized, and the probability that the SVM correctly predicts "urgent" data should be maximized. So, the selected model needs optimization. The cost matrix will be used as an optimization tool. It is a tool for reallocating the mistakes and minimizing specific types of classification errors in ML classification problems. Cost matrices are employed to selectively reduce classification errors that are associated with detrimental consequences for the system [51]. The confusion matrix considers that all the different mistakes are equally important, which is not true for most manufacturing systems. It has default settings that determine that all misclassifications have the same cost. In our case, it is extremely important to correctly detect "urgent" data in order to ensure that the robotic cell will not stop operating. The probability that "urgent" data will be correctly predicted should be prioritized against the probability that "alert" and "good" data will be correctly predicted. A trial and error method is applied in order to find the suitable costs of the pinpointed cells. Since the suitable costs are found, this new model is retrained. In Figure 16, the confusion matrix of the modified SVM model (right confusion matrix) is illustrated side by side with the SVM model without modifications in the settings of the cost matrix (left confusion matrix) in order to make the comparison.

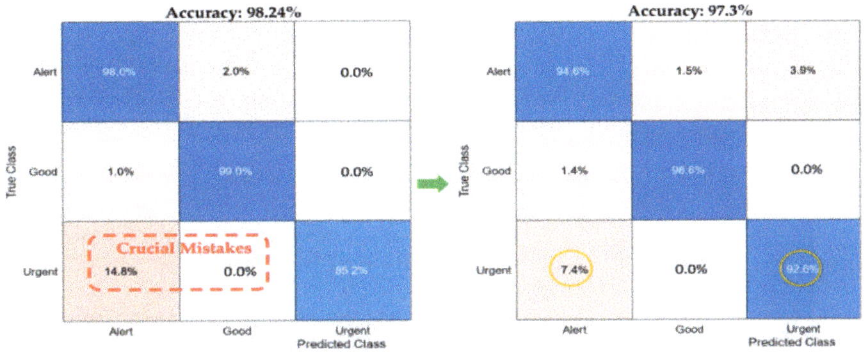

Figure 16. The retrained SVM model side by side with the unmodified SVM (developed by the authors).

From Figure 17, it can be observed that the accuracy of the modified SVM model is 97.3%. It is still a good accuracy as it is a little less than before, which was 98.2%. In the left confusion matrix, the important mistakes are circled. The modified model predicts 92.6 of times correctly "urgent" and only 7.4 of times predict "urgent" data as "alert" data. With the new settings, the percentage of predicting "urgent" data as "alert" decreased to half.

Figure 17. The testing results (developed by the authors).

However, there is a trade off, as the probability of predicting "alert" data as "urgent" data is now 3.9% compared to previously when it was 0%. However, this mistake does not affect the reliability of our model much. In case we want to further optimize the performance of our model, this can be achieved by fine tuning the model's hyperparameters.

Hyperparameters can strongly affect the performance of ML algorithms. Instead of manually selecting hyperparameter options, the Classification Learner app automates this process by trying different combinations of hyperparameter values for a given ML model type. The goal of optimization is to find the set of hyperparameter values that minimize the classification error. The app offers three different optimization methods to perform hyperparameter tuning, and the Bayesian optimization method is used for this research. More specifically, in the left confusion matrix, the original testing results are illustrated; in the middle confusion matrix, the training results after the deployment of the cost matrix is presented; and in the right confusion matrix, the testing results after the deployment of the cost matrix and the fine tuning of hyperparameters are depicted. The optimizable hyperparameters of this ML model are the following: (i) Kernel function, (ii) Box constraint level, (iii) Kernel scale, (iv) Multiclass method, and (v) Standardize data.

Therefore, it can be observed that the goal of the PdM approach has been achieved. Concretely, the tested ML model correctly predicts (100%) "urgent" data and 96% and 96.4% of the time correctly predicts "good" and "alert" data, respectively. The classification of "urgent" data has been optimized, and the results for the classification for "good" and "alert" data are adequate.

6. Discussion and Results

The implementation of a PdM for the detection and classification of the critical component of a robotic cell was presented analytically. Key performance indicators (KPIs) will be presented to assess the performance of the previous implementation. The KPIs of the ML classification problems are accuracy, recall, precision, and F1 score. The statistical parameters that are used in the equations of the KPIs are the following: TP = True Positive, TN = True Negative, FP = False Positive, FN = False Negative, TPR = True Positive Rate, FNR = False Negative Rate, and PPV = Positive Predictive Values. The accuracy is a metric that represents the percentage of the correct observations of the algorithm, and it is calculated by the following equation:

$$\text{Accuracy} = \frac{\text{Total No.of Correct Observations}}{\text{Total No.of Observations}} = \frac{\text{TP} + \text{TN}}{\text{TP} + \text{FP} + \text{TN} + \text{FN}} \tag{6}$$

It is stressed that accuracy is ineffective in the case of imbalanced datasets and by extension can lead to wrong data interpretation. On the other hand, the recall and precision metrics are mostly used when we are concerned more about predicting a specific class, and the F1 score is the harmonic mean of precision and recall. Recall basically tells us what percentage of all the points that are actually positive are correctly predicted as positive. Precision basically tells us what percentage of all points predicted to be positive by our model were actually positive, it represents a relation between them. In this research, the misclassification of "urgent" data will greatly affect the performance of the ML model and extend the performance of the bearing and the whole robotic cell. Thus, we are more concerned about the recall metric since we want data that are actually "urgent" to be predicted/classified correctly, i.e., as urgent data. The recall metric is estimated by the following equation:

$$\text{Recall} = \frac{\text{TP}}{\text{TP} + \text{FN}} = \text{TPR} \tag{7}$$

In Table 4, the accuracy and recall metrics are presented in order to assess the results of ML.

Table 4. ML model training and testing results.

	Original Training		Original Testing		1st Optimization Training (Cost Matrix)		Testing after 1st Optimization		2nd Optimization Training (Hyperpar.)		Testing after 2nd Optimization	
Accuracy	98.24%		95.1%		97.3%		95.5%		97.8%		96.3%	
Recall	TPR	FNR	TPR	FNR	TPR	FNR	TPR	FNR	TPR	FNR	TPR	FNR
"Good" data	99%	1%	96%	4%	98.6%	1.4%	96%	4%	98.8%	1.2%	96%	4%
"Alert" data	98%	2%	98.8%	1.2%	94.6%	5.4%	96.4%	3.6%	96.6%	3.4%	96.4%	3.6%
"Urgent" data	85.2%	14.8%	58.3%	41.7%	92.6%	7.4%	83.3%	16.7%	88.9%	11.1%	100%	0%

The results demonstrate that the original testing results are satisfactory for the classifications of "good" and "alert" data, but they are not sufficient for "urgent" data. Therefore, the ML model requires further optimization of the hyperparameters. The optimization process has been performed in two levels. Firstly, by using the cost matrix, the correct classification of "urgent" data is regarded as the most important. Secondly, by fine tuning the hyperparameters, the recall metric has been further optimized until it reaches 100% for the classification of "urgent" data. After the two optimizations, it can be observed that the proposed methodology can improve the reliability of the robotic cell by successfully training an ML algorithm to classify the run to failure vibration data of its critical component. The most challenging tasks in a PdM approach are the selection of the features and ML models. Preprocessing and preparation of data are vital issues that are unique each time and depend on the available data and the application. The most time consuming step, accounting for 70–90% of the total PdM approach, is data preparation, but it is highly important as it has the greatest impact on the results. It has to be stressed that the generalization of methods is an important issue. Although the presented approach is focused on Comau SMART NJ-370-3.0 robots, the model can be altered so that it corresponds to other similar robotic manipulators. Regarding the training of the machine learning model, the applied method is adequately generalized, so that it can be followed for training other predictive models either for the same robotic arm (e.g., for other critical components such as electric motors) or for other robotic cells/manipulators. In any case, minor modifications are still required since there is no method that fits all systems.

7. Conclusions and Future Work

In this research work, the reliability of manufacturing systems and especially in the robotic domain was studied. The scope of companies is to ensure reliable components and processes that will offer reliable products to the customers replying to the increasing demands of society. Each process should be implemented considering the safety measures to protect human life and the quality of the equipment. Model based approaches such as the RBD and FTA can be considered initial and important methods for the reliability assessment of manufacturing systems. The type of connection between the several components that comprise the whole robotic system has a huge impact on the reliability of the system. Parallel connections are proposed for critical components in order to ensure that the breakdown of a component will not cause the overall breakdown of the robotic cell. A comprehensive FTA of the robotic cell was developed, and its limitations were discussed. For this reason, the interest is focused on digital technologies to improve the reliability and productivity of manufacturing systems. The DT along with PdM approaches are promising approaches for industries in order to simulate, control, and monitor their equipment, ensuring high reliability of their equipment.

For future work, it becomes apparent that the impact of the human factor on the reliability of manufacturing systems is an issue that should be further investigated. The core of the Industry 5.0 revolution will be the symbiosis and the coexistence of humans and machines, highlighting the importance of reliable communication and cooperation between them. This research work will be further elaborated in the future toward making the predictive maintenance approach online by integrating the digital twin. In this way, synchronous communication between the virtual model and the physical equipment will be feasible. Furthermore, as part of future research, the authors plan different configurations of robots, such as collaborative robotic arms and hybrid cells, which involve the coexistence of human operators within the cell. Regarding the experimentation with different failures, currently, we are in the process of collecting additional data from the robotic arms in order to expand the training of the predictive models to other components. More specifically, this process involves the execution of R2F (run to failure) experiments. With regard to data management, due to the vast amount of data produced daily, edge computing will be integrated in order to minimize the computational load on the cloud layer and fully utilize the inherent intelligence of the embedded systems at the shop-floor level.

Author Contributions: Conceptualization, D.M. and J.A.; investigation, S.T.; resources, S.T.; writing—review and editing, J.A.; supervision, D.M. All authors have read and agreed to the published version of the manuscript.

Funding: This research received no external funding.

Data Availability Statement: Not applicable.

Conflicts of Interest: The authors declare no conflict of interest.

References

1. Ghodsian, N.; Benfriha, K.; Olabi, A.; Gopinath, V.; Arnou, A.; el Zant, C.; Charrier, Q.; el Helou, M. Toward designing an integration architecture for a mobile manipulator in production systems: Industry 4.0. *Procedia CIRP* **2022**, *109*, 443–448. [CrossRef]
2. Mourtzis, D. *Design and Operation of Production Networks for Mass Personalization in the Era of Cloud Technology*; Elsevier: Amsterdam, The Netherlands, 2021; pp. 1–393. [CrossRef]
3. Mourtzis, D.; Synodinos, G.; Angelopoulos, J.; Panopoulos, M. An augmented reality application for robotic cell customization. *Procedia CIRP* **2020**, *90*, 654–659. [CrossRef]
4. Niku, S.B. *Introduction to Robotics: Analysis, Control, Applications*; John Wiley & Sons: Hoboken, NJ, USA, 2020.
5. Kampa, A. The Review of Reliability Factors Related to Industrial Robo. *Robot. Autom. Eng. J.* **2018**, *3*, 624. [CrossRef]
6. Fazlollahtabar, H.; Niaki, S.T.A. *Reliability Models of Complex Systems for Robots and Automation*; CRC Press: Boca Raton, FL, USA, 2017. [CrossRef]
7. Mourtzis, D.; Tsoubou, S.; Angelopoulos, J. A conceptual framework for the improvement of robotic cell reliability through Industry 4.0. In Proceedings of the 32nd International Conference on Flexible Automation and Intelligent Manufacturing (FAIM 2023), Porto, Portugal, 18–22 June 2023.
8. Lazarova-Molnar, S.; Mohamed, N. Reliability Assessment in the Context of Industry 4.0: Data as a Game Changer. *Procedia Comput. Sci.* **2019**, *151*, 691–698. [CrossRef]
9. Friederich, J.; Lazarova-Molnar, S. Towards Data-Driven Reliability Modeling for Cyber-Physical Production Systems. *Procedia Comput. Sci.* **2021**, *184*, 589–596. [CrossRef]
10. Deloitte. Predictive Maintenance. Taking Pro-Active Measures Based on Advanced Data Analytics to Predict and Avoid Machine Failure. Analytics Institute. 2017. Available online: https://www2.deloitte.com/content/dam/Deloitte/de/Documents/deloitte-analytics/Deloitte_Predictive-Maintenance_PositionPaper.pdf (accessed on 20 June 2020).
11. Carvalho, T.P.; Soares, F.A.A.M.N.; Vita, R.; da Francisco, R.; Basto, J.P.; Alcalá, S.G.S. A systematic literature review of machine learning methods applied to predictive maintenance. *Comput. Ind. Eng.* **2019**, *137*, 106024. [CrossRef]
12. Sullivan, G.; Pugh, R.; Melendez, A.P.; Hunt, W.D. *Operations & Maintenance Best Practices—A Guide to Achieving Operational Efficiency*; Pacific Northwest National Laboratory (PNNL): Richland, WA, USA, 2010.
13. Achouch, M.; Dimitrova, M.; Ziane, K.; Sattarpanah Karganroudi, S.; Dhouib, R.; Ibrahim, H.; Adda, M. On Predictive Maintenance in Industry 4.0: Overview, Models, and Challenges. *Appl. Sci.* **2022**, *12*, 8081. [CrossRef]
14. Bi, Z.M.; Miao, Z.; Zhang, B.; Zhang, C.W.J. The state of the art of testing standards for integrated robotic systems. *Robot. Comput. Integr. Manuf.* **2020**, *63*, 101893. [CrossRef]
15. Garcia, E.; Jimenez, M.A.; De Santos, P.G.; Armada, M. The evolution of robotics research. *IEEE Robot. Autom. Mag.* **2007**, *14*, 90–103. [CrossRef]
16. Ma, Y. Design of flexible maintenance robot based on Gas Insulated Substation. *J. Phys. Conf. Ser.* **2021**, *1865*, 022052. [CrossRef]
17. De Luca, A.; Book, W.J. Robots with Flexible Elements. In *Springer Handbook of Robotics*; Siciliano, B., Khatib, O., Eds.; Springer: Cham, Switzerland, 2016. [CrossRef]
18. Wei, X.; Ye, J.; Xu, J.; Tang, Z. Adaptive Dynamic Programming-Based Cross-Scale Control of a Hydraulic-Driven Flexible Robotic Manipulator. *Appl. Sci.* **2023**, *13*, 2890. [CrossRef]

19. Gao, Z.; Wanyama, T.; Singh, I.; Gadhrri, A.; Schmidt, R. From Industry 4.0 to Robotics 4.0—A Conceptual Framework for Collaborative and Intelligent Robotic Systems. *Procedia Manuf.* **2020**, *46*, 591–599. [CrossRef]
20. Frisk, J. Robot Development towards Flexibility—The Four Robot Revolutions—OpiFlex. 2020. Available online: https://www.opiflex.se/en/publicity/four-robot-revolutions-flexible-robots/ (accessed on 20 October 2022).
21. Liu, Y.; Wang, L.; Makris, S.; Krüger, J. Smart robotics for manufacturing. *Robot. Comput. Integr. Manuf.* **2023**, *2023*, 102535. [CrossRef]
22. Marina, K. *Reliability Management of Manufacturing Processes in Machinery Enterprises*; Tallin University of Technology: Tallin, Estonia, 2012. Available online: https://digikogu.taltech.ee/en/Item/e17f1928-f8e7-4a2e-81ab-585bd19ccef4 (accessed on 20 October 2022).
23. Chryssolouris, G. *Manufacturing Systems: Theory and Practice*; Springer Science & Business Media: Cham, Switzerland, 2019.
24. Kumar, S.; Singh, R. Rank order clustering and imperialist competitive optimization based cost and RAM analysis on different industrial sectors. *J. Manuf. Syst.* **2020**, *56*, 514–524. [CrossRef]
25. Gu, X. The impact of maintainability on the manufacturing system architecture. *Int. J. Prod. Res.* **2017**, *55*, 4392–4410. [CrossRef]
26. Birolini, A. *Reliability Engineering*; Springer: Berlin/Heidelberg, Germany, 2017. [CrossRef]
27. Lazarova-Molnar, S.; Mohamed, N.; Shaker, H.R. Reliability modeling of cyber-physical systems: A holistic overview and challenges. In Proceedings of the 2017 Workshop on Modeling and Simulation of Cyber-Physical Energy Systems (MSCPES), Pittsburgh, PA, USA, 21 April 2017; pp. 1–6. [CrossRef]
28. Bai, B.; Xie, C.; Liu, X.; Li, W.; Zhong, W. Application of integrated factor evaluation–analytic hierarchy process–T-S fuzzy fault tree analysis in reliability allocation of industrial robot systems. *Appl. Soft. Comput.* **2022**, *115*, 108248. [CrossRef]
29. Michał, G. *Industrial Robots and Cobots: Everything You Need to Know about Your Future Co-Worker*; INKPAD: Carmel, IN, USA, 2018.
30. Sharma, S.P.; Sukavanam, N.; Kumar, N.; Kumar, A. Reliability analysis of complex robotic system using Petri nets and fuzzy lambda-tau methodology. *Eng. Comput.* **2010**, *27*, 354–364. [CrossRef]
31. Kumar, N.; Borm, J.-H.; Kumar, A. Reliability analysis of waste clean-up manipulator using genetic algorithms and fuzzy methodology. *Comput. Oper. Res.* **2012**, *39*, 310–319. [CrossRef]
32. Khodabandehloo, K. Analyses of robot systems using fault and event trees: Case studies. *Reliab. Eng. Syst. Saf.* **1996**, *53*, 247–264. [CrossRef]
33. Catelani, M.; Ciani, L.; Venzi, M. Sensitivity analysis with MC simulation for the failure rate evaluation and reliability assessment. *Measurement* **2015**, *74*, 150–158. [CrossRef]
34. Stavropoulos, P.; Mourtzis, D. Digital twins in Industry 4.0. In *Design and Operation of Production Networks for Mass Personalization in the Era of Cloud Technology*; Elsevier: Amsterdam, The Netherlands, 2022; pp. 277–316. [CrossRef]
35. Kritzinger, W.; Karner, M.; Traar, G.; Henjes, J.; Sihn, W. Digital Twin in manufacturing: A categorical literature review and classification. *IFAC Pap.* **2018**, *51*, 1016–1022. [CrossRef]
36. Negri, E.; Fumagalli, L.; Macchi, M. A Review of the Roles of Digital Twin in CPS-based Production Systems. *Procedia Manuf.* **2017**, *11*, 939–948. [CrossRef]
37. Saracco, R. Digital twins: Bridging physical space and cyberspace. *Computer* **2019**, *52*, 58–64. [CrossRef]
38. Mourtzis, D. Simulation in the design and operation of manufacturing systems: State of the art and new trends. *Int. J. Prod. Res.* **2020**, *58*, 1927–1949. [CrossRef]
39. Phanden, R.K.; Sharma, P.; Dubey, A. A review on simulation in digital twin for aerospace, manufacturing and robotics. *Mater. Today Proc.* **2021**, *38*, 174–178. [CrossRef]
40. Mourtzis, D.; Vlachou, E.; Milas, N.; Xanthopoulos, N. A cloud-based approach for maintenance of machine tools and equipment based on shop-floor monitoring. *Procedia CIRP* **2022**, *41*, 655–660. [CrossRef]
41. Wang, J.; Gao, R.X. Innovative smart scheduling and predictive maintenance techniques. In *Design and Operation of Production Networks for Mass Personalization in the Era of Cloud Technology*; Elsevier: Amsterdam, The Netherlands, 2022; pp. 181–207. [CrossRef]
42. Wang, Y.; Zhao, Y.; Addepalli, S. Remaining Useful Life Prediction using Deep Learning Approaches: A Review. *Procedia Manuf.* **2020**, *49*, 81–88. [CrossRef]
43. Saidi, L.; ben Ali, J.; Bechhoefer, E.; Benbouzid, M. Wind turbine high-speed shaft bearings health prognosis through a spectral Kurtosis-derived indices and SVR. *Appl. Acoust.* **2017**, *120*, 1–8. [CrossRef]
44. Brownlee, J. How to choose a feature selection method for machine learning. *Mach. Learn. Mastery* **2019**, *10*.
45. Kabir, S. An overview of fault tree analysis and its application in model based dependability analysis. *Expert Syst. Appl.* **2017**, *77*, 114–135. [CrossRef]
46. Yang, C.; Ma, J.; Wang, X.; Li, X.; Li, Z.; Luo, T. A novel based-performance degradation indicator RUL prediction model and its application in rolling bearing. *ISA Trans.* **2022**, *121*, 349–364. [CrossRef] [PubMed]
47. Lessmeier, C.; Kimotho, J.K.; Zimmer, D.; Sextro, W. Condition monitoring of bearing damage in electromechanical drive systems by using motor current signals of electric motors: A benchmark data set for data-driven classification. In Proceedings of the PHM Society European Conference, Bilbao, Spain, 5–8 July 2016; Volume 3.
48. Toma, R.N.; Prosvirin, A.E.; Kim, J.M. Bearing fault diagnosis of induction motors using a genetic algorithm and machine learning classifiers. *Sensors* **2020**, *20*, 1884. [CrossRef]

49. Community Download | SOLIDWORKS. Available online: https://www.solidworks.com/support/community-download#no-back (accessed on 8 April 2023).
50. Xu, J.; Zhang, Y.; Miao, D. Three-way confusion matrix for classification: A measure driven view. *Inf. Sci.* **2020**, *507*, 772–794. [CrossRef]
51. Gutzwiller, K.J.; Chaudhary, A. Machine-learning models, cost matrices, and conservation-based reduction of selected landscape classification errors. *Landsc. Ecol.* **2020**, *35*, 249–255. [CrossRef]

electronics

MDPI

Article

Methodical Approach to Proactivity Using a Digital Twin of Production Process

Fedor Burčiar, Pavel Važan, Bohuslava Juhásová and Martin Juhás *

Institute of Applied Informatics, Automation and Mechatronics, Faculty of Material Science and Technology in Trnava, Slovak University of Technology in Bratislava, 91724 Trnava, Slovakia; fedor.burciar@stuba.sk (F.B.); pavel.vazan@stuba.sk (P.V.); bohuslava.juhasova@stuba.sk (B.J.)
* Correspondence: martin_juhas@stuba.sk

Abstract: Real-time simulation and digital twin (DT) as a part of Industry 4.0 are becoming increasingly relevant, especially when considering production cycles. Most issues with production cycles arise from having a demand for customized production orders, while having nonmodular production lines with a medium-to-high complexity in the decision-making process. All these conditions lead to a possibility of unpredictable consequences. Being able to predict behavior and possible failure scenarios before the production starts has proven to save both costs and time. With an introduction of5 a new ISO standard which is solely focused on DT creation and sets a starting point for future research, researchers are finally able to focus on creating DT prototypes built for specific scenarios while maintaining the core concepts. This paper focuses on proposing strategies for DT and real-time simulation integration into production cycles, based on the new standards, which can be generalized and applied on a multitude of different systems with minimal changes. The proposed solutions offer different levels of human interaction with the Human–Machine Interfaces used in Cyber–Physical Systems created as a part of DT. Applicability of the solution has been verified based on the results of experiments carried out on the WITNESS Horizon simulation platform with utilization of the custom Order Manipulation Interface (OMI) application.

Keywords: data integration; digital twin; proactive simulation; WITNESS Horizon

Citation: Burčiar, F.; Važan, P.; Juhásová, B.; Juhás, M. Methodical Approach to Proactivity Using a Digital Twin of Production Process. *Electronics* **2023**, *12*, 3335. https://doi.org/10.3390/electronics12153335

Academic Editors: Luis Gracia, Juan Ernesto Solanes Galbis, Jaime Valls Miro and Franco Cicirelli

Received: 20 June 2023
Revised: 29 July 2023
Accepted: 2 August 2023
Published: 4 August 2023

1. Introduction

The digital twin (DT) is one of the basic components of the Industry 4.0 concept. It is clear from this concept that DT is influenced by its connection with other core components such as Cyber–Physical Systems (CPS), the Internet of Things (IoT), artificial intelligence (AI), machine learning (ML), Big Data and cloud solutions. All these technologies, from different points of view and at different levels of complexity, support or are related to Smart Manufacturing (SM) [1–3].

This article presents the possibility of using the current hot trend of digitization in the industrial environment—a digital twin with the aim of integrating the process of proactive simulation for the purpose of real-time analysis of incoming production orders. The task is to identify possible problems during the subsequent execution of orders in the production process itself, which will enable timely adoption of appropriate countermeasures.

The main idea and potential contribution of the article is the proposal of an original solution for data integration between the control MES and the simulation environment. It is a solution to a specific problem involving communication between the control MES created in the AVEVA InTouch environment, which ensures the control of a real Physical Production System—a hybrid production line AFB Factory, and a digital twin represented by a simulation model implemented in the WITNESS Horizon environment. The focus on such a combination of technologies is unique and not reported in the scientific literature. Our own custom Order Manipulation Interface created in MATLAB ensures the data transfer and order management in our solution.

In the introduction of the presented article, the reader will become acquainted with the standards for the implementation of a digital twin. Subsequently, the problem of data integration between MES and DT in the form of a simulation model is specified, and our proposed solution is presented in the form of the original Manual Order Rearrangement method. In the next section, the digital model representing DT is described in detail. In the experimental part, the feasibility of our proposal is declared based on four different experiments. At the end of the article, the fundamental advantages, but also the disadvantages of our solution, are presented, with an outline of the concept of Automated Order Rearrangement, which has the ambition to move the offered solution to a higher level.

The idea of the digital twin can be described as a digital model of a certain part or the entire production process. In production, we need the DT model to be used for process-level monitoring, i.e., physical and virtual entities as well as processes in real space and time, as DT allows us to create a detailed digital image with real data tracking. The connection of the physical and real environment makes it possible to optimize the activities of physical objects, continuous analysis of collected data, monitoring of the production process or its prediction. It also allows us to evaluate and maintain the operational capability of individual production equipment with utilization of predictive maintenance. Digital twin accelerates and facilitates decision-making processes in production. The use of DT in production helps to increase the overall efficiency of production, optimize processes and maximize the use of resources. On the other hand, it is necessary to take into account the fact that an enterprise will benefit from a digital twin depending on many factors. In particular, the amount of work, employees, software, systems and computers involved in the implementation of simulations causes this technology to generate very high costs. Modelling is an expensive issue, and only the profit from resultant optimization, which is never guaranteed in every case, is able to compensate for these costs.

Currently, we can say that the use of DT is mainly in the field of prototyping, which includes modeling, simulation, verification, evaluation and confirmation of a physical artifact using a simulation replica [4]. The role of digital twin is to create virtual models for physical objects that will be used to simulate their behavior [5]. Such models can reflect the state of physical entities via data sensing. These data are then used to predict, estimate and analyze dynamic changes in the production process. Thus, physical objects would respond to changes according to the optimized scheme provided by the simulation [6]. The mentioned models are able to collect data and communicate via SCADA and MES systems with other levels of company management to ensure an efficient and sustainable production. Collecting data from a real system is therefore a crucial prerequisite for the creation of DT.

An International Standard ISO 23247 was defined and published in 2021. This standard deals with automation systems and integration and provides a digital twin implementation framework for manufacturing. According to this standard, the digital twin framework for manufacturing is fit for purpose digital representation of an observable manufacturing element (OME) with synchronization between the element and its digital representation [7]. According to this standard, we would be able to design a usable digital twin. The standard defines that digital representation of OMEs can include both static and dynamic information, as is shown in Figure 1. Information that does not change during the manufacturing process is classified as static. For example, the serial number of a piece of material is static. However, the shape of the material, if it changes during manufacturing processes, is dynamic [8].

Thus, a digital twin can persist throughout the life cycle of a physical system to enable continuity of information, better communication across life-cycle stages, and continuous documentation of the physical system [9].

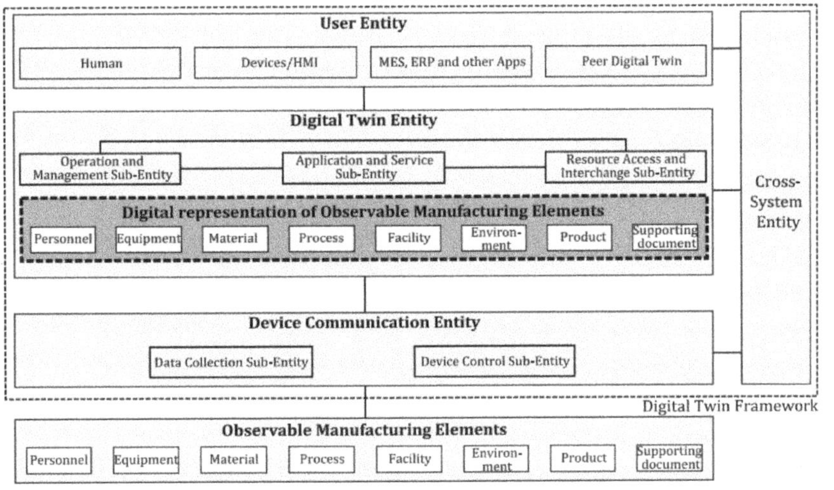

Figure 1. Types of OMEs in reference architecture [8].

Commercial solutions of digital twins for manufacturing plants are commonly based on data-driven models that have been created based on data measured in the enterprises for which they are intended [10,11]. Digital twin designed in this way, based on real production data, relies on black-box models that are built to capture the relationships between production input and output parameters. These systems can also be used to obtain production forecasts or to detect certain production anomalies. We can say that such DTs require expert supervision and are therefore more difficult to expand [12]. Data-driven DT applications are fully dependent on data obtained from the process level of manufacturing control and from monitoring systems to provide information about the current state of the manufacturing process [13].

New trends in the digitization of industry have led to the development of a simulation-based digital twin (SBDT). This method uses a simulation of a first-principles model (FPM) to capture the dynamics of production. The essence of this solution is that the simulation model—first-principles model of the device—is run in parallel with the production process. Then, the dynamic model parameter estimation methods adjust the model results by comparing the measurements from the production process with the results obtained by the model, thus ensuring that the simulated state is constantly adapting to the current state of production. So, the basic FPM SBDT is continuously synchronized with the operating device. The advantage of such models is that they provide us with measured information about the production process. We can further process such data and use them in the prediction towards production, also for offline and online optimization of production. Of course, the data are also stored in data warehouses where, after processing, we can look for various knowledge that can later be used in the production process [12–14].

There are many articles which show some knowledge about digital twins. Carvalho and da Silva in 2021 published the systematic literature review Sustainability Requirements of Digital Twin-Based Systems [14]. DT is closely related with virtual reality like that stated in 2023 by Spyrou et al. in Virtual Reality-Based Digital Twins [15]. Some articles deal with the utilization of special algorithms for simulation models used in the DT environment [16]. Liu and Zhang in 2023 presented in their paper how to apply digital twins in the automotive industry [17]. It is really necessary to take into consideration the connection between DT and Big Data Towards Smart Manufacturing and Industry 4.0 [2].

Currently, in the process of implementing the Industry 4.0 concept, we encounter the concept of Smart Manufacturing. Smart Manufacturing represents a collaborative, fully integrated manufacturing system that responds in real time to meet the changing conditions and demands in the factory, in the supply network, and in the needs of the customers [18]. Digital twins of manufacturing applications are used in Smart Manufacturing for modeling and simulation, data analysis and optimization to ensure the optimization of such manufacturing. The abovementioned ISO 23247 standard is intended to facilitate the implementation of digital twin. The recent article of Shao from 2021 shows how the ISO 23247 standard can be implemented for different manufacturing applications [19].

2. Methodology

The first and the most important question to arise from the initial analysis of the issue presented in this paper has been the highest achievable level of data integration between the MES system and the simulation platform of choice. These entities are located on the opposing ends of the communication pipeline. The level of data formatting variance they provide, or can understand and interpret, often depends on the individual software. In this paper, we focus on proposing strategies for breaching this gap without the need of any major formatting being done by humans.

The proposed solution is focused on achieving different degrees of automation for data flow between the physical and digital entity. The solution is in accordance with the ISO 23247-1 standard and represents an approach to DT creation, which can be generalized and therefore applied to a wider variety of production systems with minor adjustments based on the requirements of the problem at hand. As every production system is different, areas that require adjustments include data acquisition methods, data processing methods, digital model (DM) adjustments and bridging interfaces. It is important to note that our solution is aimed at achieving proactivity in production; therefore, only the current status of the physical production line is needed to yield valid results. The solution discussed in this paper is proposed with the goal of making production more efficient through an adjustment and management of incoming production orders.

Manual Order Rearrangement—MOR

This method we proposed revolves around being partially automated with certain operations being handled by an operator through different instances of custom data processing interfaces built specifically for this method. This method can be applied to production control, provided there are three major components with at least three minor bridging interfaces between these components. The existence of an MES with a possibility of MES data access is the first requirement that needs to be met. The MES stores all the production data used for transfer between itself and the simulator of choice. Aside from storing the data, the MES also contains an interface for production order management in which an operator can load specific orders from the database and start the production process. As the production orders are loaded into MES, a file containing the order data is generated and sent to the PC for further processing and simulation. This process is handled by a custom script implemented into the MES for this specific operation, and it happens before the production starts. The second major component required for this method to work is the Order Manipulation Interface (OMI), which an operator can use to ensure that the data are interpreted correctly. It is also possible to generate a large number of variations within this software to ensure optimal simulation outcomes. As the operator has full control over data within said software, the OMI also becomes the last control point before sending all the data into the simulation process. The last major component required for this method is the production process simulator loaded with a DM of the corresponding physical production system (PPS). It is quite obvious that a fundamental condition and essence of DT and PPS connection is the ability of two-way data transfer between them. Process data are gradually loaded into the simulator in the form of production orders, which contain all the necessary data for simulation. The data provided consist of a number of products required to be made of each type as well as their arrival time into the production system. The simulator then runs all the variations provided by the operator and signals the ability or inability of the production order to be carried out fully. After the simulation ends, full statistics data are provided to the operator in addition to the simulation log containing raw simulation data for further analysis as well as order data preformatted for import into MES. Afterwards, the simulation data are analyzed in detail, and the best outcome is chosen and imported into the MES for production. MES loads the new simulated order and displays a prompt to the operator, who can then decide to start the production process.

The key to achieving proactivity in production using the MOR method is that all the simulation runs must be completed before the production is started (Figure 2).

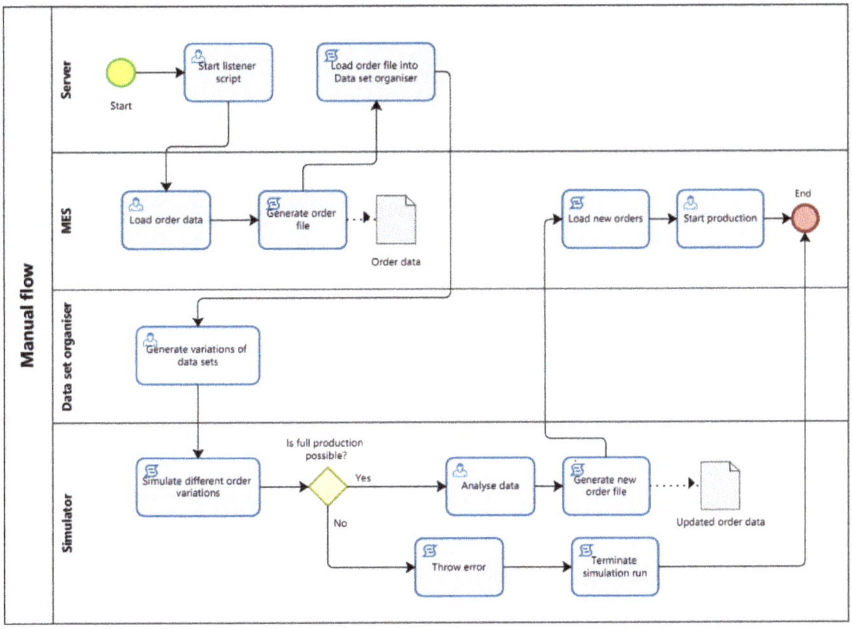

Figure 2. Conceptual model for a manual data flow approach.

It is also important to note that a simulation run is considered a success if all the inputted production orders have been fulfilled while none of the alarms have been set off during the simulation run. The alarms include a lack of resources in any of the tanks inside the model, an insufficient number of bottles for filling and predicted machine breakdowns. If any of the alarms are set off during the simulation or the model did not finish all of the orders within the preset amount of time, an appropriate message is displayed to the operator, and the simulation run is terminated.

3. Building a Digital Model

The DM used for these methods is fundamentally identical, barring the differences in input data processing, which are described further in this section. The DM contains various abstractions and substitutions for real-world processes while providing functionally identical results. The substitution of production processes allows the creation of different variations within individual machine tasks without the necessity to remove or add an entire workstation. The digital model is represented by a complex simulation model of a physical production system located in the Laboratory of Control Systems—Agro, Food & Beverage Factory (AFB Factory) by FESTO (Figure 3).

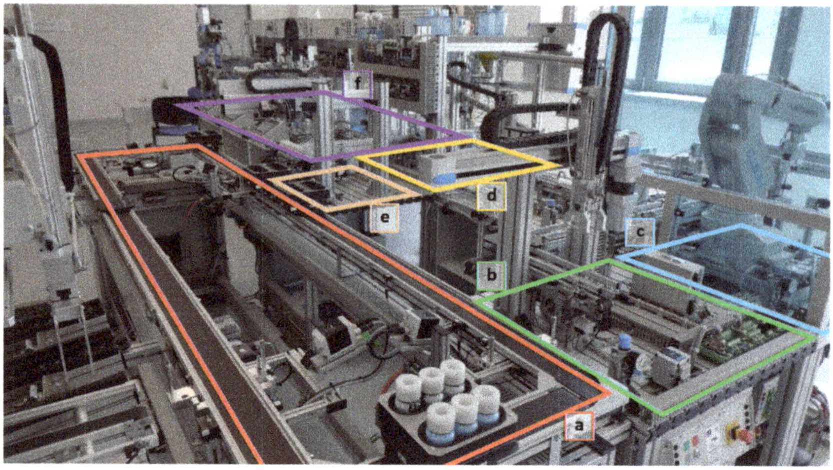

Figure 3. Agro, Food & Beverage Factory (AFB Factory) by FESTO—(**a**) conveyor; (**b**) unpackaging; (**c**) recycling; (**d**) filling; (**e**) packaging; (**f**) preprocessing.

The simulation model, shown in Figure 4, was created in the WITNESS Horizon simulation platform and realistically reflects the entire closed hybrid production process provided by this automated production line.

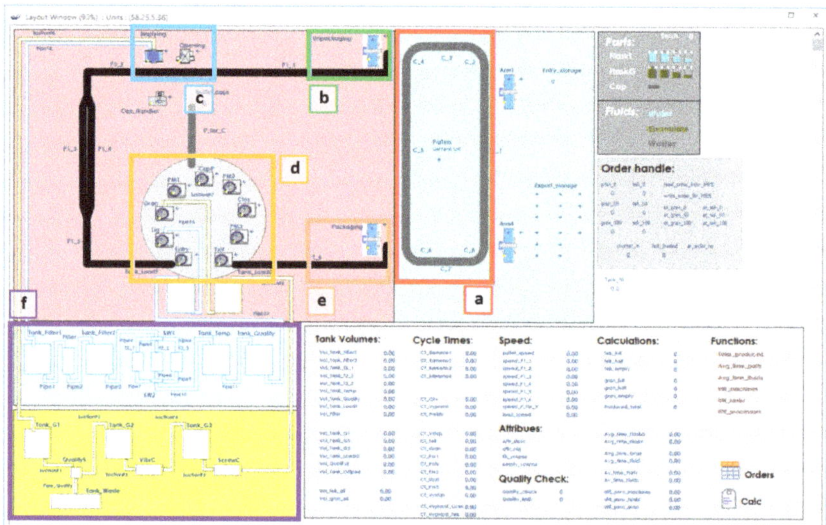

Figure 4. Simulation model of AFB Factory—(**a**) conveyor; (**b**) unpackaging; (**c**) recycling; (**d**) filling; (**e**) packaging; (**f**) preprocessing.

The model consists of two major parts. The first part is a discrete production model which is in accordance with the ISO 23247-1 standard, simulating the handling process for bottles filled with liquid or solid material. This section of the model contains bottle handling machines along with a transport system for moving the products between these machines. The best showcase for a substitution used in this section is the bottle filling machine, which is a single workstation in the physical production system—Filling Station of AFB Factory, and this filling workplace is shown in Figure 5.

Figure 5. Filling Station of AFB Factory—(**a**) bottle entry; (**b**) liquid filling; (**c**) granulate filling; (**d**) cap placing; (**e**) cap closing; (**f**) bottle exit.

The workplace, physically realized as a rotating table supplemented by multiple industrial manipulators, is in digital form realized as a series of individual workstations, each representing a singular task carried out by this machine (Figure 6).

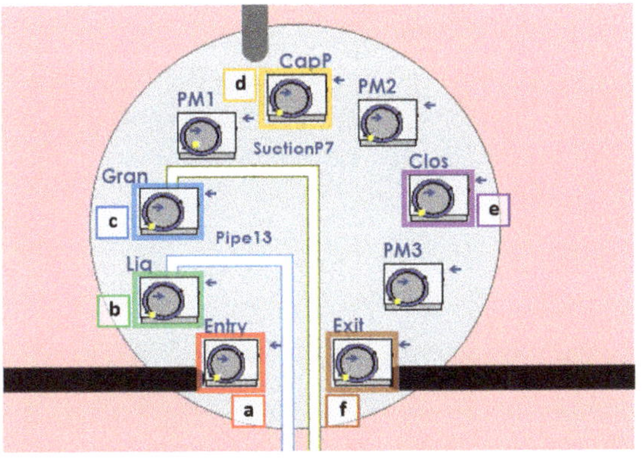

Figure 6. Simulation model—substitution for a Filling Station—(**a**) bottle entry; (**b**) liquid filling; (**c**) granulate filling; (**d**) cap placing; (**e**) cap closing; (**f**) bottle exit.

The other part of the model is a production preprocessing section which follows the ISO 15926-14 standard [20] for liquid handling with adjustments made for the specific PPS at our disposal. This section consists of two separate process lines.

The blue process line in Figure 7 is a model of a liquid material filtration, mixing, heating and quality check process with various tanks and processing units connected by a series of pipelines (Figure 8).

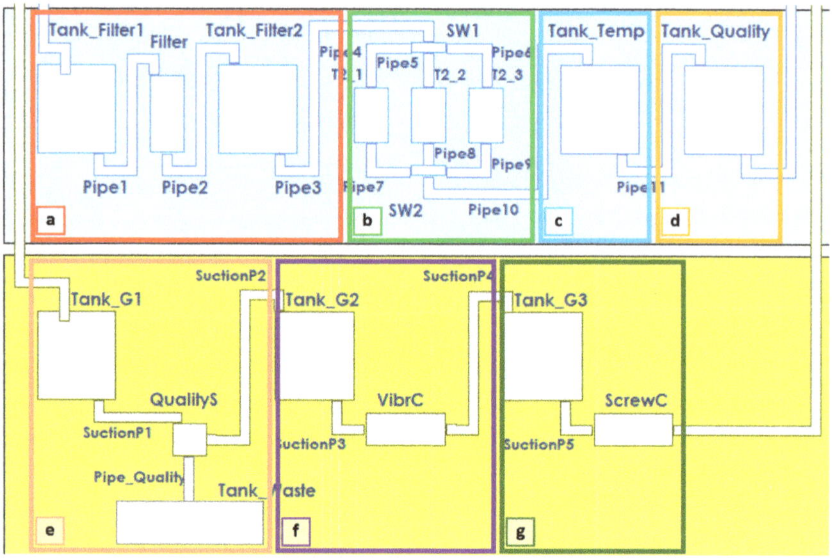

Figure 7. Digital model of material preprocessing stations—(**a**) liquid filtering; (**b**) liquid mixing; (**c**) liquid heating; (**d**) liquid quality check; (**e**) granulate quality control; (**f**) granulate cleaning; (**g**) granulate weighing.

Figure 8. Liquid material preprocessing in AFB Factory—(**a**) liquid filtering; (**b**) liquid mixing; (**c**) liquid heating; (**d**) liquid quality check.

The yellow process line in Figure 7 handles granulate material by filtering pieces of inappropriate size and quality (Figure 9). Both of these process lines feed liquid and solid material into the Filling Station in the main production process (Figure 5).

Figure 9. Solid material—granulate—preprocessing in AFB Factory—(**e**) granulate quality control; (**f**) granulate cleaning; (**g**) granulate weighing.

Data Integration between the MES and the Simulator

The production line AFB Factory allows to be controlled in two ways—autonomous mode, where production orders (required number of six-packs, number of bottles with liquid/solid material in each six-pack, amount of liquid/solid material in each bottle) are processed by the Filling Station control system (PLC), or in external mode, where the production orders are processed by the MES. In this case study, the external mode of production line control is used. All production orders are processed by the MES created in the AVEVA InTouch environment, which GUI is shown in Figure 10.

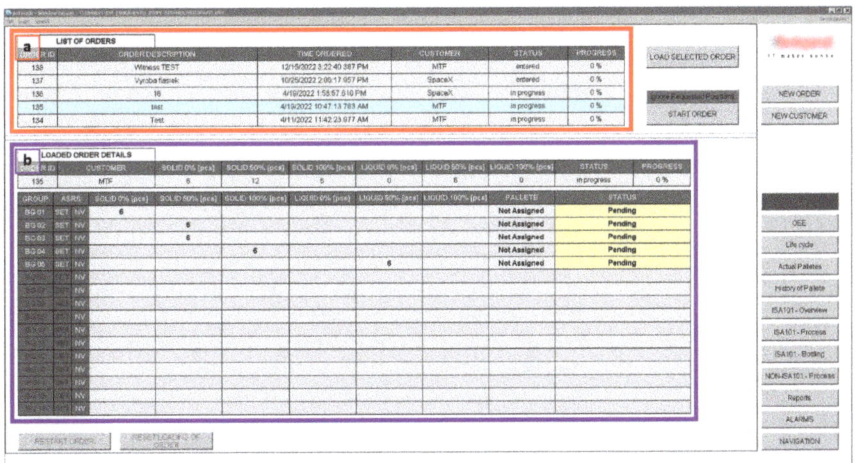

Figure 10. Intouch Manufacturing Execution System (MES)—(**a**) list of all orders; (**b**) orders details.

When it comes to data exchange between two systems, data integration is the first question that stands out almost immediately. For this problem, we proposed a method that simplifies the data format to a level which is accepted by both systems. Both MES (Figure 10) and the simulator are able to extract and read data from text or CSV files, with data being converted to numeric values, and depending on their position within their respective rows or columns, these values are interpreted accordingly.

To ensure that these files are being shared within the system properly, it is important to establish and maintain a stable connection between the communicating entities. Our solution to this problem was to have both MES and the simulation platform on the same local network. Having the two platforms connected locally, it is possible to carry out the communication using interfaces from either of the methods mentioned in this section. The operator can access the data stored on the MES server or simulation platform using a remote desktop protocol (RDP) from the user PC. As all the files being shared and accessed by both entities are located in one of the shared folders on the local network, it is possible to run custom maintenance scripts in the background which monitor their creation and dispose of the unnecessary files. The data transformation and formatting were carried out by custom OMI application created in MATLAB as a MATLAB App. The custom OMI GUI interface and data format during the order transformation are shown in Figure 11.

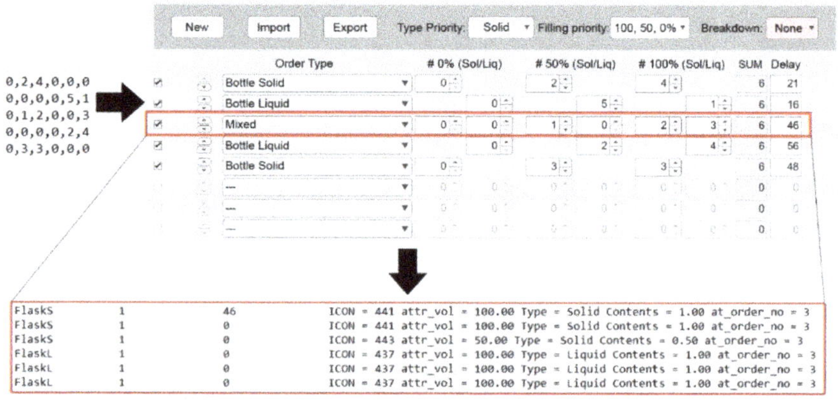

Figure 11. Data transformation from CSV to simulation input using dedicated OMI.

4. Experiments and Results

As proof of our concepts, we decided to run a case study with the proposed MOR method and use it as a starting point for the AOR method in the future research and development. With the goal of simulating multiple different scenarios without the need of manipulating resources in the physical production system, we have emulated and used different status data for storage tanks alongside the initial data gathered from the PPS. Using emulated data has granted us an access to a multitude of different scenarios, which would have otherwise required long periods of time for setting up a PPS for the specific scenario. Monitoring the flow of data from the MES to the simulator and back to the MES has been set as a main goal of this case study. During the case study, we decided to focus on two important parameters of the entire process, the first one being the time it takes for the process of order reorganization and the immediate simulation to finish, and the second one being the ability to finish the production order successfully. The two selected parameters are also the key points of future optimization with the AOR method mentioned in this paper.

The first optimization parameter could formally be defined as

$$X = N*(O + e) + \sum_{i=1}^{n} T_i + sim, \tag{1}$$

where:

X—full length of the simulation process including the use of OMI and data transfer between the interfaces and the simulator (in seconds);

N—number of orders;

O—time required for specifying singular order (in seconds);

e—human error (in seconds);

T—time required to transfer the order data between MES, interfaces and the simulator (in seconds);

sim—length of a simulation run (in seconds).

When taking the second parameter into consideration, it is binary in nature, but during a simulation run there are factors which influence its state, such as volume of resources remaining in the resource tanks. During the initiation process, we could define it as is shown in Box 1.

Box 1. Pseudocode of the parameter—an ability to finish the production order successfully

```
V1 = Volume_tank1 + Volume_tank2 + Volume_tank3 + Volume_MainTank
V2 = resources_in_pipes
R = requested_resources
if V1 > R OR V1 > R × 0.85 AND V2 > R × 0.15
    Production = true;
else
    Production = false;
end if
```

Our analysis of the production system has shown that the minimum amount of resources available in the storage tanks has to be higher than 85% of the resources requested in the production order, while the remaining 15% can be covered by the resources located in the pipelines of the production system. These values are reflected in the IF statement above.

The volume of resources in tanks is dynamically monitored during the simulation process. If at any point the volume of resources in the main tank reaches a sub 5% level, the simulation run is aborted, and an error is thrown.

After inputting the production orders in the MES, a text file containing the order data is created and loaded into the OMI. All the required order simulation attributes, such as content type, volume, number and real-time delay for every incoming order can be adjusted in the OMI, and every variation can be exported into an individual file. At export, the OMI offers an option to automatically run a simulation with preloaded resource and tank status data in the model. All the simulation data are logged into a file for postsimulation analysis. If the simulation process runs successfully, an export file is created which is then automatically loaded into the MES, and the production orders are updated within the order interface.

During the thorough testing phase of our proposed method, we carried out 4 experiments, while each of these individual sets were focused on a different aspect of the production process at hand. All the proposed experiments and their iterations have had a production requirement of 15 pallets with 6 products each, unless stated otherwise. The results of all the following experiments have been compared with the results from the existing physical system and have shown upwards of 97% match between the systems. The minor discrepancies between the results have been caused mainly by a human error while operating the physical production system among other smaller scale effects, such as multiple simultaneous processes running on the PC and others.

4.1. Experiment A

The first experiment consisted of 60 isolated iterations, divided into 4 categories. The input attribute we have iterated on was the arrival interval of production orders. The order arrival intervals specified in Table 1 are intervals between each individual order arriving in the production system, while the "All orders at start" scenario serves as a baseline scenario for Experiments A and B. The proposed categories for order arrival intervals are listed in Table 1.

Table 1. Production orders arrival intervals.

Scenario Name	Time Interval [s]
All orders at start	0
Short Arrival Interval	20–60
Medium Arrival Interval	80–120
Long Arrival Interval	130–170

Throughout this experiment, we have monitored the average time spent in the system for two types of products under different circumstances. The results of this experiment are shown in Figure 12. From the data presented in this figure, we have also deduced that prolonging the arrival interval for production orders directly impacts the average speed of production, which could also be an indicator of a bottleneck existing in the production system. When using the "All orders at start" scenario as a baseline, the arrival intervals between 20 and 60 s show a 14% decrease in the time required to finish a single product on average. When setting a time interval of arriving orders between 80 and 120 s, the results show up to 48% decrease in time spent in the system, while the slowest arrival intervals have shown up to 66.6% time-saving capability when compared to the baseline scenario.

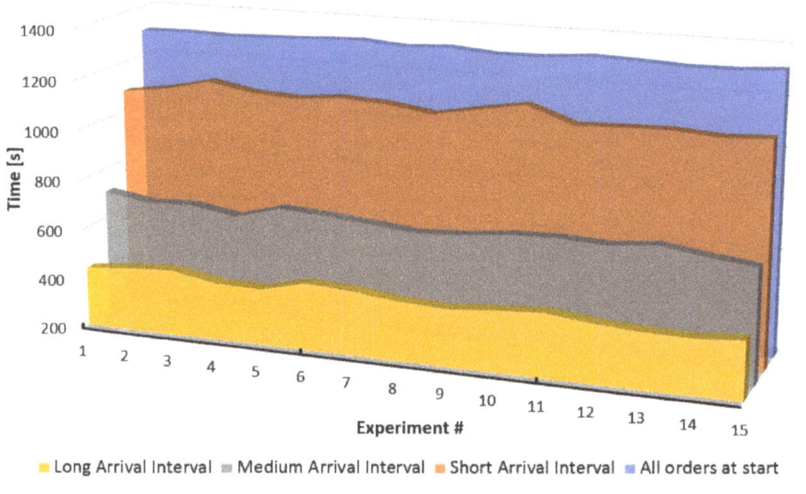

Figure 12. Effect of arrival intervals on production speed of individual products.

While these results have shown incremental improvements, it was necessary to test the impact of these changes on the full production run, with a full production order in mind.

4.2. Experiment B

Following the results analysis of the first experiment and consideration of their effects on the full production cycle, we proposed the second experiment. During this experiment, the main focus was set on the impact of different order arrival intervals on the full length of the production process. The arrival intervals were divided into four categories in accordance with Table 1. The results of the second experiment are presented in Figure 13.

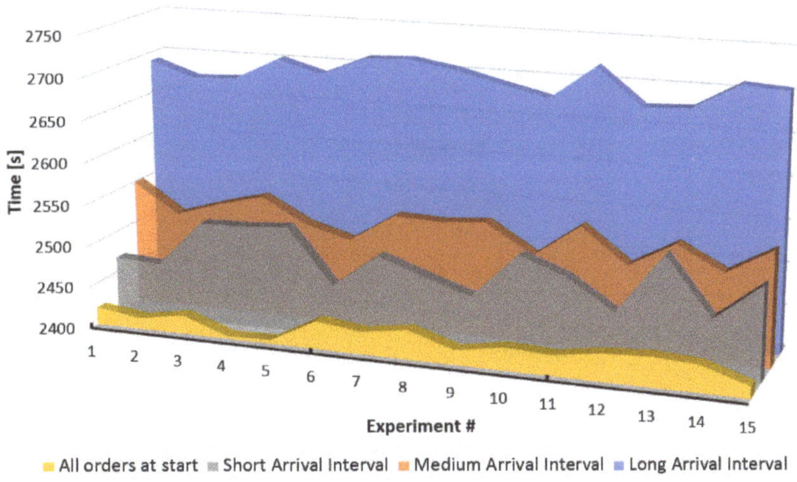

Figure 13. Effect of arrival intervals on the length of the production process.

The results analysis of this experiment has shown that adjustments to order interval has an opposite effect on the full length of the production process, in contrast to the singular product results. While the long arrival intervals benefit the production of single products by cutting their production time down to a third, when compared to the baseline scenario, prolonged order arrival intervals increase the length of the entire production process by up to 10% on average. These results were expected, as the time differences between the short and long intervals can be up to eight times as long in the most extreme cases, which leads to a large accumulation of time the production system spends idle over the longer period. Interpretation of the results of this experiment can be subjective and vary based on the needs and requirements of any production system in question. Trying to find a good balance between the lower individual production times for products and the length of the production in its entirety is an approach worth considering.

4.3. Experiment C

The focus of our third proposed experiment has been set on monitoring the time required for data exchange between MES and the simulation platform using the MOR method. A total of 150 iterations were proposed for this experiment, 50 for each of the three order types: 5-pallet, 10-pallet and 15-pallet orders. During this experiment, an operator has been involved while operating the OMI. The human error is reflected in the results of this experiment, largely caused by the lack of inconsistency during the order manipulation within OMI. The results of the third experiment are presented in Figure 14.

From the data shown in this figure, we have deduced that the time required to transfer data from MES to the simulation platform, run the simulation and then transfer data back to the MES scales linearly with the size of the incoming production orders, while being heavily impacted by the human factor in the process. The increasing time required for order management can be seen as a negative, especially while having the ability to create production orders larger than 15 pallets. The human factor in this process could start causing larger delays in production.

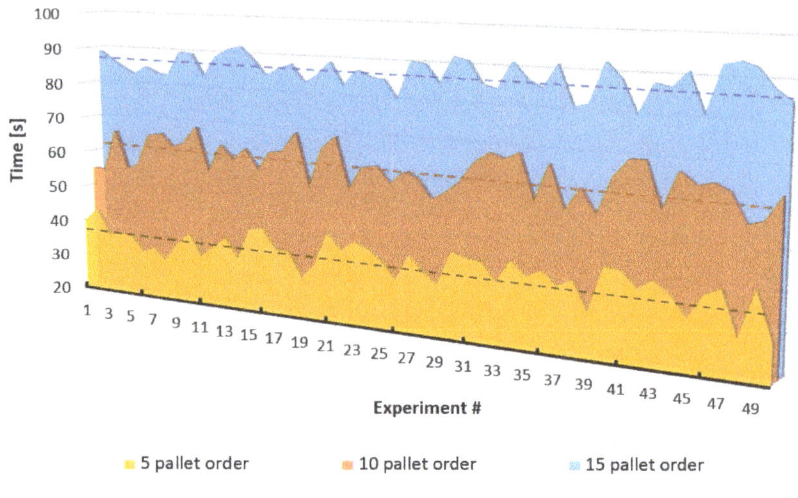

Figure 14. Time required for data exchange between MES and simulation platform.

4.4. Experiment D

For the final experiment, we opted for testing the limit of a specific workstation in the physical production system, which we identified to be a spot in the system where the bottlenecking occurs. The workstation in question is the Unpackaging station (Figure 15), which removes pallets from the transport system and moves them to the Recycling station.

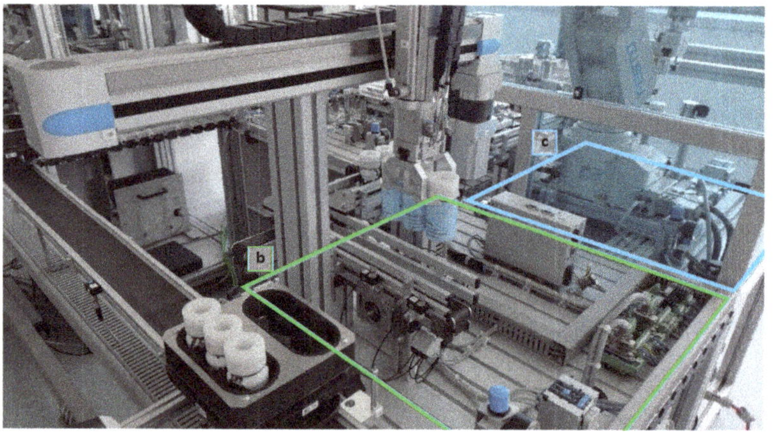

Figure 15. Unpackaging Station of AFB Factory—(**b**) unpackaging; (**c**) recycling.

For this experiment, based on the submodel in Figure 16, we have only run iteration where the order arrival interval was greater than zero. This is due to the workstation having an almost 100% blockage rate with all the orders arriving instantly at the start of the production, locking up an entire production system and requiring manual handling of products. The remaining iterations of this experiment have shown that increasing the arrival interval leads to reducing the blockage ration of this workstation to near-null values. The problematic bottleneck presented in Figure 16, which was also a part of our previous research [21], is found to be caused by the recycling station. This station handles products individually and performs two different operations on each product, while the unpackaging station moves the products onto the conveyor belt in batches of three products at a time. There have been multiple solutions proposed as alternatives to manipulating the incoming work orders. These solutions include introducing a parallel identical recycling station, which would double the rate at which products flow through this section of the production system. Increasing storage capacities and adjusting the cycle times for different machines can also be viewed as potential alternatives to the solution. All of these mentioned alternatives have been deemed inefficient for the problem at hand but have not been discarded, in case of their requirement for future research.

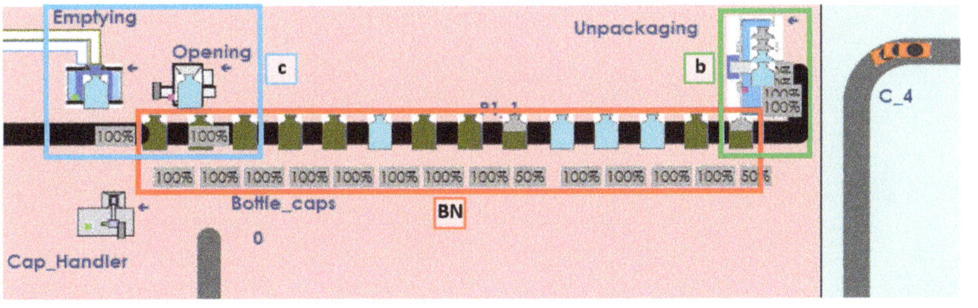

Figure 16. Simulation model—bottleneck of AFB Factory—(**b**) unpackaging; (**c**) recycling; (**BN**) bottleneck.

The data presented in Figure 17 show that, with short arrival interval (described in Table 1), the block rates have stayed at roughly 50%. Having these intervals increased to medium length, the percentage did not improve very much, sitting at around a 40% block rate, but increasing the intervals a bit further has proven to make a much bigger difference, reducing the block rate of this workstation to 1.67% on average. The results of this experiment have brought up a possibility of a breakpoint existing and a possibility to further optimize the flow of production. This will be a matter of further research.

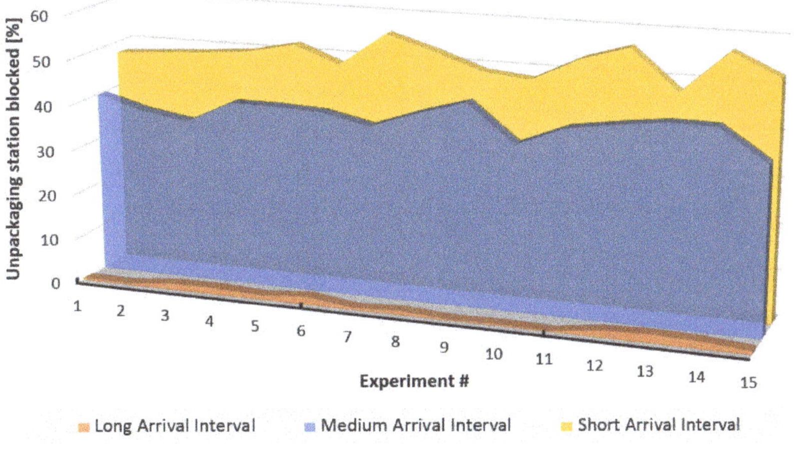

Figure 17. Block rate percentage showcase for Unpackaging machine.

5. Conclusions and Future Research

This paper describes possibilities for integrating a production system with the WITNESS Horizon 23.0 simulation software. The solution mentioned in this paper was proposed with two main goals in mind. The first goal was to use a digital twin to analyze the production orders sent by the MES as well as to check their feasibility. The other goal was to research and test the maximum possible level of data integration between the MES and the simulation platform. The proposed solution does achieve these goals to different extents, while the benefits and disadvantages of its implementation can be obviously found.

The MOR—Manual Order Rearrangement—method, while being able to handle all the requests and meet all the requirements of data integration between the two systems, has shown clear disadvantages of incorporating a human element into the integration process, mainly in terms of execution speed and consistency, which has been caused by increasing the number of orders required to be processed at the same time. This method also comes with a downside of having the operator's ability to instantly set the production in motion based on a simple inspection of the production system through an HMI.

The disadvantages of the MOR method could be eliminated by a concept of AOR—Automated Order Rearrangement. This fully automated algorithm is aimed at achieving full integration between the PPS and the proposed DM. The main difference from the MOR method is the fact that all the important decision-making is shifted from the operator to the simulator itself. The level of automation proposed in this concept does not require the OMI as was needed in the MOR, but instead is replaced by a listener script, which runs on the server and monitors the creation of specific data files and performs further actions based on their type. The only point where the operator takes any actions is during the initiation process and starting the production process. All remaining actions are handled autonomously by the simulator and its bridging interfaces. The only operator task is to perform a final inspection of the production orders and proceed to initiate the production process (Figure 18).

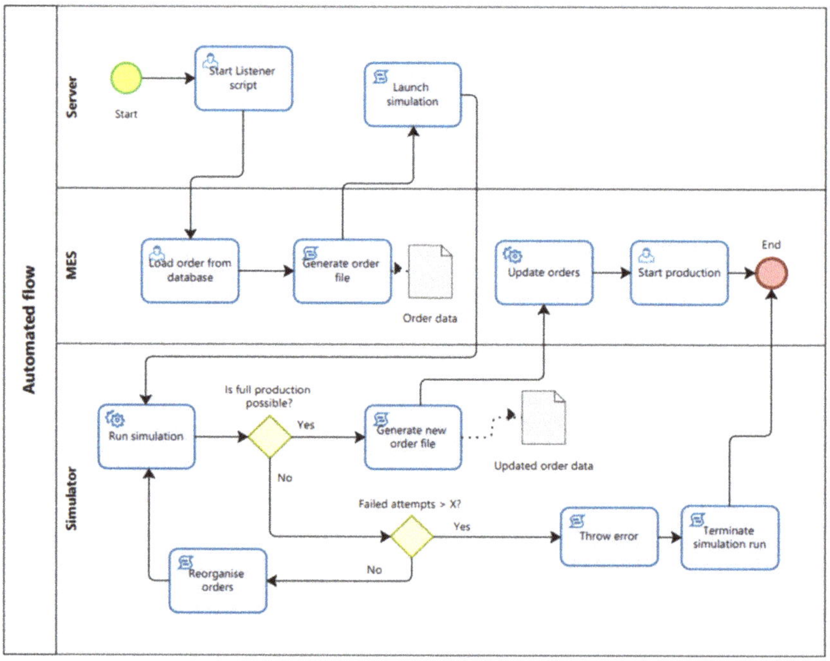

Figure 18. Conceptual model of an automated data flow method proposal.

Author Contributions: Conceptualization, F.B., P.V. and B.J.; formal analysis, P.V., B.J. and M.J.; funding acquisition, P.V.; investigation, F.B. and B.J.; methodology, F.B., P.V. and M.J.; project administration, P.V.; resources, P.V.; software, F.B.; supervision, P.V. and M.J.; validation, F.B.; visualization, M.J. and F.B; writing—original draft, F.B., B.J. and M.J.; writing—review and editing, P.V. and M.J. All authors have read and agreed to the published version of the manuscript.

Funding: This research was funded by the VEGA agency, grant number 1/0176/22 "Proactive control of hybrid production systems using simulation-based digital twin". This research was funded by the KEGA agency, grant number 027STU-4/2022 "Integration of the requirements of practice in the automotive industry with the teaching of subjects within the study programs Process Automation and Informatization in Industry and Industrial Management".

Data Availability Statement: Data sharing is not applicable to this article.

Conflicts of Interest: The authors declare no conflict of interest. The funders had no role in the design of the study; in the collection, analyses, or interpretation of data; in the writing of the manuscript; or in the decision to publish the results.

References

1. Moyne, J.; Iskandar, J. Big Data Analytics for Smart Manufacturing: Case Studies in Semiconductor Manufacturing. *Processes* **2017**, *5*, 39. [CrossRef]
2. Qi, Q.; Tao, F. Digital Twin and Big Data Towards Smart Manufacturing and Industry 4.0: 360 Degree Comparison. *IEEE Access* **2018**, *6*, 3585–3593. [CrossRef]
3. Jia, W.; Wang, W.; Zhang, Z. From Simple Digital Twin to Complex Digital Twin Part II: Multi-Scenario Applications of Digital Twin Shop Floor. *Adv. Eng. Inform.* **2023**, *56*, 101915. [CrossRef]
4. Hartmann, D.; Van der Auweraer, H. Digital Twins. In *Progress in Industrial Mathematics: Success Stories*; Cruz, M., Parés, C., Quintela, P., Eds.; Springer International Publishing: Cham, Switzerland, 2021; pp. 3–17.
5. Hochhalter, J.D. *Coupling Damage-Sensing Particles to the Digital Twin Concept*; NASA/TM; National Aeronautics and Space Administration, Langley Research Center: Hampton, VA, USA, 2014.
6. Rosen, R.; von Wichert, G.; Lo, G.; Bettenhausen, K.D. About The Importance of Autonomy and Digital Twins for the Future of Manufacturing. *IFAC-PapersOnLine* **2015**, *48*, 567–572. [CrossRef]
7. *ISO 23247-1*; Automation Systems and Integration—Digital Twin Framework for Manufacturing—Part 1: Overview and General Principles. International Organization for Standardization: Geneva, Switzerland, 2021.
8. *ISO 23247-1*; Automation Systems and Integration—Digital Twin Framework for Manufacturing—Part 3: Digital Representation of Manufacturing Elements. International Organization for Standardization: Geneva, Switzerland, 2021.
9. Shao, G.; Hightower, J.; Schindel, W. Credibility Consideration for Digital Twins in Manufacturing. *Manuf. Lett.* **2023**, *35*, 24–28. [CrossRef]
10. Brenner, B.; Hummel, V. Digital Twin as Enabler for an Innovative Digital Shopfloor Management System in the ESB Logistics Learning Factory at Reutlingen—University. *Procedia Manuf.* **2017**, *9*, 198–205. [CrossRef]
11. Pantelides, C.C.; Renfro, J.G. The Online Use of First-Principles Models in Process Operations: Review, Current Status and Future Needs. *Comput. Chem. Eng.* **2013**, *51*, 136–148. [CrossRef]
12. Martínez, G.S.; Sierla, S.; Karhela, T.; Vyatkin, V. Automatic Generation of a Simulation-Based Digital Twin of an Industrial Process Plant. In Proceedings of the IECON 2018—44th Annual Conference of the IEEE Industrial Electronics Society, Washington, DC, USA, 21–23 October 2018.
13. Martínez, G.S.; Karhela, T.A.; Ruusu, R.J.; Sierla, S.A.; Vyatkin, V. An Integrated Implementation Methodology of a Lifecycle-Wide Tracking Simulation Architecture. *IEEE Access* **2018**, *6*, 15391–15407. [CrossRef]
14. Carvalho, R.; da Silva, A.R. Sustainability Requirements of Digital Twin-Based Systems: A Meta Systematic Literature Review. *Appl. Sci.* **2021**, *11*, 5519. [CrossRef]
15. Spyrou, O.; Hurst, W.; Verdouw, C. Virtual Reality-Based Digital Twins: A Case Study on Pharmaceutical Cannabis. *Big Data Cogn. Comput.* **2023**, *7*, 95. [CrossRef]
16. Nica, E.; Popescu, G.H.; Poliak, M.; Kliestik, T.; Sabie, O.-M. Digital Twin Simulation Tools, Spatial Cognition Algorithms, and Multi-Sensor Fusion Technology in Sustainable Urban Governance Networks. *Mathematics* **2023**, *11*, 1981. [CrossRef]
17. Liu, J.; Zhang, K. Design and Simulation Debugging of Automobile Connecting Rod Production Line Based on the Digital Twin. *Appl. Sci.* **2023**, *13*, 4919. [CrossRef]
18. What Is Smart Manufacturing?—Definition from WhatIs.Com. Available online: https://www.techtarget.com/iotagenda/definition/smart-manufacturing-SM (accessed on 20 June 2023).
19. Shao, G. *Use Case Scenarios for Digital Twin Implementation Based on ISO 23247*; NIST: Gaithersburg, MD, USA, 2021.
20. *ISO 15926-2:2003*; Industrial Automation Systems and Integration—Integration of Life-Cycle Data for Process Plants Including Oil and Gas Production Facilities—Part 2: Data Model. International Organization for Standardization: Geneva, Switzerland, 2003.
21. Burčiar, F.; Važan, P. Integration of a Digital Twin into Production Line Control. In *Cybernetics Perspectives in Systems*; Silhavy, R., Ed.; Springer International Publishing: Cham, Switzerland, 2022; pp. 302–311. [CrossRef]

electronics

MDPI

Article

Mission-Conditioned Path Planning with Transformer Variational Autoencoder

Kyoungho Lee †, Eunji Im † and Kyunghoon Cho *

Department of Information and Telecommunication Engineering, Incheon National University, Incheon 22012, Republic of Korea; kno022603@inu.ac.kr (K.L.); twintwin0243@inu.ac.kr (E.I.)
* Correspondence: ckh0923@inu.ac.kr
† These authors contributed equally to this work.

Abstract: This paper introduces a novel deep learning framework for robotic path planning that addresses two primary challenges: integrating mission specifications defined through Linear Temporal Logic (LTL) and enhancing trajectory quality via cost function integration within the configuration space. Our approach utilizes a Conditional Variational Autoencoder (CVAE) to efficiently encode optimal trajectory distributions, which are subsequently processed by a Transformer network. This network leverages mission-specific information from LTL formulas to generate control sequences, ensuring adherence to LTL specifications and the generation of near-optimal trajectories. Additionally, our framework incorporates an anchor control set—a curated collection of plausible control values. At each timestep, the proposed method selects and refines a control from this set, enabling precise adjustments to achieve desired outcomes. Comparative analysis and rigorous simulation testing demonstrate that our method outperforms both traditional sampling-based and other deep-learning-based path-planning techniques in terms of computational efficiency, trajectory optimality, and mission success rates.

Keywords: deep-learning-based control synthesis; formal methods; mission-based path planning

Citation: Lee, K.; Im, E.; Cho, K. Mission-Conditioned Path Planning with Transformer Variational Autoencoder. *Electronics* **2024**, *13*, 2437. https://doi.org/10.3390/electronics13132437

Academic Editors: Luis Gracia, Juan Ernesto Solanes Galbis and Jaime Valls Miro

Received: 10 May 2024
Revised: 18 June 2024
Accepted: 19 June 2024
Published: 21 June 2024

1. Introduction

Path planning is a cornerstone of robotics, evolving from simple two-dimensional navigation to addressing more complex systems such as robot manipulators [1–3] and challenging scenarios [4–6]. This evolution underscores the necessity for sophisticated path-planning algorithms capable of navigating both the physical aspects of environments and the intricate requirements of diverse tasks.

Translating mission specifications, often articulated in human language, into computational models presents a significant challenge in path planning. Formal methods such as Linear Temporal Logic (LTL), Computation Tree Logic (CTL), and μ-calculus are pivotal in this area. LTL, in particular, is favored for its flexibility and expressive power in defining complex missions [7–9], offering a structured yet adaptable framework for encoding mission objectives.

Additionally, the quest for trajectories that balance cost-effectiveness with computational efficiency is critical. For instance, in environments with variable communication strengths, it is crucial to find low-cost paths that minimize exposure to areas with poor connectivity. Traditional methods like Rapidly Exploring Random Tree Star (RRT*) [10] are effective but can be computationally demanding, especially under numerous constraints.

The integration of deep learning into path planning offers a promising alternative, excelling in deriving optimal paths directly from data, thus mitigating the computational drawbacks of conventional methods. These techniques have broadened their utility across various domains, enhancing control strategies for robot manipulators [1] and addressing complex challenges in autonomous vehicle navigation [11,12]. The versatility and computational efficiency of deep learning approaches continue to propel advancements in the field of robotics.

This paper introduces a novel deep learning framework for robotic path planning that seamlessly integrates Linear Temporal Logic (LTL) formulas for mission specification with advanced trajectory optimization techniques. Our model employs a Conditional Variational Autoencoder (CVAE) and a Transformer network to innovatively generate control sequences that adhere to LTL specifications while optimizing cost efficiency. This integration marks a significant advancement in the fusion of deep learning with formal methods for path planning.

Key contributions of our approach include:

1. Application of the Transformer Network:We utilize the Transformer network to interpret LTL formulas and generate control sequences [13]. This allows for the effective handling of complex mission specifications.
2. Conditional Variational Autoencoder (CVAE): The CVAE is employed to navigate complex trajectory manifolds [14], providing the capability to generate diverse and feasible paths that meet the mission requirements.
3. Anchor Control Set: Our framework includes an anchor control set—a curated collection of plausible control values. At each timestep, the method selects and finely adjusts a control from this set, ensuring precise trajectory modifications to achieve desired objectives.
4. Incorporation of a Gaussian Mixture Model (GMM): The integration of a GMM to refine outputs enhances our framework's capacity to handle uncertainties, thereby improving both the precision and reliability of path planning under LTL constraints.

These contributions collectively advance efficient robotic path planning by providing near-optimal solutions that satisfy given LTL formulas.

As illustrated in Figure 1, our method synthesizes a control sequence distribution, enhanced by a GMM, for a given test scenario that adheres to the LTL formula $\phi = \Diamond(a \wedge \Diamond(b \wedge (\Diamond c)))$. This formula requires sequentially visiting regions a, b, and c. The figure displays trajectories sampled from the output control sequence distribution generated by the proposed approach. It is notable that these trajectories navigate through low-cost areas (depicted in blue) while avoiding obstacles and fulfilling the specified LTL requirements.

Figure 1. Illustrative example of trajectories generated using the proposed method in a test scenario. The mission, specified by the Linear Temporal Logic (LTL) formula $\phi = \Diamond(a \wedge \Diamond(b \wedge (\Diamond c)))$, requires sequential visits to regions a, b, and c.

Our contributions establish new benchmarks for cost efficiency and computational performance in robotic path planning. The effectiveness and superiority of our model compared to existing deep-learning-based strategies are demonstrated through rigorous comparative simulations, showcasing its potential to significantly influence the field.

2. Related Work

Path planning is a foundational element of robotics, requiring a balance between low-cost trajectories, complex dynamics, and precise mission specifications. The literature offers a diverse range of strategies addressing these challenges with varying degrees of success.

Finite Deterministic Systems: Research in finite deterministic systems has explored optimal controls with varied cost functions, such as minimax for bottleneck path problems [15] and weighted averages for cyclic paths [16]. However, these approaches often struggle in continuous path-planning scenarios due to limitations in integrating robot dynamics and the necessity for high-resolution discretization.

Sampling-based Motion Planning: Sampling-based methods, such as Rapidly Exploring Random Tree (RRT) [17], have addressed the integration of temporal logic and complex dynamics. The Rapidly Exploring Random Graph (RRG) [18] and Rapidly Exploring Random Tree Star (RRT*) [19] demonstrate utility in optimizing motion planning but face scalability and efficiency challenges as complexity increases.

Multi-layered Frameworks: Multi-layered frameworks that blend discrete abstractions with automata for co-safe LTL formulas [20–22] guide trajectory formation using sampling-based methods. Despite advancements, these approaches often rely heavily on geometric decomposition, which limits their computational efficiency.

Optimization Methods: Optimization techniques, especially those utilizing mixed-integer programming, aim to achieve optimal paths under LTL constraints [23,24]. Although effective, these methods encounter scalability issues when dealing with complex LTL formulas and a growing number of obstacles. The cross-entropy-based planning algorithm [25] enhances efficiency but also struggles with extensive LTL formulas.

Learning from Demonstration (LfD): LfD has increasingly integrated temporal logic to enhance autonomous behaviors, employing strategies such as Monte Carlo Tree Search (MCTS) adjusted with STL robustness values to enhance constraint satisfaction [26]. This integration illustrates LfD's potential in continuous control scenarios [27], with significant developments in blending formal task specifications within LfD skills using STL and black-box optimization for skill adaptation [28].

Trajectory Forecasting: Recent advances in trajectory forecasting have utilized deep learning to predict future movements based on past data, aligning closely with LfD principles. This research employs models such as Gaussian Mixture Models (GMMs) and Variational Autoencoders with Transformer architectures to produce action-aware predictions [29,30]. These approaches push the envelope toward models that seamlessly integrate global intentions with local movement strategies for improved adaptability and accuracy [31].

3. Preliminaries

This section introduces the foundational concepts and notations critical for understanding our approach to path planning under LTL specifications. Establishing a clear framework is essential for a comprehensive presentation of the system model, dynamics, and temporal logic that articulates the desired path properties. We will outline the mathematical formulations that underpin our system's model, explain the dynamics governing the system, and detail the principles of LTL that are crucial for defining and evaluating trajectory objectives. This groundwork is vital for understanding the complexities of autonomous systems and their operational criteria, preparing the ground for a detailed exploration of our proposed method.

3.1. System Model

To establish a foundation for our system model, we first introduce essential notations:

- $\mathcal{X} \subset \mathbb{R}^n$: The system's state space.

- $\mathcal{X}_{obs} \subset \mathbb{R}^n$: Space occupied by obstacles.
- $\mathcal{X}_{free} = \mathcal{X} \setminus \mathcal{X}_{obs}$: Free space not occupied by obstacles.
- $\mathcal{U} \subset \mathbb{R}^m$: Set of feasible controls.
- $\mathcal{W} \subset \mathbb{R}^{n_w}$: Workspace in which the system operates.
- $h : \mathcal{X} \rightarrow \mathcal{W}$: Mapping function from the state space to the workspace.

The system's dynamics are described by the following equation:

$$\dot{x}_t = f(x_t, u_t), \tag{1}$$

where $x_t \in \mathcal{X}_{free}$ represents the state of the system, $u_t \in \mathcal{U}$ denotes the control input, and f is a continuously differentiable function.

Given a control signal $\mathbf{u}$ over a time interval $[0, T]$, the resulting trajectory $\mathbf{x}(x_0, \mathbf{u})$ starts from the initial state x_0. The state of the system along this trajectory at any given time $t \in [0, T]$ is denoted by $\mathbf{x}(x_0, \mathbf{u}, t)$.

For discrete analysis, the trajectory $\mathbf{x}(x_0, \mathbf{u})$ is sampled at time increments $\Delta t \in \mathbb{R}^+$, expressed as:

$$\mathbf{x}_{\Delta t}(x_0, \mathbf{u}) = \{\mathbf{x}(x_0, \mathbf{u}, i\Delta t)\}_{i=0}^{i_f}, \tag{2}$$

where $i_f \in \mathbb{N}$ is the final time step, chosen based on the trajectory analysis requirements. This sampling ensures that the discrete representation accurately captures the essential dynamics of the trajectory over the analysis period, balancing computational efficiency with simulation accuracy.

3.2. *Linear Temporal Logic (LTL)*

LTL is a formalism used to express properties over linear time [32]. It utilizes atomic propositions (APs), Boolean operators, and temporal operators. An atomic proposition is a simple statement that is either true or false. Essential LTL operators include $\bigcirc$ (next), U (until), $\square$ (always), $\Diamond$ (eventually), and $\Rightarrow$ (implication). The structure of LTL formulas adheres to a grammar outlined in [33].

In our framework, $\Pi = \{\pi_0, \pi_1, \ldots \pi_N\}$ denotes the set of all atomic propositions. An LTL trace, represented as σ, is a sequence of atomic propositions. LTL typically deals with infinite traces, with Σ^ω representing all possible infinite traces originating from $\Sigma = 2^\Pi$. A trace σ satisfies a formula ϕ if it is expressed as $\sigma \models \phi$.

For this study, we focus on finite-time path planning using syntactically co-safe LTL (sc-LTL) formulas [34], which are particularly suited for finite scenarios. A sc-LTL formula ϕ ensures that any infinite trace satisfying ϕ also has a finite prefix that satisfies ϕ. All temporal logic formulas discussed in this paper adhere to the sc-LTL format.

3.2.1. Automaton Representation

Given a set of atomic propositions Π and a syntactically co-safe LTL formula ϕ, a non-deterministic finite automaton (NFA) can be constructed [35]. For instance, for the formula $\phi = \Diamond(a \land \Diamond(b \land \Diamond(c)))$, an example of the resulting NFA is depicted in Figure 2. This NFA can be converted into a deterministic finite automaton (DFA), which is more suitable for computational processes. A DFA is described by the tuple $\mathcal{A}_\phi = (Q, \Sigma, \delta, q_{init}, Q_{acc})$, where:

- Q : Set of states
- $\Sigma = 2^\Pi$: Alphabet, where each letter is a set of propositions
- $\delta : Q \times \Sigma \rightarrow Q$: Transition function
- $q_{init} \subseteq Q$: Initial state(s)
- $Q_{acc} \subseteq Q$: Accepting states

A trace σ from a DFA is accepted if, at any point, it leads to one of the accepting states (i.e., $\sigma_i \cap Q_{acc} \neq \emptyset$). Thus, a trace satisfies the sc-LTL formula ϕ (denoted as $\sigma \models \phi$) if it is accepted by the DFA $\mathcal{A}_\phi$.

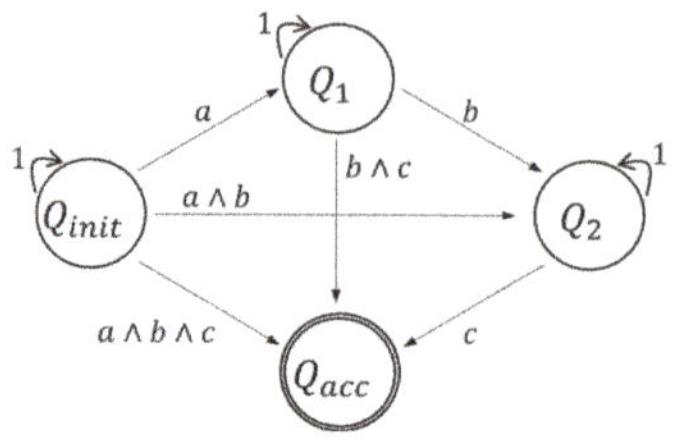

Figure 2. Example NFA for the sc-LTL formula $\phi = \Diamond(a \wedge \Diamond(b \wedge \Diamond(c)))$. The diagram illustrates four states and the transitions based on the input alphabets.

3.2.2. LTL Semantics over Trajectories

In this work, we define regions of interest within the workspace, $\mathcal{W}$, as $P = \{P_1, \ldots P_n\}$. These regions of interest are specified by the user. Each atomic proposition, π_j, from the set Π, corresponds to a specific region of interest, P_j. We employ a labeling function, $L : \mathcal{W} \to 2^{\Pi}$, to map each point in the workspace to a set of atomic propositions that are valid at that location. For any $\pi_i \in \Pi$, the negation $\neg\pi_i$ holds true for all points $\{w \in \mathcal{W} \mid \pi_i \notin L(w)\}$. Notably, π_0 remains true in all areas of the workspace except for the defined regions of interest and obstacles.

For a discretized trajectory, represented as $\mathbf{x}_{\Delta t}(x_0, \mathbf{u}) = \mathrm{x}_0, \mathrm{x}_1, \ldots \mathrm{x}_m$, which originates from x_0 and follows the control inputs $\mathbf{u}$ at each time step Δt, the trajectory trace can be defined as follows [20]:

$$trace(\mathbf{x}_{\Delta t}(\mathrm{x}_0, \mathbf{u})) = L(h(\mathrm{x}_0)), L(h(\mathrm{x}_1)), \ldots L(h(\mathrm{x}_m)). \tag{3}$$

This trace captures the sequence of atomic propositions valid at each point along the trajectory, reflecting the dynamic interaction with the workspace.

Figure 3 illustrates an example of a trajectory and its associated trace. This visual representation aids in understanding how the discrete segments of a trajectory map to their corresponding traces. For a given trajectory trace $trace(\mathbf{x}_{\Delta t}(\mathrm{x}_0, \mathbf{u})) = \tau_0, \tau_1, \ldots \tau_m$, we define the automaton state sequence $\mathcal{A}_\phi(trace(\mathbf{x}_{\Delta t}(\mathrm{x}_0, \mathbf{u}))) = q_0, q_1, \ldots q_m$ with each q_k specified as:

$$q_k = \begin{cases} \delta(q_{init}, \tau_0) & \text{if } k = 0 \\ \delta(q_{k-1}, \tau_k) & \text{if } k > 0 \end{cases}. \tag{4}$$

A trajectory $\mathbf{x}_{\Delta t}(\mathrm{x}_0, \mathbf{u})$ complies with the LTL formula ϕ, denoted by $\mathbf{x}(\mathrm{x}_0, \mathbf{u}) \models_{\Delta t} \phi$, if the automaton sequence reaches a subset of the accepting states Q_{acc}.

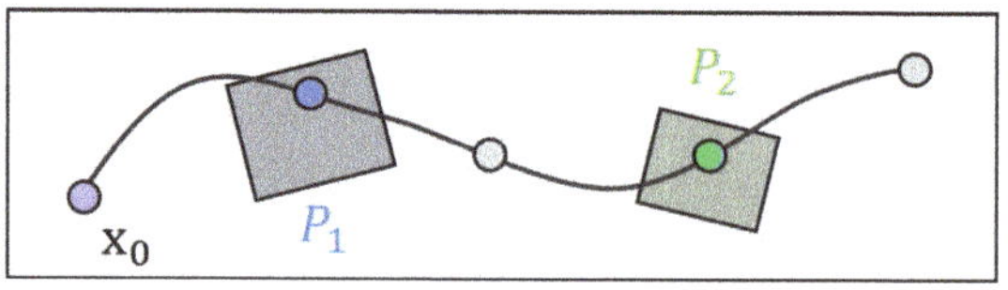

Figure 3. A trace defined over a discretized trajectory: For given $\mathbf{x}_{\Delta t}(\mathrm{x}_0, \mathbf{u}) = \mathrm{x}_0, \mathrm{x}_1, \ldots \mathrm{x}_5$, its trace is a sequence with 6 elements $\{\pi_0, \neg\pi_1, \neg\pi_2\}, \{\pi_0, \neg\pi_1, \neg\pi_2\}, \{\neg\pi_0, \pi_1, \neg\pi_2\}, \{\pi_0, \neg\pi_1, \neg\pi_2\}, \{\neg\pi_0, \neg\pi_1, \pi_2\}, \{\pi_0, \neg\pi_1, \neg\pi_2\}$.

4. Proposed Method

Our approach primarily focuses on optimizing the accumulated cost $J(\mathrm{x}_0, \mathbf{u})$, which is the line integral of a cost function c over a trajectory, mathematically expressed as:

$$J(\mathrm{x}_0, \mathbf{u}) = \frac{1}{T} \int_0^T c(\mathbf{x}(\mathrm{x}_0, \mathbf{u}, t)) dt, \tag{5}$$

where $c : \mathcal{X} \rightarrow \mathbb{R}^+$ is a bounded and continuous cost function, $\mathbf{u}$ represents the control signal from $t = 0$ to $t = T$, and x_0 is the initial state. Mission tasks are defined using a syntactically co-safe LTL formula, with each atomic proposition associated with a specific region of interest.

This paper introduces a novel deep learning framework for robotic path planning that significantly advances the synthesis of near-optimal control sequences. Our method is designed to meet specific mission requirements, adhere to system dynamics (as defined in Equation (1)), and optimize cost efficiency (as outlined in Equation (5)).

At the core of our innovative approach is the integration of a Conditional Variational Autoencoder (CVAE) with Transformer networks, creating an end-to-end solution that represents a significant leap forward in path-planning research. The CVAE plays a crucial role in learning the distribution within the latent space of optimal control sequences, enabling the generation of sequences that satisfy LTL constraints while minimizing costs.

Our methodology leverages convolutional neural networks (CNNs) to transform environmental inputs—such as cost maps, regions of interest, and obstacle configurations—into an image-like format, thus optimizing the processing of spatial information.

A distinctive feature of our research is the introduction of an anchor control set. Instead of directly generating a control sequence, our method selects an appropriate control from the anchor control set at each timestep. This selection and subsequent refinement are facilitated by a Gaussian Mixture Model (GMM), which effectively accounts for environmental uncertainties. This approach enables more precise control predictions and enhances the system's robustness against dynamic and unpredictable conditions.

The process begins with the Transformer's decoder generating an initial anchor control value, which is then refined by the GMM to incorporate minor uncertainties. This integration, bolstered by learning from the latent distribution, significantly improves the precision and reliability of control sequence predictions. Our structured approach innovatively addresses uncertainties, thereby enhancing the robustness of our path-planning framework.

In summary, the proposed method offers several key advantages:

1. End-to-end approach: By employing a Transformer network to encode LTL formulas, our method eliminates the need for the discretization processes and graph representations typically required in previous studies. This streamlined approach simplifies the encoding and handling of complex specifications directly within the network architecture.
2. Step-by-step uncertainty consideration: Our approach meticulously addresses uncertainties within the path-planning process. The latent space is designed to account for major uncertainties, while the selection of controls from the anchor control set and their subsequent refinement through the GMM framework effectively manage minor uncertainties, enhancing the robustness and reliability of the trajectory planning.

Subsequent sections will delve deeper into our methodology, particularly focusing on the innovative implementation of anchor controls within the GMM framework and its profound implications. Through this detailed exploration, we aim to provide a clear understanding of the significant advancements our strategy introduces to the field of path planning.

4.1. Data Components

This section outlines the input configurations employed in our deep learning framework, designed to facilitate the interpretation of LTL formulas. To simplify the association of LTL formulas with spatial regions, regions of interest within the operational environment are denoted alphabetically, starting with a.

Our framework utilizes two primary data components: the state image X and the solution control sequence U. The state image X consists of multiple layers, each representing different environmental features in a format readily processed by the neural network. As illustrated in Figure 4, these layers include the costmap, obstacles, regions of interest, and the initial position, with each layer stacked to provide a comprehensive environmental context.

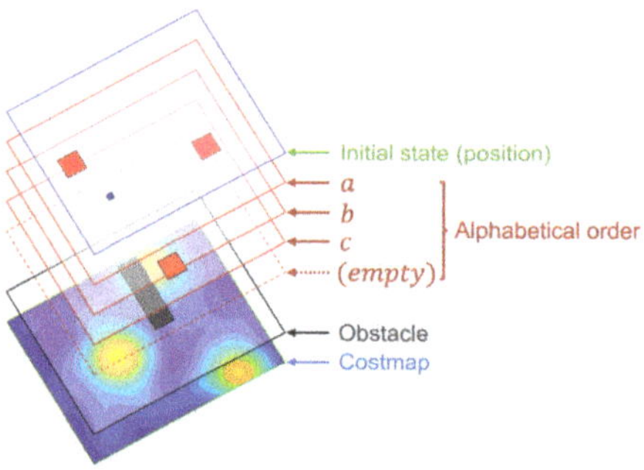

Figure 4. Configuration of the state image X for regions of interest $\{a, b, c\}$. Layers are sequentially arranged to depict the costmap, obstacles, regions of interest, and the initial state.

The generation of control sequences is guided by methodologies from our prior research [36], which align with our system dynamics as defined in Equation (1) and the specifications of co-safe temporal logic. Specifically, the adopted approach focuses on identifying low-cost trajectories that comply with given co-safe temporal logic specifications, with LTL semantics evaluated against the trajectories to ensure adherence to necessary specifications.

Our data generation strategy is specifically tailored to accommodate environmental constraints and LTL objectives relevant to our study. This strategy is depicted in Figure 5, illustrating how environmental parameters and LTL formulas are transformed into output control sequences. When the length of generated sequences falls short of the maximum designated length, dummy control values are utilized as placeholders to maintain uniform sequence length, aiding in standardizing the training process across different scenarios.

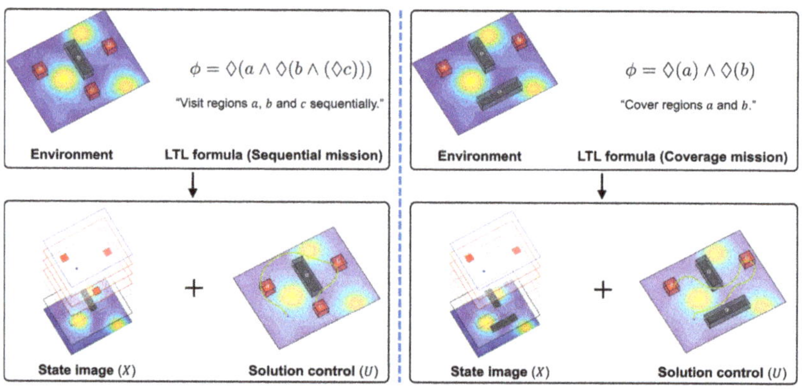

Figure 5. Visual representation of the data generation methodology, highlighting the integration of state images and control sequences derived from distinct LTL formulas.

4.2. Anchor Control Set

In our proposed model, we utilize an anchor control set $\mathbf{A} = \{\mathbf{a}^k\}_{k=1}^{K}$, consisting of a predefined, fixed set of control sequences. Each anchor control, $\mathbf{a}^k$, is a sequence of control inputs $[\mathrm{u}_0^k, \mathrm{u}_1^k, \dots \mathrm{u}_{H_A-1}^k]$ that spans a designated time horizon H_A. It is important to note that this time horizon H_A is not necessarily equivalent to the time horizon of the final solution's control sequence.

The use of longer sequences for each anchor control, rather than single timestep controls, is motivated by the difficulty of capturing significant behavioral trends with overly granular, single-step data. In the control generation stage of our network, which will be elaborated on in subsequent sections, controls are selected in bundles of H_A rather than individually per timestep. This approach simplifies the decoder's prediction tasks compared to methods that operate on a per-timestep basis, thereby enhancing both the efficiency and efficacy of our model.

To construct the anchor control set, we derived it from a dataset using the k-means clustering algorithm. The distance between two anchor controls, necessary for the clustering process, is calculated as follows [29]:

$$d(\mathbf{a}^i, \mathbf{a}^j) = \sum_{t=0}^{H_A} \|\mathrm{u}_t^i - \mathrm{u}_t^j\|^2. \tag{6}$$

This metric ensures that the controls within our set are optimally spaced to effectively cover diverse potential scenarios.

4.3. Proposed Architecture

The architecture of our proposed deep learning network is depicted in Figure 6. This comprehensive end-to-end system processes inputs from the environmental image and LTL formula to the final generation of the control sequence.

- Data components (1st row): The input layer consists of the multi-channeled state image X, the initial state x_0, the LTL formula ϕ, and the solution control sequence U. These components establish the context and objectives for path planning.
- Training phase (2nd row): During training, the network utilizes the solution control sequence U from the dataset to train the Conditional Variational Autoencoder (CVAE). This enables the network to effectively learn the latent distribution, facilitating accurate prediction of the control sequence $\hat{U}$ that adheres to the LTL specifications.
- Testing phase (3rd row): In the testing phase, the architecture demonstrates how latent samples are converted into predicted control sequences, validating the trained model's efficacy in real-world scenarios.

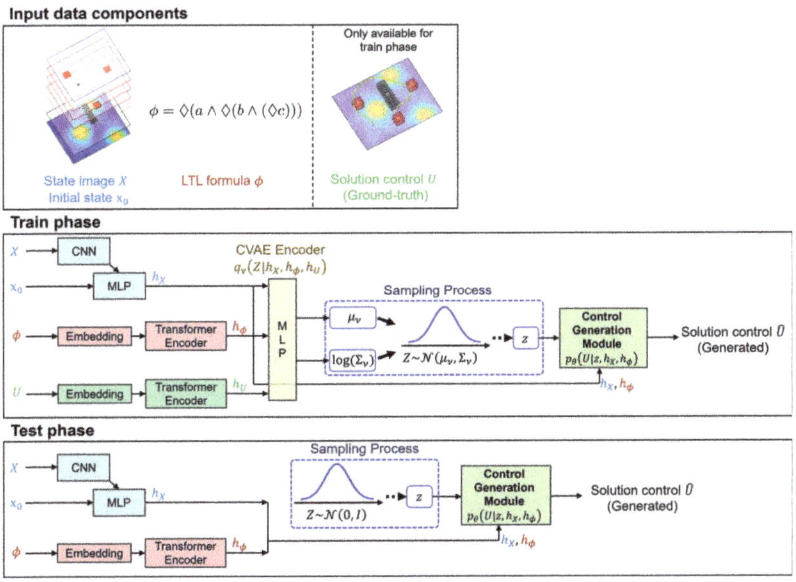

Figure 6. Overview of the proposed end-to-end deep learning network, illustrating the flow from input data components through the training and testing phases to the output control sequences.

This network not only streamlines the transition from input to output but also ensures that all elements, from environmental conditions to control strategies, are integrated within a unified framework. By detailing each phase of the network, we provide a clear pathway from data ingestion to practical application, highlighting the network's capacity to adapt and respond to complex path-planning demands.

In the encoding stage, the network processes the input data using specialized components. A CNN encodes the state image, while Transformer encoders [13] handle the encoding of control sequences and LTL formulas. The LTL formulas are encoded by transforming each character into an embedded representation using a predefined set of alphabet and operator symbols. The resulting encoded outputs—h_X for the state image X and initial state x_0, h_ϕ for the LTL formula ϕ, and h_U for the solution control sequence U—are then integrated to facilitate the learning process.

A key feature of our network is the implementation of a CVAE, chosen for its efficacy in handling high-dimensional spaces and versatility with various input configurations. The CVAE is instrumental in generating output control sequences by exploring the latent space. During training, it learns a probability distribution representing potential control sequences, conditioned on the encoded state image h_X and LTL formula features h_ϕ.

Our CVAE model includes three crucial parameterized functions:

- The recognition model $q_\nu(Z|h_X, h_\phi, h_U)$ approximates the distribution of the latent variable Z based on the input features and the control sequence. It is modeled as a Gaussian distribution, $\mathcal{N}(\mu_\nu(h_X, h_\phi, h_U), \Sigma_\nu(h_X, h_\phi, h_U))$, where μ_ν and Σ_ν represent the mean and covariance determined by the network.
- The prior model $p_\theta(Z|h_X, h_\phi)$ assumes a standard Gaussian distribution, $\mathcal{N}(0, I)$, simplifying the structure of the latent space.
- The generation model $p_\theta(U|z, h_X, h_\phi)$ calculates the likelihood of each control sequence element u_i based on the latent sample z and the encoded inputs, computed as the product of conditional probabilities over the sequence's length $N_A \times H_A$. This model is implemented in the Control Generation Module depicted in Figure 7.

A sample z drawn from the recognition model is fed into the decoder, which then generates the predicted control sequence. The length of this control sequence is $N_A \times H_A$, reflecting the selection of N_A anchor controls, each with a time length of H_A.

4.4. Control Generation Module

The architecture of our proposed control generation module is depicted in Figure 7. This module efficiently synthesizes the entire control sequence distribution from the latent sample z and encoded information h_X, h_ϕ in a single step, utilizing a non-autoregressive model to enhance efficiency and coherence. The GMM projection networks share parameters across all calculations, ensuring consistency.

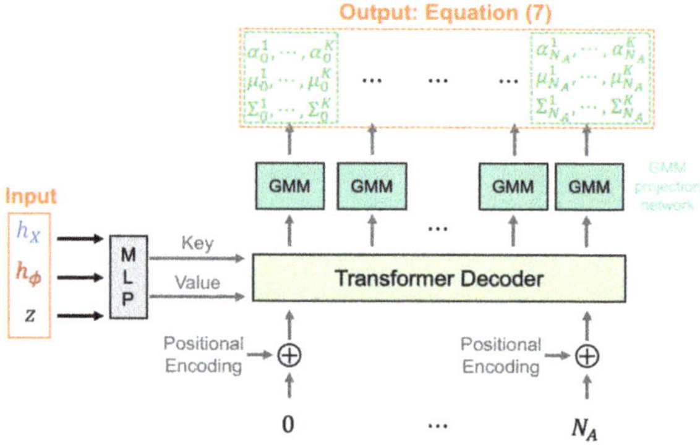

Figure 7. Schematic of the control decoder architecture, illustrating how the distribution of the output control sequence is generated from the latent sample z and encoded information h_X, h_ϕ.

In this model, a Transformer decoder utilizes sinusoidal positional encodings to integrate time information as the query, while the latent vector, combined with the encoded state image and LTL formula features, acts as the key and value. This configuration, coupled with a GMM mixture module, enables the Transformer decoder to generate the output control sequence distribution as defined by the following equation:

$$p_\theta(U|z, h_X, h_\phi) = \prod_{t=0}^{N_A} \sum_{k=1}^{K} \alpha_t^k \mathcal{N}(\tilde{u}_t | \mathbf{a}^k + \mu_t^k, \Sigma_t^k). \quad (7)$$

In this formulation:

- α_t^k, μ_t^k, and Σ_t^k are the mixture coefficients, means, and covariances of the GMM, respectively, produced by the GMM projection network.
- $\mathbf{a}^k$ represents the anchor control from the set $\mathbf{A}$.
- K is the number of mixture components, equal to the number of anchor controls, demonstrating the model's capability to represent complex distributions of control sequences.
- Each $\tilde{u}_t$ spans the time horizon H_A.

This approach uses the GMM to integrate the latent variable z, historical state image data h_X, and LTL formula features h_ϕ, creating a probabilistic space where potential control sequences are distributed around the anchor control $\mathbf{a}^k$. This serves as a central reference point, enabling the identification of feasible control sequences within the operational domain. Unlike static models, $\mathbf{a}^k$ and the GMM adapt predictions to varying conditions and uncertainties inherent in dynamic environments, enhancing the model's flexibility.

To maintain focus on the model's predictive capability and avoid unnecessary complexity, we present the GMM parameters directly without delving into the detailed functional dependencies on θ. This straightforward presentation underscores the model's utility in forecasting control sequences that are both feasible and optimized according to the computed probability distributions.

4.5. Loss Function for Training Phase

The training of our CVAE is governed by the Evidence Lower Bound (ELBO) loss function, which is initially formulated as:

$$\mathbb{E}_{q_\nu(Z|h_X,h_\phi,h_U)}[\log p_\theta(U|z, h_X, h_\phi)] - \mathcal{D}_{KL}(q_\nu(z|h_X, h_\phi, h_U)||p_\theta(z|h_X, h_\phi)). \quad (8)$$

To better suit our application's specific requirements, we adapt the ELBO function and define the loss function as follows:

$$-\sum_{t=0}^{N_A} \log(p_\theta(\tilde{u}_t|z, h_X, h_\phi)) + \lambda \cdot \mathcal{D}_{KL}\Big(\mathcal{N}(\mu_\nu(h_X, h_\phi, h_U), \Sigma_\nu(h_X, h_\phi, h_U))||\mathcal{N}(0, I)\Big), \quad (9)$$

where $\tilde{u}_t$ represents an element of the control sequence U, N_A is the number of anchor controls, and λ is a scaling factor used to balance the terms. The Kullback-Leibler divergence ($\mathcal{D}_{KL}$) measures how one probability distribution diverges from a second, reference probability distribution. We set $\lambda = 1$, optimizing parameters ν and θ by minimizing this loss function.

The first term of Equation (9), which leverages Equation (7), is detailed as follows:

$$\log\left(p_\theta(\tilde{u}_t|z, h_X, h_\phi)\right) = \sum_{t=0}^{N_A}\sum_{k=1}^{K} \mathbf{1}(k = \hat{k}_t)\left[\log \alpha_t^k + \log \mathcal{N}(\tilde{u}_t|\mathbf{a}^k + \mu_t^k, \Sigma_t^k)\right]. \quad (10)$$

This expression represents a time-sequence extension of the standard GMM likelihood fitting [37]. The notation $\mathbf{1}(\cdot)$ is the indicator function, and $\hat{k}_t$ is the index of the anchor control that most closely matches the ground-truth control, measured using the $l2$-norm distance. This hard assignment of ground-truth anchor controls circumvents the intractability of direct GMM likelihood fitting, avoids the need for an expectation-maximization procedure, and allows practitioners to precisely control the design of anchor controls as discussed in [29]. This formulation underlines our methodology for estimating the probability distribution of control sequences, essential for ensuring that the model effectively handles the diversity of potential solutions and manages uncertainties.

4.6. Test Phase

During the test phase, the control decoder operates by processing a latent sample z, drawn from the prior distribution. This sample is deterministically transformed into a control sequence distribution as defined in Equation (7). From this distribution, the solution control sequence is generated.

The generation of the control sequence is a continuous process that persists until one of the following conditions is met: the sequence satisfies the specified LTL constraints, a collision with an obstacle occurs, or the sequence moves beyond the boundaries set by the cost map.

5. Experimental Results

This section details the outcomes from a series of simulations and experiments using the Dubins car model, which adheres to the following kinematic equations:

$$\dot{x} = v\cos(\theta), \quad \dot{y} = v\sin(\theta), \quad \dot{\theta} = \omega, \tag{11}$$

where (x, y) represents the car's position, θ the heading angle, and v and ω the linear and angular velocities, respectively. It is important to note that the symbol θ is used elsewhere in this manuscript to denote different concepts unrelated to its usage here as the vehicle's heading.

We conducted three distinct sets of simulation experiments to comprehensively evaluate the proposed method's effectiveness and versatility. The first set involved generated costmaps to test the method's performance in controlled environments, focusing on its ability to navigate based on cost efficiency. The second set utilized real-world data, incorporating a traffic accident density map from Helsinki, to demonstrate the method's applicability and performance in real scenarios. The third set involved autonomous driving contexts, where the method demonstrated stable control sequence generation amidst the dynamic movement of surrounding vehicles.

The datasets for learning, including costmaps, were created as follows:

- First and second experiments: Gaussian process regression was employed to generate training costmaps, each containing no more than four regions of interest and no more than eight obstacles. Using the dynamic model defined in Equation (1), near-optimal control sequences were computed based on the method described in [36]. The resulting dataset comprised 800 costmaps, each facilitating the generation of 1500 control sequences, thereby capturing a wide range of environmental scenarios. To enhance the robustness and generalizability of our model, variability was introduced in the data generation phase by randomly varying the starting positions, placements of regions of interest, obstacle configurations, and assignments of LTL formulas for each dataset instance. This approach was designed to simulate a diverse set of potential operational scenarios, thereby preparing the model to handle a wide range of conditions effectively.
- Last experiment: In the final autonomous driving experiment, the costmap was generated from the highD dataset [38]. High costs were assigned to areas where other vehicles were present and to out-of-track areas. In this experiment, three types of LTL formulas were used: lane change to the left, lane keeping, and lane change to the right. Each data instance consists of a costmap, an LTL formula, and a control sequence. The LTL formula was selected as the closest match from the dataset based on the control sequence. For example, if the vehicle changes lanes to the left in the data, an

LTL formula related to "lane change to the left" is selected. The dataset comprised 1,000,000 instances. Please refer to the relevant subsection for a detailed explanation.

For network input, images were standardized to 128×128 pixels to comply with the memory capacity limitations of our GPU hardware. This resolution strikes a balance between retaining essential environmental details and maintaining computational feasibility. The network was trained over 300 epochs to ensure adequate learning depth, with a batch size of 32 to optimize the balance between memory usage and convergence stability. An initial learning rate of 1×10^{-3} and a weight decay of 1×10^{-5} were empirically set to provide an optimal compromise between training speed and minimizing the risk of overfitting.

In the experimental setup, the number of anchor controls K was defined as 20, and the anchor control set $\mathbf{A}$ was established using the entire training data.

Simulation experiments were conducted on an AMD R7-7700 processor with an RTX 4080 Super GPU, and the proposed network was implemented using PyTorch (version 2.2.1) [39].

The results for each experiment are described in the subsequent subsections.

5.1. The Generated Costmap

Figure 8 showcases the test costmap, synthesized using the same methods as those for the training costmaps. The costmap features regions of interest, marked with red boxes labeled with alphabetic identifiers, and obstacles are indicated by gray boxes.

In our experimental setup, we aimed to assess the robustness and effectiveness of our system across various LTL missions. These missions were categorized into sequential missions (ϕ_{toy1} and ϕ_{toy4}) and coverage missions (ϕ_{toy2} and ϕ_{toy3}). A mission was deemed incomplete if the system either exceeded the maximum allowed sequence length or encountered a collision, thereby failing to meet the mission criteria. Each row in the figure corresponds to a set of four subfigures, each varying by the initial position. Trajectories generated from the output distribution (as defined in Equation (7)) are displayed as red lines in each subfigure.

The proposed method strategically generates control sequences that traverse low-cost areas, depicted in blue, to effectively complete the LTL missions. Notably, these sequences successfully avoid collisions even in environments with obstacles. For coverage missions, as shown in Figure 8b,c, the solution paths differ in the order they visit regions of interest, which varies according to the starting position. For example, in Figure 8c, the sequences in each subfigure visit the regions in various orders, such as "c->b->a", "a->b->c", "a->b->c", and "b->c->a".

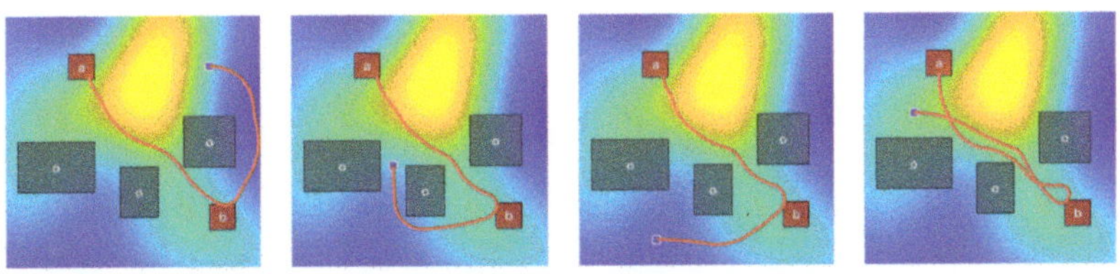

(a)$\phi_{toy1} = \Diamond(a \wedge \Diamond(b))$, "Visit regions a and b sequentially."

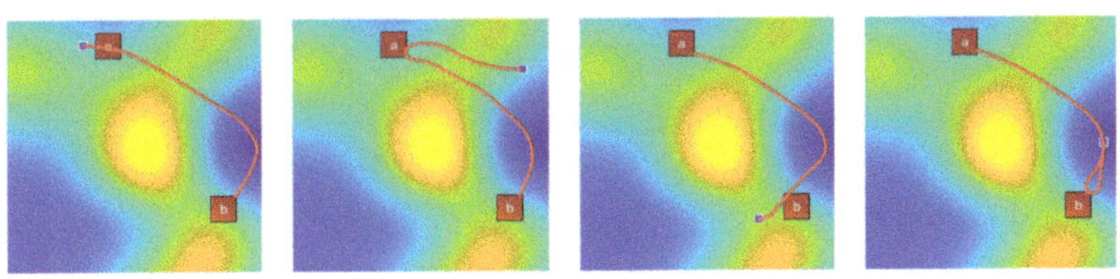

(b)$\phi_{toy2} = \Diamond(a) \wedge \Diamond(b)$, "Cover regions a and b."

Figure 8. *Cont.*

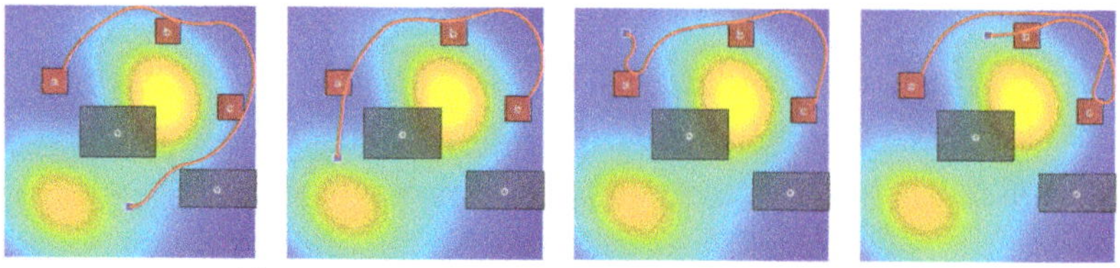

(c) $\phi_{toy3} = \Diamond(a) \wedge \Diamond(b) \wedge \Diamond(c)$, "Cover regions a, b and c."

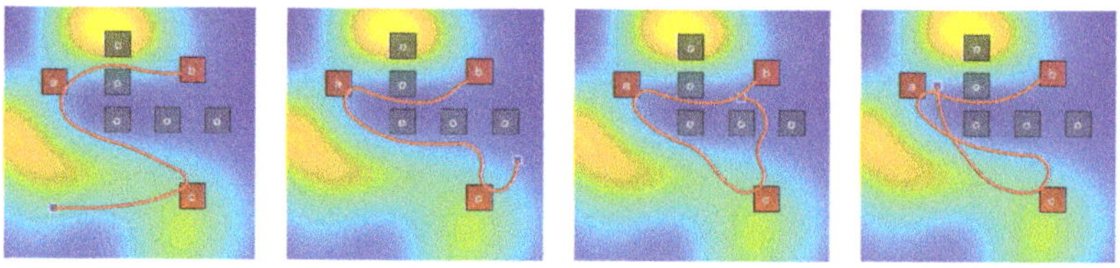

(d) $\phi_{toy4} = \Diamond(a \wedge \Diamond(b \wedge (\Diamond c)))$, "Visit regions a, b and c sequentially."

Figure 8. Solution trajectories generated by the proposed method for different LTL formulas, denoted as ϕ_{toyi}, shown in each subfigure.

Figure 9 presents solution trajectories generated by the proposed network for an LTL mission specified by $\phi = \Diamond(a) \wedge \Diamond(b) \wedge \Diamond(c)$, which mandates visiting regions of interest a, b, and c at least once. In this figure, trajectories colored identically originate from the same latent sample value. The latent distribution governs the sequence in which the regions of interest are visited, ensuring compliance with the LTL mission, while the GMM component of the control decoder models the uncertainty within this sequence.

For example, in subfigure (b), the orange trajectories represent a sequence visiting a, followed by b, then c. Conversely, the green trajectories depict a sequence visiting a, c, and then b. This variability illustrates the network's ability to generate diverse solutions that not only adhere to the given LTL mission but also effectively account for uncertainties.

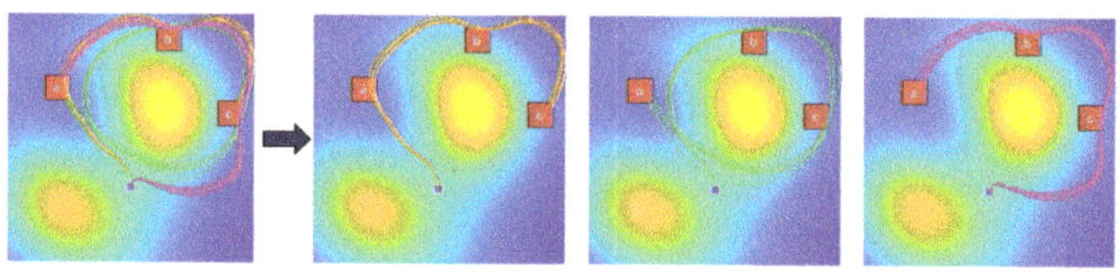

(a)

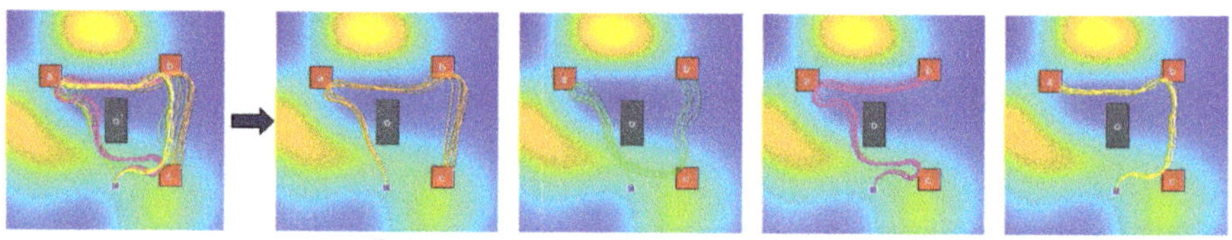

(b)

Figure 9. Solution trajectories for an LTL mission $\phi = \Diamond(a) \wedge \Diamond(b) \wedge \Diamond(c)$, requiring at least one visit to each region of interest a, b, and c. Trajectories sharing the same color are derived from the same latent sample value.

Performance evaluation of the developed path-planning approach was conducted through comparative experiments. These experiments aimed to quantify trajectory cost and mission success rates across various scenarios characterized by different lengths of sequential LTL formulas ($|\phi|$) and obstacle counts (n_{obs}). The length of a sequential LTL formula corresponds to the number of specified regions of interest.

The experimental design included 250 trials per scenario, which featured varying costmap configurations, region of interest placements, obstacle locations, initial positions, and LTL formulas. To ensure a comprehensive evaluation of the approach's robustness, these elements were systematically varied within each trial. Trials lacking feasible solution paths were excluded to maintain the integrity of the experiment.

The method's performance was benchmarked against several established deep learning models:

- MLP: A basic Multilayer Perceptron architecture.
- Seq2Seq-LSTM: A sequence-to-sequence model using LSTM networks [40].
- TCN: A Temporal Convolutional Network [41].
- TFN: A Transformer network model [13].

These models were trained to map initial conditions and LTL formulas to control sequences, with a CNN feature extractor handling image-like inputs. The LTL formula ϕ was encoded as an input sequence using the same embedding technique employed in the proposed method. Additionally, LBPP-LTL [36], a sampling-based path-planning algorithm noted for its longer computation times but guaranteed asymptotic optimality, was included as a benchmark for cost performance despite its computational intensity.

The results, summarized in Table 1, present the average trajectory cost and mission success rate for each model in the evaluated scenarios. The LBPP-LTL method serves as a baseline, with its trajectory cost normalized to 1, providing a standard for comparison despite its computational demands.

Table 1. Comparative Performance of Path Planning Approaches on Scenarios with Sequential LTL Missions. This table details trajectory costs and LTL mission success rates, categorized by the length of the LTL missions ($|\phi|$) and the number of obstacles (n_{obs}). Metrics are normalized against the LBPP-LTL benchmark, which is set with a normalized trajectory cost of 1 and a mission success rate of 100%.

	$\|\phi\| = 2, n_{obs} = 1$	$\|\phi\| = 2, n_{obs} = 3$	$\|\phi\| = 3, n_{obs} = 2$	$\|\phi\| = 3, n_{obs} = 5$
Trajectory cost (relative)				
MLP	1.391	1.401	1.417	1.445
Seq2Seq-LSTM	1.180	1.186	1.190	1.209
TCN [41]	1.187	1.193	1.198	1.215
TFN [13]	1.075	1.097	1.102	1.114
Proposed	1.081	1.086	1.093	1.107
LBPP-LTL [36]	1.000	1.000	1.000	1.000
LTL mission success rate				
MLP	92.4%	90.4%	88.8%	87.2%
Seq2Seq-LSTM	96.4%	94.4%	93.6%	92.8%
TCN [41]	96.0%	93.6%	92.8%	91.6%
TFN [13]	98.0%	95.6%	95.2%	94.0%
LBPP-LTL [36]	100%	100%	100%	100%

The experimental findings indicate that the proposed method outperforms other deep-learning-based path-planning techniques in terms of cost efficiency and success rate for missions defined by LTL. This superior performance can be primarily attributed to two novel aspects of the proposed method: (1) the adoption of advanced transformer networks for accurate sequence prediction, and (2) the effective incorporation of diversity and uncertainty into the path-planning process through latent space modeling paired with GMMs. Although the LBPP-LTL algorithm demonstrates superior trajectory cost and LTL mission success rates, its practicality is moderated by the requirement for extensive computational resources. These results highlight the capability of the proposed method to reliably approximate optimal solutions with reduced computational demands.

5.2. The Helsinki Traffic Accident Map

This section examines autonomous navigation for traffic surveillance within a designated area of Helsinki, as depicted in Figure 10. The map identifies four regions of interest with alphabetic labels and obstacles as gray regions.

For path planning, a traffic accident density map was synthesized using Gaussian process regression based on historical traffic accident data [42]. This map distinguishes areas with higher accident density as high cost and those with lower density as low cost, affecting the path-planning algorithm's cost evaluations.

(**a**)Traffic accident locations in Helsinki. (**b**)Traffic accident density map.

Figure 10. Visual representation of Helsinki's traffic landscape: (**a**) Traffic accidents marked with red dots, regions of interest alphabetically labeled, and obstacles shown in gray. (**b**) Traffic accident density map, where blue denotes low-density (low-cost) areas and red signifies high-density (high-cost) zones.

The study outlines three distinct scenarios, each associated with a unique mission profile defined by Linear Temporal Logic (LTL) formulas:

$$\begin{aligned}
&\text{Scenario1}: \phi_{h1} = \Diamond(a \wedge \Diamond(b \wedge (\Diamond c))).\\
&\text{Scenario2}: \phi_{h2} = \Diamond(b) \wedge \Diamond(c) \wedge \Diamond(d).\\
&\text{Scenario3}: \phi_{h3} = \Diamond(b \wedge ((w \vee a)\mathrm{U}(a \wedge ((w \vee b)\mathrm{U}(c))))).
\end{aligned}$$

ϕ_{h1} and ϕ_{h2} are designed for sequential and coverage missions across three distinct regions, respectively. ϕ_{h3} specifies a strict sequential mission where w represents the workspace adjacent to the regions of interest.

These formulas define the autonomous agent's mission objectives. Specifically, ϕ_{h1} mandates the agent to sequentially visit regions a, b, and c. ϕ_{h2} requires coverage of regions b, c, and d, ensuring each is visited at least once. ϕ_{h3} dictates a strict sequence for visiting regions b, a, and then c, focusing on a precise navigational order.

Figure 11 illustrates the trajectories computed by the proposed algorithm for these scenarios within the Helsinki traffic framework. The proposed method successfully generates low-cost paths that adhere to the specified LTL missions, demonstrating its effectiveness.

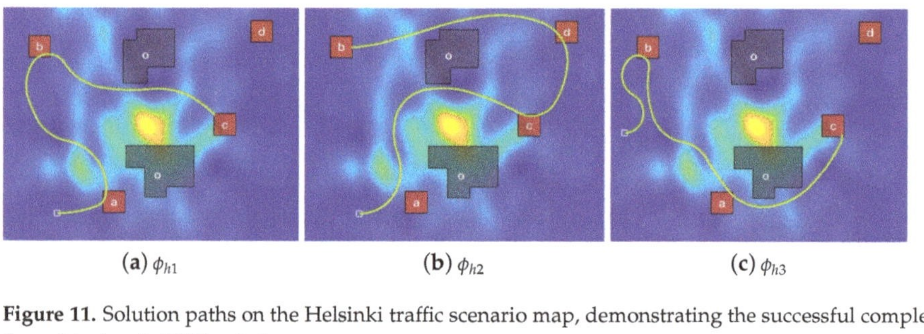

(**a**) ϕ_{h1} (**b**) ϕ_{h2} (**c**) ϕ_{h3}

Figure 11. Solution paths on the Helsinki traffic scenario map, demonstrating the successful completion of designated LTL missions.

5.3. Application to an Autonomous Driving Environment

In the dynamic landscape of autonomous driving, reactive planning is paramount for safe navigation. The solution of the proposed network was utilized as the output of the reactive planner. During the evaluation, three Linear Temporal Logic (LTL) formulas were employed (Figure 12):

- $\phi_{left} = \Diamond(R_{left}) \land \Box(R_{track}) \land \Box(\neg R_{other})$;
- $\phi_{center} = \Diamond(R_{center}) \land \Box(R_{track}) \land \Box(\neg R_{other})$;
- $\phi_{right} = \Diamond(R_{right}) \land \Box(R_{track}) \land \Box(\neg R_{other})$.

Here, R_{left}, R_{center}, and R_{right} denote temporal goal regions, R_{track} denotes the region inside the track, and R_{other} denotes regions occupied by other vehicles. The formula $\phi_{left} = \Diamond(R_{left}) \land \Box(R_{track}) \land \Box(\neg R_{other})$ signifies the goal to "reach the region R_{left} while remaining within the track region ($\Box(R_{track})$) and avoiding collisions with other vehicles ($\Box(\neg R_{other})$)."

For each situation, one of the three LTL formulas was selected, and a control sequence corresponding to the chosen LTL formula was generated. Generally, ϕ_{center} is selected, with the lane-changing formulas (ϕ_{left}, ϕ_{right}) being chosen only in specific times.

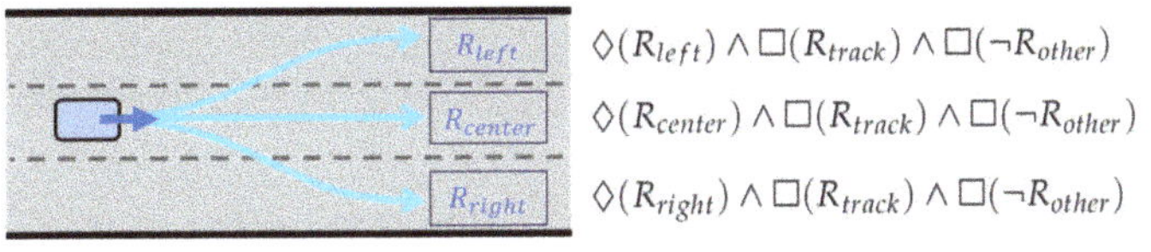

Figure 12. Three LTL formulas for the autonomous driving experiment.

Figure 13 presents snapshots from the experiment conducted using the highD dataset [38]. The decision to change lanes was made at specific points in time, allowing up to two lane changes per trial. In the figure, the ego vehicle is marked in blue, with its trajectory indicated by a blue line. Each subfigure contains three snapshots from a single trial, with lane change points indicated by arrows.

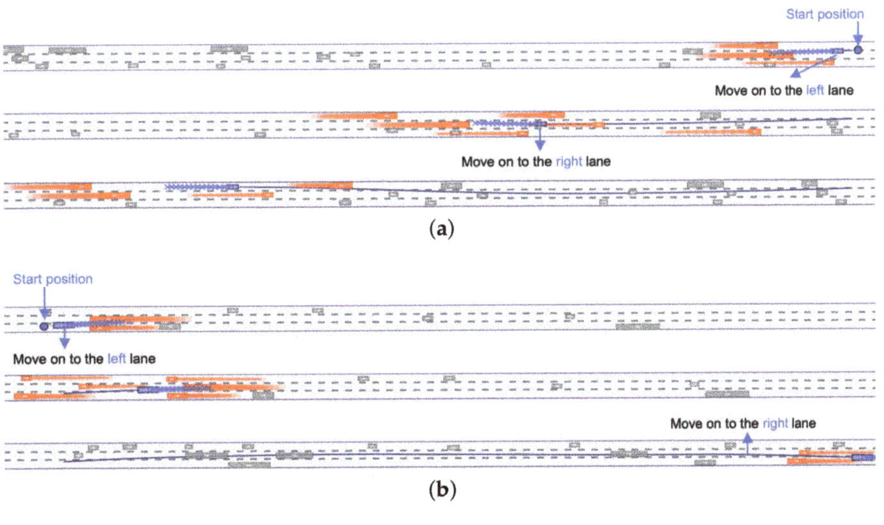

Figure 13. *Cont.*

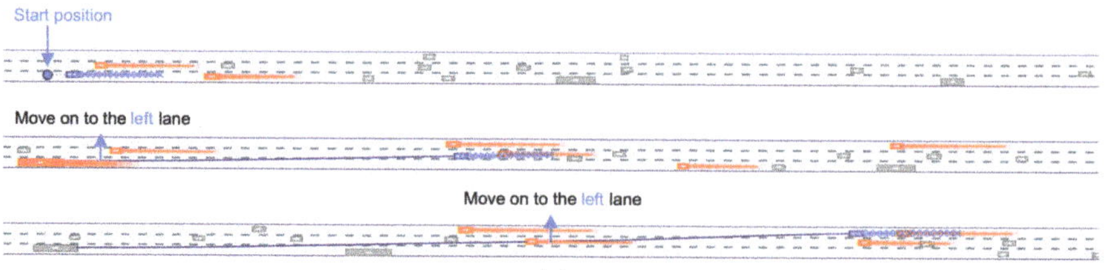

(c)

Figure 13. Snapshots of the autonomous driving experiment. The ego vehicle is marked in blue, with its trajectory indicated by a blue line. Lane change points are highlighted by arrows.

Comparison experiments with other deep learning methods were conducted. We selected a test dataset from the highD dataset, which includes 60 tracks. The test dataset specifically included track IDs 10, 20, 30, 40, and 50, which were not used during the training stage. For each track, 200 trials were conducted. Each trial involved controlling a different vehicle, ensuring fairness by using the same vehicle for each method. The success metric was defined as the controlled vehicle reaching the end of the lane without incidents (collisions or going off track). Table 2 summarizes the results. The proposed method exhibited superior safety compared to other deep learning methods.

Table 2. Success ratio (percentage) in the highD dataset.

	Track ID: 10	Track ID: 20	Track ID: 30	Track ID: 40	Track ID: 50
MLP	90.0	89.5	86.5	85.5	88.0
Seq2Seq-LSTM	91.0	90.0	89.0	88.0	89.5
TCN [41]	90.5	89.5	87.5	86.5	88.5
TFN [13]	93.5	92.0	91.0	90.0	92.5
Proposed	94.5	92.5	91.5	91.0	93.0

6. Conclusions

This study presents a pioneering path-planning approach that effectively integrates co-safe Linear Temporal Logic (LTL) specifications with an end-to-end deep learning architecture. Our method stands out for its ability to generate near-optimal control sequences by combining a Transformer encoder, which is informed by LTL requirements, with a Variational Autoencoder (VAE) enhanced by Gaussian Mixture Model (GMM) components. This architecture adeptly handles the complexities of path planning by accommodating a diverse range of tasks and managing inherent uncertainties within these processes.

Empirical evaluations demonstrate the significant advantages of our approach over existing deep learning strategies. In our experiments, the proposed method consistently outperformed other methods in terms of safety and efficiency, particularly in the context of autonomous driving scenarios using the highD dataset. Our approach achieved higher success rates in reaching the end of the lane without incidents, indicating its robustness and reliability. Furthermore, the method's adaptability and scalability were highlighted through various test cases involving both synthetic and real-world data.

The results confirm the method's suitability for a wide array of systems, significantly enhancing path-planning processes. By effectively addressing the challenges posed by complex environments and logical constraints, our approach offers a robust solution for diverse robotic applications.

Looking ahead, we aim to apply our methodology to more challenging high-dimensional path-planning problems, particularly those involving additional logical constraints and intricate operational contexts, such as multi-joint robotic manipulations. Expanding our focus to these areas is expected to yield further valuable insights into robotics and automation, enhancing the sophistication and efficiency of path-planning techniques.

The integration of deep learning with logical frameworks in our study represents a significant advancement in robotic path planning, paving the way for more complex and effective mission executions in the future.

Author Contributions: Conceptualization, K.L., E.I. and K.C.; methodology, K.L. and E.I.; validation, K.C.; data curation, K.L. and K.C.; writing—original draft preparation, K.L. and E.I.; writing—review and editing, K.C.; visualization, K.L. and E.I.; supervision, K.C. All authors have read and agreed to the published version of the manuscript.

Funding: This work was supported by Innovative Human Resource Development for Local Intellectualization program through the Institute of Information and Communications Technology Planning and Evaluation (IITP) grant funded by the Korea government (MSIT) (IITP-2024-RS-2023-00259678).

Institutional Review Board Statement: Not applicable.

Informed Consent Statement: Not applicable.

Data Availability Statement: Part of the dataset is available upon request from the authors, while another part is available in a publicly accessible repository.

Conflicts of Interest: The authors declare no conflicts of interest.

References

1. Pairet, È.; Chamzas, C.; Petillot, Y.; Kavraki, L.E. Path planning for manipulation using experience-driven random trees. *IEEE Int. Conf. Robot. Autom.* **2021**, *6*, 3295–3302. [CrossRef]
2. Lamiraux, F.; Mirabel, J. Prehensile Manipulation Planning: Modeling, Algorithms and Implementation. *IEEE Trans. Robot.* **2021**, *38*, 2370–2388. [CrossRef]
3. Xu, K.; Yu, H.; Huang, R.; Guo, D.; Wang, Y.; Xiong, R. Efficient Object Manipulation to an Arbitrary Goal Pose: Learning-based Anytime Prioritized Planning. In Proceedings of the IEEE International Conference on Robotics and Automation, Philadelphia, PA, USA, 23–27 May 2022; pp. 7277–7283.
4. Belkhouche, F. Reactive path planning in a dynamic environment. *IEEE Trans. Robot.* **2009**, *25*, 902–911. [CrossRef]
5. Eiffert, S.; Kong, H.; Pirmarzdashti, N.; Sukkarieh, S. Path planning in dynamic environments using generative rnns and monte carlo tree search. In Proceedings of the IEEE International Conference on Robotics and Automation, Paris, France, 31 May–31 August 2020; pp. 10263–10269.
6. Lin, J.; Zhou, T.; Zhu, D.; Liu, J.; Meng, M.Q.H. Search-Based Online Trajectory Planning for Car-like Robots in Highly Dynamic Environments. In Proceedings of the IEEE International Conference on Robotics and Automation, Xi'an, China, 30 May–5 June 2021; pp. 8151–8157.
7. Fainekos, G.E.; Kress-Gazit, H.; Pappas, G.J. Temporal logic motion planning for mobile robots. In Proceedings of the IEEE International Conference on Robotics and Automation, Barcelona, Spain, 18–22 April 2005.
8. Karaman, S.; Frazzoli, E. Sampling-based motion planning with deterministic μ-calculus specifications. In Proceedings of the 48h IEEE Conference on Decision and Control (CDC) held jointly with 2009 28th Chinese Control Conference, Shanghai, China, 15–18 December 2009; pp. 2222–2229.
9. Lahijanian, M.; Wasniewski, J.; Andersson, S.B.; Belta, C. Motion planning and control from temporal logic specifications with probabilistic satisfaction guarantees. In Proceedings of the IEEE International Conference on Robotics and Automation, Anchorage, AK, USA, 3–7 May 2010; pp. 3227–3232.
10. Karaman, S.; Frazzoli, E. Sampling-based algorithms for optimal motion planning. *Int. J. Robot. Res.* **2011**, *30*, 846–894. [CrossRef]
11. Wang, H.; Cai, P.; Sun, Y.; Wang, L.; Liu, M. Learning interpretable end-to-end vision-based motion planning for autonomous driving with optical flow distillation. In Proceedings of the IEEE International Conference on Robotics and Automation, Xian, China, 30 May–5 June 2021; pp. 13731–13737.
12. Hu, S.; Chen, L.; Wu, P.; Li, H.; Yan, J.; Tao, D. St-p3: End-to-end vision-based autonomous driving via spatial-temporal feature learning. In Proceedings of the European Conference on Computer Vision, Tel Aviv, Israel, 23–27 October 2022; pp. 533–549.
13. Vaswani, A.; Shazeer, N.; Parmar, N.; Uszkoreit, J.; Jones, L.; Gomez, A.N.; Kaiser, Ł.; Polosukhin, I. Attention is all you need. In Proceedings of the Advances in Neural Information Processing Systems, Long Beach, CA, USA, 4–9 December 2017.
14. Sohn, K.; Lee, H.; Yan, X. Learning structured output representation using deep conditional generative models. In Proceedings of the Advances in Neural Information Processing Systems, Montreal, QC, Canada, 7–12 December 2015; Volume 28.
15. Smith, S.L.; Tumova, J.; Belta, C.; Rus, D. Optimal path planning for surveillance with temporal logic constraints. *Int. J. Robot. Res.* **2011**, *30*, 1695–1708. [CrossRef]
16. Wolff, E.M.; Topcu, U.; Murray, R.M. Optimal Control with Weighted Average Costs and Temporal Logic Specifications. In Proceedings of the Robotics: Science and Systems, Sydney, NSW, Australia, 9–13 July 2012.
17. LaValle, S.M.; Kuffner, J.J. Randomized kinodynamic planning. *Int. J. Robot. Res.* **2001**, *20*, 378–400. [CrossRef]

18. Karaman, S.; Frazzoli, E. Sampling-based algorithms for optimal motion planning with deterministic μ-calculus specifications. In Proceedings of the IEEE American Control Conference, Montreal, QC, Canada, 27–29 June 2012.
19. Varricchio, V.; Chaudhari, P.; Frazzoli, E. Sampling-based algorithms for optimal motion planning using process algebra specifications. In Proceedings of the IEEE International Conference on Robotics and Automation, Hong Kong, China, 31 May–7 June 2014.
20. Bhatia, A.; Kavraki, L.E.; Vardi, M.Y. Sampling-based motion planning with temporal goals. In Proceedings of the IEEE International Conference on Robotics and Automation, Anchorage, AK, USA, 3–7 May 2010.
21. Plaku, E. Planning in discrete and continuous spaces: From LTL tasks to robot motions. In Proceedings of the Towards Autonomous Robotic Systems, Bristol, UK, 20–23 August 2012.
22. McMahon, J.; Plaku, E. Sampling-based tree search with discrete abstractions for motion planning with dynamics and temporal logic. In Proceedings of the IEEE/RSJ International Conference on Intelligent Robots and Systems, Chicago, IL, USA, 14–18 September 2014.
23. Karaman, S.; Sanfelice, R.G.; Frazzoli, E. Optimal control of mixed logical dynamical systems with linear temporal logic specifications. In Proceedings of the IEEE Conference on Decision and Control, Cancun, Mexico, 9–11 December 2008.
24. Wolff, E.M.; Topcu, U.; Murray, R.M. Optimization-based control of nonlinear systems with linear temporal logic specifications. In Proceedings of the IEEE International Conference on Robotics and Automation, Hong Kong, China, 31 May–7 June 2014; pp. 5319–5325.
25. Livingston, S.C.; Wolff, E.M.; Murray, R.M. Cross-entropy temporal logic motion planning. In Proceedings of the 18th ACM International Conference on Hybrid Systems: Computation and Control, Seattle, WA, USA, 14–16 April 2015.
26. Aloor, J.J.; Patrikar, J.; Kapoor, P.; Oh, J.; Scherer, S. Follow the rules: Online signal temporal logic tree search for guided imitation learning in stochastic domains. In Proceedings of the IEEE International Conference on Robotics and Automation, London, UK, 29 May–2 June 2023; pp. 1320–1326.
27. Wang, Y.; Figueroa, N.; Li, S.; Shah, A.; Shah, J. Temporal Logic Imitation: Learning Plan-Satisficing Motion Policies from Demonstrations. *arXiv* **2022**, arXiv:2206.04632.
28. Dhonthi, A.; Schillinger, P.; Rozo, L.; Nardi, D. Optimizing demonstrated robot manipulation skills for temporal logic constraints. In Proceedings of the IEEE/RSJ International Conference on Intelligent Robots and Systems, Kyoto, Japan, 23–27 October 2022; pp. 1255–1262.
29. Chai, Y.; Sapp, B.; Bansal, M.; Anguelov, D. Multipath: Multiple probabilistic anchor trajectory hypotheses for behavior prediction. *arXiv* **2019**, arXiv:1910.05449.
30. Petrovich, M.; Black, M.J.; Varol, G. Action-conditioned 3D human motion synthesis with transformer VAE. In Proceedings of the IEEE/CVF International Conference on Computer Vision, Montreal, QC, Canada, 10–17 October 2021; pp. 10985–10995.
31. Shi, S.; Jiang, L.; Dai, D.; Schiele, B. Motion transformer with global intention localization and local movement refinement. In Proceedings of the Advances in Neural Information Processing Systems, New Orleans, LA, USA, 28 November–9 December 2022; Volume 35, pp. 6531–6543.
32. Choset, H.; Lynch, K.M.; Hutchinson, S.; Kantor, G.; Burgard, W.; Kavraki, L.E.; Thrun, S. *Principles of Robot Motion: Theory, Algorithms, and Implementation*; MIT Press: Cambridge, MA, USA, 2005.
33. Baier, C.; Katoen, J.P. *Principles of Model Checking*; MIT Press: Cambridge, MA, USA, 2008.
34. Sistla, A.P. Safety, liveness and fairness in temporal logic. *Form. Asp. Comput.* **1994**, *6*, 495–511. [CrossRef]
35. Kupferman, O.; Vardi, M.Y. Model checking of safety properties. *Form. Methods Syst. Des.* **2001**, *19*, 291–314. [CrossRef]
36. Cho, K. Learning-based path planning under co-safe temporal logic specifications. *IEEE Access* **2023**, *11*, 25865–25878. [CrossRef]
37. Bishop, C.M.; Nasrabadi, N.M. *Pattern Recognition and Machine Learning*; Springer: Berlin/Heidelberg, Germany, 2006; Volume 4.
38. Krajewski, R.; Bock, J.; Kloeker, L.; Eckstein, L. The highD Dataset: A Drone Dataset of Naturalistic Vehicle Trajectories on German Highways for Validation of Highly Automated Driving Systems. In Proceedings of the International Conference on Intelligent Transportation Systems, Maui, HI, USA, 4–7 November 2018; pp. 2118–2125. [CrossRef]
39. Paszke, A.; Gross, S.; Massa, F.; Lerer, A.; Bradbury, J.; Chanan, G.; Killeen, T.; Lin, Z.; Gimelshein, N.; Antiga, L.; et al. PyTorch: An Imperative Style, High-Performance Deep Learning Library. In *Advances in Neural Information Processing Systems*; Curran Associates, Inc.: Glasgow, UK, 2019; pp. 8024–8035.
40. Sutskever, I.; Vinyals, O.; Le, Q.V. Sequence to sequence learning with neural networks. *Adv. Neural Inf. Process. Syst.* **2014**, *27*, 1–9.
41. Bai, S.; Kolter, J.Z.; Koltun, V. An empirical evaluation of generic convolutional and recurrent networks for sequence modeling. *arXiv* **2018**, arXiv:1803.01271.
42. Traffic Accidents in Helsinki. 2011. Available online: http://www.hri.fi/en/dataset/liikenneonnettomuudet-helsingissa (accessed on 5 March 2024).

electronics

MDPI

Article

Design and Development of Shadow: A Cost-Effective Mobile Social Robot for Human-Following Applications

Alejandro Torrejón, Noé Zapata, Lucas Bonilla, Pablo Bustos and Pedro Núñez *

RoboLab, Robotics and Artificial Vision, University of Extremadura, 10003 Cáceres, Spain; atorrejon@unex.es (A.T.); nzapata@unex.es (N.Z.); lubonillar@unex.es (L.B.)

* Correspondence: pnuntru@unex.es

Abstract: This study explores the development and implementation of Shadow, an advanced mobile social robot designed to meet specific functional requirements. Shadow is intended to serve both as a versatile tool and a human companion, assisting in various tasks across different environments. The construction emphasizes cost efficiency and high agility, utilizing 3D printing technology exclusively. The robot features omnidirectional kinematics and a flexible power electronics system, accommodating diverse energy needs with lithium batteries that ensure at least seven hours of autonomous operation. An integrated sensor array continuously monitors the power system, tracks tilt and acceleration, and facilitates self-diagnostic functions. Rapid prototyping allows for swift iteration, testing, and refinement to align with project goals. This paper provides a comprehensive blueprint for designing cost-effective, highly agile robots using advanced manufacturing techniques. Extensive testing, including stability and sensory skills evaluations, demonstrates Shadow's adherence to its design objectives. Shadow has advanced from technology readiness level (TRL) 2 to TRL 7 within a year and is currently undergoing trials with advanced functionalities, offering significant insights into overcoming practical design challenges and optimizing robot functionality.

Keywords: mobile social robot; cost effective; 3D printing technology; orin; omnidirectional kinematics; prototype generation

Citation: Torrejón, A.; Zapata, N.; Bonilla, L.; Bustos, P.; Núñez, P. Design and Development of Shadow: A Cost-Effective Mobile Social Robot for Human-Following Applications. *Electronics* **2024**, *13*, 3444. https://doi.org/10.3390/electronics13173444

Academic Editors: Luis Gracia, Juan Ernesto Solanes Galbis and Jaime Valls Miro

Received: 29 June 2024
Revised: 19 August 2024
Accepted: 21 August 2024
Published: 30 August 2024

1. Introduction

The evolution of robotics has ushered in an era where robots are not only utilized for industrial automation but have also become integral to everyday human activities. A significant advancement is the development of social robots designed to interact with humans and assist in various tasks. Social robots are autonomous systems capable of communicating, interacting, and collaborating with people naturally and effectively. These technologies can potentially revolutionize the near future, enhancing assistance in healthcare, education, and customer service sectors [1,2]. In this context, we present Shadow, an innovative mobile social robot that embodies this trend by integrating low-cost prototyping and manufacturing techniques. Shadow is equipped with advanced sensors to improve human-assisted applications.

The demand for social robots seamlessly integrating into human environments is rapidly growing. Studies indicate that social robots can revolutionize human-robot interaction by providing companionship, enhancing productivity, and assisting in daily activities [3]. To achieve this, social robots must evolve rapidly to keep pace with technological advancements and meet user preferences and requirements. However, several factors, like scalability, limit robot designs' adaptability and effective lifespan. Current challenges include integrating advanced sensors like 360° cameras and 3D LiDARs, and robust embedded GPUs for real-time processing of deep neural network models. Closed or restricted upgrade options in commercial robots can quickly lead to obsolescence.

This paper proposes the design of the Shadow social robot guided by the following research questions: (i) What design features enhance a social robot's use and acceptability during human following in real environments? (ii) How can the robot's design adapt to different environments and function autonomously for extended periods? (iii) What basic equipment (sensors) should a social robot be equipped with to follow a person in a real environment effectively? The Shadow robot aims to address crucial questions related to human-following capabilities. It aims to offer companionship and support during extensive work tasks in various settings. This paper seeks to create a cost-effective, agile, and adaptable social robot. We employ 3D printing technology to achieve these goals, directly supporting low-cost production and rapid iterations. This technology enables the efficient and economical advancement of social robot development, facilitating prototype creation and continuous improvement.

This article is organized as follows: Section 2 provides a background on the role of social robots like Shadow, discussing various research questions related to functionality and acceptance. Section 3 outlines the requirements considered during the design and development of the robot. Section 4 describes the body design of Shadow, covering the prototyping process, the development of the mobile base and suspension systems, and the power electronics system used in the robot. It also discusses the various sensors integrated into Shadow. Section 5 presents the experimental results obtained during testing. Finally, Section 6 concludes the paper with a summary of findings and future work directions.

2. Background

The use of social robots has significantly expanded over the past decade, finding applications in various real-world settings such as healthcare, education, and customer service [4]. In healthcare, social robots like Paro and Pepper provide companionship and support to patients, particularly the elderly and those with cognitive impairments [5,6]. In education, robots like NAO and Robovie enhance learning experiences and engage students in interactive activities [7,8]. In the customer service sector, robots such as Pepper and various hotel concierge robots assist customers and improve service efficiency [9]. These examples highlight the growing acceptance of social robots and their utility in enhancing human–robot interactions across diverse environments. The Shadow robot, designed explicitly for human-following tasks, is particularly useful in care environments and customer or visitor service settings.

For social robots to be effective, they must possess several key characteristics. Firstly, they need robust human detection and interaction capabilities to understand and respond to human cues accurately [10]. Secondly, they should exhibit adaptive behaviors to cater to user needs and preferences, ensuring a personalized interaction experience [2]. Additionally, they must be designed with safety and reliability, mainly when operating near humans, to prevent accidents and ensure user trust [11]. These characteristics are essential for successfully integrating social robots into daily life, as they directly impact the robot's ability to interact meaningfully and safely with humans. Our Shadow robot is equipped with various sensors, including 360° cameras and 3D LiDAR, along with a Jetson Orin, which enables the execution of specific algorithms for human detection, the calculation of safe and socially accepted routes, and interaction with humans in the environment.

The design of robots involves several critical considerations to ensure functionality and adaptability across various applications. Robot design has been revolutionized by 3D printing technology, allowing for rapid prototyping and customization of complex structures at a reduced cost [12–14]. Modular design approaches enable the creation of flexible systems that can be easily updated and expanded with new capabilities as needed [15,16]. Furthermore, incorporating advanced sensors is crucial for enhancing the robot's perception and interaction capabilities, allowing it to operate effectively in dynamic environments [17,18]. Shadow leverages rapid prototyping through 3D printing, with tests and validations at each design stage. Additionally, Shadow is designed modularly to allow easy access to each component for replacement, upgrade, or repair. The arrangement of the sensors has also been carefully considered in the final system design.

Robot Comparison

As part of the design process of Shadow, we analyzed and compared several well-known commercial robots available for purchase and some custom-made robots built in research labs [4]. The comparison shown in the Table 1 considers only the functionalities offered by these units and advertised by the manufacturers.

Table 1. Comparison of feature availability among different robots. This table highlights the presence or absence of various characteristics, as offered by those units and advertised by the manufacturers. ✓ available; ∼ depends on model or conditions; × not available.

Feature/Robots	**Shadow**	**Morphia [19]**	**TIAGo[20]**	**WaPOCHI [21]**	**Dinerbot T5 [22]**	**Bellabot [23]**	**Amy Waitress [24]**	**Hobbit [25,26]**	**Giraff**
Omnidirectional movement	✓	×	∼	×	×	×	×	×	×
Autonomous Navigation	✓	✓	✓	✓	✓	✓	✓	✓	✓
Detection of people	✓	✓	✓	✓	×	×	×	✓	✓
Object Manipulation	∼	×	∼	×	×	×	×	✓	×
Video Calling	×	✓	∼	×	×	×	×	✓	✓
Transportation	✓	✓	✓	✓	✓	✓	✓	✓	✓
Tracking	✓	✓	✓	✓	×	×	×	✓	✓
Expansible	✓	×	∼	×	×	×	×	×	∼
Low-cost focus	✓	✓	×	×	×	✓	✓	✓	✓

One of the key aspects of Shadow's design is its omnidirectional movement capability, which allows it to navigate in all directions with great agility. This feature is essential for maneuvering in complex and narrow environments. In contrast, most of the other compared robots, such as Morphia [19], WaPOCHI [21], Dinerbot T5 [22], Bellabot [23], Amy Waitress [24], Hobbit [25,26], and Giraff [27], lack this capability and rely on more traditional movements. TIAGo [20,28,29] has similar capabilities but they depend on the specific model or conditions.

All the robots analyzed, including Shadow, Morphia, TIAGo, WaPOCHI, Dinerbot T5, Bellabot, Amy Waitress, Hobbit and Giraff, feature autonomous navigation. This functionality enables robots to move independently within a defined environment, using sensors and algorithms to avoid obstacles and follow predefined routes. Autonomous navigation is critical for ensuring that robots can operate without constant human supervision, making them more efficient and practical for various applications.

Shadow, along with Morphia, TIAGo, WaPOCHI, Hobbit, and Giraff, includes the ability to detect people, which is essential for social interactions and human-assisted tasks. The capability to detect people allows these robots to interact meaningfully with their environment and the humans within it. However, Dinerbot T5, Bellabot, and Amy Waitress do not offer this functionality, potentially limiting their usefulness in applications where human interaction is crucial. The absence of this feature in some robots restricts their potential in settings where recognizing and responding to human presence is important.

Object manipulation is an advanced feature that allows robots to interact with their environment physically. Hobbit excels in this area, providing significant capabilities for handling objects. Shadow and TIAGo have limited object manipulation capabilities that depend on the model or conditions. On the other hand, Morphia, WaPOCHI, Dinerbot T5, Bellabot, Amy Waitress, and Giraff lack this capability, restricting their functionality to tasks that do not require direct physical manipulation. The ability to manipulate objects is precious in industrial and service applications where handling and moving items are necessary.

Video calling is a valuable feature for remote communication and telepresence. Although Shadow does not currently include this capability, it is designed to support it in the future, as it is equipped with the necessary components, such as a camera, microphone, and screen. In contrast, robots like Morphia, TIAGo, Hobbit, and Giraff already offer video-calling functionality, making them suitable for remote assistance and communication with distant users. However, WaPOCHI, Dinerbot T5, Bellabot, and Amy Waitress lack this feature, which may limit their effectiveness in scenarios requiring remote interaction. Incorporating video-calling capabilities would enhance the versatility of these robots, making them more effective in environments where visual and audio communication is crucial.

All the compared robots, including Shadow, have transportation capabilities. This feature allows robots to carry objects from one place to another within a defined environment, which is fundamental for logistics, services, and customer care applications. Efficient transportation of items is necessary in various settings, and the ability to perform this task makes these robots highly valuable for tasks involving movement and delivery of goods.

The ability to track and follow a specific person is an essential feature for assistive and social robots. Shadow, Morphia, TIAGo, WaPOCHI, Hobbit, and Giraff include this functionality, which is critical for applications where the robot needs to maintain proximity to a human user. Dinerbot T5, Bellabot, and Amy Waitress lack this capability, limiting their use in applications where human tracking is essential. Tracking capabilities ensure that robots can provide continuous assistance and support by staying close to the user.

Expandability is another important aspect of robot design. Shadow is designed to be expandable, allowing for the addition of new components and upgrades. TIAGo offers limited expandability, depending on the model, while Giraff has some expandable capabilities. Morphia, WaPOCHI, Dinerbot T5, Bellabot, Amy Waitress, and Hobbit are not expandable, which may limit their ability to adapt to new technologies and future needs. Expandability ensures that robots can be updated and improved, extending their usefulness and relevance.

Lastly, a low-cost focus is a significant consideration for making robots accessible for various applications. Shadow and several other robots, such as Morphia, Bellabot, Amy Waitress, Hobbit, and Giraff, are designed with a low-cost focus, making them accessible for various applications. TIAGo and other more advanced models do not emphasize cost reduction, which may make them less accessible for some users or applications where budget is a primary concern. The focus on cost efficiency allows for broader adoption and deployment of robotic technologies in different fields.

For a more extensive but similar comparison, see [30]. The table shows significant similarities in many of the compared functionalities. However, the day-to-day use of robots in research labs involves more subtle aspects that condition their long-term availability, such as adding more powerful computers, connectivity, software updates, part replacement, adaptation to new sensors, warranty, etc.

Shadow addresses the deficiencies found in many commercial robots, such as TIAGo, WaPOCHI, and Dinerbot T5. These robots often come with closed software and operating systems customized by the manufacturer, making upgrades to sensors, hardware, and processing components difficult. They also suffer from challenging maintenance procedures and high costs, with no option for users to create or customize the robot to their specific needs, and sometimes even require a subscription for the use of different functions. Shadow, on the other hand, provides solutions to these problems by offering an open platform that allows for easy customization and upgrades, making it more adaptable and user-friendly at a lower cost. This is particularly valuable to researchers, educators, and developers.

3. Requirements

As mentioned above, Shadow is a low-cost social robot that requires great agility and responsiveness in its movements. It must be able to adapt to a dynamic environment with people and interact with them. In addition to being physically stable to operate reliably and continuously, with a minimum autonomy of 7 h, the design of the robot must be human-friendly and safe, it needs to have the necessary sensors to locate and recognize people and must reach a minimum speed of 3 km/h to follow a walking person.

Another important requirement is the size, which must be large enough to accommodate all the necessary technology and, at the same time, small enough to move freely in the environment. The maximum size allowed is 625 mm wide and 2030 mm high, as these are the minimum door dimensions according to [31]

Completing the section, the robot must be easy to upgrade, maintain, and manufacture and have the necessary technologies to perform its task in real time.

4. Shadow Robot

Shadow is a robot with a design that ensures cost effectiveness without compromising functionality. This balance is achieved through 3D printing, enabling rapid prototyping and customization, allowing the creation of complex structures at a reduced cost. As highlighted by [13], additive manufacturing technologies like 3D printing transform the robot design and production landscape, making developing sophisticated robots on a budget feasible. Another crucial aspect is the acceptability of Shadow's movement within its environment, addressing the growing demand for lighter, more agile designs akin to biological movement [32]. The recent availability of high-powered wheel-motor units and custom-configured lithium batteries has enabled more compact, lightweight, and efficient mobile bases. Additionally, the design includes sensors for high-level behaviors like people detection and tracking in complex environments, underscoring their significance in advancing robotic capabilities [33].

Therefore, constructing our social robot (Figure 1) addresses these challenges. Shadow leverages a quick prototyping cycle enabled by large-format 3D printers (Creality CR SO 60 PRO, Creality Store, Shenzhen, China) and a modular power electronics design, identifying and resolving several design challenges to ensure the final product meets its objectives. The iterative nature of rapid prototyping refines robot designs, enhancing functionality and reliability [13,34].

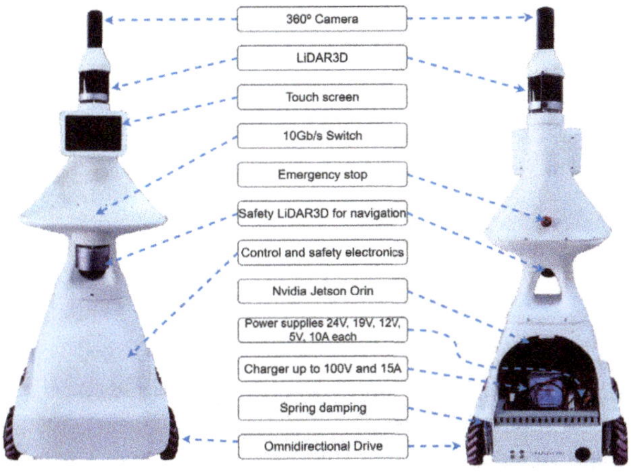

Figure 1. Front and rear view of the Shadow robot. The image shows the main sensors and equipment of the social robot.

Shadow is equipped with omnidirectional kinematics (Mecanum wheels and Drivers, UU Motor Technology Company Ltd., Chanzhou, China), allowing it to navigate complex environments smoothly. A versatile power electronics system complements this design feature and can adapt to varying energy requirements. Lithium batteries were chosen for their high energy density and reliability, ensuring a minimum of seven hours of autonomous operation. Additionally, an array of sensors continuously monitors the power system's status, tilt, and acceleration, supporting a self-diagnostic function that enhances the robot's reliability and performance. Shadow integrates LiDAR (Helios and BPearl, RoboSense Technology Co., Ltd. Shenzhen, China) and 360° camera (Theta Z1, Ricoh Company, Ltd., Tokio, Japan) for complete environmental perception, supported by a high-capacity NVIDIA Jetson Orin (Jetson Orin, Nvidia Corporation, Santa Clara, California) for executing specific algorithms. The robot also features a touch screen for future interactions and a tray on the front for use during tracking tasks.

4.1. Prototyping

Agile methodologies, such as rapid prototyping, have been utilized in the manufacturing of Shadow. This prototyping phase is a critical step in developing any advanced robotic system. Rapid prototyping using 3D printing technology was employed for the Shadow robot to achieve cost efficiency and design flexibility. This iterative design process involved multiple steps, from initial concept models to functional prototypes. Emphasis was placed on using large-format 3D printers, which allowed for the creation of complex structures and components with high precision. The advantages of this approach include the ability to quickly test and refine the design, illustrating the effectiveness of rapid prototyping in modern robotic engineering.

We iterated over a series of prototypes to meet Shadow's specific design requirements. This process allowed us to detect inappropriate design decisions that led to undesirable situations, which only became apparent once the prototype was built and tested. Two significant sources of error identified were the configuration of the volume inside the plastic casing and the vibrations transmitted to the tray. By addressing these issues, we were able to improve the overall design and functionality of the robot.

The 3D printing technology revolutionized our approach to robot design, enabling rapid prototyping and customization of complex structures at a reduced cost [12–14]. This method provided the flexibility needed to iterate on designs quickly and efficiently. Each prototype underwent rigorous testing and validation, ensuring design flaws were identified and corrected early in development. The benefits of this approach are evident in the precision and reliability of the final product.

Furthermore, the iterative prototyping process enabled us to refine the robot's design continuously. Large-format 3D printers allowed us to create detailed and accurate models, facilitating swift adjustments and enhancements. This approach improved the design and ensured that Shadow met all the specified requirements, including robustness, flexibility, and cost effectiveness.

The result of the first year of work on this robot is shown in Figure 2 as a series of prototypes. Each iteration brought us closer to a final design that effectively balances functionality, adaptability, and user requirements.

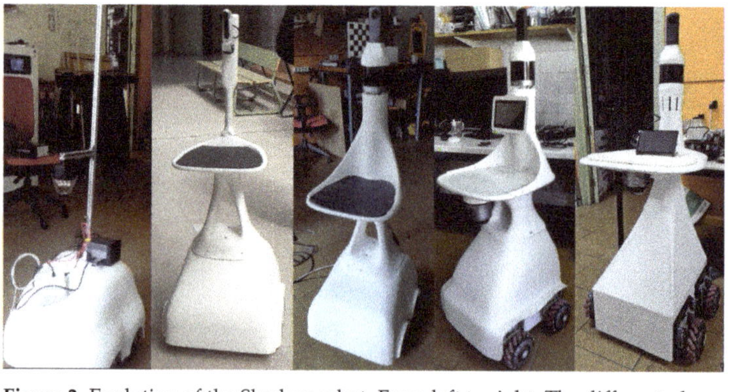

Figure 2. Evolution of the Shadow robot. From left to right: The different phases of the construction of the Shadow robot, from its initial version to its final version, with an omnidirectional base and a touchscreen for interaction.

4.2. Body Design

The body of Shadow was conceived as one sizable printable piece that serves as both the supporting structure and the functional shape for external (human-robot interaction; HRI) and internal (electronics and cables guiding) requirements. However, the size limitation of our 3D printer (500 × 500 × 600 mm) forced us to divide the body into three pieces and a small connecting element. This segmentation posed challenges in ensuring the structural integrity and alignment of the components, which were addressed through precise design and robust connectors.

The three main body sections of the robot were meticulously designed to interlock seamlessly, forming a robust and cohesive structure. Each section was printed separately, enabling precise attention to be given to the specific requirements of each part, such as sensor placement, accessibility to electronic components, and the routing of cables. A small connecting element played a critical role in maintaining the alignment and stability of the entire assembly, thereby ensuring that the structural and functional integrity of the robot remained uncompromised.

Additionally, this modular design allows for scalability in the construction of the robot. This means that certain elements, like the lower section housing the electronics and wheels, can remain unchanged, while other parts can be modified or replaced to introduce new functionalities or features. For instance, modifications might include the addition, removal, or expansion of sensors and actuators, enhancing the robot's adaptability to different tasks or environments.

4.3. Mobile Base

Shadow has been designed with omnidirectional kinematics to achieve high mobility using four Mecanum wheels in a rectangular configuration. This design choice allows the robot to move in any direction without changing its orientation, providing a significant advantage in navigating complex environments. Additionally, this type of natural movement is more readily accepted by people [32], aligning with the robot's primary objective of following a person seamlessly and intuitively.

Figure 3 illustrates the Mecanum wheels and the coordinate systems used in the omnidirectional base. The Mecanum wheel, shown in Figure 3a, allows the robot to move in any direction by varying the speed and direction of each wheel. Each wheel has rollers set at a 45 degree angle to the wheel's plane, allowing forward, backward, and lateral motion to be combined into a single movement. Figure 3b details the coordinate systems that describe the robot's omnidirectional movement, showing the wheels' positions and the rollers' orientation.

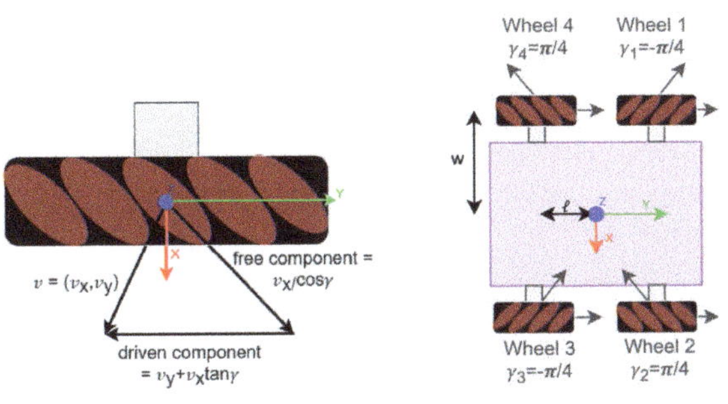

(a) (b)

Figure 3. Omnidirectional kinematics. (**a**) Mecanum wheel. (**b**) Coordinate system in the omnidirectional base.

The inverse kinematics equations required to control the robot were derived following the methodologies, as outlined in [35,36]. These equations are crucial for converting the desired movements of the robot into the specific rotational speeds for each wheel. As shown in Figure 3a, at the center of the wheel, the linear velocity $v = (v_x, v_y)$ is the sum of the velocity components along the driving direction and the sliding direction:

$$\begin{bmatrix} v_x \\ v_y \end{bmatrix} = v_{drive} \begin{bmatrix} 0 \\ 1 \end{bmatrix} + v_{slide} \begin{bmatrix} cos\gamma \\ sin\gamma \end{bmatrix} \tag{1}$$

where γ denotes the angle at which free sliding occurs, allowed by the passive rollers on the wheel's circumference; v_{drive} is the driving speed; and v_{slide} is the sliding speed. Solving Equation (1) for v_{drive} and v_{slide} we obtain

$$\begin{aligned} v_{drive} &= v_y - v_x \tan\gamma \\ v_{slide} &= \frac{v_x}{\cos\gamma} \end{aligned} \tag{2}$$

When the robot is moving with velocity $v = \begin{bmatrix} \omega_z & v_x & v_y \end{bmatrix}^\top$, each wheel u_i has an angular speed given by

$$u_i = \begin{bmatrix} \frac{1}{r_i} & \frac{tan\gamma_i}{r_i} \end{bmatrix} \begin{bmatrix} x_i & 0 & 1 \\ y_i & 1 & 0 \end{bmatrix} \begin{bmatrix} \omega_z \\ v_x \\ v_y \end{bmatrix} \tag{3}$$

with x_i, y_i being the coordinates of wheel u_i with respect to the center of the robot, γ_i is the angles of each roller, and r_i is the radius of each wheel. From right to left, the first transformation expresses the linear velocity at the wheel in the robot's center b. The second transformation calculates the driving angular velocity using Equation (2).

To obtain the final inverse kinematics equation, the position coordinates of each wheel and the angle of its roller, $\pm 45°$, are substituted into Equation (3). As an example, for wheel u_1 with $\gamma = \frac{-\pi}{4}$,

$$u_1 = \begin{bmatrix} \frac{1}{r_i} & \frac{-1}{r_i} \end{bmatrix} \begin{bmatrix} -w & 0 & 1 \\ l & 1 & 0 \end{bmatrix} \begin{bmatrix} \omega_z \\ v_x \\ v_y \end{bmatrix} = \begin{bmatrix} -w\text{-}l & -1 & 1 \end{bmatrix} \frac{1}{r_1} \begin{bmatrix} \omega_z \\ v_x \\ v_y \end{bmatrix} \tag{4}$$

Each u_i vector is stacked as rows in a matrix to obtain Equation (5). This equation links the desired velocity of the robot's center, v_x, v_y, ω_z, to the linear speed of the wheels, u_i. The geometric parameters w and l denote the semi-distance between wheels and the semi-distance between axes, respectively.

$$\begin{bmatrix} u_1 \\ u_2 \\ u_3 \\ u_4 \end{bmatrix} = \frac{1}{r} \begin{bmatrix} -w - l & -1 & 1 \\ w + l & 1 & 1 \\ w + l & -1 & 1 \\ -l - w & 1 & 1 \end{bmatrix} \begin{bmatrix} \omega_z \\ v_x \\ v_y \end{bmatrix} \tag{5}$$

By setting v_z and v_y to zero, the equation sends all the wheels' speeds to the same value, making the robot move forward. For lateral speed $v_y \neq 0$, wheels in the same diagonal receive the same sign in the speed magnitude. For rotation, wheels on the same side receive the same sign and a magnitude scaled by the geometric parameters.

This omnidirectional configuration has been translated to the real robot using four Mecanum motor wheels. Each wheel includes a 150 W hub motor controlled by one of the two 2-axis drivers provided by the same manufacturer.

4.4. Materials

In fused deposition modeling (FDM) printing, a variety of materials are available, each offering unique characteristics such as resistance to external elements, toughness, flexibility, and hardness. The materials selected for testing include PLA (*polylactic acid*),

ABS (*acrylonitrile butadiene styrene*), TPU (*thermoplastic polyurethane*) HARDNESS+, and PC (*polycarbonate*), with all plastics manufactured by Smart Materials 3D.

- PLA: is a cost-effective, easy-to-print, and cheap material. However, it has a low thermal resistance and can become malleable at temperatures of around 65 °C.
- ABS: offers better mechanical and thermal performance compared to PLA. It is more challenging to print, particularly for long-duration prints, due to warping, where the first layer may lift off the print bed. Despite this, ABS is tougher and more heat-resistant than PLA.
- TPU HARDNESS+: this material is more impact-resistant than both PLA and ABS and offers good flexibility. It is also relatively easy to print, though it comes at a higher cost. TPU's properties make it suitable for applications requiring durable parts.
- PC: polycarbonate is known for its exceptional rigidity and strength. However, it is brittle and challenging to print with, often resulting in imperfections and inaccuracies. These defects can create stress concentration points, leading to potential fractures under load.

Initially, PLA was chosen for constructing the robot's body due to its ease of printing, low cost, and adequate structural properties.

In Figure 4, two types of simulations are presented: static displacement analysis and static strain analysis. These tests were conducted to evaluate the robot's ability to support its own weight, as well as additional loads. The first test involved applying a gravity force on the Shadow, the second applied a distributed force of 40 kgf on the tray, while the third applied a distributed force of 10 kgf. The results indicate that the structure of the robot, constructed from PLA, can support these weights without exhibiting significant or hazardous deformation.

However, the high torque generated by the wheels imposed significant stress on the chassis–wheel connections, leading to issues such as wheel axle penetration when using PLA and ABS. Additionally, PC was deemed unsuitable due to its printing difficulties. After extensive testing under prolonged operational conditions, TPU was selected for its superior durability and flexibility, which are crucial for maintaining structural integrity under stress, as shown in Figure 5b.

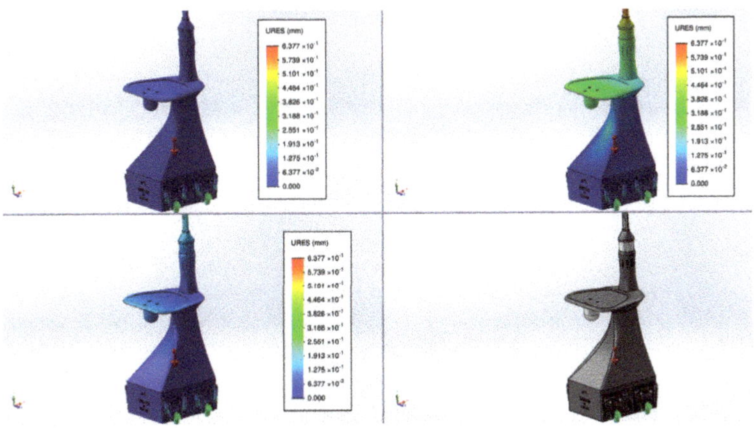

(**a**)

Figure 4. *Cont.*

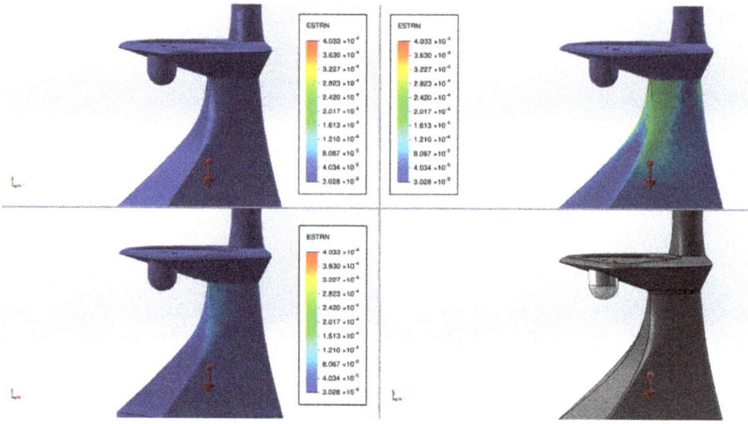

(**b**)

Figure 4. Simulations of the Shadow robot built with PLA are presented. From left to right and top to bottom, the tests include the robot under its own weight in gravity, with an additional weight of 40 kgf on the tray, with a weight of 10 kgf on the tray, and the model. (**a**) Simulation of the static Shadow displacement. Scale: 6.377×10^{-1} to 0 mm. (**b**) Simulation of static unitary Shadow deformation. Scale: 4.033×10^{-4} to 3.028×10^{-9} equivalent strain.

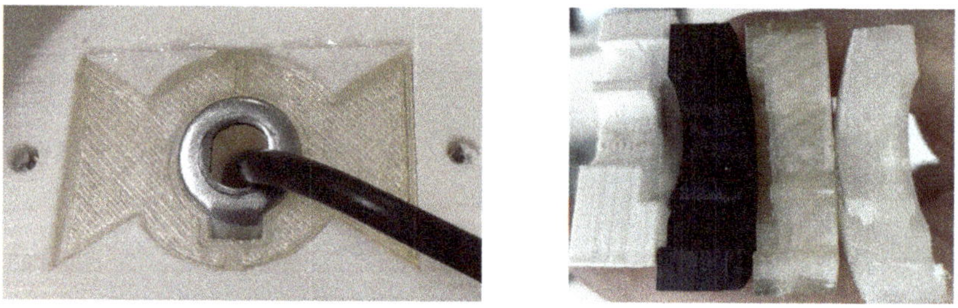

(**a**) (**b**)

Figure 5. Wheel fixation solution and materials. (**a**) Kite tail-shaped element inserted in the robot's chassis. (**b**) State of wear of the materials after the test. From left to right: PLA, ABS, TPU HARDNESS+ and polycarbonate.

4.5. Suspension System

In our first prototype, the wheels were directly attached to the chassis. This design led to premature wear of the plastic part of the chassis holding the wheel's axis. To mitigate this, we introduced an intermediate element made of a more resistant material, as shown in Figure 5a. Additionally, the generation and transmission of vibrations caused by the fixed attachment were problematic, highlighting the need for a more effective solution. Consequently, the design of Shadow's suspension system became crucial for ensuring stability and smooth operation across various conditions.

To address these issues, we implemented a robust suspension system designed to manage weight distribution and absorb shocks, enhancing the robot's durability and improving its interaction with the environment. This system allows for more precise and reliable human-following capabilities by minimizing the impact of uneven terrain.

During testing of the initial prototypes in real-world conditions, we encountered significant issues related to vibration. These vibrations were transmitted to the tray and the head, where the camera was mounted, rendering the tray unsuitable for carrying items such as medicines, bottles, or other tall objects. We identified three main causes of these problems: (i) misalignment of the Mecanum wheels; (ii) instability in the four-wheel configuration, often causing one wheel to lose contact with the ground; and (iii) the rigid connection of the motor wheels to the body. We resolved these issues by decoupling the wheels from the chassis through a micro-adjustable suspension system.

Figure 6a shows the initial design with the wheel directly attached to the chassis. The final design was engineered to support the robot's weight while maintaining flexibility and responsiveness. In addition to decoupling the wheels from the chassis, shock absorbers and springs that could handle the dynamic loads encountered during operation were integrated. The placement and configuration of these components were optimized to ensure even weight distribution and to minimize vibrations that could affect the robot's sensors and electronics. Our design is shown in Figure 6b and the implementation in Figure 6c.

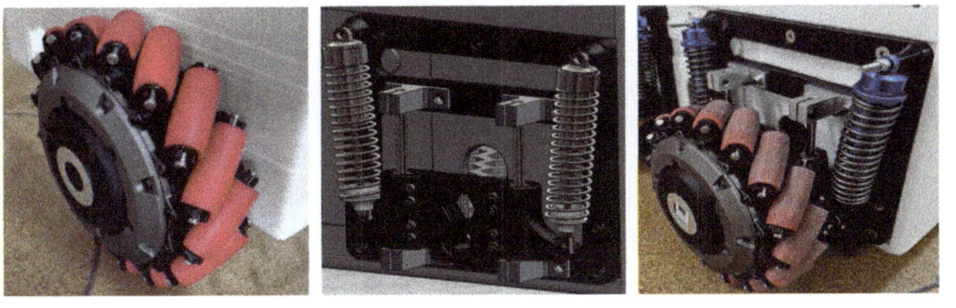

(**a**) (**b**) (**c**)

Figure 6. Before and after views of the wheel suspension system. (**a**) Wheel without damping system. (**b**) Design of the damping system. (**c**) Wheel with damping system.

This suspension system plays a vital role in managing the robot's stability and performance, reducing the impact of vibrations and ensuring more reliable operation in various scenarios; see Section 5.1.

However, a static unit deformation analysis and static displacement analysis were performed on this damping system using different materials, including PLA, ABS, and TPU HARDNESS+. The analysis involved fixing the joint to the chassis and applying a vertical force of 60 kgf on the wheel axle, along with a torque force of 10 Nm. The motor's maximum load capacity is 50 kgf, with a peak torque of 7 Nm, as shown in Figure 7.

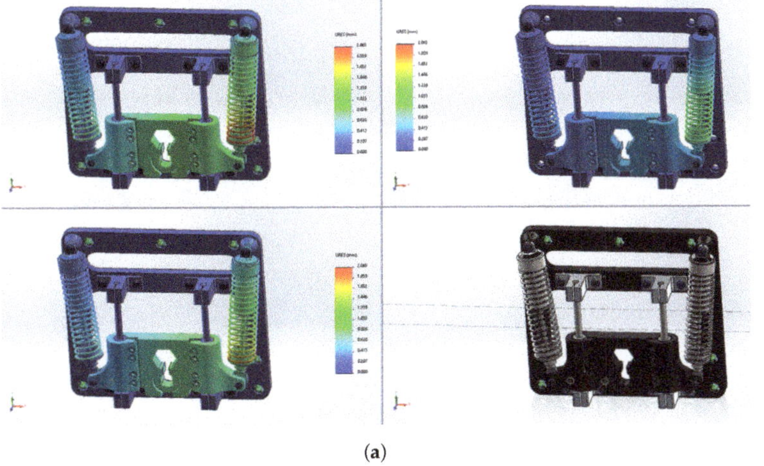

(**a**)

Figure 7. *Cont.*

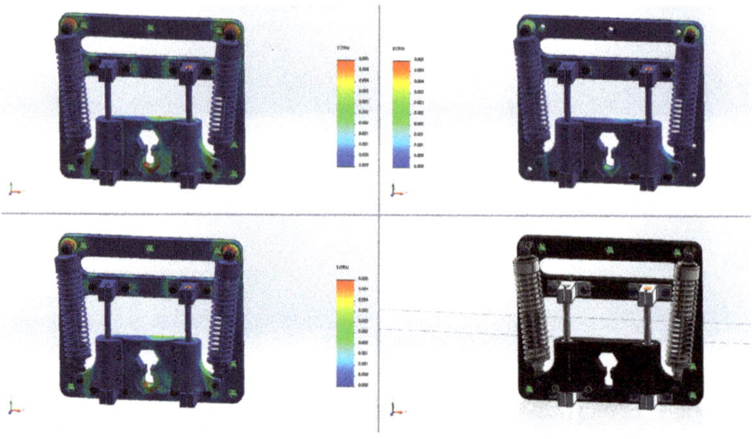

(b)

Figure 7. Simulations of the damping system under a vertical force of 60 kgf on the wheel axle combined with a torque of 10 Nm are presented. The results are organized from left to right and top to bottom, showing tests with TPU HARDNESS+, PLA, ABS, and the model. (**a**) Simulation of the static damping system displacement. Scale: 2.065 to 0 mm. (**b**) Simulation of static unitary damping system deformation. Scale: 0.005 to 0 equivalent strain.

The results indicate that the designed part can withstand these forces. However, TPU HARDNESS+ exhibits more deformation compared to PLA and ABS, primarily due to its greater flexibility. Despite this deformation, TPU HARDNESS+ remains harder and more durable under these conditions, as demonstrated in Figure 5b.

4.6. Power Electronics

The power electronics that drive Shadow have been designed to overcome the typical limitations of commercial robots, which often feature closed or poorly documented systems. Ensuring a robot's longevity and adaptability requires an infrastructure that allows for the integration of new sensors and computing resources. These additional elements draw energy at various voltages, which the robot's battery system must provide, and these requirements may not have been anticipated in the initial design.

We developed an extractable power electronics tray that offers multiple power buses to address this challenge. This tray can be easily resized by replacing the power supplies, ensuring flexibility and scalability. This modularity is crucial for extending Shadow's operational life by accommodating technological advancements and changing mission requirements.

The primary goal of this design is to provide a robust and versatile power system that can support a wide range of devices. The tray includes several power buses with different voltage and current capabilities, as outlined in Table 2. This comprehensive distribution system ensures that all components, from high-power motors to delicate sensors, receive the appropriate power.

Table 2. Voltages and maximum currents provided by the various power buses in Shadow's power electronics system, ensuring flexible and scalable power distribution for diverse components.

	Battery	**Motors**	**Control**	**Supply**	**Supply**	**Supply**	**Supply**	**Supply**
Voltage	48 V	48 V	24 V	48 V	24 V	19 V	12 V	5 V
Max. current	22 A	13 A	5 A	20 A	10 A	10 A	10 A	10 A

Figure 8 shows a detailed layout of Shadow's power system. On the left side, the 1 kWh lithium battery occupies the lowest position in the chassis. This placement helps maintain a low center of gravity, improving the robot's stability. Above the battery, the control buttons and charging socket are indicated, facilitating user interaction and recharging operations. A detailed view of the power electronics tray is provided on the right side of Figure 8. The tray includes various power supplies delivering voltages of 48 V, 24 V, 19 V, 12 V, and 5 V, each capable of supplying different amperages as needed. This configuration currently powers the four 150 W wheel motors, an NVIDIA Orin unit, two 3D LiDARs, a 360° RGB camera, and other smaller sensors and devices. The tray also houses the motor controllers and fuses, ensuring safe and reliable operation. The distribution terminals are marked, showing how power is routed to different robot components. This modular and organized layout allows for easy maintenance and upgrades, ensuring Shadow can adapt to evolving technological needs.

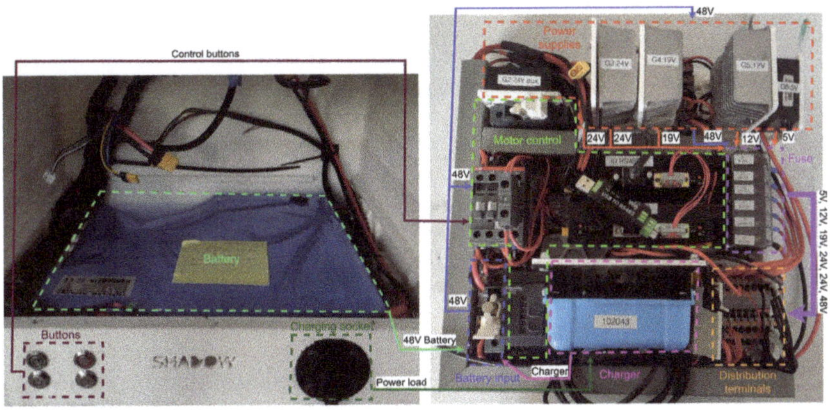

Figure 8. Detailed layout of Shadow's power system. The left side shows the 1 kWh lithium battery at the lowest position in the chassis for stability, along with control buttons and a charging socket. The right side displays the power electronics tray, featuring various power supplies, motor controllers, and distribution terminals, highlighting the modular and organized design for easy maintenance and upgrades.

4.7. Perception System

The ability of a robot to perceive its environment and respond appropriately is crucial for effective operation, especially in applications involving human interaction. Shadow has various advanced sensors that allow it to detect and follow people, navigate complex environments, and perform tasks autonomously. All sensors in Shadow are implemented using RoboComp [37] and the cognitive architecture CORTEX [38], and their distribution is divided into two sets: internal and external.

The integration of RoboComp provides a robust framework for sensor data processing and hardware abstraction, enabling seamless communication and coordination among the various sensors. The cognitive architecture CORTEX allows for easy upgrades and integration of new sensors, ensuring that Shadow can adapt to evolving technological advancements and diverse operational needs. By leveraging RoboComp and CORTEX, Shadow can achieve high levels of performance and reliability in its perception and interaction capabilities.

- Internal sensors. Internal sensors measure the robot's internal state and are critical for maintaining operational efficiency and safety. These sensors include:
  - Voltmeter and ammeter on each power bus: These sensors monitor the voltage and current on each power bus, ensuring that all components receive the correct power levels and helping to detect any irregularities that might indicate potential issues.

- Battery status and charge monitoring: These sensors track the charge level and overall health of the battery, providing essential information to prevent overcharging or deep discharge, which could damage the battery.
- Temperature sensors: Placed at several points in the Shadow, these sensors monitor the temperature of key components to prevent overheating and ensure optimal operating conditions.
- AHRS-IMU (Attitude and Heading Reference System—Inertial Measurement Unit): This sensor provides data on the robot's orientation, acceleration, and angular velocity, which are crucial for maintaining stability and accurate navigation (WT901B, Witmotion, Shenzhen, China).

A dedicated embedded processor reads these internal sensors. This processor continuously collects data from all internal sensors and creates a comprehensive data structure representing the robot's current internal state. This data structure is then published and made available to other robot subsystems, enabling real-time monitoring and dynamic adjustments as needed. This architecture, supported by CORTEX, ensures that Shadow can maintain optimal performance and respond swiftly to any internal anomalies, enhancing its reliability and safety during operation.

- External sensors. External sensors give Shadow access to the outside world, enabling it to perceive and interact with its environment effectively. These sensors include:
  - 3D LiDARs: Shadow is equipped with two 3D LiDARs (Helios and Bpearl models, from Robosense) that provide comprehensive coverage of the surrounding environment. The first LiDAR, placed on the head of the robot, has a conventional configuration with 32 elements, covering angles from 10° upwards to −55° downwards. This sensor is essential for detecting obstacles and mapping the environment at various heights. The second LiDAR is a dome-type model that offers extensive coverage of 90 × 360 solid degrees, ensuring that Shadow can detect obstacles and navigate safely in almost all directions. This configuration provides near-complete coverage of the volume surrounding the robot, making it highly effective in dynamic and complex environments.
  - 360° RGB camera: This camera provides a 4 K H264 compressed stream constructed from two 180° fisheye cameras placed back to back. This setup allows for a full panoramic view, essential for tasks requiring a comprehensive visual context, such as people tracking and semantic navigation.

Figure 9 presents the output from the 360° RGB camera with LiDAR depth overlay on a jet colormap, which illustrates Shadow's environmental mapping, showing a 360° indoor view with depth information in colors representing different distances. With these external sensors, accurate human tracking is possible.

As one of the main objectives of Shadow is to perform navigation focused on people tracking, we have chosen that the LiDAR data should be registered together with the 360° RGB image. This integration allows all detected visual elements to be accurately positioned in 3D space. Given the post-processing applied by the camera manufacturer to provide high-quality images and the unique front–back configuration of the two fisheye cameras, several steps are necessary to project an arbitrary LiDAR 3D point onto the 360° image. The use of the CORTEX cognitive architecture [38] provides a robust framework for integrating and processing sensory data in real time, facilitating accurate 3D positioning of visual elements detected by the LiDARs and 360° camera. CORTEX enables the seamless fusion of these data streams, improving the robot's ability to navigate and interact with its environment effectively, detecting and tracking people in its surroundings, and ensuring high precision in tracking and spatial awareness.

Figure 9. The 360° RGB camera output with LiDAR depth overlay on a jet colormap, demonstrating Shadow's environmental mapping capabilities. The image shows a panoramic indoor view with depth information in various colors, indicating different distances from the LiDAR.

The 360° camera is treated as two fisheye 180° cameras placed back to back, combining images into an equirectangular frame of reference. This approach allows for a seamless panoramic view. To achieve this integration, we first define a 3D coordinate system centered at each camera, $\mathfrak{C}_f$ for the front camera and $\mathfrak{C}_b$ for the back camera. This setup ensures accurate spatial alignment of visual data from both cameras, facilitating comprehensive environmental mapping and object detection within Shadow's cognitive architecture.

A 3D point obtained by the LiDAR is transformed into the corresponding camera coordinate system and projected onto the fisheye image plane. This process involves translating the LiDAR data points to the camera's frame of reference, ensuring the spatial relationship between the points is maintained. Each 3D point is then mapped onto the 2D image plane of the fisheye camera, which captures a wide field of view. This transformation allows the integration of depth information from the LiDAR with the visual data from the 360° camera, providing a comprehensive understanding of the environment.

Since all 2D pixels in the fisheye camera have 3D coordinates, an image pixel (x, y), normalized between the values $[-1, 1]$ in each of its 2D coordinates, has the following 3D coordinates:

$$p_x = x, \quad p_y = \frac{r}{\tan(\frac{r \cdot a}{2})}, \quad p_z = y \tag{6}$$

where $r = \|(x, y)\|$ and a is the field of view. These coordinates represent the projection of the 2D fisheye image pixels into 3D space, allowing for accurate spatial representation. Next, we compute a transformation to obtain coordinates in a longitude/latitude system:

$$la = \arctan(\frac{p_z}{\|(p_x, p_y)\|}), \quad lo = \arctan(p_y, p_x) \tag{7}$$

Finally, the equirectangular coordinates are obtained as follows:

$$e_x = \frac{lo}{\pi}, \quad e_y = \frac{la * 2}{\pi} \tag{8}$$

These equirectangular coordinates are normalized and must be scaled to the image size of the 360° camera. This scaling ensures that the projected points align accurately with the visual data, enabling precise integration of depth and visual information for comprehensive environmental mapping and interaction; see Figure 9.

Combining the projected points with object detectors or semantic segmentation makes it possible to assign an approximate position in 3D space to those visual elements. However, the size of the point cloud and the 360° image makes an all objects, all the time policy not advisable for real-time operation. Instead, we have introduced an attention mechanism that works similarly to an orientable camera but with 360° coverage and no mechanical delay. This mechanism is based on a server component for each LiDAR and the camera. These components read the data streams from the devices at maximum frequency and offer an RPC (Remote Procedure Call) interface with parameters defining the desired vertical slice of the 3D point cloud or an arbitrary region of the global image at a specified resolution. The agents of the CORTEX architecture handle this processing, ensuring efficient and real-time data integration. As shown in Figure 10, this approach allows real-time people (or object) detection.

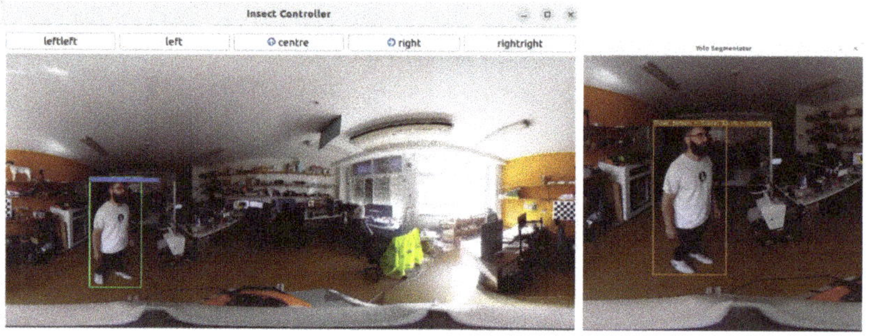

(a) (b)

Figure 10. (**a**) Global 360° image stream from Shadow's 360° camera, showing a panoramic view of the environment; and (**b**) target selected with ROI output, highlighting the identified person for tracking.

According to specific CORTEX agents, two types of tracking can be executed simultaneously to enhance Shadow's object detection and tracking capabilities. First, foveal tracking is initiated by requesting a global, low-resolution image region from the detectors. Once a target is identified, the region of interest (ROI) is progressively adapted and tracked, with a PID (Proportional Integral Derivative) controller maintaining its position and size. Second, peripheral attention to non-target, unexpected objects is managed by requesting a large-size, low-resolution region from the server, which is then processed by the detectors. Both tracking modes and the additional degrees of freedom the attention system provides are integrated into the tracking architecture for optimal performance.

5. Experimental Results

Shadow's capabilities were evaluated through a series of experimental tests. These experiments were designed to validate the complete system, ensuring all components function seamlessly together and meet the high-level objectives outlined in the design phase. The experimental results include validating the suspension system, sensor calibration and data fusion, and navigation.

5.1. Suspension System Validation

The performance of Shadow's suspension system was validated through a series of rigorous tests designed to assess its effectiveness in reducing vibrations. A three-axis accelerometer was placed on the chassis with a sampling rate of 4 ms, and the robot was driven through several forward, lateral, diagonal, and rotational movements at 800 mm/s and 300 mm/s. Table 3 shows the movements' sequence and speeds.

Table 3. Sequence of movement in the vibration test.

Speed/Movement	1	2	3	4	5	6	7	8	9	10	11
Linear (y-axis) speed (mm/s)	300	0	0	0	−800	0	0	0	300	−800	0
Side (x-axis) speed (mm/s)	0	0	300	0	0	0	−800	0	300	−800	0
Rotational speed (rad/s)	0	1	0	1	0	1	0	0.5	0	0	0.5
Execution time (s)	10	6.25	10	1.25	3.75	6.25	3.75	0.25	5	3.75	1.25

Figure 11a shows the results of these tests for our original design without the damping system. The three series represent the x, y, and z axes, with time on the abscissa and displacement in millimeters per second squared (mm/s^2) on the ordinate. High vibration values were observed in all three axes, most prominently in the z-axis (up–down direction) at a forward speed of 800 mm/s.

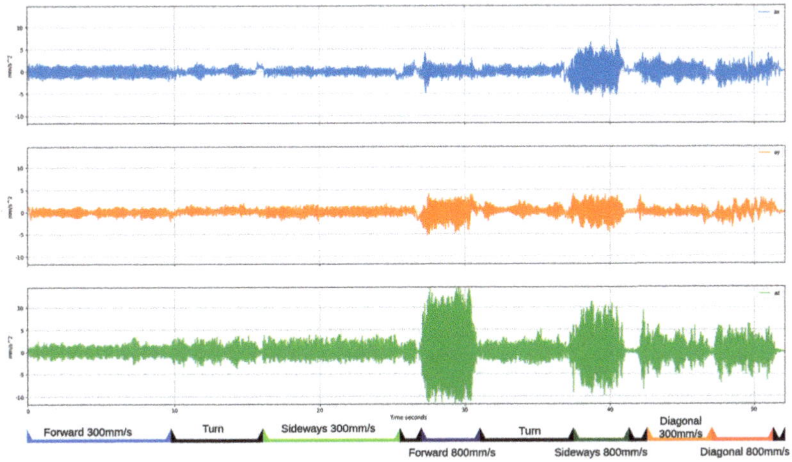

(**a**)

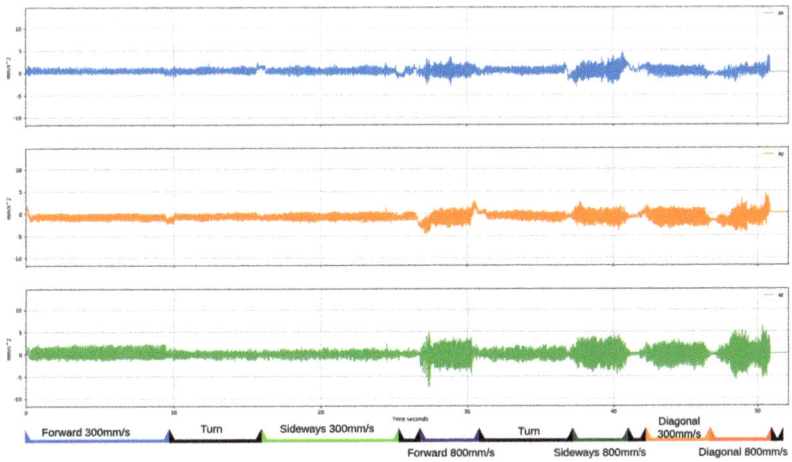

(**b**)

Figure 11. *Cont.*

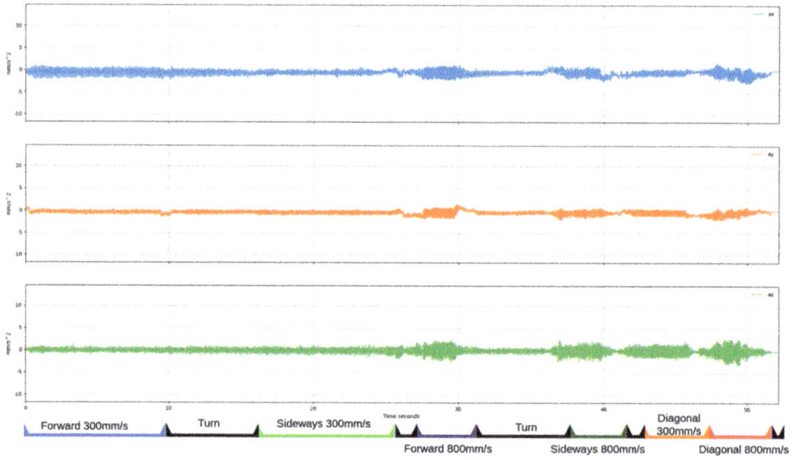

(c)

Figure 11. Acceleration comparison. Acceleration comparison. (**a**) Acceleration without damping system. (**b**) Acceleration of damping system with 468 N/m springs. (**c**) Acceleration of damping system with 1288 N/m springs.

After these results, a new design was undertaken to include a suspension system with each wheel attached to a supporting plastic element of TPU HARDNESS+ that moves vertically along two steel rods. The movement is constrained by two shock absorbers that link it to the chassis. The steel rods are fixed to the chassis using metal elements that can be adjusted in position, effectively modifying the orientation of the wheels concerning the chassis. The shock absorbers are filled with 650 viscosity paraffin oil.

A new series of tests with different spring values were performed (see Table 4); the first value of 468 N/m is the default setting for the shock absorber, while the second value of 1288 N/m was calculated based on an estimated weight of approximately 50 kg for Shadow. This calculation assumes a uniform weight distribution across the eight springs, with a desired deformation of 50%, or about 50 mm, as shown in Equation (9):

$$k = \frac{F}{\Delta l} = \frac{m * g}{\Delta l} = \frac{\frac{50}{8} * 9.8}{0.05} = \frac{61.25\ N}{0.05\ m} = 1225\ \frac{N}{m} \tag{9}$$

The tests performed with this suspension system showed a drastic reduction in the vibrations in the robot's base that were transmitted to the tray; see Figure 11b,c. The reduction in standard deviation obtained concerning the chassis mounting was as shown in Table 5.

Table 4. Spring characteristics.

Parameter	Spring 1	Spring 2
Step	9.5 mm	6.06 mm
Useful spires	10	16.5
Wire diameter	1.25 mm	2 mm
Length	100 mm	100 mm
Constant k	468 N/m	1288 N/m
Materials	INOX-AISI 302	INOX-AISI 302

With this data, a Fast Fourier Transform (FFT) was computed with a time window of 1 s and a time step of 0.5 s (FFT video with 1 s time window and 0.5 s time step https://youtu.be/DWQJhnZFJD8, accessed on 22 August 2024). The results also confirm the drastic reduction in vibrations in all relevant modes.

Table 5. Improvement of the standard deviation concerning chassis mounting.

System/Axis	X	Y	Z
Damping system with 468 N/m springs	64.31%	10.94%	118.02%
Damping system with 1288 N/m springs	90.1%	129.87%	333.31%

5.2. Sensor Calibration and Data Fusion

This subsection discusses the outcomes of calibrating the 3D LiDARs and the 360° RGB camera. To visualize the calibration results, a video demonstrating a person moving within the environment was recorded. The video shows the alignment of the LiDAR point cloud with the 360° camera imagery, highlighting the effectiveness of the calibration (the video can be accessed at the following link: https://youtu.be/jXQAF8chnhk, accessed on 22 August 2024). Figure 12 presents a screenshot from the demonstration video, displaying the 3D map superimposed on the 360° image. The depth is indicated by a color scale, providing a clear visualization of the spatial alignment between the LiDAR data and the camera imagery.

Figure 12. Output from the 360° RGB camera with LiDAR depth overlay on a jet colormap, demonstrating the calibration results. The colors represent different depth levels, with warmer colors indicating closer distances and cooler colors indicating farther distances.

The accuracy of the 3D point projections and visual data alignment was qualitatively assessed. Although detailed quantitative error metrics are not presented here due to the dynamic nature of the testing environment and the complexity of the data, the visual alignment in the recorded video provides clear evidence of the high calibration accuracy. The calibration results are consistent with expected performance, ensuring reliable sensor integration.

5.3. People following Navigation

This subsection presents the results of Shadow's people following capabilities, as demonstrated in a video (the video can be accessed at the following link: https://youtu.be/_vndgz-sviE, accessed on 22 August 2024). The video shows Shadow following a person, highlighting the smooth movement of its omnidirectional base. Initially, the video shows the configuration and placement of sensors on the robot, including the 3D LiDARs and the 360° RGB camera.

Shadow uses a basic A* path-planning algorithm, dynamically adding the target's pose based on the detected person's movements. The robot adjusts its path using a social elastic band mechanism, adapting to environmental changes to maintain a safe and socially aware following distance [39]. Figure 13 shows a screenshot of the robot during the following of a person in the corridors of the Polytechnic School of the University of Extremadura, Spain.

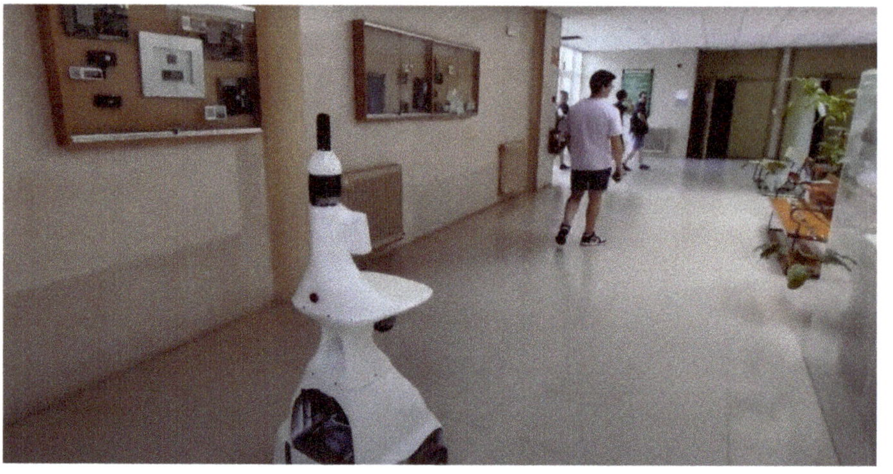

Figure 13. A screenshot of Shadow following a person, maintaining a safe distance, and demonstrating smooth movements of its omnidirectional base (https://youtu.be/_vndgz-sviE, accessed on 22 August 2024).

The smoothness and naturalness of Shadow's movements were qualitatively assessed through visual observations in various real-world tests. Evaluators focused on the robot's ability to maintain a constant and safe distance from the person while tracking them naturally. The video demonstrates Shadow's ability to follow a person with smooth, natural, and uninterrupted motion, attributed to the omnidirectional kinematics and the navigation mechanism. This visual evidence supports the conclusion that Shadow's motion is fluid and natural, enhancing its suitability for socially aware navigation.

To quantify the smoothness and naturalness of Shadow's movement, 20 evaluators (8 roboticists and 12 non-roboticists) were asked to rate their observations on a Likert scale from 1 to 5, where 1 represented "very poor" and 5 represents "excellent". The ratings focused on two key aspects: smoothness of movement and naturalness of movement. Table 6 summarizes the results of the questionnaires.

Table 6. Mean and variance of evaluator ratings for Shadow's movement smoothness and naturalness.

Metric	Mean	Variance
Smoothness	4.45	0.26
Naturalness	4.50	0.26

The results from the evaluators indicate that Shadow's movements are perceived as smooth and natural. These observations initially confirm the effectiveness of the Shadow's omnidirectional kinematics in providing a fluid and socially aware navigation experience.

5.4. Survey on Acceptance and Usability of the Shadow Robot

A survey was conducted to evaluate the acceptance and usability of the Shadow robot among medical and therapeutic professionals. The study included fifteen participants, all without prior knowledge of robotics. The survey utilized a Likert scale to assess various aspects of the robot's design and functionality. The questions posed to the participants were as follows:

- Ergonomic design: Is the robot designed ergonomically and comfortable for users?
- User safety: Does the design of the robot ensure user safety?
- Work efficiency: Does the robot enhance the efficiency of healthcare personnel's work?
- Visual appeal: Is the robot's design visually appealing?
- Adaptability to work environments: Does the robot's design adapt well to different healthcare work environments?
- Dimensional suitability: Are the robot's dimensions appropriate and do they meet the ergonomic needs of healthcare staff?
- Overall satisfaction: Are you generally satisfied with the design of the robot?

The survey results, see Figure 14, highlight a generally neutral perception of the Shadow robot's design, with specific areas receiving more varied feedback. The moderate mean scores and variability in responses, particularly in aspects like adaptability and dimensions, indicate that while the robot is generally acceptable, specific areas may require refinement. Addressing these areas could enhance user satisfaction and overall usability, making the robot more suitable for diverse healthcare environments. Further studies and continuous feedback collection will be crucial in guiding these improvements.

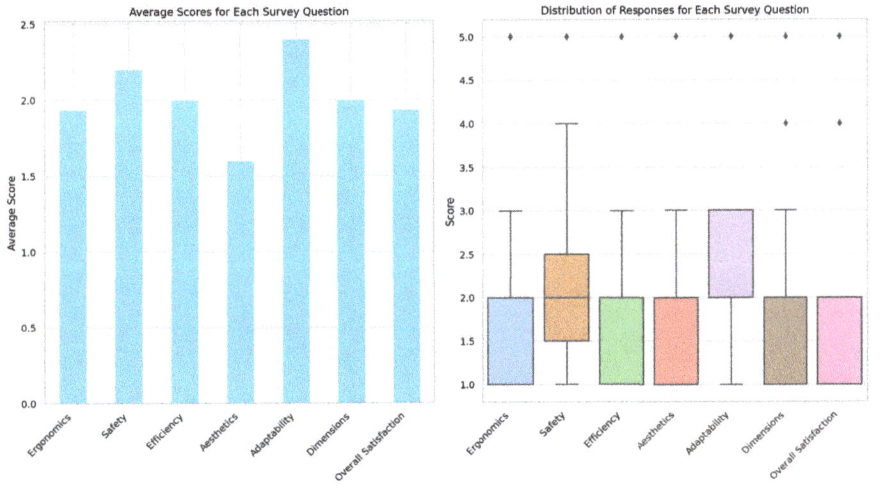

Figure 14. Survey results.

6. Conclusions

The development and implementation of Shadow, a mobile social robot, demonstrate the successful integration of advanced manufacturing techniques, omnidirectional kinematics, and a flexible power electronics system to meet specific functional requirements. Shadow utilizes 3D printing technology to achieve cost efficiency and high agility, making it a versatile tool and human companion for various environments. Integrating a comprehensive sensor array and rapid prototyping methodology allowed for continuous monitoring, swift iteration, and refinement, aligning with the project goals and overcoming practical design challenges.

Experimental tests validated the system, including the suspension system, sensor calibration, data fusion, and navigation. The suspension system effectively reduced vibrations, enhancing stability and durability. Sensor calibration and data fusion, facilitated by the CORTEX cognitive architecture, ensured accurate 3D positioning of visual elements, improving environmental mapping and interaction capabilities. In addition, the navigation tests highlighted the effectiveness of Shadow's omnidirectional kinematics for human-following tasks.

In future work, the possibility of adding a robotic arm for manipulation is proposed. Thanks to its modular design in three pieces and the available power buses, only one or two additional parts would need to be designed, while retaining the most complex part, the lower base, which houses the wheels and power electronics.

Additionally this study highlights the unique features and advantages of the Shadow system; a detailed performance comparison with other existing service robots remains outside the scope of this work. Future research could focus on conducting comprehensive performance evaluations to benchmark Shadow against other robots in terms of tracking ability, speed, accuracy, and other relevant metrics.

Overall, Shadow has progressed from technology readiness level (TRL) 2 to TRL 7 within a year, showing its advanced functionalities and readiness for real-world applications. This study provides a comprehensive blueprint for creating cost-effective, highly agile robots, offering valuable insights into optimizing robot functionality and overcoming design challenges. The successful implementation of Shadow underscores the potential of combining advanced manufacturing techniques with robust cognitive architectures to develop efficient and versatile robotic systems.

Author Contributions: Conceptualization, A.T., P.B. and P.N.; methodology, A.T.; software, L.B. and N.Z.; validation, A.T., N.Z. and P.B.; formal analysis, A.T.; investigation, A.T.; resources, N.Z.; data curation, A.T. and P.N.; writing—original draft preparation, A.T.; writing—review and editing, P.N.; visualization, L.B.; supervision, P.N.; project administration, P.N.; funding acquisition, P.B. and P.N. All authors have read and agreed to the published version of the manuscript.

Funding: This work has been partially funded by TED2021-131739-C22, supported by Spanish MCIN/AEI/10.13039/501100011033 and the European Union's NextGenerationEU/PRTR, by the Spanish Ministry of Science and Innovation PDC2022-133597-C41 and by FEDER Project 0124 EUROAGE MAS 4 E (2021–2027 POCTEP Program).

Data Availability Statement: The data presented in this study are available on request from the corresponding author. The data are not publicly available due to privacy and ethical restrictions.

Conflicts of Interest: The authors declare no conflicts of interest.

References

1. Breazeal, C.L. *Designing Sociable Robots*; MIT press: Cambridge, MA, USA, 2004.
2. Dautenhahn, K. Socially intelligent robots: Dimensions of human–robot interaction. *Philos. Trans. R. Soc. B Biol. Sci.* **2007**, *362*, 679–704. [CrossRef] [PubMed]
3. Breazeal, C.; Takanishi, A.; Kobayashi, T. Social Robots that Interact with People. In *Springer Handbook of Robotics*; Springer: Berlin/Heidelberg, Germany, 2008; pp. 1349–1369.
4. Mahdi, H.; Akgun, S.A.; Saleh, S.; Dautenhahn, K. A survey on the design and evolution of social robots—Past, present and future. *Robot. Auton. Syst.* **2022**, *156*, 104193. [CrossRef]
5. Wada, K.; Shibata, T.; Saito, T.; Tanie, K. Effects of robot-assisted activity for elderly people and nurses at a day service center. *Proc. IEEE* **2007**, *92*, 1780–1788. [CrossRef]
6. Ragno, L.; Borboni, A.; Vannetti, F.; Amici, C.; Cusano, N. Application of social robots in healthcare: Review on characteristics, requirements, technical solutions. *Sensors* **2023**, *23*, 6820. [CrossRef]
7. Manzi, F.; Peretti, G.; Di Dio, C.; Cangelosi, A.; Itakura, S.; Kanda, T.; Ishiguro, H.; Massaro, D.; Marchetti, A. A robot is not worth another: Exploring children's mental state attribution to different humanoid robots. *Front. Psychol.* **2020**, *11*, 2011. [CrossRef] [PubMed]
8. Egido-García, V.; Estévez, D.; Corrales-Paredes, A.; Terrón-López, M.J.; Velasco-Quintana, P.J. Integration of a social robot in a pedagogical and logopedic intervention with children: A case study. *Sensors* **2020**, *20*, 6483. [CrossRef] [PubMed]
9. Reis, J.; Melão, N.; Salvadorinho, J.; Soares, B.; Rosete, A. Service robots in the hospitality industry: The case of Henn-na hotel, Japan. *Technol. Soc.* **2020**, *63*, 101423. [CrossRef]
10. Fong, T.; Nourbakhsh, I.; Dautenhahn, K. A survey of socially interactive robots. *Robot. Auton. Syst.* **2003**, *42*, 143–166. [CrossRef]
11. Goodrich, M.A.; Schultz, A.C. *Human-Robot Interaction: A Survey*; Now Publishers Inc.: Norwell, MA, USA, 2008; Volume 1.
12. Gibson, I.; Rosen, D.; Stucker, B. *Additive Manufacturing Technologies*; Springer: Berlin/Heidelberg, Germany, 2010.
13. Gupta, A.; Singh, V. A review of emerging technologies for rapid prototyping. In Proceedings of the 11th International Advances in Applied Physics and Materials Science Congress & Exhibition, Fethiye, Turkey, 17–21 October 2021 ; AIP Publishing: Melville, NY, USA, 2023.
14. Sharma, A. (Ed.) *Advances in 3D Printing*; IntechOpen: London, UK, 2023.

15. Yim, M.; Shen, W.M.; Salemi, B.; Rus, D.; Moll, M.; Lipson, H.; Klavins, E.; Chirikjian, G.S. Modular self-reconfigurable robot systems [grand challenges of robotics]. *IEEE Robot. Autom. Mag.* **2007**, *14*, 43–52. [CrossRef]
16. Murata, S.; Kurokawa, H.; Kokaji, S. Self-reconfigurable robots. *IEEE Robot. Autom. Mag.* **2002**, *14*, 71–78. [CrossRef]
17. Siciliano, B.; Khatib, O. *Springer Handbook of Robotics*; Springer Science & Business Media: Berlin/Heidelberg, Germany, 2008.
18. Spong, M.W.; Hutchinson, S.; Vidyasagar, M. *Robot Modeling and Control*; John Wiley & Sons: Hoboken, NJ, USA, 2006.
19. Wengefeld, T.; Schuetz, B.; Girdziunaite, G.; Scheidig, A.; Gross, H.M. The morphia project: First results of a long-term user study in an elderly care scenario from robotic point of view. In Proceedings of the ISR Europe 2022, 54th International Symposium on Robotics, VDE, Munich, Germany, 20–21 June 2022; pp. 1–8.
20. PALROBOTICS. TIAGO. 2023. Available online: https://pal-robotics.com/es/robots/tiago/ (accessed on 24 June 2024).
21. Honda. WaPOCHI. 2022. Available online: https://global.honda/jp/stories/046/ (accessed on 24 June 2024).
22. KEENON. DinerbotT5. 2022. Available online: https://www.keenonrobot.com/EN/index/Page/index/catid/6.html (accessed on 24 June 2024).
23. PUDU. Bellabot. 2023. Available online: https://www.pudurobotics.com/es/products/bellabot (accessed on 24 June 2024).
24. experthubrobotics. AmyWaitress. 2023. Available online: https://experthubrobotics.com/premium-robots/csj/amy-waitress (accessed on 24 June 2024).
25. Fischinger, D.; Einramhof, P.; Wohlkinger, W.; Papoutsakis, K.; Mayer, P.; Panek, P.; Koertner, T.; Hofman, S.; Argyros, A.; Vincze, M.; et al. HOBBIT—The Mutual Care Robot. In Proceedings of the 2013 IEEE/RSJ International Conference on Intelligent Robots and Systems (IROS 2013), Tokyo, Japan, 3–8 November 2013.
26. Bajones, M.; Fischinger, D.; Weiss, A.; Wolf, D.; Vincze, M.; de la Puente, P.; Körtner, T.; Weninger, M.; Papoutsakis, K.; Michel, D.; et al. Hobbit: Providing fall detection and prevention for the elderly in the real world. *J. Robot.* **2018**, *2018*, 1754657. [CrossRef]
27. González-Jiménez, J.; Galindo, C.; Ruiz-Sarmiento, J. Technical improvements of the Giraff telepresence robot based on users' evaluation. In Proceedings of the 2012 IEEE RO-MAN: The 21st IEEE International Symposium on Robot and Human Interactive Communication, Paris, France, 9–13 September 2012; pp. 827–832. [CrossRef]
28. Chebotareva, E.; Magid, E.; Carballo, A.; Hsia, K.H. Basic User Interaction Features for Human-Following Cargo Robot TIAGo Base. In Proceedings of the 2020 13th International Conference on Developments in eSystems Engineering (DeSE), Virtual Conference, 14–17 December 2020; pp. 206–211. [CrossRef]
29. Megalingam, R.K.; Naick, V.S.; Manoharan, S.K.; Sivananthan, V. Analysis of Tiago Robot for Autonomous Navigation Applications. In Proceedings of the 2021 Second International Conference on Electronics and Sustainable Communication Systems (ICESC), Coimbatore, India, 4–6 August 2021; pp. 257–261. [CrossRef]
30. Palacín, J.; Rubies, E.; Clotet, E. The Assistant Personal Robot Project: From the APR-01 to the APR-02 Mobile Robot Prototypes. *Designs* **2022**, *6*, 66. [CrossRef]
31. *UNE56801-2008*; UNE 56801:2008: Unidad de Hueco de Puerta de Madera. Terminología, Definiciones y Clasificación. AENOR: Madrid, España, 2008.
32. Guillén-Ruiz, S.; Bandera, J.P.; Hidalgo-Paniagua, A.; Bandera, A. Evolution of Socially-Aware Robot Navigation. *Electronics* **2023**, *12*, 1570. [CrossRef]
33. Siegwart, R.; Nourbakhsh, I.R.; Scaramuzza, D. *Introduction to Autonomous Mobile Robots*, 2nd ed.; Intelligent Robotics and Autonomous Agents; MIT Press: Cambridge, MA, USA, 2014.
34. Ebert-Uphoff, I.; Gosselin, C.M.; Rosen, D.W.; Laliberte, T. Rapid prototyping for robotics. In *Cutting Edge Robotics*; IntechOpen: London, UK , 2005; pp. 17–46.
35. Lynch, K.M.; Park, F.C. *Modern Robotics: Mechanics, Planning, and Control*, 1st ed.; Cambridge University Press: New York, NY, USA, 2017.
36. Maulana, E.; Muslim, M.A.; Hendrayawan, V. Inverse kinematic implementation of four-wheels mecanum drive mobile robot using stepper motors. In Proceedings of the 2015 International Seminar on Intelligent Technology and Its Applications, ISITIA 2015—Proceeding, Surabaya, Indonesia, 20–21 May 2015; pp. 51–55. [CrossRef]
37. Manso, L.; Bachiller, P.; Bustos, P.; Núñez, P.; Cintas, R.; Calderita, L. RoboComp: A Tool-Based Robotics Framework. In *Simulation, Modeling, and Programming for Autonomous Robots: Second International Conference, SIMPAR 2010, Darmstadt, Germany, 15–18 November 2010*; Springer: Berlin/Heidelberg, Germany, 2010; Volume 6472 LNAI. [CrossRef]
38. García García, J.C.; Núñez Trujillo, P.M.; Bachiller Burgos, P.; Bustos García, P. Towards the design of efficient and versatile cognitive robotic architecture based on distributed, low-latency working memory. In Proceedings of the IEEE International Conference on Autonomous Robot Systems and Competitions (ICARSC 2022), Santa Maria da Faira, Portugal, 29–30 April 2022.
39. Pérez, G.; Zapata-Cornejo, N.; Bustos, P.; Núñez, P. Social Elastic Band with Prediction and Anticipation: Enhancing Real-Time Path Trajectory Optimization for Socially Aware Robot Navigation. *Int. J. Soc. Robot.* **2024** . [CrossRef]

MDPI AG
Grosspeteranlage 5
4052 Basel
Switzerland
Tel.: +41 61 683 77 34

Electronics Editorial Office
E-mail: electronics@mdpi.com
www.mdpi.com/journal/electronics

www.ingramcontent.com/pod-product-compliance
Lightning Source LLC
Chambersburg PA
CBHW061443210926
51850CB00008B/1596
* 9 7 8 3 7 2 5 8 2 3 8 9 5 *